DR. BILLY NG

JESUS

REVOLUTION

2

All scripture quotations are taken from the *King James Version* of the Holy Bible.

JESUS REVOLUTION 2

Library of Congress Control No: 2017909239
ISBN-10: 0-9651139-3-0
ISBN-13: 978-0-9651139-3-9
Printed in the United States of America

DEDICATION

To Jesus Christ, Beloved Son of God;

Laura Ng, Beloved daughter of God;

and all my readers, Beloved children of God.

FOREWORD

The radical Grace Revolution has now spread worldwide. Many people may fear the word 'radical' equating it to some form of extremism. But radical simply means 'of or pertaining to the root'. The root of Grace is Jesus. Grace is a person and His name is Jesus. Without Jesus, there is no Grace. Therefore, Grace is not another doctrine or topic for us to understand and expound upon. As such, Jesus did not come to teach grace but to be Grace. Grace is a person who desires to have an intimate relationship with us. Grace is Jesus.

The word 'revolution' involves the overthrow of something old in favor of something new. The old are formulas on how to please God based on our obedience. The new is that God is already pleased with us because of Jesus' obedience. We throw off old for new and self-works for Jesus' works. Therefore, the Grace Revolution is all about Jesus wanting to have an intimate relationship with us based on His obedience. We did not start this revolution nor can we. The revolution began with Jesus and it will end with Jesus.

When the Roman soldiers dug the hole for the cross, little did they know that they were digging the grave for self-works. When the nails were hammered into Jesus, it nailed the law to the cross. We read this in *Colossians 2:14, Blotting out the handwriting of ordinances that was against us, which was contrary to us, and took it out of the way, nailing it to his cross.* When the cross thudded down into the freshly dug hole, Grace was lifted up on high. As Jesus' blood rivulets ran crookedly down the cross, it made us straight. As His blood stained the cross, it washed us clean. Because sin was nailed to the cross, we walk away free. Forever separated from our sins! Grace severed us from the law. Jesus unburdened the heavy load of the law and self-works off our shoulders forever.

This book greatly expands on our knowledge of who we are in Christ. Thank-you for joining me again on this thrilling journey to know ourselves as we are known by Jesus. Let the Jesus Revolution expand! Welcome to Jesus Revolution 2! Trending hashtags: #JesusRevolution

And I, brethren, when I came to you, came not with excellency of speech or of wisdom, declaring unto you the testimony of God. For I determined not to know anything among you, save Jesus Christ, and him crucified.

1 Corinthians 2:1-2

Jesus is in heaven, not works.

Billy Ng

CONTENTS

To The Reader

This book is the second book in the Jesus Revolution trilogy. Once again, this book is heavy on scripture and is intended as such. While you can read Jesus Revolution 2 independently of Jesus Revolution 1, this book does assume that you have some basic familiarity with Jesus as Grace.

Let us define Grace again. Grace is simply 'the unmerited gift or blessing brought to man by Jesus Christ'. The gift is Jesus Himself! Jesus is the unmerited gift of love from God to you. This book will provide you with many fresh revelations of Grace. With each revelation, I encourage you to spend time with Jesus because He desired to spend time with you first. Let Jesus speak to you about His finished work for you. The finished work of Christ simply means that His work in redeeming you has been completed, it stands completed, and it will always be completed. There is nothing that you can add to His completed work.

This book has been divided into 37 chapters. You can read the chapters in any order that you like. The sole message for each chapter is always Jesus as Grace. I hope that by the end of this book, you will not only see Jesus as the Son of God but as your brother, and as your best friend as well. When you find out how much Jesus loved you first, you will fall in love with Him all over again. You will want to spend a lot of your time with Him, not because you have to but because you absolutely long and desire to.

Just like John, who leaned on Jesus' bosom and changed his name to 'the one whom Jesus loved', you will also desire to incline your whole self towards Jesus. You will want to nestle with Him every second of your life as you become enthralled and captivated by His unmerited love for you. And as you spend time with Him, you will gradually come to the realization that you are exactly as He is. You do not become more like Him because you are already as He is. You cannot have more of Him because He gave all of Himself to you already. You cannot get closer to Him or deeper in Him because He already lives in you. However, what you will apprehend is full awareness of who you are in Him. Then, just like John, you can confidently say that you too are 'the one whom Jesus loves'.

❧ 1 ❧

JESUS AND JUBILEE

The key foundation of Grace is resting upon the finished work of Jesus. It is because of Jesus' finished work on the cross that we win the prize before the race began. It is because of Jesus that all our sins were forgiven even before we were born. Every sin was dealt with at the cross by the blood of Jesus. Every debt that mankind owed to the law was paid for by Jesus. Jesus gave the same free gift of righteousness to the whole world – to both believers and unbelievers. Believers accept, become united with Jesus, and thank Him for His free gift. Unbelievers reject Jesus, they are not in union with Jesus, and ignore His free gift.

While all believers accept Jesus' free gift, they tend to disagree on how free is Jesus' free gift! There are some who cannot believe that Jesus actually paid it all for them. To them, the free gift is not completely free. The finished work is not completely finished. Jesus' work is insufficient so they continue to labor to pay back what Jesus already paid for. For them, their labors complete the work that Jesus only started.

Then there are others who believe that Jesus finished the work completely and perfectly and hence, there is nothing left to be added to it. The free gift is free indeed. They operate out of rest in Jesus. They recognize that they are complete in Him and it is from this position of completeness that they begin their work. If they fail in what they do, they are still complete. They still have the prize. Their completeness is in Jesus. Their labors add nothing to their completeness. They further acknowledge that Jesus, not their labors, affects the outcome of situations. They trust implicitly in Jesus' assurance that all outcomes will be good because He is good. It is from resting in Jesus that they bear His fruit. They do not struggle to produce their own fruit but they bear the fruit of Jesus' supply.

This rest can be found in *Leviticus 25:1-7, And the Lord spake unto Moses in mount Sinai, saying, Speak unto the children of Israel, and say unto them, When ye come into the land which I give you, then shall the land keep a sabbath unto the Lord. Six years thou shalt sow thy field, and six years thou shalt prune thy vineyard, and gather in the fruit thereof; But in the seventh year shall be a sabbath of rest unto the land, a sabbath for the Lord: thou shalt neither sow thy field, nor prune thy vineyard. That which groweth of its own accord of thy harvest thou shalt not reap, neither gather the grapes of thy vine undressed: for it is a year of rest unto the land. And the sabbath of the land shall be meat for you; for thee, and for thy servant, and for thy maid, and for thy hired servant, and for thy stranger that sojourneth with thee, And for thy cattle, and for the beast that are in thy land, shall all the increase thereof be meat.* A jubilee is made up of seven years. At the time this commandment was given, the Jewish calendar year began in the month of Nisan (around March to April in our calendar). After Herod took control of Jerusalem, the Jewish calendar year was changed to begin in the month of Tishri (around September to October).

When the Israelites finally entered and possessed their new land, they were told to work and to collect the harvest for six years straight. Each year, beginning in March, the Israelites would harvest their crops. Barley and flax were the first crops to be harvested. Then in May, wheat and early figs. From June to September, fruits would be collected. Grapes first, then olives, followed by dates, summer figs, and pomegranates. The sowing season would begin again when the rains came in October and would run until December. Barley, wheat, and flax would be sowed again for the next year.

However, God commanded them not to work at all in the seventh year! They were to let the land rest. They would neither sow their fields nor prune their vineyards. Anything that grew that year would be left uncollected. There would be no sowing nor reaping. It was a year of rest. In that year of rest, with no work, God assured them that there would be a super abundance of food. There would be more than enough food, not only for their families, but also for their servants and other travelers staying with them. There would be more than enough grain for their animals. So even though they were not producing, they were told that their supply would keep coming. The Israelites, living under the law, could not believe their ears. They were well schooled in the law - if you do not work, then you do not eat! If they did not sow, then they would not reap. If they did not reap, then how would they survive? Their performance mattered. The outcome depended on them. After all, God helps those who help themselves, right? This one year rest out of every seven years did not made any sense at all, just as the extra manna on the sixth day to feed them on the seventh! So they ignored it. The Israelites lived in the new land for a total of 490 years and never once did they allow the land to rest.

Not only were the Israelites told to let the land rest once every seven years, but after forty-nine years, to let the land rest in the fiftieth year as well. Hence, they were not to plow, sow, or reap for two consecutive years (the 49th and 50th year)! We see this in *Leviticus 25:8,10-11, And thou shalt number seven sabbaths of years unto thee, seven times seven years; and the space of the seven sabbaths of years shall be unto thee forty and nine years. And ye shall hallow the fiftieth year, and proclaim liberty throughout all the land unto all the inhabitants thereof: it shall be a jubilee unto you. A jubilee shall that fiftieth year be unto you: ye shall not sow, neither reap that which groweth of itself in it, nor gather the grapes in it of thy vine undressed.*

Seven Sabbath years (7x7=49) is equal to forty-nine years. The year after that, the fiftieth year, is called the year of jubilee. Letting the land fallow for one year out of seven was already illogical. Letting the land fallow for two consecutive years was insupportable. Surely God's instructions to Moses must be in error! Pure and simple, God was wrong!

The Israelites missed the whole point for the rest of the land. It symbolized the rest that they would have in Jesus. God wanted them to not rely on their own efforts to produce food every year. God wanted them to rest in Him. If they sowed and reaped every year by their own efforts, the regularity of it would just lull them into believing that it was their performance that provided them with their harvest. So to break the cycle of self-works, in the perfect year or the seventh year, God would supply them with all their needs, without them having to work at all! If year seventh stood for perfection, then year forty-ninth (7x7) must be perfection squared. When perfection upon perfection came, it would manifest itself in the following year, on the fiftieth year, or the year of jubilee. Jesus is that manifestation of perfection upon perfection. He is the Year of Jubilee.

Reading from *Leviticus 25:19-24, And the land shall yield her fruit, and he shall eat your fill, and dwell therein in safety. And if ye shall say, What shall we eat the seventh year? behold, we shall not sow, nor gather in our increase: Then I will command my blessing upon you in the sixth year, and it shall bring forth fruit for three years. And ye shall sow the eighth year, and eat yet of old fruit until the ninth year; until her fruits come in ye shall eat of the old store. The land shall not be sold for ever: for the land is mine; for ye are strangers and sojourners with me. And in all the land of your possession ye shall grant a redemption for the land.*

In the forty-eighth year (equivalent to the sixth year), all the harvest whether it be grain or fruits, would be harvested. But it would not be a natural harvest. It would be a super-abundant harvest, blessed by God to last three years! They were to eat out of this supernatural increase. There was no need to work as God would supply them. They could sow but they did not need to. If they chose to sow, they would not be allowed to reap when the grains matured the following year.

In the forty-ninth year (or the seventh year), even though the fields would be full of grain and the vineyards heavy with grapes, they would be left uncollected. When the sowing season came, there would be no tilling nor planting. In the fiftieth year (or the eighth year), the year of jubilee, sowing would be allowed again. By now the un-harvested grain planted two years ago has self-sown. Being uncollected, the ripe grain seeds would have fallen to the ground and sowed itself naturally. So, while sowing was allowed in the fiftieth year, there was really no need to sow as the plants had self-sown. In the fifty-first year, without any sowing, there would be a rich harvest for the Israelites to gather in.

God will take care of us! It is not the land, it is not the crops, it is not our efforts that will take care of us. It is Jesus at work for us! When we rest in Him, the land would yield its fruit without struggle. We would eat our fill as Jesus is always more than sufficient. **Our abundant life depends solely on Jesus' unmerited provision. Everything we need is already supplied by Jesus. Our part is to rest in His work and to receive His super-abundant blessings. Resting in Jesus is a spiritual activity. We need to be spiritually aware of the provisions that He has already provided.**

Because of Adam, the ground became cursed. It fell, together with Adam. *Genesis 3:19* states, *In the sweat of thy face shalt thou eat bread, till thou return unto the ground;* Sweat and toil were required for the ground to produce. There was no rest in it. But we read in *Luke 22:44, And being in an agony he prayed more earnestly: and his sweat was as it were great drops of blood falling down to the ground.* Because of Jesus' sweat and blood on the ground, the curse has now been reversed. Grace redeemed the ground. We do not have to sweat anymore to produce bread. The ground will produce because of what Jesus has accomplished. Gethsemane replaced Eden! The second garden replaced the first.

In the temple, every priest was to be clothed in linen garments. They were not to clothe themselves in anything else besides linen. Linen was cool and caused no sweat. We read about this in a future temple in *Ezekiel 44:17-18, And it shall come to pass, that when they enter in at the gates of the inner court, they shall be clothed with linen garments; and no wool shall come upon them, whiles they minister in the gates of the inner court, and within. They shall have linen bonnets upon their heads, and shall have linen breeches upon their loins; they shall not gird themselves with anything that causeth sweat.* Self-works produce sweat. But to rest in Jesus meant no sweat! Jesus confirmed this in *Matthew 4:4, But he answered and said, It is written, Man shall not live by bread alone, but by every word that proceedeth out of the mouth of God.* The old bread, which was the stony law, causes sweat and we cannot live by it. But man shall live by the new Bread that proceeds out of God's mouth. This new Bread is Jesus and He gives us eternal life. Let us rest in Him. *Hebrews 4:1* states, *Let us therefore fear, lest, a promise being left us of entering into his rest, any of you should seem to come short of it.* We should very much fear if we do not enter into this Rest, who is Jesus!

The work that we now do becomes restful work as Jesus works through us. He is our Provider. For only Jesus can provide food for thousands in the desert as we read in *Matthew 14:17-21, But Jesus said unto them, They need not depart; give ye them to eat. And they say unto him, We have here but five loaves, and two fishes. He said, Bring them hither to me. And he commanded the multitude to sit down on the grass, and took the five loaves, and the two fishes, and looking up to heaven, he blessed, and brake, and **gave** the loaves to his disciples, and the disciples to the multitude. And they did all eat, and were filled: and they took up of the fragments that remained twelve baskets full. And they that had eaten were about five thousand men, beside women and children.*

The number 2 in Hebrew is *bet*, written as a 'house with a roof and walls with an always open door'. The number 5 is *hei* or Grace. Nobody need depart from the Provider. Jesus is the always the open door of the house of Grace! Just as He provided manna and quails which blew in from the sea, in His hands the 2 fish and 5 loaves multiplied. His disciples, after distributing what was given to them by Jesus, had to come back to Him again and again, to receive more food. Jesus gave and gave and after everyone had eaten their fill, there were twelve baskets of food left over. We saw a similar provision back in *Genesis 24:20, So she quickly emptied her jar into the trough, ran back to the well to draw more water, and drew enough for all his camels.* Rebekah, a shadow of the disciples, went back again and again to the well to fetch living water for all the camels. Drink the Living Water and eat the Bread of Life to your fill for Jesus is always more than enough!

But the Israelites could not see Grace. They toiled under the law and never followed the commandment to let the land rest. They never observed the Jubilee for the land too. They rejected their Rest and their Provider. As such, they did not see God's supply. We read in *Leviticus 26:33-35, And I will scatter you among the heathen, and will draw out a sword after you: and your land shall be desolate, and your cities waste. Then shall the land enjoy her sabbaths, as long as it lieth desolate, and ye be in your enemies' land; even then shall the land rest, and enjoy her sabbaths. As long as it lieth desolate it shall rest; because it did not rest in your sabbaths, when ye dwelt upon it.* And in *2 Chronicles 36:20-21, And them that had escaped from the sword carried he away to Babylon; where they were servants to him and his sons until the reign of the kingdom of Persia: To fulfil the word of the Lord by the mouth of Jeremiah, until the land had enjoyed her sabbaths: for as long as she lay desolate she kept sabbath, to fulfil threescore and ten years.*

The Israelites lived in the land for 490 years, missing a total of 70 (490/7) Sabbatical years for the land. As they broke the law, they were punished for it. Their punishment was captivity for a period of exactly 70 years. During this period, the land rested. The land did not come short of its rest. Once these 70 years of rest for the land had been completed, God restored, and brought them back home from exile. We read this in *Jeremiah 29:11, For I know the thoughts that I think toward you, saith the LORD, thoughts of peace, and not of evil, to give you an expected end.* But their return, their expected end, would be markedly different than their going. We read further in *Jeremiah 31:21, Set up the roadmarks, establish the signposts. Keep the highway in mind, the road you have traveled. Return, O Virgin Israel, return to these cities of yours.* On their return home, they would have roadmarks (*tsiyyun*) and signposts (*tamrur*). Both *tsiyyun* and *tamrur* are guideposts or pillars that symbolized the cross of Jesus that guides, not only the Jews, but all of us back home. Therefore, let us not come short of His rest. Let us enter 100% into Jesus' rest!

❧ 2 ❧

JESUS AND CIRCUMCISION

The familiar definition of faith is found in *Hebrews 11:1-2, Now faith is the substance of things hoped for, the evidence of things not seen. For by it the elders obtained a good report.* Since Jesus was the Unseen One and the One Hoped For by the elders of old, faith is therefore the substance and evidence of Jesus. He is not a wish or a perhaps, but an assurance or a guarantee of a good report. So when we say that we have faith we are saying that we trust in the immutable and unchangeable person of Jesus. *1 Peter 1:7-9* states, *That the trial of your faith, being much more precious than of gold that perisheth, though it be tried with fire, might be found unto praise and honour and glory at the appearing of Jesus Christ: Whom having not seen, ye love; in whom, though now ye see him not, yet believing, ye rejoice with joy unspeakable and full of glory: Receiving the end of your faith, even the salvation of your souls.* Our faith begins and ends with Jesus. The end of our faith is when we meet our Faith, who is Jesus! Faith cannot be separated from Jesus for Jesus is Faith perfected. Jesus is the manna that will come in the morning. He is our Faith-certainty.

Abraham discovered this faith in *Romans 4:1-16, What shall we say then that Abraham our father, as pertaining to the flesh, hath found? For if Abraham were justified by works, he hath whereof to glory;* **but not before God**. *For what saith the scripture? Abraham believed God, and it was counted unto him for righteousness. Now to him that worketh is the reward not reckoned of grace, but of debt. But to him that worketh not, but believeth on* *him that justifieth the ungodly, his faith is counted for righteousness... for we say that faith was reckoned to Abraham for righteousness. How was it then reckoned? when he was in circumcision, or in uncircumcision? Not in circumcision, but in uncircumcision. And he received the sign of circumcision, a seal of the righteousness of the faith which he had yet being uncircumcised: that he might be the father of all them that believe, though they be not circumcised; that righteousness might be imputed unto them also... For the promise, that he should be the heir of the world, was not to Abraham, or to his seed, through the law, but through the righteousness of faith... **Therefore it is of faith, that it might be by grace**; to the end the promise might be sure to all the seed; not to that only which is of the law, but to that also which is of the faith of Abraham; who is the father of us all,*

Abraham, the patriarch of all the Jews, was not justified by his works. God owed him nothing. His reward, if based on his works, would have been death. But Abraham was not justified by works but by faith in God. Works may be glorious to men but not before God! Abraham became heir of the world, not by the law, but by his faith in God. Jesus actually appeared to him in a vision in *Genesis 15:1,6, the word of the LORD came unto Abram in a vision... And he believed in the Lord; and he counted it to him for righteousness.* Abram simply believed in the Word of the Lord and that was counted unto him for righteousness. Many times, Abraham did not even do what God told him to do but it was his faith in God that mattered. **No one was ever justified before God by his or her works.**

So, what about the act of circumcision? Did Abraham get blessed by this act or was he blessed unconditionally by God? Abraham was seventy-five years old when he left all and went to a new land that God showed him. We read in *Genesis 12:3-4, in thee shall all families of the earth be blessed...and Abram was seventy and five years old when he departed out of Haran.* He was uncircumcised at that time, yet God blessed him richly. Not only was Abraham richly blessed but he was also promised the Seed, Jesus Christ, in whom all families of the earth would be blessed. God made an unconditional covenant with him to bless him before he was circumcised. We call that covenant the Abrahamic Covenant. It was many years later, when Abraham was ninety-nine years old that he was given the sign of circumcision. Only after that did he become circumcised. The blessings were given to him and righteousness was imputed to him before any works on his part. God promised to bless him and that was why he was blessed. He received righteousness and blessings before his circumcision.

This event can be found in *Genesis 17:1-11, And when Abram was ninety years old and nine, the Lord appeared to Abram, and said unto him, I am the Almighty God; walk before me, and be thou perfect. And I will make my covenant between me and thee, and will multiply thee exceedingly…and thou shalt be a father of many nations… And I will make thee exceeding fruitful, and I will make nations of thee, and kings shall come out of thee. And I will establish my covenant between me and thee and thy seed after thee in their generations for an everlasting covenant, to be a God unto thee, and to thy seed after thee. And I will give unto thee, and to thy seed after thee, the land wherein thou art a stranger, all the land of Canaan, for an everlasting possession…This is my covenant, which ye shall keep, between me and you and thy seed after thee; Every man child among you shall be circumcised. And ye shall circumcise the flesh of your foreskin; and it shall be a token of the covenant betwixt me and you.*

Circumcision was not a covenant but a token or sign of the covenant already given by God to Abraham. God was good to Abraham both before and after circumcision. The promises that God gave to Abraham were not based on circumcision but through righteousness of faith. Circumcision, a self-work, added nothing to Abraham. If the promises were fulfilled based upon circumcision, then faith in God would not be necessary. Therefore it was only by faith, that it might be only by Grace, that Abraham was blessed. The promise to Abraham was that he would be the heir of the world (people and land) through his Seed, Jesus. The Gospel is always inclusive, never exclusive. It was God's plan from the start that through Jesus would come redemption and forgiveness of sins for the whole world. It would be called the New Covenant and would be by faith, that it might be only by Grace, that all people in all lands would be blessed.

We continue in *Romans 4:17-25, God, who quickeneth the dead, and calleth those things which be not as though they were… And being not weak in faith, he considered not his own body now dead, when he was about an hundred years old, neither yet the deadness of Sara's womb: He staggered not at the promise of God through unbelief; but was strong in faith, giving glory to God; And being fully persuaded that, what he had promised, he was able also to perform. And therefore it was imputed to him for righteousness. Now it was not written for his sake alone, that it was imputed to him; But for us also, to whom it shall be imputed, if we believe on him that raised up Jesus our Lord from the dead…for our justification.* God 'quickened the dead' meant that He made the dead alive. He (not our faith) called things into existence which cannot exist. Abraham and Sarah's reproductive organs were stone cold dead as in *Isaiah 51:1-2, Look to the rock from which you were cut and to the quarry from which you were hewn; look to Abraham, your father, and to Sarah, who gave you birth.* Abraham could not 'work' to get himself a son. Rock and quarry do not produce life. Abraham and Sarah were impotent, helpless, and unable. Circumcision did not and cannot produce Isaac. Abraham's faith was that God was able to perform what he could not. The *hei* or Grace which was added to their names showed that they were 'born again by Grace' in their old age. **Similarly, we were spiritually dead, unable, impotent, and helpless to justify ourselves. But the resurrection of Jesus imputed righteousness and justification to all those who believe in Him. The resurrected Jesus declares us alive and justified!**

Another instance of this can be found in *John 4:49-53, The nobleman saith unto him, Sir, come down ere my child die. Jesus saith unto him, Go thy way; thy son liveth. And the man believed the word that Jesus had spoken unto him, and he went his way. And as he was now going down, his servants met him, and told him, saying, Thy son liveth. Then inquired he of them the hour when he began to amend. And they said unto him, Yesterday at the seventh hour the fever left him. So the father knew that it was at the same hour, in the which Jesus said unto him, Thy son liveth: and himself believed, and his whole house.* Grace spoke in the seventh hour and the 'like-dead' child became alive again. The child now lived and like Abraham, would reproduce one day. The child is just like us. We too move from death to life. It is because of our faith in Jesus, that justification or righteous standing before God is imputed to us. We are born again into this righteousness. **It is solely by birth and not by works that we attain our righteous identity in Jesus.** In the grafting in process, we were the dead branches grafted into the Living Tree, Jesus. The dead became alive. We did nothing in the seventh hour but rest and receive this Grace! Jesus spoke. We believed. Therefore we live. Just as the nobleman. And his son. And his whole household.

Acts 17:28 states, *For in him we live, and move, and have our being; as certain also of your own poets have said, For we are also his offspring.* We become His offspring. We become heirs to all of God's promises. We are blessed because God imputes righteousness, without works, upon us. Because of Jesus, God will not and cannot impute sin upon us because Jesus paid for all of our sins; past, present, and future. We, who are in Jesus, are sinless and live for eternity with Him.

Paul reminded us again in *Colossians 2:11-14, In whom also ye are circumcised with the circumcision made without hands, in putting off the body of the sins of the flesh by the circumcision of Christ: Buried with him in baptism, wherein also ye are risen with him through the faith of the operation of God, who hath raised him from the dead. And you, being dead in your sins and the uncircumcision of your flesh, hath he quickened together with him, having forgiven you all trespasses; Blotting out the handwriting of ordinances that was against us, which was contrary to us, and took it out of the way, nailing it to his cross.* Because of the finished work of Jesus on the cross, the handwriting of ordinances or the law, was blotted out. The law was contrary to us because we could not fulfill all its requirements by our fleshly works.

Physical circumcision was a work while spiritual circumcision is a gift. Jesus was *the stone cut out without hands* from *Daniel 2:34* that gave us our spiritual circumcision made without hands or self-works. Because of our faith in Jesus and His circumcision (death, burial, and resurrection), we are considered spiritually circumcised. He knifed the sinful carnal nature off us and gave us complete forgiveness of sins. **We were dead people but now made alive by Jesus. As Jesus is, so are we. He is alive, so are we.**

This 'new life' symbolism by circumcision was also important in Moses' time. Before the law was given, we have this curious incident described in *Exodus 4:22-26, And thou shalt say unto Pharaoh, Thus saith the Lord, Israel is my son, even my firstborn: And I say unto thee, Let my son go, that he may serve me: and if thou refuse to let him go, behold, I will slay thy son, even thy firstborn. And it came to pass by the way in the inn, that the Lord met him, and sought to kill him. Then Zipporah took a sharp stone, and cut off the foreskin of her son, and cast it at his feet, and said, Surely a bloody husband art thou to me. So he let him go: then she said, A bloody husband thou art, because of the circumcision.* Did God not ask Moses to lead His people out of Egypt? Why then is God trying to kill him now? Is God schizophrenic? Was it because Moses and his son were uncircumcised?

God wanted to take His people out of Egypt and He chose Moses to do it. Circumcised or not, all the Israelites would come out. It was the goodness of God that would lead them out of captivity and not the 'work' of circumcision. We read in *Joshua 5:4-5, All the people that came out of Egypt, that were males, even all the men of war, died in the wilderness by the way, after they came out of Egypt. Now all the people that came out were circumcised: but all the people that were born in the wilderness by the way as they came forth out of Egypt, them they had not circumcised.*

Before the exodus, God judged the firstborn in Egypt. The nation of Israel, being the firstborn of God in Egypt, had to be protected. Therefore, all the Israelites were circumcised signifying being saved by Christ. Jesus, as their spiritual circumcision, was the only way to be saved. *Deuteronomy 10:16* states this clearly, *Circumcise therefore the foreskin of your heart, and be no more stiffnecked.* It was really the circumcision of their hearts that saved them, not their physical circumcision. Hence, all the males were circumcised when they came out of Egypt. But they did not understood their spiritual circumcision. They turned circumcision into a work. Circumcision 'the work' did not save them as they perished in the wilderness. *Psalm 90:9-10* states, *For all our days are passed away in thy wrath: we spend our years as a tale that is told. The days of our years are threescore years and ten; and if by reason of strength they be fourscore years, yet is their strength labour and sorrow; for it is soon cut off, and we fly away.* Because of the law which brought God's wrath on sin, they did not live long enough to enter the Promised Land. The next generation of Israelites were brought in instead. Their circumcision in the new land of rest was a shadow of Jesus. Without Jesus, there would be no rest and no new life.

Moses' wife was a Gentile. She was the daughter of Jethro, the priest of Midian. We read of them in *Exodus 2:21-22, And Moses was content to dwell with the man: and he gave Moses, Zipporah his daughter. And she bare him a son, and he called his name Gershom.* At the time of her marriage to Moses, she probably abhorred the bloody practice of physical circumcision as practiced by the Jews. And Moses, even though he was a Jew, was brought up by the Egyptians and was not circumcised. We learned this in *Exodus 6:30, And Moses said before the Lord, Behold, I am of uncircumcised lips, and how shall Pharaoh hearken unto me?* The original Hebrew word for uncircumcised as used here was '*arel*' or '*orlah*', literally meaning 'uncircumcised foreskin'. His uncircumcised lips indicated his uncircumcised penis.

Hence, both Moses and Zipporah knew about circumcision but did not put much emphasis on it. That is why Moses delayed circumcising Gershom, his first born son. But because of what God said about the firstborn in Egypt dying, Gershom was now in danger of death. If he remained uncircumcised, he would be killed together with all the other firstborn in Egypt. So that night, at the inn or camp, Zipporah quickly cut off his foreskin. Gershom's life would now be spared. When she flung the foreskin at 'his' feet, we automatically assume that it was Moses' feet and that he was the bloody husband. But Moses, her husband, was not bloody, only Gershom. The Hebrew word, translated as husband here is '*ḥātān*' meaning bridegroom (not husband). This statement of course prefigured Jesus, our bridegroom, who became bloody for us. Jesus was present at this event and Zipporah effectively admitted to having a circumcision of her heart to Him. Jesus became her bridegroom of blood. In the last statement, in Hebrew, the word circumcision, *A bloody husband thou art, because of the circumcision* is plural, i.e. circumcisions. Moses, Zipporah, Gershom, and the other son, Eliezer (also uncircumcised), were all saved that night because of circumcisions of their hearts by faith. Because of Jesus, we are all spared. Because of His blood, not the blood of circumcision, we all gain new life.

Paul put it best in *Philippians 3:2,5-9, Beware of dogs, beware of evil workers, beware of the concision. Circumcised the eighth day, of the stock of Israel, of the tribe of Benjamin, an Hebrew of the Hebrews; as touching the law, a Pharisee; concerning zeal, persecuting the church; touching the righteousness which is in the law, blameless. But what things were gain to me, those I counted loss for Christ. Yea doubtless, and I count all things but loss for the excellency of the knowledge of Christ Jesus my Lord...and do count them but dung (skubalon), that I may win Christ, And be found in him, not having mine own righteousness, which is of the law, but that which is through the faith **of** Christ, the righteousness which is of God by faith:*

The dogs here were the evil workers who held onto their concision or '*katatomé*'. *Katatomé* in Greek, simply meant mutilation or a false circumcision. **Self-works brought skin to the fore. The righteousness which comes from self-works and the law is a mutilation of the righteousness which is of God by faith.** It is false. Paul, circumcised in the flesh by the foreskin and of great Hebrew stock, took no pride in his Pharisaical heritage garnered by his righteous self-works. He counted it all as *skubalon* or literally, shit! In fact, he wished that those who continued to harass believers in Jesus (like Titus the Greek in *Galatians 2:3-5*) with the self-work of circumcision would not stop at just cutting off their penis foreskins but to go all the way and cut off their entire penis, as in *Galatians 5:12, I wish those upsetting you also will emasculate themselves!* This damnable teaching of adding to Jesus' finished work is heresy.

For those who contend that in *Acts 16:3* (Paul circumcising Timothy who was half Greek half Jew) or *Acts 21:26* (shaving heads and purifying rituals) it was clearly acts *for the Jews*. To reach the Jews with the gospel, Paul circumcised Timothy or participated in traditions (*to the Jews I became as a Jew in order to win the Jews*)! Paul really loved his fellow Jews as we know from *Romans 9:2-4, I have great sorrow and unceasing anguish in my heart. For I could wish that I myself were cursed and cut off from Christ for the sake of my people, those of my own race, the people of Israel.* He could say that being first filled with Christ love!

We find Paul's summation statement on circumcision in *1 Corinthians 7:19-20, Circumcision is nothing and uncircumcision is nothing. Keeping God's commands is what counts. Each person should remain in the situation they were in when God called them.* Both circumcision and uncircumcision is nothing! If a person is circumcised (keeps the law) let him continue keeping the law. For the law would lead him to Jesus. If a person is uncircumcised (does not keep the law), let him continue *not* keeping the law! Do not focus on works, which is 'nothing'. Focus on Jesus' work, which is 'everything'.!

Man's ways stink, pervert, and mutilate Jesus' perfection. So let us stop shoveling our warm penis foreskins and other crap on Jesus. Stop adding our filth to Jesus, thinking that we are helping Him. True righteousness only comes from Jesus as He is the righteousness of God. *Haggai 2:8-9* states, *The silver is mine, and the gold is mine, saith the Lord of hosts. The glory of this latter house shall be greater than of the former, saith the Lord of hosts.* Silver and gold stood for redemption and righteousness respectively. The glory of Grace (the latter house) is much greater than the law (the former house). Grace is much greater because redemption and righteousness are now given by Jesus Himself to us freely. We find great peace in putting our faith in Jesus' faith, the faith **of** Christ, and not in our penises!

❧ 3 ❧

JESUS AND FEASTS

There were seven feasts given by God to Moses on mount Sinai. The Hebrew word for feast is '*moed*', meaning a fixed time or season. Every year, at the appointed season, Jews would have a holy convocation, an assembly, or '*miqrā*'. They would be called out to rehearse something that would occur in the future. At the same time, they would also look back at what God had done in the past. *Isaiah 46:9-10* puts it succinctly, *Remember the former things of old: for I am God, and there is none else; I am God, and there is none like me, Declaring the end from the beginning, and from ancient times the things that are not yet doned...and I will do all my pleasure:* These appointed times of the year are His feasts. All the feasts are for His pleasure. They are not Jewish feasts, but God's feasts on God's calendar.

To see the significance of these feasts, let us begin in *Leviticus 23:1,4-6, And the Lord spake unto Moses, saying, Speak unto the children of Israel, and say unto them, Concerning the feasts of the Lord, which ye shall proclaim to be holy convocations, even these are my feasts...In the fourteenth day of the first month at even is the Lord's passover. And on the fifteenth day of the same month is the feast of unleavened bread unto the Lord: seven days ye must eat unleavened bread.* The first feast is called the Passover. The second is the feast of Unleavened Bread.

A more detailed explanation of these first two feasts can be found in *Exodus 12:1-14, And the Lord spake unto Moses and Aaron in the land of Egypt, saying, This month shall be unto you* *the beginning of months: it shall be the first month of the year to you. Speak ye unto all the congregation of Israel, saying, In the tenth day of this month they shall take to them every man **a lamb**, according to the house of their fathers, a lamb for an house: And if the household be too little for **the lamb**, let him and his neighbour next unto his house take it according to the number of the souls; every man according to his eating shall make your count for the lamb. **Your lamb** shall be without blemish, a male of the first year: ye shall take it out from the sheep, or from the goats: And ye shall keep it up until the fourteenth day of the same month: and the whole assembly of the congregation of Israel shall kill it in the evening.*

*And they shall take of the blood, and strike it on the two side posts and on the upper door post of the houses, wherein they shall eat it. And they shall eat the flesh in that night, roast with fire, and unleavened bread; and with bitter herbs they shall eat it. Eat not of it raw, nor sodden at all with water, but roast with fire; his head with his legs, and with the purtenance thereof. And ye shall let nothing of it remain until the morning; and that which remaineth of it until the morning ye shall burn with fire...it is the Lord's passover. For I will pass through the land of Egypt this night, and will smite all the firstborn in the land of Egypt, both man and beast; and against all the gods of Egypt I will execute judgment: I am the Lord. And the blood shall be to you for a token upon the houses where ye are: and **when I see the blood, I will pass over you**, and the plague shall not be upon you to destroy you, when I smite the land of Egypt. And this day shall be unto you for a memorial; and ye shall keep it a feast to the Lord throughout your generations; ye shall keep it a feast by an ordinance forever.*

Passover or in Hebrew '*Pesach*' means to pass through and over, or to spare. This feast was so important that God changed Israel's calendar in order for Passover to become the first month of the year for them. This month was called Nisan. On the tenth day of Nisan, every man would take an unblemished lamb, a male of the first year, for his house. The lamb would be kept until the fourteenth, when the lamb would be sacrificed at sundown. In a lunar calendar, sundown marks the beginning of a new day. Notice that 'a lamb' became 'the lamb' which became 'your lamb' which was kept for five days, signifying Grace! If there were too few members in his household, then he would share the lamb with his neighbors. They would eat the lamb together in one house, as in *Exodus 12:46, It must be eaten inside the house; take none of the meat outside the house. Do not break any of the bones.* Hence, Passover fell on the 14th of Nisan. All the other feasts would be numbered from this feast. For example, the next feast, the feast of unleavened bread, fell on the next day, or on the 15th of Nisan.

The blood of the sacrificed lamb would be struck on the outside two side posts and the upper door post of their houses. It was on the outside for God to see. The Israelites would then roast the lamb whole and consume it completely. They were forbidden to eat the lamb raw or boiled. **Note that having the lamb and then killing it accomplishes nothing unless the blood of the lamb is also applied to the doorposts. Only when God sees the blood of the lamb, then God's wrath on sin would pass over them. The blood of the lamb was for God to see, not the inhabitants. Also, God did not inspect the worthiness of each inhabitant in the house. It was the worthiness of the lamb, not the people, that mattered to God.** Whether they cowered in fright or praised God inside the house, the blood of the lamb was all that mattered. As such, the firstborn of all Israel were saved. Passover was therefore the feast of salvation for the Jews. Interestingly, some rabbis have taught that *two* bloods were put on the doorposts! One of the lamb and the more important one of circumcision. The circumcision blood was necessary to earn redemption from Egypt!

For believers, the explanation is equally simple. Jesus rode into Jerusalem on the back of a donkey on the tenth of Nisan. Jesus died on the fourteenth of Nisan after Pilate, at Gabbatha, announced that he had found no fault or guilt in Him. He was the young one year old lamb for He died *in the midst* of His days as in *Psalm 102:24.* **However, just knowing that Jesus is the unblemished Lamb of God sacrificed for the whole world accomplishes nothing. For we still have to receive Him! It is His life, death, and blood that makes us righteous forever.** After Jesus, no more sacrifices were needed. We read in *1 Peter*

1:18-19, Forasmuch as ye know that ye were not redeemed with corruptible things, as silver and gold, from your vain conversation received by tradition from your fathers; But with the precious blood of Christ, as of a lamb without blemish and without spot.

Jesus is always more than sufficient for every member in a household. He is to be shared with the neighbors as well. Salvation by faith is offered freely to all. But not everyone wants it. But for those of us who would accept this free gift, we would be given a new life. We call this our 'born again' redemptive experience. Our 'old man' died and we are transformed into the 'new man'. We passed over death and became new creations, with a new life. Just like the blood splattered door posts, dripping to form a cross, Jesus on the cross is still the only solution to sin. Any offering that is raw (Jesus did not start the work of redeeming us) or boiled (Jesus did not finish the work of redeeming us) is not a burnt (Jesus finished the work of redeeming us) sin offering. We know that the fiery judgment of God on sins consumes the entire offering. That is also why the lamb had to be roasted and eaten whole. The head, the legs, and the entrails were all to be consumed. Jesus is to be taken whole, and none of His bones were to be broken, as in *Psalm 34:20, He keepeth all his bones: not one of them is broken.*

Passover is therefore a shadow of Jesus as we read in *Luke 22:7-20, Then came the day of unleavened bread, when the passover must be killed. And he sent Peter and John, saying, Go and prepare us the passover, that we may eat. And they said unto him, Where wilt thou that we prepare? And he said unto them, Behold, when ye are entered into the city, there shall a man meet you, bearing a pitcher of water; follow him into the house where he entereth in. And ye shall say unto the goodman of the house, The Master saith unto thee, Where is the guestchamber, where I shall eat the passover with my disciples? And he shall shew you a large upper room furnished: there make ready.. And when the hour was come, he sat down, and the twelve apostles with him. And he said unto them, With desire I have desired to eat this passover with you before I suffer...And he took the cup, and gave thanks, and said, Take this, and divide it among yourselves...And he took bread, and gave thanks, and brake it, and gave unto them, saying,*

This is my body which is given for you: this do in remembrance of me. Likewise also the cup after supper, saying, This cup is the new testament in my blood, which is shed for you.

The man carrying the pitcher of living water entered into the house of the goodman. In those days, no man carried water, only women did. But Jesus was the Man who carried Living Water in Him. The guest chamber is our heart. Jesus entered into our hearts and furnished it anew. He finished the work. There He had Passover. He desired to have Passover with us as He is our Passover. *1 Corinthians 5:7* states, *For even Christ our passover is sacrificed for us.* That is why Pharaoh had to let the Israelites free after the Passover lamb was sacrificed. All the other former plagues had no power over Pharaoh until the blood of the lamb was shed. Only then did Pharaoh lost all power over the Israelites. Similarly for us, sin no longer has any power over us because of Jesus' shed blood. Also, His broken body removed all our sicknesses. Sin and sicknesses has to let us go as Jesus, our Passover, became our salvation and our healer.

After the last supper on Passover, *Matthew 26:30* states, *And when they had sung an hymn, they went out into the mount of Olives.* The hymns that they sung were the psalms, possibly *Psalm 118:24-29, This is the day which the Lord hath made; we will rejoice and be glad in it. Save now, I beseech thee, O Lord: O Lord, I beseech thee, send now prosperity. Blessed be he that cometh in the name of the Lord: we have blessed you out of the house of the Lord. God is the Lord, which hath shewed us light: bind the sacrifice with cords, even unto the horns of the altar. Thou art my God, and I will praise thee: thou art my God, I will exalt thee. O give thanks unto the Lord; for he is good: for his mercy endureth forever.* But because of the veil over their eyes, they could not see that Jesus was the sacrifice bound with cords to the horns of the altar. Give thanks and praises to Jesus for He is good!

But we do not have the veil any longer. We can see clearly. The next night's feast after Passover was called the feast of unleavened bread. This was the second feast. As leaven symbolized sin, Jewish tradition required the removal of all leaven from their homes. The process is highly significant. Wives would thoroughly clean the house of leaven but would purposefully leave 10 small leavened pieces of bread hidden throughout the house. These pieces of 'sin' would then be 'discovered' by husbands and children. Using only light from candles (Light of Jesus), whenever a piece of sin was discovered, it would be swept up with a feather (Holy Spirit) into a wooden spoon (cross of Jesus). These 10 pieces of sin (the law) would then be wrapped up in a linen cloth (the finished work of Jesus), taken to the synagogue, and there burned (Jesus judged for all our sins).

All bread that was to be eaten with the lamb had to be unleavened. The unleavened bread, together with the bitter herbs, would be dipped into a sweet sauce or paste. The bitter herbs reminded the Israelites of their slavery while the sweetness of the sauce, their redemption.

Of course, Jesus is our Unleavened Bread as He is without sin. **He tasted the bitter on the cross so that we would be able to savor sweet redemption. Jesus, who was without sin, bore our sins and took the bitter judgment of God on sins.** He died for us on the fourteenth of Nisan and was buried on the fifteenth. He is the true Manna from heaven. The manna in the wilderness lasted for only one day, except on the day before the Sabbath. When kept by human efforts, it stank and maggots grew in it. We read in *John 6:32-33 and 48-50, Then Jesus said unto them, Verily, verily, I say unto you, Moses gave you not that bread from heaven; but my Father giveth you the true bread from heaven. For the bread of God is he which cometh down from heaven, and giveth life unto the world. I am that bread of life. Your fathers did eat manna in the wilderness, and are dead. This is the bread which cometh down from heaven, that a man may eat thereof, and not die.* The true Bread from heaven is Jesus. He was buried but He never stank nor bred worms. As He is unleavened, so are we. *1 Corinthians 5:7-8* states, *Purge out therefore the old leaven, that ye may be a new lump, as ye are unleavened. For even Christ our passover is sacrificed for us: Therefore let us keep the feast, not with old leaven, neither with the leaven of malice and wickedness; but with the unleavened bread of sincerity and truth.*

This old leaven of malice and wickedness was cleaned out by Jesus in *Matthew 21:12-15, And Jesus went into the temple of God, and cast out all them that **sold and bought** in the temple, and overthrew the tables of the moneychangers, and the seats of them that sold doves, And said unto them, It is written, My house shall be called the house of prayer; but ye have made it a den of thieves. And the blind and the lame came to him in the temple; and he healed them…and the children crying in the temple, and saying, Hosanna to the Son of David.* The Pharisees controlled the sale of animals used for sacrifices and the tables where currencies were changed. They made it into a religious den of thievery and larceny. Jesus cleaned out the temple by flipping and whipping (*John 2:15*) up a mess of fleeing Pharisees, oxen, sheep, doves, and tables. Crap was everywhere and on everything, a symbol that the defiled temple would be overturned soon, as in *Jeremiah 7:11, Has this house, which bears my Name, become a den of robbers to you?*

And into this chaotic mess, the blind and the lame came to Jesus to be healed. But not only were they healed but Hosanna-ed! Hosanna means 'save us'. Jesus met the people in their mess and saved them! The cleaning of the temple was actually to show us that salvation cannot be *sold and bought*. Only Jesus can whip and flip all sinful crap from us! The temple was actually not only for Jews but also for Gentiles. In *1 Kings 8:41* and *2 Chronicles 6:32*, Solomon dedicated the temple also for foreigners/Gentiles to pray towards it. In *Isaiah 56:6*, foreigners who gave burnt offerings and sacrifices at the temple were also accepted. Jesus, as the new and forever living Temple, is always for ALL.

This is a fulfillment of *Zechariah 14:20-21, On that day, Holy to the LORD will be written on the horses' bells. The pots in the house of the LORD will be as the basins before the altar. Every pot in Jerusalem and in Judah will be holy to the LORD of hosts… No longer will there be merchants in the house of the LORD of hosts on that day.* We see a small preview of the Millennial reign of Christ here. Every pot, not only those in the temple, becomes holy. Even the bells that horses have on their heads are just as holy as the crown on the high priest's head that reads 'Holy to the Lord'. There will be no merchants or traders in the temple. Jesus threw out the religious leavened crap so that everybody, every messed up pothead, could come to the true Temple which was Himself! Jesus, the Lamb of God, took away the sins of the world!

The third feast is found in *Leviticus 23:9-11, And the Lord spake unto Moses, saying, Speak unto the children of Israel, and say unto them, When ye be come into the land which I give unto you, and shall reap the harvest thereof, then ye shall bring a sheaf of the firstfruits of your harvest unto the priest: And he shall wave the sheaf before the Lord, to be accepted for you: on the morrow after the sabbath the priest shall wave it.* The previous feast of unleavened bread was exactly seven days long. This feast of firstfruits was to be done 'on the morrow after the Sabbath' or Saturday evening to Sunday evening. Sabbath is from Friday evening to Saturday evening. Somewhere in those seven days of unleavened bread would be a Saturday-Sunday and that day would be the feast of firstfruits. The first cut from the sickle produced the first grains. This referred to the barley harvest. The Israelites were to bring this early barley harvest to the priest who would then wave and heave the offering before the Lord, symbolizing the cross. Their offerings of first sheaves blessed the rest of the harvest. It was an acknowledgement of the good land and the harvest that God had given to them.

Jesus is our firstfruit. He was the kernel of wheat mentioned in *John 12:24, Verily, verily, I say unto you, Except a corn of wheat fall into the ground and die, it abideth alone: but if it die, it bringeth forth much fruit.* He died to give us life. Because of Jesus, we would all be 'secondfruits' one day. This is clearly stated in *1 Corinthians 15:20-23, But now is Christ risen from the dead, and become the firstfruits of them that slept. For since by man came death, by man came also the resurrection of the dead. For as in Adam all die, even so in Christ shall all be made alive. But every man in his own order: Christ the firstfruits; afterward they that are Christ's at his coming.* Again in *1 Thessalonians 4:16-17, For the Lord himself shall descend from heaven with a shout, with the voice of the archangel, and with the trump of God: and the dead in Christ shall rise first: Then we which are alive and remain shall be caught up together with them in the clouds, to meet the Lord in the air: and so shall we ever be with the Lord,* and *Colossians 1:18, he is the beginning and the firstborn from among the dead.*

Jesus is the first sheaf waved before God. He was resurrected on the seventeenth of Nisan. He was victorious over death and one day, He will come back for us. We call this event the rapture as Jesus comes for us in the clouds. The dead in Christ are resurrected and taken up first. Then we, who are alive, would be caught up together with them. Because of Jesus, we get to be with Him forever, as in *Ephesians 2:6, And hath raised us up together, and made us sit together in heavenly places in Christ Jesus.* Jesus even gave a small example of this coming day in *Matthew 27:52-53, And the graves were opened; and many bodies of the saints which slept arose, And came out of the graves after his resurrection, and went into the holy city, and appeared unto many.* These believers, though without glorified bodies, were resurrected and were seen by many. We know from *1 Corinthians 3:17, for the temple of God is holy, and that is what you are,* and *Romans 11:16, For if the firstfruit be holy, the lump is also holy: and if the root be holy, so are the branches,* that we are holy because He is holy.

Exactly fifty days after the feast of firstfruits is the fourth feast. This feast is known as the feast of weeks, as it is the day after seven Sabbaths. It is also the end of the summer wheat harvest. We read this in *Leviticus 23:15-17* and *21, And ye shall count unto you from the morrow after the sabbath, from the day that ye brought the sheaf of the wave offering; seven sabbaths shall be complete: Even unto the morrow after the seventh sabbath shall ye number fifty days; and ye shall offer a new meat offering unto the Lord. Ye shall bring out of your habitations two wave loaves of two tenth deals: they shall be of fine flour; they shall be baken with leaven; they are the firstfruits unto the Lord.   And ye shall proclaim on the selfsame day, that it may be an holy convocation unto you: ye shall do no servile work therein.*

For the Jews, the feast of weeks celebrated the day when Moses received the law from God. On Mount Sinai, the thunderings (in Hebrew *qol* meaning voices) and the lightnings (in Hebrew *lappid* meaning burning torch) fell upon the people. Immediately after the law was given, 3000 souls died as we read in

Exodus 32:28, And the children of Levi did according to the word of Moses: and there fell of the people that day about three thousand men. The Levites killed their brothers defending the law. About 1400 years later, Caiaphas the Sadducee Levitical high priest would deliver his Jewish brother, Jesus, to be killed as well. All to defend the law that would ultimately kill them.

For believers, fifty days after the resurrection of Jesus the Firstfruit, is Pentecost. The two wave loaves, baked with leaven, and offered up before God represent Jews and Gentiles saved by their faith in Jesus. Baked with leaven, sinful man was made new by the fine flour of Jesus. New Bread → new man → new life! In the upper room, cloven tongues like as of fire came down and sat upon each of them. Immediately after that, the Holy Spirit spoke through Peter and 3000 souls lived, as we read in *Acts 2:41, Then they that gladly received his word were baptized: and the same day there were added unto them about three thousand souls.* The 3000 souls were a small token of the coming fall harvest. There was also a specific command not to do any work on this day. **Jesus sent the Holy Spirit to remind us of our righteousness in Him. It was a gift of righteousness and not a work to righteousness. It is not by our works but our rest in Jesus, our Jubilee, that mattered.**

The fifth feast is the feast of trumpets. We read this in *Leviticus 23:23-24, In the seventh month, in the first day of the month, shall ye have a sabbath, a memorial of blowing of trumpets, an holy convocation.* To obtain a trumpet or *shofar*, a male sheep has to die. Its horn becomes a trumpet. But what is the use of a trumpet? Its use is found in *Numbers 10:1-9, And the Lord spake unto Moses, saying, Make thee two trumpets of silver; of a whole piece shalt thou make them: that thou mayest use them for the calling of the assembly, and for the journeying of the camps. And when they shall blow with them, all the assembly shall assemble themselves to thee at the door of the tabernacle of the congregation. And if they blow but with one trumpet, then the princes, which are heads of the thousands of Israel, shall gather themselves unto thee. When ye blow an alarm, then the camps that lie on the east parts shall go forward. When ye blow an alarm the second time, then the camps that lie on the south side shall take their journey: they shall blow an alarm for their journeys. But when the congregation is to be gathered together, ye shall blow, but ye shall not sound an alarm. And the sons of Aaron, the priests, shall blow with the trumpets; and they shall be to you for an ordinance for ever throughout your generations. And if ye go to war in your land against the enemy that oppresseth you, then ye shall blow an alarm with the trumpets; and ye shall be remembered before the Lord your God, and ye shall be saved from your enemies. Also in the day of your gladness, and in your solemn days, and in the beginnings of your months, ye shall blow with the trumpets...*

In addition to the shofar, God commanded that another two trumpets be made, of silver, signifying redemption. When the trumpets blew: (1) faithful Jews would leave the harvest field, assemble and gather together for prayers in the temple; (2) Jews would journey forth to a new place; (3) it was to announce a day of gladness; and (4) they would prepare for war.

For believers, when the trumpets blow, all those in Christ would be changed. *1Corinthians 15:42-44,51-53* states, *So also is the resurrection of the dead. It is sown in corruption; it is raised in incorruption: It is sown in dishonour; it is raised in glory: it is sown in weakness; it is raised in power: It is sown a natural body; it is raised a spiritual body. There is a natural body, and there is a spiritual body.   Behold, I shew you a mystery; We shall not all sleep, but we shall all be changed, In a moment, in the twinkling of an eye, at the last trump: for the trumpet shall sound, and the dead shall be raised incorruptible, and we shall be changed. For this corruptible must put on incorruption, and this mortal must put on immortality.* The dead would be raised up. Those alive would be changed. All would be given new glorious, powerful, incorruptible, and immortal bodies. New Covenant believers would be assembled and then taken out of this world. It would be a day of exceeding gladness. It would also be a day when the people who were left behind would have to endure the tribulation/war period.

The sixth feast is the day of atonement. We read this in *Leviticus 23:26-28, And the Lord spake unto Moses, saying, Also on the tenth day of this seventh month there shall be a day of atonement: it shall be an holy convocation unto you; and ye shall afflict your souls, and offer an offering made by fire unto the Lord. And ye shall do no work in that same day: for it is a day of atonement, to make an atonement for you before the Lord your God.* On the day of atonement or *Yom Kippur*, considered as the holiest day by the Jews, the high priest of Israel would offer sacrifices on his own behalf, as well as sacrifices on behalf of all the Israelites. *Leviticus 16:14* states, *And he shall take of the blood of the bullock, and sprinkle it with his finger upon the mercy seat eastward; and before the mercy seat shall he sprinkle of the blood with his finger seven times.* The blood of the sacrificed animals would be sprinkled upon and in front of the mercy seat. If God rejected the high priest and his offerings, then all of Israel would be rejected. It was a day where the Jews literally lived or died. It was a most solemn day.

For believers, in the fiftieth year or the year of jubilee, Perfection upon Perfection arrived. Jesus was revealed. He is our Jubilee, now made manifest. *Leviticus 25:9-10* states, *Then shalt thou cause the trumpet of the jubilee to sound on the tenth day of the seventh month, in the day of atonement shall ye make the trumpet sound throughout all your land. And ye shall hallow the fiftieth year, and proclaim liberty throughout all the land unto all the inhabitants thereof: it shall be a jubilee unto you; and ye shall return every man unto his possession, and ye shall return every man unto his family.* On the tenth day of the seventh month, on the day of atonement, trumpets were blown. Jesus had arrived. Liberty was announced throughout the land. A new High Priest came who would always be accepted by God. He was the perfect offering. He atoned for the sins of the whole world. He was the one-time sprinkled blood atop the mercy seat. He was also the seven times sprinkled blood before the mercy seat, seven being the number for perfection. Perfect redemption came for all. Seven plus one is eight. The number eight signified a new beginning. Because He came, every man's possession was restored, every broken relationship was restored, and every family was united together again. It was a new beginning for all. The law for people to do no work at all on the day of atonement is now clear. The finished work of Jesus precludes any additional work. And just as His first coming, the day of atonement also symbolized Jesus' second coming. But this time in power, at the end of the tribulation period.

The seventh feast can be found in *Leviticus 23:33-34,36,* and *42-43, The fifteenth day of this seventh month shall be the feast of tabernacles for seven days unto the Lord. Seven days ye shall offer an offering made by fire unto the LORD: on the eighth day shall be an holy convocation unto you; and ye shall offer an offering made by fire unto the LORD: it is a solemn assembly (atsereth);and ye shall do no servile work therein. And ye shall take you on the first day the boughs of goodly trees, branches of palm trees, and the boughs of thick trees, and willows of the brook; and ye shall rejoice before the LORD your God seven days. And ye shall keep it a feast unto the LORD seven days in the year. It shall be a statute forever in your generations: ye shall celebrate it in the seventh month. Ye shall dwell in booths seven days; all that are Israelites born shall dwell in booths: That your generations may know that I made the children of Israel to dwell in booths, when I brought them out of the land of Egypt.*

This feast of Tabernacles or Booths was to commemorate the shelters that God provided for the Jews when they came out of Egypt. *Isaiah 4:5-6* states, *And the Lord will create upon every dwelling place of mount Zion, and upon her assemblies, a cloud and smoke by day, and the shining of a flaming fire by night: for upon all the glory shall be a defence. And there shall be a tabernacle for a shadow in the daytime from the heat, and for a place of refuge, and for a covert from storm and from rain.* God's shelter was a secure place of protection. He would be their defense. He would 'shadow' them from the heat of the day and keep them warm during the cool of the night. Everyone would be shielded with a leafy cloud covering. We see this in *Psalm 105:39, He spread a cloud for a covering; and fire to give light in the night.* Under the law, the Israelites were told to build temporary shelters, booths, or *sukkah*, to remind themselves of God's goodness. The roof of the shelter would be branches and leaves weaved together in such a manner that would provide shade from the sun, yet let cool air in when night fell. Also, during this feast, the Israelites had to take the branches of four plants, group them together and wave it before God. After Israel entered the Promised Land, the feast of Tabernacles became a feast of ingathering. The fall harvest of corn, wine, and fruits were gathered in. That is why the *sukkah* is usually decorated inside with fruits from the fall harvest.

We read in *Mark 11:8-9, And many spread their garments in the way: and others cut down branches off the trees, and strawed them in the way. And they that went before, and they that followed, cried, saying, Hosanna; Blessed is he that cometh in the name of the Lord:* Jesus riding into Jerusalem from the east fulfilled *Ezekiel 43:4, The glory of the LORD entered the temple through the gate facing east.* It also fulfilled the 600+ years old prophecy of His coming and death found in *Daniel 9:25-26.* We are the branches that worship Him, *hosanna* meaning 'save us'. Jesus came to save us. He is our King, as in *2 Kings 9:13, Then they hasted, and took every man his garment, and put it under him.* Jesus as Grace is always above, never below. *Psalm 68:4* states, *Sing unto God, sing praises to his name: extol him that rideth upon the heavens by his name JAH, and rejoice before him.* Jesus rides upon the heavens or the clouds. It is as prophesied in *Zechariah 9:9, See, your king comes to you, righteous and victorious, lowly and riding on a donkey, on a colt, the foal of a donkey.*

For believers, Jesus has become our Booth and our Tabernacle. With Jesus as our Tabernacle, we can finally understand *Isaiah 25:6-8, And in this mountain shall the Lord of hosts make unto all people a feast of fat things, a feast of wines on the lees, of fat things full of marrow, of wines on the lees well refined. And he will destroy in this mountain the face of the covering cast over all people, and the vail that is spread over all nations. He will swallow up death in victory; and the Lord God will wipe away tears from off all faces; and the rebuke of his people shall he take away from off all the earth: for the Lord hath spoken it.* One day, in Jesus' Millennial Kingdom, there will be no veil of the law which brought death. Death will be swallowed up instead. There will be a feast of fat and refined things. He will wipe away our tears of gratitude. Everything will be made new. We will be glad and rejoice in His salvation.

The feast of Tabernacles would last for seven days. On the eighth day, there would be a solemn assembly or *atsereth,* with burnt, grain, drink, and sin offerings. For present-day Jews, this eighth day is known as *Simchat Torah* or 'rejoicing in the *Torah*'. It marks the completion of another yearly cycle of reading through the Torah, re-rolling the *Torah* scroll, and beginning again in *Genesis/Bereshit.* In Hebrew, *atsereth* is spelled Ayin Tsade Reysh Tav, meaning 'those who know the Prince on the cross' will be gathered together with Him. Jesus is our Tabernacle now and in His future Millennial Reign. We read of this in *Revelation 21:3, And I heard a great voice out of heaven saying, Behold, the tabernacle of God is with men, and he will dwell with them, and they shall be his people, and God himself shall be with them, and be their God.* In the Millennial Reign, we dwell on earth with Jesus for 1000 years.

There is another feast called the feast of dedication or *Hanukkah* (*Chanukah*). It was not given by God to Moses on mount Sinai, but was prophesied by Daniel in *Daniel 8:9,11, And out of one of them came forth a little horn, which waxed exceeding great, toward the south, and toward the east, and toward the pleasant land. Yea, he magnified himself even to the prince of the host, and by him the daily sacrifice was taken away, and the place of his sanctuary was cast down.* In the year 167 BC, the Greek King of the Seleucid empire, Antiochus IV Epiphanes (the 'little horn' is the antichrist, of which Antiochus IV is a small reflection), started to openly persecute the Jews (prophesied in *Daniel 11:21-39*). Antiochus ransacked the temple in Jerusalem, stole its treasures, raised up an altar to Zeus, and sacrificed pigs on the altar of burnt offerings in the temple. This led to a revolt by the Jews, called the Maccabean revolt, which resulted in the overthrow of the Greeks in Judea and its surrounding areas. The temple in Jerusalem was liberated but because of the Greeks' profanity, had to be rededicated. According to Jewish tradition, when the time came for rededicating the temple, very little oil was left that had not been defiled. This oil was to keep the golden menorah fire continuously lit at night. Only one day's supply of oil was left, but miraculously, lasted for 8 days. This accounts for the 8+1 branched

Hanukkah menorah used by Jews for this feast. This feast can be found in *John 10:22-23, And it was at Jerusalem the feast of the dedication, and it was winter. And Jesus walked in the temple in Solomon's porch.*

Jesus walked into the temple during the feast of dedication, symbolizing that the true Light of the World had come. *John 8:12* states, *Then spake Jesus again unto them, saying, I am the light of the world: he that followeth me shall not walk in darkness, but shall have the light of life.* The everlasting light in the temple is Jesus as He is the eternal Light of Life. We read in *Exodus 40:24-25, And he put the candlestick in the tent of the congregation, over against the table, on the side of the tabernacle southward. And he lighted the lamps before the Lord; as the Lord commanded Moses.* The menorah was put on the south side of the tabernacle, south signifying warmth and brightness, just as Jesus is.

We see the details of the menorah in *Exodus 25:31-33,37, And thou shalt make a candlestick of pure gold: of beaten work shall the candlestick be made: his shaft, and his branches, his bowls, his knops, and his flowers, shall be of the same. And six branches shall come out of the sides of it; three branches of the candlestick out of the one side, and three branches of the candlestick out of the other side: Three bowls made like unto almonds, with a knop and a flower in one branch; ...so in the six branches that come out of the candlestick. And in the candlestick shall be four bowls made like unto almonds, with their knops and their flowers. And thou shalt make the seven lamps thereof: and they shall light the lamps thereof, that they may **give light over against it.***

Jesus is the Central Branch of the gold menorah, from which three branches branch out to the right and three to the left (3+1+3). He is the middle shaft that supplies light to all the six branches of the lamp. As such, the center shaft wick is always lit first. All the wicks point inwards (they give light over against *it*; 'it' referring to the center shaft). Jesus is our Light and everything points towards Him. The menorah is a one piece gold lampstand standing 5.3 feet tall resembling the almond tree which is the first flowering tree of the year. The almond buds and flowers symbolize

Jesus because He is the source of all growth and He is the scent that pleases God. Almond in Hebrew is *shaked* meaning to watch. It is as though the trees in the bible, from the gopher, acacia, oak, cedar, myrtle, sycamore, palm, fig, and olive trees, to name a few, incline towards and watch Jesus, the central Tree of Life!

We read further in *Zechariah 4:2-3,7, And said unto me, What seest thou? And I said, I have looked, and behold a candlestick all of gold, with a bowl upon the top of it, and his seven lamps thereon, and seven pipes to the seven lamps, which are upon the top thereof: And two olive trees by it, one upon the right side of the bowl, and the other upon the left side thereof... and he shall bring forth the headstone thereof with shoutings, crying, Grace, grace unto it.* In Zechariah's vision, there were two olive trees continuously filling up a big bowl with olive oil. The oil from this big bowl would in turn flow down seven pipes to fill the seven oil trays/bowls, one on top of each branch of the menorah.

The two olive trees in Zechariah's time were Joshua (high priest) and Zerubbabel (governor). But Jesus is both eternal High Priest and King. Hence, Jesus is 'both' the olive trees. He supplies all the oil to all the lamps. The two witnesses identified in *Revelation 11:4, These are the two olive trees, and the two candlesticks standing before the God of the earth,* will similarly have Jesus' power supplied to them! God revealed to us in *Revelation 1:12-13, I saw seven golden candlesticks; And in the midst of the seven candlesticks one like unto the Son of man, clothed with a garment down to the foot, and girt about the paps with a golden girdle,* that the golden candlesticks actually stood for people with Jesus at their center. As we are attached to Him, His golden oil flows into us. We become sons and daughters of Golden Oil. Just like Zerubbabel, we say "Grace! Grace!" to all of it.

Jesus is the appointed time and the fulfillment of all the feasts. He is the beginning and the ending of all the feasts. We read in *Colossians 2:16-17, Let no man therefore judge you in meat, or in drink, or in respect of an holyday, or of the new moon, or of the sabbath days: Which are a shadow of things to come; but the body is of Christ.* Every feast was a shadow of Jesus. The real is always Jesus!

❧ 4 ❧

JESUS AND WELLS

Wells give water and life. Even wilderness and desert places become alive where there are wells. We start by reading *Genesis 29:1-3,7-10, Then Jacob went on his journey, and came into the land of the people of the east. And he looked, and behold a well in the field, and, lo, there were three flocks of sheep lying by it; for out of that well they watered the flocks: and a great stone was upon the well's mouth. And thither were all the flocks gathered: and they rolled the stone from the well's mouth, and watered the sheep, and put the stone again upon the well's mouth in his place. And he said, Lo, it is yet high day, neither is it time that the cattle should be gathered together: water ye the sheep, and go and feed them. And they said, We cannot, until all the flocks be gathered together, and till they roll the stone from the well's mouth; then we water the sheep. And while he yet spake with them, Rachel came with her father's sheep: for she kept them. And it came to pass, when Jacob saw Rachel the daughter of Laban his mother's brother, and the sheep of Laban his mother's brother, that Jacob went near, and rolled the stone from the well's mouth, and watered the flock of Laban his mother's brother.*

When Jacob was thirsty, he happened upon a well in a field. There were shepherds and three flocks of sheep lying by the well. The water from the well would nourish and give them life. But the well was covered by a big stone! Life was available for the flocks but because of the law of stone, they all had to wait for the stone to be lifted. The shepherds were as described by *Titus 2:13,*

Looking for that blessed hope, and the glorious appearing of the great God and our Saviour Jesus Christ; They were sitting and waiting around for the stone to be removed because they did not have the rights to the well. Laban and his daughter, Rachel, had the rights. When Rachel finally showed up, the stone was rolled away. The stone which covered the well was a shadow of the law. It was for a period of time before being rolled away by Jesus.

We see this same stone in *John 11:5-7,38-44, Now Jesus loved Martha, and her sister, and Lazarus. When he had heard therefore that he was sick, he abode two days still in the same place where he was. Then after that saith he to his disciples, Let us go into Judaea again. Jesus therefore again groaning in himself cometh to the grave. It was a cave, and a stone lay upon it. Jesus said, Take ye away the stone. Martha, the sister of him that was dead, saith unto him, Lord, by this time he stinketh: for he hath been dead four days. Jesus saith unto her, Said I not unto thee, that, if thou wouldest believe, thou shouldest see the glory of God? Then they took away the stone from the place where the dead was laid. And Jesus lifted up his eyes, and said, Father, I thank thee that thou hast heard me. And I knew that thou hearest me always: but because of the people which stand by I said it, that they may believe that thou hast sent me. And when he thus had spoken, he cried with a loud voice, Lazarus, come forth. And he that was dead came forth, bound hand and foot with graveclothes: and his face was bound about with a napkin. Jesus saith unto them, Loose him, and let him go.*

The two days where Jesus stayed across the Jordan before He left for Judea on the third day to raise up Lazarus, portends that the rapture will happen any day from AD2033-AD3032. Jesus groaned in Himself when He reached the grave. For He saw that Lazarus was caught behind the stone! Everyone stunk behind the stony law because the law showed us how stinky we really are. And just like Martha, we have to roll away the law of stone to see the glory of God. Jesus called Lazarus specifically by name, otherwise all the dead would have been raised up as well. But to emphasize how bound up he was, John wrote that Lazarus came hopping out of the grave, bound hand and foot with grave clothes, and with the deathly veil still upon his face. Lazarus was bound but Grace set him loose and gave him Life.

Jesus gave us access to the Living Water, which was Himself. But even though we may now have access to the water, there were still bad shepherds who would drive us away from this Living Water. We read this in *Exodus 2:15-19, But Moses fled from the face of Pharaoh, and dwelt in the land of Midian: and he sat down by a well. Now the priest of Midian had seven daughters: and they came and drew water, and filled the troughs to water their father's flock. And the shepherds came and drove them away: but Moses stood up and helped them, and watered their flock.* It was ironic that Moses, who drove away the bad shepherds, would ultimately bring the law that closed the mouth of the well. The law of stone would multiply bad shepherds, herding and multiplying sin, until all creation groaned and travailed in pain under the weight of the stony law, waiting for the day when the rapture would take place. *Romans 8:22-23* states, *For we know that the whole creation groaneth and travaileth in pain together until now. And not only they, but ourselves also, which have the firstfruits of the Spirit, even we ourselves groan within ourselves, waiting for the adoption, to wit, the redemption of our body.*

For the next thirty-eight years, after the law was given on mount Sinai, the people suffered and died. None of the first generation of Israelites, bar Joshua and Caleb, which came out of Egypt entered the Promised Land. The law of stone kept them out of their new life. We read of this in *Deuteronomy 2:14, And the space in which we came from Kadesh-barnea, until we were come over the brook Zered, was thirty and eight years; until all the generation of the men of war were wasted out from among the host, as the Lord sware unto them.* They carried the law with them for thirty-eight years, succumbing to it, until they all died. This was the same period of time that the paralytic spent at the pool of Bethesda in *John 5.* For thirty-eight years, he was maimed and immobilized by the law, until Grace came.

God wants us to just receive His blessings. It is He who gives us power, strength, youthfulness, healing, and wholeness. It is all unmerited favor. Not earned. Our part is to be still, rest, and receive what He had already done for us. *Psalm 46:10* states, *Be still (raphah or let drop), and know that I am God: I will be exalted among the heathen, I will be exalted in the earth.* And then again in *Isaiah 40:28-31, the everlasting God, the Lord, the Creator of the ends of the earth, fainteth not, neither is weary?... He giveth power to the faint; and to them that have no might he increaseth strength. Even the youths shall faint and be weary, and the young men shall utterly fall: But they that wait upon the Lord shall renew their strength; they shall mount up with wings as eagles; they shall run, and not be weary; and they shall walk, and not faint.*

And yet again in *Genesis 32:24-28, And Jacob was left alone; and there wrestled a man with him until the breaking of the day. And when he saw that he prevailed not against him, he touched the hollow of his thigh; and the hollow of Jacob's thigh was out of joint, as he wrestled with him. And he said, Let me go, for the day breaketh. And he said, I will not let thee go, except thou bless me. And he said unto him, What is thy name? And he said, Jacob. And he said, Thy name shall be called no more Jacob, but Israel: for as a prince hast thou power with God and with men, and hast prevailed.* Jacob, being full of his own strength, wrestled with Jesus all night. He could not be blessed until Jesus touched the socket of his hip and wrenched it out of place. Only then was he blessed as a prince and his name was changed to Israel. From his name, a whole nation would be called as such. When he utterly fell, Jesus renewed his strength. When he could no longer walk, Jesus made him mount up with wings as eagles. When he could not, then he was ready to receive from the One who could. In the natural we walk but can never fly. But when we *raphah* and let Jesus the Exalted One take over, then we can fly!

That is the also the reason why Jesus was displeased with His disciples in *Mark 10:13-15, And they brought young children to him, that he should touch them: and his disciples rebuked those that brought them. But when Jesus saw it, he was much displeased, and said unto them, Suffer the little children to come unto me, and forbid them not: for of such is the kingdom of God. Verily I say unto you, Whosoever shall not receive the kingdom of God as a little child, he shall not enter therein.* We are not talking about childlike faith or childish faith here. **It is not about how much faith we have but about how we can receive as a little child from God. Little children cannot give back. They are many times, helpless, and can only receive. We are to receive Grace as a little child.** We saw in *Matthew 18:3, And said, Verily I say unto you, Except ye be converted, and become as little children, ye shall not enter into the kingdom of heaven.* Adults are in a position to give back, but little children can only receive. Of such, meaning like children who cannot pay back, is the kingdom of God. For what can we give back to God which is not His to begin with as in *1 Chronicles 29:14, For all things come from you, and of your own have we given you.* God gives. God supplies. We receive. Even baby Jesus received milk from Mary that God provided at creation!

Let us read from *Deuteronomy 1:21-23, Behold, the Lord thy God hath set the land before thee: go up and possess it, as the Lord God of thy fathers hath said unto thee; fear not, neither be discouraged. And ye came near unto me every one of you, and said, **We will send men before us**, and they shall search us out the land, and bring us word again by what way we must go up, and into what cities we shall come. And the saying pleased me well: and I took twelve men of you, one of a tribe.* God gave the Israelites the land, the cities, the houses, and the fruit of the land. It was to be their place of rest, a place where they would be supplied and blessed. But they could not receive this good news as a child. Instead they sent out the twelve spies! They had to verify God's word. **God did not send out spies into the land nor had He need to!** The people were against receiving freely from God. Much like the law, they wanted spies and God gave them the spies. They wanted man's works instead of God's Word. Hence, by their own works, they did not enter the Promised Land.

But their children, because of their young age and ability to receive freely from God, entered into the Promised Land. We read this in *Deuteronomy 1:35-39, Surely there shall not one of these men of this evil generation see that good land, which I sware to give unto your fathers, Save Caleb the son of Jephunneh; he shall see it, and to him will I give the land that he hath trodden upon, and to his children, because he hath wholly followed the Lord...*

But Joshua the son of Nun, which standeth before thee, he shall go in thither: encourage him: for he shall cause Israel to inherit it. Moreover your little ones, which ye said should be a prey, and your children, which in that day had no knowledge between good and evil, they shall go in thither, and unto them will I give it, and they shall possess it, and *Numbers 14:24* states, *But my servant Caleb, because he had another spirit with him, and hath followed me fully, him will I bring into the land whereinto he went; and his seed shall possess it.* Hence, only their children entered in together with Caleb and Joshua. They had a different spirit. A spirit of Grace! **They saw unmerited Grace winning the battles over the giants that their parents feared.**

Of course, the greatest well-story was the one of the Samaritan woman by the well. We read it in *John 4:3-29, He left Judaea, and departed again into Galilee. And he **must needs go** through Samaria. Then cometh he to a city of Samaria, which is called Sychar, near to the parcel of ground that Jacob gave to his son Joseph. Now Jacob's well was there. Jesus therefore, being wearied with his journey, sat thus on the well: and it was about the sixth hour. There cometh a woman of Samaria to draw water: Jesus saith unto her, Give me to drink. (For his disciples were gone away unto the city to buy meat.) Then saith the woman of Samaria unto him, How is it that thou, being a Jew, askest drink of me, which am a woman of Samaria? for the Jews have no dealings with the Samaritans. Jesus answered and said unto her, If thou knewest **the gift of God**, and who it is that saith to thee, Give me to drink; thou wouldest have asked of him, and he would have given thee living water. The woman saith unto him, Sir, thou hast nothing to draw with, and the well is deep: from whence then hast thou that living water?...Jesus answered and said unto her, Whosoever drinketh of this water shall thirst again: But whosoever drinketh of the water that I shall give him shall never thirst; but the water that I shall give him shall be in him a well of water springing up into everlasting life. The woman saith unto him, Sir, give me this water, that I thirst not, neither come hither to draw.*

Jesus saith unto her, Go, call thy husband, and come hither. The woman answered and said, I have no husband. Jesus said unto her, Thou hast well said, I have no husband: For thou hast had five husbands; and he whom thou now hast is not thy husband: in that saidst thou truly. The woman saith unto him, Sir, I perceive that thou art a prophet. Our fathers worshipped in this mountain; and ye say, that in Jerusalem is the place where men ought to worship. Jesus saith unto her, Woman, believe me, the hour cometh, when ye shall neither in this mountain, nor yet at Jerusalem...God is a Spirit: and they that worship him must worship him in spirit and in truth. The woman saith unto him, I know that Messias cometh, which is called Christ: when he is come, he will tell us all things. Jesus saith unto her, I that speak unto thee am he (in Greek, **I AM**, *the speaking to you*). *And upon this came his disciples, and marvelled that he talked with the woman: yet no man said, What seekest thou? or, Why talkest thou with her? The woman then left her waterpot, and went her way into the city, and saith to the men, Come, see a man, which told me all things that ever I did: is not this the Christ?*

Although Jesus' ministry was primarily for the Jews, He went to Samaria just for this one woman. He *'must needs go'* through Samaria for this woman. Even today, He still *'must needs go'* and seek the lost. The setting was important as it was by Jacob's well. We know that his father, Isaac, dug the wells that the Philistines had filled up. We saw this in *Genesis 26:18, And Isaac digged again the wells of water, which they had digged in the days of Abraham his father; for the Philistines had stopped them after the death of Abraham.* Wells give life saving water but the Philistines had filled them up with earth. This earth covering was symbolic of wrong teaching which brought dryness, hardness and ultimately, death. Jacob dug wells as his father Isaac did. But the wells were soon filled up with earth again. Law invaded the waters and covered it up. It gave no life whatsoever.

The Jews considered the Samaritans a sect. Samaritans worship at their temple on mount Gerizim and not at the temple in Jerusalem On top of this, this Samaritan woman had no repute as she came to fetch water in the afternoon instead of in the morning. She had no friends as she was alone. She had no husband although she had five previous husbands. She had no honor because she was

living with a man. She had no living water for she was always
thirsty. And it was precisely that she had nothing that she could
receive *the gift of God* or Grace. Jesus was fully aware of who she
was but did not condemn her. She was fornicating yet Jesus
complimented her. The sixth man in her life was no good for her.
The number six stands for man. But now Jesus would be the
perfect or seventh man in her life! Jesus would fill her with living
water an be her 'husband'! She was a picture of the beloved bride
at the well, just as Zipporah, Rebekah, and Rachel.

The natural well could never permanently quench the thirst
of the people. That was why Jesus sat on it. There was no need to
go to Gerizim or Jerusalem for Jesus Himself had come near. The
woman drank from I AM, and became filled with Living Water.
**She no longer had any need for her water pot so she left it
behind. We cannot quench our inside thirst with outside water.
Only Jesus can quench us on the inside. Grace does not fill up
the thirst-gap caused by wrong teaching. Wrong teaching, by
definition, is wrong. Grace replaces wrong teaching, not just
fill up its gaps. The woman, now filled with right teaching, left
her wrong teaching pot behind.** She now had no fear, no shame,
no self consciousness, no need for Jerusalem or mount Gerizim,
and no thirst for she was filled on the inside with Jesus. So filled
and un-shamed that she went straight back into the city and
evangelized the inhabitants thereof.

This Samaritan woman reminds us of Achsah from *Judges
1:12,15, He that smiteth Kirjathsepher, and taketh it, to him will I
give Achsah my daughter to wife...thou hast given me a south
land; give me also springs of water. And Caleb gave her the upper
springs and the nether springs.* Othniel (lion of God of Judah or
Jesus) after conquering Kirjathsepher (city of writing or the
Torah/Law) married us! We were not only given land (new life)
but springs of water as well. These upper and lower springs in
Negev were Wells of Life or Grace. So let us drink Jesus, the
everlasting Spring of Living Water!

❧ 5 ❧

JESUS AND HIS UNCOMMON BLOOD

Jesus is uncommon. Jesus is unique. Most of us do not seem to realize that Jesus is incomparable to anyone else. Even Peter made the mistake of thinking that Jesus was just the same as Moses and Elijah, in *Matthew 17:1-5, And after six days Jesus taketh Peter, James, and John his brother, and bringeth them up into an high mountain apart, And was transfigured before them: and his face did shine as the sun, and his raiment was white as the light. And, behold, there appeared unto them Moses and Elias talking with him. Then answered Peter, and said unto Jesus, Lord, it is good for us to be here: if thou wilt, let us make here three tabernacles; one for thee, and one for Moses, and one for Elias. While he yet spake, behold, a bright cloud overshadowed them: and behold a voice out of the cloud, which said, This is my beloved Son, in whom I am well pleased; hear ye him.*

Peter, James, and John must have been the ones whom Jesus promised in *Luke 9:27, who would not see death till they saw the Kingdom of God come with power.* For they saw Jesus as the Shekinah Glory before they died! The high mountain was probably Mount Hebron as David wrote in *Psalm 133:1,3, Behold, how good and how pleasant it is for brethren to dwell together in unity! As the dew of Hermon, and as the dew that descended upon the mountains of Zion: for there the LORD commanded the blessing, even life forevermore.* Jesus as the Dew of Hermon descended in Zion, where all the children of God has life forevermore. We all know that the sequential names of Peter (*petros* or stone), James (*Jacob* or supplant), and John (*Yah* or Gracious), signified that the stony law would be replaced or supplanted by Grace. For Jesus is the Kingdom of God, as in *Luke 17:21, behold, the kingdom of God is within you.* Right after the transfiguration, Peter mentioned that he would build three tabernacles. God corrected him by pointing out that Jesus was His beloved Son 'in whom I am well pleased' and for Peter to listen to Him only. Only one new tabernacle was needed. Jesus fulfilled *Isaiah 42:1, Here is My Servant, whom I uphold, My Chosen One, in whom My soul delights.* **Moses represented the law while Elijah the prophets, as in *Romans 3:21, But now the righteousness of God without the law is manifested, being witnessed by the law and the prophets.* Both of them were servants. But Jesus was the Son. He would always be greater than the law or the prophets. There was no need to add Moses (who told us to listen to Jesus) and Elijah to Jesus as that would result in a mixture. Jesus has been and will always be uncommon. At the end, the disciples saw no one except Jesus.**

A short while later, Jesus Himself reaffirmed His exalted position. There is no equal to Him. We read this in *Matthew 17:25-27, What thinkest thou, Simon? of whom do the kings of the earth take custom or tribute? of their own children, or of strangers? Peter saith unto him, Of strangers. Jesus saith unto him, Then are the children free. Notwithstanding, lest we should offend them, go thou to the sea, and cast an hook, and take up the fish that first cometh up; and when thou hast opened his mouth, thou shalt find a piece of money: that take, and give unto them for me and thee.*

This simple exchange between Jesus and Peter was not so much about the payment of the temple tax as it was about who Jesus was. When Jesus asked Peter to whom do kings collect taxes from, Peter replied that kings collected taxes from the common people. Uncommon people do not pay taxes! That is why kings do not tax their own sons. Why? Because their sons were not common. **The law required the tax but Jesus, being the King's Son, was above the law. Grace is always higher than the law. Jesus has always been uncommon. He did not have to pay any tax as the Son of the King!** But Jesus still paid the tax that He was

not required to in order to fulfill all the requirements of the law.
Jesus also paid the tax for Peter. The only way whereby we, like
Peter, can become sons and daughters too is by allowing Jesus to
pay the price for us. Jesus lifts us up to His uncommon status.

We read in *Matthew 12:6,41-42, But I say unto you, That in
this place is one greater than the temple. The men of Nineveh
shall rise in judgment with this generation, and shall condemn it:
because they repented at the preaching of Jonas; and, behold, a
greater than Jonas is here. The queen of the south shall rise up in
the judgment with this generation, and shall condemn it: for she
came from the uttermost parts of the earth to hear the wisdom of
Solomon; and, behold, a greater than Solomon is here.* Jesus
Himself stated clearly that He is greater than the temple, greater
than Jonah, and greater than Solomon. Solomon was a king, Jonah
was a prophet, and the temple had priests. But none compared to
Jesus! He was greater than any king, any prophet. any priest. He
was greater because He was uncommon. He was unique and
unequalled! Because Jesus was not just another man, His blood is
similarly uncommon. This uncommon scarlet thread runs
throughout the whole bible. The scarlet thread represents the
uncommon blood of Jesus which was shed for the remission or
cancellation of all sins. Greater than any sin! Where the scarlet
blood of Jesus is, there is no guilt or condemnation.

We literally encounter this thread in *Joshua 2:1-4,6,9-
11,17-19, And Joshua the son of Nun sent out of Shittim two men to
spy secretly, saying, Go view the land, even Jericho. And they
went, and came into an harlot's house, named Rahab, and lodged
there. And it was told the king of Jericho, saying, Behold, there
came men in hither to night of the children of Israel to search out
the country. And the king of Jericho sent unto Rahab, saying, Bring
forth the men that are come to thee...But she had brought them up
to the roof of the house, and hid them with the stalks of flax, which
she had laid in order upon the roof. And she said unto the men, I
know that the LORD hath given you the land, and that your terror
is fallen upon us, and that all the inhabitants of the land faint
because of you. For we have heard how the LORD dried up the
water of the Red sea for you, when ye came out of Egypt; and what*

ye did unto the two kings of the Amorites...our hearts did melt, neither did there remain any more courage in any man, because of you: for the LORD your God, he is God in heaven above, and in earth beneath.   And the men said unto her... Behold, when we come into the land, thou shalt bind this line of **scarlet thread** *in the window which thou didst let us down by: and thou shalt bring thy father, and thy mother, and thy brethren, and all thy father's household, home unto thee. And it shall be, that whosoever shall go out of the doors of thy house into the street, his blood shall be upon his head, and we will be guiltless.*

    This well known story of Rahab the Gentile, centered around her whole household being saved by a line of scarlet thread tied to the window of her house. In Hebrew, line and hope is *tiqvah.* Salvation from death was due solely to that scarlet thread, which represented the blood of Jesus. Our hope is in His bloodline. In *Psalm 22:6, But I am a worm (tola),* Jesus equated Himself to the tola worm, *Coccus ilicis,* an insect whose dried body is used to make a red dye. Interesting enough, the tola worm, before giving birth to her young would affix herself to the trunk of a tree. Her eggs would be protected under her body until they hatched. As she died, her body, her eggs, and the tree surrounding her body would be stained an indelible crimson, reminding us of *Isaiah 1:18, though your sins be as scarlet, they shall be as white as snow; though they be red like crimson (tola), they shall be as wool.*

    It did not matter that Rahab was a prostitute, who her parents and siblings were, how great her faith was, or that she hid the spies and helped them escape. If she or anyone of her family left the house where the scarlet thread was, they would be killed. Only those in the house with the scarlet thread would be saved. The scarlet robe in *Matthew 27:28, And they stripped him, and put on him a scarlet robe,* has the same symbolism. For only the blood of Jesus mattered, as we know from *Hebrews 9:22, And almost all things are by the law purged with blood; and without shedding of blood is no remission.* No Jesus' scarlet crimson blood → no remission or cancellation of sins! No Jesus → no Hope!

    It is also interesting to note that the two spies who were sent out to view Jericho ended up viewing naked women inside

Jericho's whorehouse. Rahab had to hide them under stalks of flax and had to remind them who their God was! The seeds of the flax plant can either be eaten or pressed to make linseed oil but the stalks themselves yield the fiber which is used to make linen. As priests wore linen, and Jesus is our High Priest, He kept the two spies safe under Him. Jesus is our food and our refuge.

We read of the attack on Jericho in *Joshua 6:20-24, So the people shouted when the priests blew with the trumpets: and it came to pass, when the people heard the sound of the trumpet, and the people shouted with a great shout, that the wall fell down flat, so that the people went up into the city, every man straight before him, and they took the city. And they utterly destroyed all that was in the city, both man and woman, young and old, and ox, and sheep, and ass, with the edge of the sword... And the young men that were spies went in, and brought Rahab, and her father, and her mother, and her brethren, and all that she had; and they brought out all her kindred, and left them without the camp of Israel. And they burnt the city with fire, and all that was therein: only the silver, and the gold, and the vessels of brass and of iron, they put into the treasury of the house of the Lord.*

Months before Jericho was even attacked, many rams were sacrificed and their horns made into trumpets or *shofars*. **The ram had to die to obtain its horn, symbolizing the death of Jesus. When the priests blew the horns, the walls of Jericho fell down flat. Walls and gates were places of judgment. But they always fall flat against Grace. Jesus was and is always the reason for our victories.** Amidst the destruction of Jericho, Rahab was saved and she lived with the Israelites the rest of her life. All of Jericho was condemned but Rahab! Grace was scandalous for it saved an undeserving harlot while the rest of Jericho burned. But to God, it was not scandalous enough. In *Matthew 1:5-6* we read, *And Salmon begat Booz of Rachab; and Booz begat Obed of Ruth; and Obed begat Jesse; And Jesse begat David the king.* God made Rahab/Rachab the harlot become part of the ancestry of Jesus! This scarlet and scandalous thread of Grace weaved itself throughout the bible. Because of the uncommon blood of Jesus, all sins were forgiven. This scandalous Grace was a rock of offence to many. It was love gone too far. But for believers like Rahab, it was power unto salvation. Grace is always a door and never a wall or a gate.

Ephesians 2:13-14 states, *But now in Christ Jesus ye who sometimes were far off are made nigh by the blood of Christ. For he is our peace, who hath made both one, and hath broken down the middle wall of partition between us.* Then again in *Colossians 1:21-22, And you, that were sometime alienated and enemies in your mind by wicked works, yet now hath he reconciled. In the body of his flesh through death, to present you holy and unblameable and unreproveable in his sight.* In Hebrew, sacrifice is *korban* and brought near is *karav*. Both share the same root word. Only with *korban* can there be *karav!* Only with Jesus' blood can we, once enemies, be reconciled to God! His blood is required, not our blood. He brought us in through the veil. He brought us into the presence of His Father. He broke down every partition that separated us from God. Jesus brought us near. And in the holy presence of God, Jesus presented us as holy, un-blameable and un-reproveable! Free from every accusation and guilt!

Nobody can accuse us of being unholy. Nobody can reprove us. Why? Because Jesus' life, death, and blood fulfilled all the requirements of the law. He finished the work for us. Satan who once had authority to accuse us for not measuring up to the standard of the law, before the throne of God, lost that authority because of Jesus' blood. The blood of the Lamb overcame him. We read this in *Revelation 12:9-11, And the great dragon was cast out, that old serpent, called the Devil, and Satan, which deceiveth the whole world: he was cast out into the earth, and his angels were cast out with him. And I heard a loud voice saying in heaven, Now is come salvation, and strength, and the kingdom of our God, and the power of his Christ: for the accuser of our brethren is cast down, which accused them before our God day and night. And they overcame him by the blood of the Lamb.*

But many people make the blood of Jesus as common as that of goats and sheep. What was uncommon or holy or *qadosh* is made into something common or *chalal.* We read this in *Hebrews 10:28-29, He that despised Moses' law died without mercy under two or three witnesses: Of how much sorer punishment, suppose ye, shall he be thought worthy, who hath trodden underfoot the Son of God, and hath counted the blood of the covenant, wherewith he was sanctified, an unholy thing, and hath done despite unto the Spirit of grace?* These people trod Jesus under their feet and treated His spilled blood as *chalal.* The blood of animals were common. It covered sins up until the point the animal was sacrificed. When the sinner who offered the sacrifice walked out of the tabernacle or temple and sinned again, another sacrifice was needed. Common blood does not remove future sins! It only covered past sins. As such, the sinner is always guilty of some thought or deed. The person who does not obey the Mosaic law dies without mercy unless he keeps on sacrificing. It is an endless process.

For example, there is a popular teaching that divides forgiveness into two parts, namely judicial forgiveness and parental forgiveness. Judicial forgiveness is explained as what the sinner received when he put his faith in Jesus. His sins were forgiven and he gained right standing before God. But his right standing before God is not assured. He can lose it the moment he sins again. He can be un-forgiven. Parental forgiveness then has to kick in. Parental forgiveness says that in order to continue having right standing before God and to have an unbroken relationship with Him, we have to do some self-work, for example confess our sins. Hence, we think that confession repairs our fellowship with God. Yet is says in *1 John 2:12, I write unto you, little children, because your sins are forgiven you for his name's sake.* As children of our Father, all our sins were forgiven. There is no broken fellowship to repair. The unbiblical teaching of parental forgiveness centers on endless self-works to maintain forgiveness. It assumes that the blood of Jesus is common and not good enough. Therefore we have to add our part to it.

That is also why the Israelites were prohibited from eating blood, as in *Leviticus 17:14, For it is the life of all flesh; the blood of it is for the life thereof: therefore I said unto the children of Israel, Ye shall eat the blood of no manner of flesh: for the life of all flesh is the blood thereof: whosoever eateth it shall be cut off.*

Because life is in the blood, eating the common blood of animals makes a life-union with death through the dead animal. But Jesus encouraged us to take His blood! We read in *John 6:53-54, Except ye eat the flesh of the Son of man, and drink his blood, ye have no life in you. Whoso eateth my flesh, and drinketh my blood, hath eternal life.* **Partaking of the uncommon blood of Jesus is to be in life-union with Eternal Life, through the living God Himself!**

Hebrews 10:17-19 states, *And their sins and iniquities will I remember no more. Now where remission of these is, there is no more offering for sin. Having therefore, brethren, boldness to enter into the holiest by the blood of Jesus.* **The blood of Jesus is uncommon. A believer in Jesus has no more conscience of sins! That is faith in the blood. It did not reconcile God to man but man to God. The blood of Jesus saves us completely. It removed past, present, and future sins!** Jesus is not coming again to die for our sins. *Romans 6:9-10* states, *Knowing that Christ being raised from the dead dieth no more; death hath no more dominion over him. For in that he died, he died unto sin once.* **It was a one-time sacrifice good for all time. God exists outside of time and has consolidated all sins of all time to be cancelled by a one-time sacrifice. If we were to commit a sin next week, Jesus will not come back next week to die again for that future sin. If we can go back in time to correct our sins from the past, we would not be able to either as Jesus had already corrected them! All our mistakes has been wiped away! The uncommon blood of Jesus cancelled all our sins for all time, past, present, and future. There is no more offering for sin because of this remission or cancellation. Our sins are remembered no more as there are no sins to remember any.**

Ephesians 1:7 states, *In whom we have redemption through his blood, the forgiveness of sins, according to the riches of his grace;* The Greek word for redemption here is *'apolutrósis'*. It is a compound of two words, *'apo'* meaning, separate one thing from another so that the union is permanently destroyed. The union will never ever happen again. The second word is *'lutron'* meaning, ransom. **Hence, the ransom that Jesus paid for us separated us permanently from sin. We can never be associated with sin**

again. Therefore, even when we sin, we are considered as not having sinned at all! The ransom was a complete onetime payment. It covered our past, present, and future sins. The ransom paid for our redemption. That is what redemption through His blood meant. Jesus' uncommon blood is always 'more' than enough.

We read this in *Hebrews 9:12-14* states, *by his own blood he entered in once into the holy place, having obtained eternal redemption for us. For if the blood of bulls and of goats, and the ashes of an heifer sprinkling the unclean, sanctifieth to the purifying of the flesh: How much **more** shall the blood of Christ, who through the eternal Spirit offered himself without spot to God, purge your conscience from dead works to serve the living God?* and again in *Hebrews 10:1-3, 12, For the law having a shadow of good things to come, and not the very image of the things, can never with those sacrifices which they offered year by year continually make the comers thereunto perfect. For then would they not have ceased to be offered? because that the **worshippers once purged should have had no more conscience of sins.** But in those sacrifices there is a remembrance again made of sins every year.   But this man, after he had offered **one sacrifice for sins forever**, sat down on the right hand of God.*

One example of this is found in *1 Kings 21* on the well known story of Naboth's vineyard which king Ahab desired. When confronted by Ahab to sell his vineyard (a symbol of us) Naboth replied in *verse 3: And Naboth said to Ahab, The LORD forbid it me, that I should give the inheritance of my fathers unto thee.* What his fathers had given to him was not for sale, just as Jesus said that He would lose none of what His Father had given to Him in *John 6:39.* Under the law, in *Leviticus 25:23-24, The land shall not be sold for ever: for the land is mine; for ye are strangers and sojourners with me. And in all the land of your possession ye shall grant a redemption for the land.* The land which God gave to the Israelites could not be sold, only redeemed, as it belonged to God. Here Naboth is symbolic of Jesus, Ahab, the Roman governors, and Jezebel symbolized the Jewish religious leaders. Jezebel influenced Ahab (who was no kinsman redeemer) to kill Naboth just as the Jewish leaders influenced Pilate to hang Jesus on the cross. Jezebel used Ahab, false witnesses, elders and leaders of the city, and a sham trial to dispose of Naboth. Similarly, the Pharisees used the Roman governors, false witnesses, other elders and leaders, and a mock trial to dispose of Jesus.

Under the law, the punishment for Ahab would be death. We read this in *1 Kings 21:19,24-25, Thus saith the LORD, In the place where dogs licked the blood of Naboth shall dogs lick thy blood, even thine. Him that dieth of Ahab in the city the dogs shall eat; and him that dieth in the field shall the fowls of the air eat. But there was none like unto Ahab, which did sell himself to work wickedness in the sight of the LORD, whom Jezebel his wife stirred up.* God Himself said that there was none so wicked as Ahab but because of Jesus'/Naboth's blood, Ahab was forgiven! Incredible! We read of this in *1 Kings 21:29,because he humbleth himself before me, I will not bring the evil in his days.* Grace is scandalous and offensive to our law soaked minds. Where is fairness and justice? We want Ahab to end up like his wife Jezebel who in *2 Kings 9:33,36, So they threw her down: and some of her blood was sprinkled on the wall, and on the horses: and he trode her under foot. In the portion of Jezreel shall dogs eat the flesh of Jezebel.* We want to see Ahab's blood splattered on a wall in a million drops, for his carcass to be eaten by dogs, and for ravens to pluck away at his rotting flesh.

Under the law, Ahab was unredeemable. But under Jesus' uncommon blood of Grace, Ahab was redeemed! It is as written in *Hebrews 12:24, You have come to Jesus, the one who mediates the new covenant between God and people, and to the sprinkled blood, which speaks of forgiveness instead of crying out for vengeance like the blood of Abel.* Jesus' uncommon blood cries out forgiveness, never vengeance! Roughly 190 years after Ahab, king Manasseh who worshipped Baal and other demonic idols, murdered innocent people, sacrificed his own son in the fire, practiced divination, sought omens, consulted mediums, and was probably responsible for the destruction of Jerusalem by the Assyrians was similarly forgiven in *2 Chronicles 33:13, And when he prayed to Him, the LORD received his plea and heard his petition; so He brought him back to Jerusalem and to his kingdom. Then Manasseh knew that the LORD is God.* His name even appeared in the genealogy of Jesus! Grace is indeed radical! For only Jesus as Grace can justify the ungodly (*Romans 4:5*).

The book of Hebrews was written for the Hebrews or the Jews. Paul, who probably wrote this book, knew the struggles the Jews had and continuously exhorted them to hold onto their confidence in Jesus' uncommon blood sacrifice. We read in *Hebrews 3:12-13, Take heed, brethren, lest there be in any of you an evil heart of unbelief, in departing from the living God.. lest any of you be hardened through the deceitfulness of sin.* The deceitfulness of sin mentioned here refers to the sin of unbelief. Because of unbelief they developed an evil heart. The Greek word for evil here is *ponéros,* meaning full of labors, annoyances, and hardships. The Jews labored onerously because they followed the law. Belief in Jesus would have given them rest but instead their hearts became full of stress, anxiety, and care.

And again in *Hebrews 10:26, For if **we** sin wilfully after that we have received the knowledge of the truth, there remaineth no more sacrifice for sins.* The 'we' here were the Jews who knew Jesus yet rejected Him. They received the knowledge of the Truth, who is Jesus, but chose the law instead. Their willful sin was their rejection of Jesus. Similarly, we can treat Jesus' finished work as unfinished too. We can continue to sacrifice after the perfect sacrifice was accepted. We can continue to work after the work was finished. We forget that the ways of the law are no longer accepted by God. The blood of animal sacrifices are no longer accepted. There remained no more sacrifice for sins. Works are no longer accepted! **There was no more offering for sins because all sins have been dealt with. There are no sins left to forgive because Jesus forgave us of every sin ever committed.** While sinning does have consequences and many times, grave consequences, it is not counted against us. Because of Jesus' blood, our hearts no longer have an evil conscience. This means that we are no longer sin conscious but righteousness conscious. We should not go back to the law.

Paul reminded Timothy of this as well. We read in *1 Timothy 4:1-2, Now the Spirit speaketh expressly, that in the latter times some shall depart from the faith, giving heed to seducing spirits, and doctrines of devils; Speaking lies in hypocrisy; having their conscience seared with a hot iron.* The people who had their conscience seared with a hot iron were those who went back to the law. They departed from the faith of Jesus. They listened to seducing spirits and doctrines of devils. Paul consistently taught the Jews, as in *Acts 21:21, teachest all the Jews which are among the Gentiles to forsake Moses, saying that they ought not to circumcise their children, neither to walk after the customs.* Paul taught the people to forsake Moses, or *apostasia*, meaning to leave or reject the law. The lying hypocrites were those who put people under the law again after Jesus had set them free. They made Jesus' *qadosh* blood into *chalal* blood. That is the doctrine of devils - to make Jesus common!

Paul went on to encourage Jews to wholeheartedly trust in Jesus. *Hebrews 12:1-2* states, *let us run with patience the race that is set before us, Looking unto Jesus the author and finisher of our faith; who for the joy that was set before him endured the cross, despising the shame, and is set down at the right hand of the throne of God.* Jesus is the author and finisher of our faith. He is the Bridegroom Runner in *Psalm 19:6, bridegroom coming out of his chamber and rejoiceth as a strong man to run a race.* His joy was in finishing the race, winning us, and then awarding us the unmerited prize to reign over sin with Him. And one day, we will reign eternally with Jesus. In that day, according to *1 Corinthians 6:3*, we even get to judge fallen angels! We may become kings and lords but Jesus is King of Kings and Lord of Lords! He will always be our King and our Lord. So, let us reject the sin which so easily beset us. That sin is the sin of unbelief. It says Jesus is neither the beginning nor the end; neither the prize nor the reason for the race. It is the sin that says Jesus did not finish the race, so we must pick up the baton and finish the race for Him. It is the sin that says we are not worthy of any prize, far less the prize to reign with Him.

Jesus also encouraged the Jews to not fall back into the law. We read in *Matthew 10:22, And ye shall be hated of all men for my*

name's sake: but he that endureth to the end shall be saved, and
again in the dual fulfillment prophecy of *Matthew 24:9-13, And
many false prophets shall rise, and shall deceive many. And
because iniquity shall abound, the love of many shall wax cold. But
he that shall endure unto the end, the same shall be saved,* and
again in *Colossians 1:23-24, If ye continue in the faith grounded
and settled, and be not moved away from the hope of the gospel..
Now I rejoice in my sufferings for you.* At first glance, this seemed
to refer to their salvation. If they endured to the end, they would
receive salvation. If not, they would lose their salvation. That is
insane logic as they could not lose what they never had! But this
was not about salvation but about persecution. The people who
endured to the end, who despite persecution, did not return to the
law. False prophets of the law would deceive many, but could not
hoodwink these people whom Jesus loved. Because of Jesus' love
first, their love back for Jesus did not wax cold. They continued to
put their faith in Jesus despite afflictions, enmities, offenses,
betrayals, and murders. They were not silenced but held on to their
Confidence, Jesus, as in *Hebrews 3:6, But Christ as a son over his
own house; whose house are we, if we hold fast the confidence and
the rejoicing of the hope firm unto the end.* They partook of Christ
and rejoiced in Him until the end as in *Hebrews 3:14, For we are
made partakers of Christ, if we hold the beginning of our
confidence stedfast unto the end;* These are the people who held on
to what Jesus did. They did not become weary of their belief or
became faint in their minds. They remembered that it was Jesus
who endured the cross. That is how Paul rejoiced in his sufferings!

At His transfiguration on the mountain, Jesus' face shone
as the sun, His clothes were white as light, He was with Moses and
Elijah, a bright cloud overshadowed Hebron, and God the Father
announced that Jesus was His Beloved Son. At His disfiguration
on the cross, Jesus' face was unrecognizable, His garments were
stripped off Him, He was with two thieves, darkness
overshadowed Golgotha, and lowly centurions exclaimed that He
was the Son of God. It was Jesus who first endured the suffering,
the mocking, the beatings, the shame, the pain, and the crucifixion.
Let us never forget what Jesus went through for us.

❧ 6 ❧

JESUS AND BOAZ

God delights in showing us that He is just and good. This is illustrated in *Luke 18:1-7, And he spake a parable unto them to this end, that men ought always to pray, and not to faint; Saying, There was in a city a judge, which feared not God, neither regarded man: And there was a widow in that city; and she came unto him, saying, Avenge me of mine adversary. And he would not for a while: but afterward he said within himself, Though I fear not God, nor regard man; Yet because this widow troubleth me, I will avenge her, lest by her continual coming she weary me. And the Lord said, Hear what the unjust judge saith. And shall not God avenge his own elect, which cry day and night unto him, though he bear long with them? I tell you that he will avenge them speedily.*

From a self-works perspective, the widow should be congratulated for her persistence in troubling the unjust judge. For her perseverance paid off and the judge adjudicated her justice, albeit from his own selfish viewpoint for he did not want to be wearied by the woman. So bother God until He answers you! However, from God's perspective, the unjust judge was well, unjust! He took a long time to make up his mind but God our Father is not like that. God is a speedy prayer-answering God. In fact, during the millennial rule of Jesus, He answers before we can even ask from Him, as in *Isaiah 65:24, And it shall come to pass, that before they call, I will answer; and while they are yet speaking, I will hear.* He does not answer because we manipulated, pressed, or moved Him with our long prayers and our insistence.

He answers speedily as His mind is already made up about our wellbeing. He finds pleasure in answering our prayers because He loves us. We join Him praying His pre-prepared answer!

We read this further in *Luke 11:5-13, And he said unto them, Which of you shall have a friend, and shall go unto him at midnight, and say unto him, Friend, lend me three loaves; For a friend of mine in his journey is come to me, and I have nothing to set before him? And he from within shall answer and say, Trouble me not: the door is now shut, and my children are with me in bed; I cannot rise and give thee. I say unto you, Though he will not rise and give him, because he is his friend, yet because of his importunity he will rise and give him as many as he needeth. And I say unto you, Ask, and it shall be given you; seek, and ye shall find; knock, and it shall be opened unto you. For every one that asketh receiveth; and he that seeketh findeth; and to him that knocketh it shall be opened. If a son shall ask bread of any of you that is a father, will he give him a stone? or if he ask a fish, will he for a fish give him a serpent? Or if he shall ask an egg, will he offer him a scorpion? If ye then, being evil, know how to give good gifts unto your children: how much **more** shall your heavenly Father give the Holy Spirit to them that ask him?*

A person may give help to a friend due to his friend's importunity or continued pleading, but God is our true Friend who joyously gives to us. We do not have to plead with Him. Whether we are believers or unbelievers, His abundance and bounty is available to us all. Even though we may not know Him personally, He will still rise up and give us as many loaves of sustenance as we need. Everyone that asks from God receives from Him. Everyone that seeks Him finds Him. He will open His door to everyone who knocks. That is because He supplied, found, and opened the door for us first. The loaves of bread, symbolizing Jesus, were prepared beforehand. He is for friends and friends of friends as well. Jesus is the 'more' and He is for everyone! He never un-friended anyone,

Unfriend

Flat breads can look like flat stones. Long fish can look like serpents and eggs can appear like white scorpions. Satan tries to give us substitutes. But God, being a good Father, always supplies us with the real thing. God gave us the real Bread of Life, Jesus, even before we were born.

Let us discover more of God's unmerited provision in *Ruth 1:1-7, Now it came to pass in the days when the judges ruled, that there was a famine in the land. And a certain man of Bethlehem Judah went to sojourn in the country of Moab, he, and his wife, and his two sons. And the name of the man was Elimelech, and the name of his wife Naomi, and the name of his two sons Mahlon and Chilion, Ephrathites of Bethlehem Judah. And they came into the country of Moab, and continued there. And Elimelech Naomi's husband died; and she was left, and her two sons. And they took them wives of the women of Moab; the name of the one was Orpah, and the name of the other Ruth: and they dwelled there about ten years. And Mahlon and Chilion died also both of them; and the woman was left of her two sons and her husband. Then she arose with her daughters in law, that she might return from the country of Moab: for she had heard in the country of Moab how that the Lord had visited his people in giving them bread. Wherefore she went forth out of the place where she was, and her two daughters in law with her; and they went on the way to return unto the land of Judah.*

Times were bad in Bethlehem. Bethlehem means 'the house of bread' but there was no bread in the house of bread. In its place, widespread famine and hunger. Men, as judges, ruled based on their knowledge of right and wrong or self-works. *Judges 21:25,* states that *In those days there was no king in Israel: every man did that which was right in his own eyes.* They acted like god and replaced God. Works replaced Grace. Hence, the land which was to be a blessing became a curse. *Hebrews 6:7-8,* states *For the earth which drinketh in the rain that cometh oft upon it, and bringeth forth herbs meet for them by whom it is dressed, receiveth blessing from God: But that which beareth thorns and briers is rejected, and is nigh unto cursing; whose end is to be burned.* Instead of turning back to God, to ask and to receive from Him, they ran further away from Him to the cursed land of Moab. We read this in *Deuteronomy 23:3, An Ammonite or Moabite shall not enter into the congregation of the Lord; even to their tenth generation shall they not enter into the congregation of the Lord for ever.*

After they fled from God, their names were revealed. Elimelech meant 'my God is King' but he ran away from God, his King, and died. Naomi, his wife, meant 'pleasant' but she walked away from the Pleasant One to an unpleasant deathly land. Fleeing famine seemed the right thing to do but it also meant moving away from their unmerited Provider, Jesus. We seem to be good flee-ers, not followers. Their two sons, Mahlon and Chilion meant 'weak, sickly, wasting away, and 'coming to an end'. It was no surprise that both of them subsequently died. Their wives, Orpah and Ruth, were from the cursed Moabite land. As they were cursed, they were to have absolutely no inheritance in the Abrahamic promise.

Then, one day, Naomi heard that God had provided bread again in Bethlehem and made plans to return home. God never abandoned them, but they abandoned God based on their knowledge of right and wrong. We read of Naomi's return in *Ruth 1:8-22, And Naomi said unto her two daughters in law, Go, return each to her mother's house: the Lord deal kindly with you, as ye have dealt with the dead, and with me. The Lord grant you that ye may find rest, each of you in the house of her husband. Then she kissed them; and they lifted up their voice, and wept. And they said unto her, Surely we will return with thee unto thy people. And Naomi said, Turn again, my daughters: why will ye go with me? are there yet any more sons in my womb, that they may be your husbands? Turn again, my daughters, go your way; for I am too old to have an husband. If I should say, I have hope, if I should have an husband also to night, and should also bear sons; Would ye tarry for them till they were grown? would ye stay for them from having husbands? nay, my daughters; for it grieveth me much for your sakes that the hand of the Lord is gone out against me. And they lifted up their voice, and wept again: and Orpah kissed her mother in law; but Ruth clave unto her. And she said, Behold, thy sister in law is gone back unto her people, and unto her gods: return thou after thy sister in law. And Ruth said, Intreat me not to leave thee, or to return from following after thee: for whither thou goest, I will go; and where thou lodgest, I will lodge: thy people*

shall be my people, and thy God my God: Where thou diest, will I
die, and there will I be buried: the Lord do so to me, and more
also, if ought but death part thee and me. When she saw that she
was stedfastly minded to go with her, then she left speaking unto
her. So they two went until they came to Bethlehem. And it came to
pass, when they were come to Bethlehem, that all the city was
moved about them, and they said, Is this Naomi? And she said unto
them, Call me not Naomi, call me Mara: for the Almighty hath
dealt very bitterly with me. I went out full, and the Lord hath
brought me home again empty: why then call ye me Naomi, seeing
the Lord hath testified against me, and the Almighty hath afflicted
me? So Naomi returned, and Ruth the Moabitess, her daughter in
law, with her, which returned out of the country of Moab: and they
came to Bethlehem in the beginning of barley harvest.

We see that Naomi did not have a relationship with God at
all. Instead of seeing Him as Provider, Naomi saw God as a taker.
She told people to call her Mara, or 'bitter', as she griped bitterly,
and wrongly, about how God took her husband and her sons.
Orpah, meaning 'neck or mane', had turned her neck upon Naomi
and returned to her people. Her other daughter-in-law, Ruth,
meaning 'beautiful friend' chose to return with her. While many
people would laud Ruth's 'where you go, I will go' speech (just
like the persistent widow), the truth was that Ruth was completely
helpless. Cursed because she was a Moabitess, doubly cursed as
she was now a widow, she deserved nothing. But because of the
goodness of her God, she deserved everything. And speedily too!

We continue reading in *Ruth 2:1-16, And Naomi had a*
kinsman of her husband's, a mighty man of wealth, of the family of
Elimelech; and his name was Boaz. And Ruth the Moabitess said
unto Naomi, Let me now go to the field, and glean ears of corn
after him in whose sight I shall find grace. And she said unto her,
Go, my daughter. And she went, and came, and gleaned in the field
after the reapers: and her hap was to light on a part of the field
belonging unto Boaz, who was of the kindred of Elimelech. And
behold, Boaz came from Bethlehem, and said unto the reapers, The
Lord be with you. And they answered him, The Lord bless thee.
Then said Boaz unto his servant that was set over the reapers,

Whose damsel is this? And the servant that was set over the reapers answered and said, It is the Moabitish damsel that came back with Naomi out of the country of Moab: And she said, I pray you, let me glean and gather after the reapers among the sheaves: so she came, and hath continued even from the morning until now, that she tarried a little in the house. Then said Boaz unto Ruth, Hearest thou not, my daughter? Go not to glean in another field, neither go from hence, but abide here fast by my maidens: Let thine eyes be on the field that they do reap, and go thou after them: have I not charged the young men that they shall not touch thee? and when thou art athirst, go unto the vessels, and drink of that which the young men have drawn. Then she fell on her face, and bowed herself to the ground, and said unto him, Why have I found grace in thine eyes, that thou shouldest take knowledge of me, seeing I am a stranger?

And Boaz answered and said unto her, It hath fully been shewed me, all that thou hast done unto thy mother in law since the death of thine husband: and how thou hast left thy father and thy mother, and the land of thy nativity, and art come unto a people which thou knewest not heretofore. The Lord recompense thy work, and a full reward be given thee of the Lord God of Israel, under whose wings thou art come to trust. Then she said, Let me find favour in thy sight, my lord; for that thou hast comforted me, and for that thou hast spoken friendly unto thine handmaid, though I be not like unto one of thine handmaidens. And Boaz said unto her, At mealtime come thou hither, and eat of the bread, and dip thy morsel in the vinegar. And she sat beside the reapers: and he reached her parched corn, and she did eat, and was sufficed, and left. And when she was risen up to glean, Boaz commanded his young men, saying, Let her glean even among the sheaves, and reproach her not: And let fall also some of the handfuls of purpose for her, and leave them, that she may glean them, and rebuke her not.

Under the law, the poor and the stranger may glean from the corners of a field or glean from the field itself, but only after the reapers have already made several passes over the field. We see this in *Leviticus 19:9-10, And when ye reap the harvest of your land, thou shalt not wholly reap the corners of thy field, neither shalt thou gather the gleanings of thy harvest. And thou shalt not glean thy vineyard, neither shalt thou gather every grape of thy vineyard; thou shalt leave them for the poor and stranger: I am the Lord your God* and again in *Deuteronomy 24:19-22, When thou cuttest down thine harvest in thy field, and hast forgot a sheaf in the field, thou shalt not go again to fetch it: it shall be for the stranger, for the fatherless, and for the widow: that the Lord thy God may bless thee in all the work of thine hands. When thou beatest thine olive tree, thou shalt not go over the boughs again: it shall be for the stranger, for the fatherless, and for the widow. When thou gatherest the grapes of thy vineyard, thou shalt not glean it afterward: it shall be for the stranger, for the fatherless, and for the widow. And thou shalt remember that thou wast a bondman in the land of Egypt: therefore I command thee to do this thing.*

As Ruth was both poor and a stranger, she gleaned after the reapers. There was precious little corn left to collect after the reapers had passed over the field. What was left was probably deemed undesirable. Ruth thought herself unworthy but Grace, in the form of Boaz, found Ruth immediately! God, unlike the unjust judge, answered speedily. Boaz (meaning, in Him is strength) was a shadow of Jesus. Just as Boaz, He found us before we even knew Him. Doors opened for Ruth before she even knocked. She received before she even asked. For Jesus' strength is made perfect in Ruth's weakness.

Of all the fields that Ruth could have gleaned in, her 'hap' was to be found gleaning in Boaz's field. That was her 'hap' or her position as a child of God. Ruth thought that she deserved leftovers and scraps, but Boaz quickly changed her thinking. She was told to stay in Boaz's field, offered protection and sustenance, and was promoted from gleaner to reaper. She reaped only in the best fields together with other maidens. When she was hungry or thirsty, food and drink, prepared beforehand, were provided for her. She ate of the Bread of Life as symbolized by the bread and corn, and drank the Living Water of Life. She could eat her fill in the time of famine because her provision came from Jesus or Boaz, not the world. She received Jesus. In the end, she did not even have to reap anymore. The reapers were instructed to purposefully drop handfuls of grain for Ruth to pick up. She did not have to perform but just to receive her unmerited, abundant, no condemnation, no rebuke blessings. Jesus is always more than enough. He always overpays the debt owed. He overpaid the promises that He made. Abraham did not only become father to his wives children but was overpaid to become the father of multitudes. Joseph did not only save Pharaoh and Egypt but was overpaid to save many other nations. Ruth did not only pick up grain for herself, but was overpaid with more than enough; sufficient even for Naomi. The blessings continued from one harvest to another.

Ruth 2:17-23, So she gleaned in the field until even, and beat out that she had gleaned: and it was about an ephah of barley. And she took it up, and went into the city: and her mother in law saw what she had gleaned: and she brought forth, and gave to her that she had reserved after she was sufficed. And her mother in law said unto her, Where hast thou gleaned to day? and where wroughtest thou? blessed be he that did take knowledge of thee. And she shewed her mother in law with whom she had wrought, and said, The man's name with whom I wrought to day is Boaz. And Naomi said unto her daughter in law, Blessed be he of the Lord, who hath not left off his kindness to the living and to the dead. And Naomi said unto her, The man is near of kin unto us, one of our next kinsmen. And Ruth the Moabitess said, He said unto me also, Thou shalt keep fast by my young men, until they have ended all my harvest. And Naomi said unto Ruth her daughter in law, It is good, my daughter, that thou go out with his maidens, that they meet thee not in any other field. So she kept fast by the maidens of Boaz to glean unto the end of barley harvest and of wheat harvest; and dwelt with her mother in law.

God is pleased when He pleases us. His pleasure is to see us experience His goodness. Boaz loved Ruth first and his desire was to take care of and to bless her. He wanted to please her. When Naomi suggested to Ruth to doll herself up and to visit Boaz at the threshing floor, she was operating in the flesh. Naomi thought that was the 'right' and 'good' thing to do. Naomi did wrong but that did not stop Boaz from loving Ruth. The threshing floor separated the barley and the wheat from its chaff. We are the harvest come before the feet of Jesus. Ruth rested herself at the feet of Boaz. He spread his skirt over her and covered her fully. Unlike the law, there are no short beds and narrow covers in Jesus' garments. Jesus covered us perfectly and completely. Just like Ruth, we become perfectly virtuous and righteous under His covering.

Ruth 3:1-11, Then Naomi her mother in law said unto her, My daughter, shall I not seek rest for thee, that it may be well with thee? And now is not Boaz of our kindred, with whose maidens thou wast? Behold, he winnoweth barley to night in the threshingfloor. Wash thyself therefore, and anoint thee, and put thy raiment upon thee, and get thee down to the floor: but make not thyself known unto the man, until he shall have done eating and drinking. And it shall be, when he lieth down, that thou shalt mark the place where he shall lie, and thou shalt go in, and uncover his feet, and lay thee down; and he will tell thee what thou shalt do. And she said unto her, All that thou sayest unto me I will do. And she went down unto the floor, and did according to all that her mother in law bade her. And when Boaz had eaten and drunk, and his heart was merry, he went to lie down at the end of the heap of corn: and she came softly, and uncovered his feet, and laid her down. And it came to pass at midnight, that the man was afraid, and turned himself: and, behold, a woman lay at his feet. And he said, Who art thou? And she answered, I am Ruth thine handmaid: spread therefore thy skirt over thine handmaid; for thou art a near kinsman. And he said, Blessed be thou of the Lord, my daughter: for thou hast shewed more kindness in the latter end than at the beginning, inasmuch as thou followedst not young men, whether poor or rich. And now, my daughter, fear not; I will do to thee all that thou requirest: for all the city of my people doth know that thou art a virtuous woman.

Boaz was a kinsman or relative to Elimelech, Naomi's husband. There was a law governing widows and kinsmen. It is found in *Deuteronomy 25:5-10, If brethren dwell together, and one of them die, and have no child, the wife of the dead shall not marry without unto a stranger: her husband's brother shall go in unto her, and take her to him to wife, and perform the duty of an husband's brother unto her. And it shall be, that the firstborn which she beareth shall succeed in the name of his brother which is dead, that his name be not put out of Israel. And if the man like not to take his brother's wife, then let his brother's wife go up to the gate unto the elders, and say, My husband's brother refuseth to raise up unto his brother a name in Israel, he will not perform the duty of my husband's brother. Then the elders of his city shall call him, and speak unto him: and if he stand to it, and say, I like not to take her; Then shall his brother's wife come unto him in the presence of the elders, and loose his shoe from off his foot, and spit in his face, and shall answer and say, So shall it be done unto that man that will not build up his brother's house. And his name shall be called in Israel, The house of him that hath his shoe loosed.*

If the husband died, the widow could marry the brother or a close relative of her dead husband (levirate marriage). However, the brother or close relative has a right to say 'No'. In that case, the widow would remove the sandal of the brother and spit in his face. The brother is then released from his duty to marry her, albeit in a scandalous 'sandal-less and spit-face' unclean position. The right to redeem and marry the widow was then transferred to another who would accept the sandal. Since both Naomi and Ruth were widows, they both qualified under that category of the law. But only Ruth was a Moabitess and an outcast. That unqualified her. So under Grace, only Ruth the unqualified qualified! Boaz became her kinsman-redeemer. But there was a problem as there was another unnamed kinsman closer to Ruth than Boaz!

Ruth 3:12-18 states, *And now it is true that I am thy near kinsman: howbeit there is a kinsman nearer than I. Tarry this night, and it shall be in the morning, that if he will perform unto thee the part of a kinsman, well; let him do the kinsman's part: but if he will not do the part of a kinsman to thee, then will I do the part of a kinsman to thee, as the Lord liveth: lie down until the morning. And she lay at his feet until the morning: and she rose up before one could know another. And he said, Let it not be known that a woman came into the floor. Also he said, Bring the vail that thou hast upon thee, and hold it. And when she held it, he*

*measured six measures of barley, and laid it on her: and she went
into the city. And when she came to her mother in law, she said,
Who art thou, my daughter? And she told her all that the man had
done to her. And she said, These six measures of barley gave he
me; for he said to me, Go not empty unto thy mother in law. Then
said she, Sit still, my daughter, until thou know how the matter will
fall: for the man will not be in rest, until he have finished the thing
this day.*

Boaz protected Ruth until morning came. Then he gave her
six measures of barley. That was enough food for two months. Six
denotes man. Man could provide for Ruth for a period of time but
the seventh or perfect measure would be the Provider Himself,
Jesus. And His provision is forever as it is not based upon our
works. Like Ruth, we are told to sit still as there is nothing for us
to do. Boaz, like Jesus, will not rest until his work is finished. We
read in *Hebrews 12:2, Looking unto Jesus the author and finisher
of our faith;* Jesus started it and He will finish it. Boaz, like Jesus,
is our sabbatical or seventh year. Boaz is at work in that year, not
Ruth!

We continue reading in *Ruth 4:1-10, Then went Boaz up to
the gate, and sat him down there: and, behold, the kinsman of
whom Boaz spake came by; unto whom he said, Ho, such a one!
turn aside, sit down here. And he turned aside, and sat down. And
he took ten men of the elders of the city, and said, Sit ye down here.
And they sat down. And he said unto the kinsman, Naomi, that is
come again out of the country of Moab, selleth a parcel of land,
which was our brother Elimelech's: And I thought to advertise
thee, saying, Buy it before the inhabitants, and before the elders of
my people. If thou wilt redeem it, redeem it: but if thou wilt not
redeem it, then tell me, that I may know: for there is none to
redeem it beside thee; and I am after thee. And he said, I will
redeem it. Then said Boaz, What day thou buyest the field of the
hand of Naomi, thou must buy it also of Ruth the Moabitess, the
wife of the dead, to raise up the name of the dead upon his
inheritance. And the kinsman said, I cannot redeem it for myself,
lest I mar mine own inheritance: redeem thou my right to thyself;
for I cannot redeem it. Now this was the manner in former time in*

Israel concerning redeeming and concerning changing, for to confirm all things; a man plucked off his shoe, and gave it to his neighbour: and this was a testimony in Israel. Therefore the kinsman said unto Boaz, Buy it for thee. So he drew off his shoe. And Boaz said unto the elders, and unto all the people, Ye are witnesses this day, that I have bought all that was Elimelech's, and all that was Chilion's and Mahlon's, of the hand of Naomi. Moreover Ruth the Moabitess, the wife of Mahlon, have I purchased to be my wife, to raise up the name of the dead upon his inheritance, that the name of the dead be not cut off from among his brethren, and from the gate of his place: ye are witnesses this day.

The day came when the kinsmen met. After a short conversation, it turned out that the kinsman who was closer than Boaz was amenable to redeem a piece of land to be sold by Naomi. But when the redemption of the land was linked to him redeeming Ruth as well, he declined. Subsequently, he took off his shoe and gave it to Boaz. Boaz, now owning the redemptive rights, paid for both the land and Ruth.

But who was the unnamed kinsman that turned down Ruth? He was a man of the law and a shadow of the law itself. When Boaz sat down with him, ten elders representing the ten commandments glared at them in judgment. The law was clear where it concerned redeeming property sold. In *Leviticus 25:25, If thy brother be waxen poor, and hath sold away some of his possession, and if any of his kin come to redeem it, then shall he redeem that which his brother sold.* It was perfectly good to redeem the possession sold. But when it came to Ruth the Moabitess, it was not good as it would ruin the law's inheritance. *Romans 4:14-15*, states, *For if they which are of the law be heirs, faith is made void, and the promise made of none effect: Because the law worketh wrath: for where no law is, there is no transgression.* Under the law, we inherit the knowledge of sin and the wrath of God on sin. The law cannot redeem us as it has no redeeming qualities. The law cannot redeem Ruth because that would void *mitzvoth* 603 which was to show the cursed nature of the Moabites by not ever offering them a peace treaty.

The Moabites descended from an incestuous relationship between Lot and his eldest daughter. We read of this in *Genesis 19:36-37, Thus were both the daughters of Lot with child by their father. And the firstborn bare a son, and called his name Moab: the same is the father of the Moabites unto this day.* Although related to the Israelites, they would not help the Israelites when they came out of Egypt, choosing to curse them through Balaam. But because of the Abrahamic covenant, the Israelites continued to be blessed while the Moabites became cursed to their tenth generation, meaning, forever. In *Deuteronomy 23:3-4,* we read, *An Ammonite or Moabite shall not enter into the congregation of the Lord; even to their tenth generation shall they not enter into the congregation of the Lord for ever: Because they met you not with bread and with water in the way, when ye came forth out of Egypt; and because they hired against thee Balaam the son of Beor of Pethor of Mesopotamia, to curse thee.* The Moabites would be trodden down as straws by cattle, mixed with its dung in *Isaiah 25:10, Moab shall be trodden down under him, even as straw is trodden down for the dunghill.* Moab would be as Sodom in *Zephaniah 2:9,* a place *breeding of nettles, and saltpits, and a perpetual desolation.*

Ruth, the Moabitess, could never enter into the congregation of the Lord because of this curse. But now, because of Boaz, the curse has been reversed. She was of wrong birth but now given new birth. She was polluted and looked different than the Israelite maidens but now she was cleansed and looked much better than the Israelite maidens. She was cursed to marry a sickly man who died, who left her childless, but now she was destined to marry a strong man who would give her a child. Not any child but a child that would have kingly lineage. She was condemned by the law but now she was married to Grace. Sick to strong; unclean to clean; cursed to blessed; childless to child bearing; law to Grace!

Ruth is an exact copy of polluted Jerusalem or Gentiles made exceedingly beautiful by God in *Ezekiel 16:3-14, And say, Thus saith the Lord God unto Jerusalem; Thy birth and thy nativity is of the land of Canaan; thy father was an Amorite, and thy mother an Hittite. And as for thy nativity, in the day thou wast born thy navel was not cut, neither wast thou washed in water to supple thee; thou wast not salted at all, nor swaddled at all. None eye pitied thee, to do any of these unto thee, to have compassion upon thee; but thou wast cast out in the open field, to the lothing of thy person, in the day that thou wast born. And when I passed by thee, and saw thee polluted in thine own blood, I said unto thee when thou wast in thy blood, Live; yea, I said unto thee when thou wast in thy blood, Live. I have caused thee to multiply as the bud of the field, and thou hast increased and waxen great, and thou art come to excellent ornaments: thy breasts are fashioned, and thine hair is grown, whereas thou wast naked and bare. Now when I passed by thee, and looked upon thee, behold, thy time was the time of love; and I spread my skirt over thee, and covered thy nakedness: yea, I sware unto thee, and entered into a covenant with thee, saith the Lord God, and thou becamest mine.*

*Then **washed I thee with water**; yea, I throughly washed away thy blood from thee, and I anointed thee with oil. I clothed thee also with broidered work, and shod thee with badgers' skin, and I girded thee about with fine linen, and I covered thee with silk. I decked thee also with ornaments, and I put bracelets upon thy hands, and a chain on thy neck. And I put a jewel on thy forehead, and earrings in thine ears, and a beautiful crown upon thine head. Thus wast thou decked with gold and silver; and thy raiment was of fine linen, and silk, and broidered work; thou didst eat fine flour, and honey, and oil: and thou wast exceeding beautiful and thou didst prosper into a kingdom. And thy renown went forth among the heathen for thy beauty: for it was perfect through my comeliness, which I had put upon thee, saith the Lord God.*

Ruth was similarly washed with Living Water. She merited nothing but because of Grace, received everything. The moment Boaz redeemed Ruth, the Moabitess appendage was severed. She was now 'the woman', 'the wife', 'the builder of the house of Israel', 'the worthy' and 'the famous'. As Ruth's spirit and soul prospered, everything on her outside prospered too. *3 John 2* states, *Beloved, I wish above all things that thou mayest prosper and be in health, even as thy soul prospereth.* The Moabitess had no favor until unmerited favor made her wife. As a wife, she had favor from every side. She was so favored by God that her child with Boaz, Obed, would one day produce an offspring that would be famous in all of Israel. A child that would restore lives and be a nourishment for all people. From the sheaves dropped for her initially would ultimately come the Sheaf of Life, Jesus!

We read in *Ruth 4:13-17, So Boaz took Ruth, and she was his wife: and when he went in unto her, the Lord gave her conception, and she bare a son. And the women said unto Naomi, Blessed be the Lord, which hath not left thee this day without a kinsman, that his name may be famous in Israel. And he shall be unto thee a restorer of thy life, and a nourisher of thine old age: for thy daughter in law, which loveth thee, which is better to thee than seven sons, hath born him. And Naomi took the child, and laid it in her bosom, and became nurse unto it. And the women her neighbours gave it a name, saying, There is a son born to Naomi; and they called his name Obed: he is the father of Jesse, the father of David.*

More than 1200 years later, we read in *Matthew 1:20-21, But after he had pondered these things, an angel of the Lord appeared to him in a dream and said, Joseph, son of David, do not be afraid to embrace Mary as your wife, for the One conceived in her is from the Holy Spirit. She will give birth to a Son, and you are to give Him the name Jesus because He will save His people from their sins.* Joseph and Mary's son would be Jesus. Hence, when Ruth *fell on her face, and bowed herself to the ground, and said unto him, Why have I found grace in thine eyes, that thou shouldest take knowledge of me, seeing I am a stranger?* Jesus, her great-great-great…grandson could very well have replied, "Grace found you because you were undeserving. Grace noticed you because you were unnoticed. Take knowledge of this. You came from Moab, meaning from father Lot. But you are actually from Father God! You were never a stranger because you have always been Mine!"

❧ 7 ❧

JESUS AND JONATHAN

David was anointed by Samuel to become king with the horn of oil, symbolizing the Holy Spirit, in *1 Samuel 16:13, Then Samuel took the horn of oil, and anointed him in the midst of his brethren: and the Spirit of the LORD came upon David from that day forward.* David would be king because God had anointed him to be such!

For David, it began with Jonathan (meaning, God has given), a shadow and type of Jesus. Jonathan loved David as his own soul, and they were knitted together in the king's house. *1 Samuel 18:1-4* states, *And it came to pass, when he had made an end of speaking unto Saul, that the soul of Jonathan was knit with the soul of David, and Jonathan loved him as his own soul. And Saul took him that day, and would let him go no more home to his father's house. Then Jonathan and David made a covenant, because he loved him as his own soul. And Jonathan stripped himself of the robe that was upon him, and gave it to David, and his garments, even to his sword, and to his bow, and to his girdle.* Jonathan, being the son of the king, supplied all. David, like us, received all. Jesus loved us as His own soul. He stripped Himself of His royal robe and gave us His position with His Father. Our soiled garments were replaced with His garments of righteousness. Jesus is our protector, both near (sword) and far (bow). Whether in the near present or in the far future, He will always be there with us. He provides all we need from his girdle or supply belt. He is a personal Savior and Brother who positions us to become a king.

We see this come true in *1 Samuel 23:16-18, And David saw that Saul was come out to seek his life: and David was in the wilderness of Ziph in a wood. And Jonathan Saul's son arose, and went to David into the wood, and strengthened his hand in God. And he said unto him, Fear not: for the hand of Saul my father shall not find thee; and thou shalt be king over Israel, and I shall be next unto thee; and that also Saul my father knoweth. And they two made a covenant before the LORD.* In the meantime, we know what David thought about himself. It is found in *1 Samuel 18:18, 23, And David said unto Saul, Who am I? and what is my life, or my father's family in Israel, that I should be son in law to the king? And David said, Seemeth it to you a light thing to be a king's son in law, seeing that I am a poor man, and lightly esteemed?* David believed himself unworthy but Jonathan thought otherwise. He strengthened David, covered for him, assured him that he will be the next king, and told him that he will be next to him when he takes over the kingship. The rightful heir to the throne gifted the highest position over to a person who esteemed himself as a nobody. All David had to do to become king was to give up his raggedly garments, his poverty, and his lowly servanthood position. It was all Grace from Jonathan to David.

After becoming king of Israel, David wrote *Psalm 139:13-16, thou hast covered me in my mother's womb. I will praise thee; for I am fearfully and wonderfully made: marvellous are thy works; and that my soul knoweth right well. My substance was not hid from thee, when I was made in secret, and curiously wrought in the lowest parts of the earth. Thine eyes did see my substance, yet being unperfect; and in thy book all my members were written, which in continuance were fashioned, when as yet there was none of them.* The Spirit revealed to David that God thought, saw, wrote, and spoke him into existence. Let there be - David! Only after that did God wrought and knitted him together in the womb. *Ezekiel 12:28* states, *the word which I have spoken shall be done, saith the Lord GOD.* And just as He did with David, God spoke, Let there be - us! And you and I came into being! God spoke us into existence to love us. God made us and we are His, as in *Psalm 100:3, It is he who made us, and we are his.* We became alive before we were formed in the womb! Then in the womb, our parents DNA come together to build a physical us! Each one of us is unique, as in *Ecclesiastes 11:5, As thou knowest not what is the way of the spirit, nor how the bones do grow in the womb of her that is with child: even so thou knowest not the works of God who maketh all.* While we do know the human genome, we still do not know why DNA does what it does. In time, God also knitted His Son Jesus together in Mary's womb to redeem us.

God is a covenant maker and keeper. He makes the covenant and then He keeps the covenant that He made. All the benefits of the covenant that He makes and keeps flow toward us. It is the kindness of the Lord who enlarges the covenant to cover not only David but the whole house of David. David would in turn show the same kindness to Jonathan's household. We read this in and *1 Samuel 20:14-17, And thou shalt not only while yet I live shew me the **kindness of the LORD**, that I die not: But also thou shalt not cut off thy kindness from my house for ever: no, not when the LORD hath cut off the enemies of David everyone from the face of the earth. So Jonathan made a covenant with the house of David, saying, Let the LORD even require it at the hand of David's enemies. And Jonathan caused David to swear again, because he loved him: for he loved him as he loved his own soul.* God's presence would be with David. David, when he became king, upheld his covenant with Jonathan. For the King's covenant was built upon kindness or *checed,* meaning Grace! Regardless whether it was from Jonathan to David or David back to Jonathan, Grace flowed unilaterally, from the strong to the weak! The strong provided all. The weak received all. There is no meeting half-way. One gives all. The other receives all.

Let us discover more about *checed* in *2 Samuel 4:4, And Jonathan, Saul's son, had a son that was lame of his feet. He was five years old when the tidings came of Saul and Jonathan out of Jezreel, and his nurse took him up, and fled: and it came to pass, as she made haste to flee, that he fell, and became lame. And his name was Mephibosheth.* Jonathan had a son by the name of Mephibosheth. His nurse, not knowing of God's plan to make David king, must have thought that soldiers were coming to kill off

Saul's entire household. In their haste to escape, young
Mephibosheth fell and became lame, on both his feet. He is
representative of mankind before Jesus came. Fallen, in hiding,
poor, weak, unable to walk, fearful, depressed, and guilty. But
God's magnificent thoughts about him changed all of that.

We take up the story in *2 Samuel 9:1-13, And David said,
Is there yet any that is left of the house of Saul, that I may shew
him kindness for Jonathan's sake? And there was of the house of
Saul a servant whose name was Ziba. And when they had called
him unto David, the king said unto him, Art thou Ziba? And he
said, Thy servant is he. And the king said, Is there not yet any of
the house of Saul, that I may shew the kindness of God unto him?
And Ziba said unto the king, Jonathan hath yet a son, which is
lame on his feet. And the king said unto him, Where is he? And
Ziba said unto the king, Behold, he is in the house of Machir, the
son of Ammiel, in Lodebar. Then king David sent, and fetched him
out of the house of Machir, the son of Ammiel, from Lodebar. Now
when Mephibosheth, the son of Jonathan, the son of Saul, was
come unto David, he fell on his face, and did reverence. And David
said, Mephibosheth. And he answered, Behold thy servant! And
David said unto him, Fear not: for I will surely shew thee* **kindness**
*for Jonathan thy father's sake, and will restore thee all the land of
Saul thy father; and thou shalt eat bread at my table continually.
And he bowed himself, and said, What is thy servant, that thou
shouldest look upon such a dead dog as I am? Then the king called
to Ziba, Saul's servant, and said unto him, I have given unto thy
master's son all that pertained to Saul and to all his house. Thou
therefore, and thy sons, and thy servants, shall till the land for him,
and thou shalt bring in the fruits, that thy master's son may have
food to eat: but Mephibosheth thy master's son shall eat bread
alway at my table. Now Ziba had fifteen sons and twenty servants.
Then said Ziba unto the king, According to all that my lord the
king hath commanded his servant, so shall thy servant do. As for
Mephibosheth, said the king, he shall eat at my table, as one of the
king's sons. And Mephibosheth had a young son, whose name was
Micha. And all that dwelt in the house of Ziba were servants unto*

Mephibosheth. So Mephibosheth dwelt in Jerusalem: for he did eat continually at the king's table; and was lame on both his feet.

David was now king. Meanwhile, Mephibosheth was hiding out in Lodebar, meaning 'no pasture and no promise'. Where there is no Jesus there is nothing to feed on. But David inquired 'where is he?' and then searched for him. Jesus searches for us too for He *is the kindness and love of God* in *Titus 3:4.* Never to berate, humiliate, or to put the fear of God in us! He wants to give us pure *unconditional* blessings based on Grace. As Mephibosheth could not walk on his own self, he was carried by Grace into the presence of David. David restored Mephibosheth's lands and even provided manual help for him. Others would bring him food and drink. Ziba, who had fifteen sons and twenty servants would now serve Mephibosheth. Mephibosheth received all because of Grace.

This reminds us of a significant event about eighteen years earlier in *1 Samuel 30:1-6,11-15,18-19, And it came to pass, when David and his men were come to Ziklag on the third day, that the Amalekites had invaded the south, and Ziklag, and smitten Ziklag, and burned it with fire; And had taken the women captives, that were therein: they slew not any, either great or small, but carried them away, and went on their way. So David and his men came to the city, and, behold, it was burned with fire; and their wives, and their sons, and their daughters, were taken captives. Then David and the people that were with him lifted up their voice and wept, until they had no more power to weep. And David's two wives were taken captives, Ahinoam the Jezreelitess, and Abigail the wife of Nabal the Carmelite. And David was greatly distressed; for the people spake of stoning him, because the soul of all the people was grieved, every man for his sons and for his daughters: but David encouraged himself in the LORD his God.   And they found an Egyptian in the field, and brought him to David, and gave him bread, and he did eat; and they made him drink water; And they gave him a piece of a cake of figs, and two clusters of raisins: and when he had eaten, his spirit came again to him: for he had eaten no bread, nor drunk any water, three days and three nights. And David said unto him, To whom belongest thou? and whence art*

thou? And he said, I am a young man of Egypt, servant to an
Amalekite; and my master left me, because three days ago I fell
sick...And David said to him, Canst thou bring me down to this
company? And he said, Swear unto me by God, that thou wilt
neither kill me, nor deliver me into the hands of my master, and I
will bring thee down to this company.   And David recovered all
that the Amalekites had carried away: and David rescued his two
wives. And there was nothing lacking to them, neither small nor
great, neither sons nor daughters, neither spoil, nor any thing that
they had taken to them: David recovered all.

David and his men lost all to the Amalekites, including
their families. Despite losing everything, David encouraged
himself in the Lord. For he knew that Grace always had the best
for him! Did not Grace remember him when his own father forgot
about him when Samuel came to anoint the next king? David's
answer came in the form of the Egyptian servant who guided him
into the Amalekites camp. After a triumphant victory, David
recovered all that he lost. The Egyptian servant, a Gentile, who
was left to die received Grace as well. First, he received freedom
from his old master the Amalekites after drinking the Water of Life
and eating the raisins/dried grapes. Second, in his new life, he
received the blessing of physical healing after eating the bread and
figs - just as Hezekiah's boils were healed with the fig poultice in
Isaiah 38:21. It was all Grace and David remembered this Grace as
he now addressed Mephibosheth.

Mephibosheth thought of himself as being a dead dog and a
servant. But this was expunged as he was promoted to sit, rest, and
dine with the king continuously at the king's table. There was no
need for him to lift or mend himself so he could crawl or limp to
the king's table. He was fetched and carried there every time!
Nobody body-shamed him as he sat with the king. He was on par
with all the other mighty men of David. His son Micha was
similarly promoted. You and I are there as well. All the multitudes
of sons and daughters of God, feasting together with Jesus who
bought and brought us all in, exactly as written in *Ephesians 2:6-8,*
And hath raised us up together, and made us sit together in
heavenly places in Christ Jesus: That in the ages to come he might

shew the exceeding riches of his **grace in his kindness** *toward us through Christ Jesus. For by grace are ye saved through faith; and that not of yourselves: it is the gift of God.*

We can now also understand the curious statement found in *2 Samuel 5:8, And David said on that day, Whosoever getteth up to the gutter, and smiteth the Jebusites, and the lame and the blind, that are hated of David's soul, he shall be chief and captain. Wherefore they said, The blind and the lame shall not come into the house.* If David really hated lame and blind people, Mephibosheth would not have been permitted to enter his palace as he was lame. So who were the lame and blind that David hated? Well, those were the idols that the Jebusites worshipped. These idols could not walk nor could they see. Lame and blind idols cannot sit and dine with Jesus but lame and blind men can and will.

At the king's table, Mephibosheth could finally say his name meaning aloud, 'shame no more'! The King is not ashamed of us. He claimed *Isaiah 61:7, For your shame ye shall have double.* He would be doubly honored for his past shame. There was no humiliation and embarrassing reminder of wrongs and sins. God does not cover sins. He obliterates them completely. But at God's table, a reminder of the Lord's supper, there is even more! For those who feast with and on Jesus's body are healed as well. God does not just cover lameness (or blindness) and shove it under the table so that it is out of His sight. He provides new legs as well as new life in Him! No longer a lame dead dog! But fit to sit and dine with the King! Inheritance assured. Life for death. Beauty for our ugliness.

Meanwhile, Ziba the servant of Mephibosheth, wanted more. So he ingratiated himself by working harder and trying to earn favor from the king. We saw this when David was fleeing Jerusalem due to Absalom trying to usurp his throne, in *2 Samuel 16:1-4, And when David was a little past the top of the hill, behold, Ziba the servant of Mephibosheth met him, with a couple of asses saddled, and upon them two hundred loaves of bread, and an hundred bunches of raisins, and an hundred of summer fruits, and a bottle of wine. And the king said unto Ziba, What meanest thou by these? And Ziba said, The asses be for the king's household to ride on; and the bread and summer fruit for the young men to eat; and the wine, that such as be faint in the wilderness may drink. And the king said, And where is thy master's son? And Ziba said unto the king, Behold, he abideth at Jerusalem: for he said, To day shall the house of Israel restore me the kingdom of my father. Then said the king to Ziba, Behold, thine are all that pertained unto Mephibosheth. And Ziba said, I humbly beseech thee that I may find grace in thy sight, my lord, O king.* Ziba met David on his own two feet with his own provision. Then, lying through his teeth about Mephibosheth coveting David's kingdom, Ziba through his self-works and fraudulent words conned his way to possess Mephibosheth's lands.

However, we get to hear the truth from Mephibosheth's mouth in *2 Samuel 19: 25-27,29-30, And it came to pass, when he was come to Jerusalem to meet the king, that the king said unto him, Wherefore wentest not thou with me, Mephibosheth? And he answered, My lord, O king, my servant deceived me: for thy servant said, I will saddle me an ass, that I may ride thereon, and go to the king; because thy servant is lame. And he hath slandered thy servant unto my lord the king; but my lord the king is as an angel of God: do therefore what is good in thine eyes. And the king said unto him...Thou and Ziba divide the land. And Mephibosheth said unto the king, Yea, let him take all, forasmuch as my lord the king is come again in peace unto his own house.* After Absalom was killed, Mephibosheth finally got to meet with David. When asked by David as to why he did not accompany him when he was fleeing Jerusalem, Mephibosheth simply replied that he had been purposefully left behind by Ziba. He had no intention to betray David. He was lame and he could not saddle his donkey by himself.

And how do we know that Mephibosheth was telling the truth and not Ziba? Well, let us read *1 Kings 3:16-27, Then came there two women, that were harlots, unto the king, and stood before him. And the one woman said, O my lord, I and this woman dwell in one house; and I was delivered of a child with her in the house. And it came to pass the third day after that I was delivered, that this woman was delivered also: and we were together; there was no stranger with us in the house, save we two in the house. And this woman's child died in the night; because she overlaid it. And she arose at midnight, and took my son from beside me, while thine handmaid slept, and laid it in her bosom, and laid her dead child in my bosom. And when I rose in the morning to give my child suck, behold, it was dead: but when I had considered it in the morning, behold, it was not my son, which I did bear. And the other woman said, Nay; but the living is my son, and the dead is thy son. And this said, No; but the dead is thy son, and the living is my son. Thus they spake before the king. Then said the king, The one saith, This is my son that liveth, and thy son is the dead: and the other saith, Nay; but thy son is the dead, and my son is the living. And the king said, Bring me a sword. And they brought a sword before the king. And the king said, Divide the living child in two, and give half to the one, and half to the other. Then spake the woman whose the living child was unto the king, for her bowels yearned upon her son, and she said, O my lord, give her the living child, and in no wise slay it. But the other said, Let it be neither mine nor thine, but divide it. Then the king answered and said, Give her the living child, and in no wise slay it: she is the mother thereof.*

These two stories parallel each other. When Solomon asked for a sword to cut the baby in two, the real mother, having compassion and love for her baby, relinquished her baby and said, "give her the child." The Sword, which is Jesus, still saves! The real mother ceded so that her son would live. Even though David ruled that Mephibosheth's land be split in two, Mephibosheth said, "give Ziba the land." Mephibosheth was willing to give up all his lands and possessions. All Mephibosheth really wanted was David on the throne! Similarly, all we want and need is Jesus on the throne! For in Jesus we have everything. *JESUS + 0 = EVERYTHING.* Without Jesus, we have nothing, even if we have everything. *0 = EVERYTHING – JESUS.*

Mephibosheth knew that if he had David, he would have everything. Look at what happened to him in *2 Samuel 21:1-3,6-10, Then there was a famine in the days of David three years, year after year; and David inquired of the LORD. And the LORD answered, It is for Saul, and for his bloody house, because he slew the Gibeonites. And the king called the Gibeonites, and said unto them; What shall I do for you? And they answered the king, Let seven men of his sons be delivered unto us, and we will hang them up unto the LORD in Gibeah of Saul, whom the LORD did choose. And the king said, I will give them. But the king spared Mephibosheth, the son of Jonathan the son of Saul, because of the LORD'S oath that was between them, between David and Jonathan the son of Saul. But the king took the two sons of Rizpah...and the five sons of Michal...And he delivered them into the hands of the Gibeonites, and they hanged them in the hill before the LORD. And Rizpah... took sackcloth, and spread it for her upon the rock, from the beginning of harvest until water dropped upon them out of heaven, and suffered neither the birds of the air to rest on them by day, nor the beasts of the field by night.*

Famine was a curse as a result of breaking the law. In this case, an oath made by Joshua (*Joshua 9:3*) more than 400 years before David's time to let the Gibeonites live was broken by Saul. The curse of the law was death to seven male descendants of Saul, of which Mephibosheth was the most prominent. But he was spared by David. Other descendants of Saul were hung on the hill instead. The law brought death. Seven stood for perfection. At Golgotha, Jesus the Perfect Sacrifice, would be hung on a hill for us. He brought the curse of the law to an end. Neither the birds of the air nor beasts of the field, signifying satan and his demons, could touch Him. Because of Jesus, satan the usurper was severely weakened in his power. Jesus is the Rock as in *Deuteronomy 32:4, He is the Rock, His work is perfect; For all His ways are justice, A God of truth and without injustice; Righteous and upright is He.* Rain began to fall after His perfect work. It brought the drought and the famine to an end. We, like Mephibosheth, were spared from death. The end of the cursed law brought in the rain and reign of Grace!

⊱ 8 ⊰

JESUS AND MODECAI

Jesus not only saves us but raises us up. The book of Esther is about an extravagant God who saves us, rewards us, and then elevates us up to Jesus' level. It is a book about Grace triumphing over law.

Let us start at the beginning. The Persian armies under King Ahaseurus (in Greek, King Xerxes) were fighting the Greeks. He was planning to invade Greece in the third year of his reign. Before this event, he called all his princes, nobles, and servants to a grandiose feast at his palace in Shushan. They would feast and plot strategy for six months. After that, a seven day banquet would be held in the garden court of the palace. The splendor of the palace was unequaled in richness and beauty. We read this in *Esther 1:1-7, Now it came to pass in the days of Ahasuerus, (this is Ahasuerus which reigned, from India even unto Ethiopia, over an hundred and seven and twenty provinces:) That in those days, when the king Ahasuerus sat on the throne of his kingdom, which was in Shushan the palace, In the third year of his reign, he made a feast unto all his princes and his servants; the power of Persia and Media, the nobles and princes of the provinces, being before him: When he shewed the riches of his glorious kingdom and the honour of his excellent majesty many days, even an hundred and fourscore days. And when these days were expired, the king made a feast unto all the people that were present in Shushan the palace, both unto* great *and small, seven days, in the court of the garden of the king's palace; Where were white, green, and blue, hangings, fastened with cords of fine linen and purple to silver rings and pillars of marble: the beds were of gold and silver, upon a pavement of red, and blue, and white, and black, marble. And they gave them drink in vessels of gold, (the vessels being diverse one from another,) and royal wine in abundance, according to the state of the king.*

Ahaseurus, in a small way, symbolized God here. He is described as purposefully extravagant here to show a purposefully extravagant God! We catch a glimpse of His majesty, stateliness, and greatness. The colors in His garden signified divinity, royalty, and primacy. He gave to all out of His abundance. He gave according to His state as the King. He gave liberally. He lavished His riches upon His people. His chosen people were the Jews as symbolized by queen Vashti. They would be blessed by the King to the envy of the Gentiles. Sadly, just as queen Vashti rejected the king, the Jews rejected God's calling. Ahaseurus sent chamberlain after chamberlain. God sent prophet after prophet, but the Jews rejected Him choosing to follow the law instead. Because of their consistent rejection of Jesus, their blessedness would now be suspended. In their place, the Gentiles would be blessed. The royal estate of the Jews would be given to another.

We read this in *Esther 9-19, Also Vashti the queen made a feast for the women in the royal house which belonged to king Ahasuerus. On the seventh day, when the heart of the king was merry with wine, he commanded Mehuman, Biztha, Harbona, Bigtha, and Abagtha, Zethar, and Carcas, the seven chamberlains that served in the presence of Ahasuerus the king, To bring Vashti the queen before the king with the crown royal, to shew the people and the princes her beauty: for she was fair to look on. But the queen Vashti refused to come at the king's commandment by his chamberlains: therefore was the king very wroth, and his anger burned in him. Then the king said to the wise men, which knew the times, (for so was the king's manner toward all that knew law and judgment: And the next unto him was Carshena, Shethar, Admatha, Tarshish, Meres, Marsena, and Memucan, the seven princes of Persia and Media, which saw the king's face, and which sat the first in the kingdom;) What shall we do unto the queen* Vashti

*according to law, because she hath not performed the
commandment of the king Ahasuerus by the chamberlains? And
Memucan answered before the king and the princes, Vashti the
queen hath not done wrong to the king only, but also to all the
princes, and to all the people that are in all the provinces of the
king Ahasuerus. For this deed of the queen shall come abroad unto
all women, so that they shall despise their husbands in their eyes,
when it shall be reported, The king Ahasuerus commanded Vashti
the queen to be brought in before him, but she came not. Likewise
shall the ladies of Persia and Media say this day unto all the king's
princes, which have heard of the deed of the queen. Thus shall
there arise too much contempt and wrath. If it please the king, let
there go a royal commandment from him, and let it be written
among the laws of the Persians and the Medes, that it be not
altered, That Vashti come no more before king Ahasuerus; and let
the king give her royal estate unto another that is better than she.*
     We continue reading in *Esther 2:1-15, After these things,
when the wrath of king Ahasuerus was appeased, he remembered
Vashti, and what she had done, and what was decreed against her.
Then said the king's servants that ministered unto him, Let there be
fair young virgins sought for the king: And let the king appoint
officers in all the provinces of his kingdom, that they may gather
together all the fair young virgins unto Shushan the palace, to the
house of the women unto the custody of Hege the king's
chamberlain, keeper of the women; and let their things for
purification be given them: And let the maiden which pleaseth the
king be queen instead of Vashti. And the thing pleased the king;
and he did so. Now in Shushan the palace there was a certain Jew,
whose name was Mordecai, the son of Jair, the son of Shimei, the
son of Kish, a Benjamite; Who had been carried away from
Jerusalem with the captivity which had been carried away with
Jeconiah king of Judah, whom Nebuchadnezzar the king of
Babylon had carried away. And he brought up Hadassah, that is,
Esther, his uncle's daughter: for she had neither father nor mother,
and the maid was fair and beautiful; whom Mordecai, when her
father and mother were dead, took for his own daughter. So it
came to pass, when the king's commandment and his decree was*

heard, and when many maidens were gathered together unto
Shushan the palace, to the custody of Hegai, that Esther was
brought also unto the king's house, to the custody of Hegai, keeper
of the women. And the maiden pleased him, and she obtained
kindness of him; and he speedily gave her her things for
purification, with such things as belonged to her, and seven
maidens, which were meet to be given her, out of the king's house:
and he preferred her and her maids unto the best place of the
house of the women. Esther had not shewed her people nor her
kindred: for Mordecai had charged her that she should not shew it.
And Mordecai walked every day before the court of the women's
house, to know how Esther did, and what should become of her.
Now when every maid's turn was come to go in to king Ahasuerus,
after that she had been twelve months, according to the manner of
the women, (for so were the days of their purifications
accomplished, to wit, six months with oil of myrrh, and six months
with sweet odours, and with other things for the purifying of the
women;) Then thus came every maiden unto the king; whatsoever
she desired was given her to go with her out of the house of the
women unto the king's house. In the evening she went, and on the
morrow she returned into the second house of the women, to the
custody of Shaashgaz, the king's chamberlain, which kept the
concubines: she came in unto the king no more, except the king
delighted in her, and that she were called by name.

Now when the turn of Esther, the daughter of Abihail the
uncle of Mordecai, who had taken her for his daughter, was come
to go in unto the king, she required nothing but what Hegai the
king's chamberlain, the keeper of the women, appointed. And
Esther obtained favour in the sight of all them that looked upon
her. So Esther was taken unto king Ahasuerus into his house royal
in the tenth month, which is the month Tebeth, in the seventh year
of his reign. And the king loved Esther above all the women, and
she obtained grace and favour in his sight more than all the
virgins; so that he set the royal crown upon her head, and made
her queen instead of Vashti. Then the king made a great feast unto
all his princes and his servants, even Esther's feast; and he made a

release to the provinces, and gave gifts, according to the state of the king.

The king started to look for a new bride. Fair maidens from all over the kingdom were taken into the palace. We were all brought into the kingdom. We do not need to bring anything with us as the King is our provision and provider. From all the maidens, one stood out. Her name was Esther or in Hebrew, Hadassah. Hadassah meant myrtle or sweet fragrance. Hadassah is us. We have Modecai, who is a figure of Jesus, to take care of us. With Modecai, Hadassah found favor with Hegai, who gave her seven choice maidens and the best place in the house of the women. Hegai, as the Holy Spirit gave us perfect spiritual gifts called *charismata* or Grace gifts. Hegai dressed Hadassah in Jesus' righteousness, perfumed her with Jesus' oil of myrrh or *mor*, and immersed her in Jesus' fragrance. When Hadassah went into the king's house she required and had need of nothing else. The King, seeing Jesus on Hadassah, loved Hadassah above all the other women. She obtained grace and favor in his sight. Hadassah became queen and a feast was thrown in her honor. Hadassah was given what was once reserved only for Vashti. Gifts were given according to the abundance of the king and not according to the needs of the people. Similarly, when we approach God, we require and have need of nothing as well. We definitely do not need our works. We are loved above all others because we have Jesus. He is all in all and when we have Him, we have everything. Jesus is the appointed One. Because of Jesus, we have unmerited favor. Because of Grace, we are given more grace. At God's banqueting table, we get to sit with the King and partake of His extravagant goodness and bountiful blessings. The Gentiles were given what was originally for the Jews.

While all of this was going on, enemies rose up, and tried to kill the king and the new queen. But Modecai stepped in and the perpetrators were caught and subsequently, hung from a tree. We read this in *Esther 2: 19-23, And when the virgins were gathered together the second time, then Mordecai sat in the king's gate. Esther had not yet shewed her kindred nor her people; as Mordecai had charged her: for Esther did the commandment of*

Mordecai, like as when she was brought up with him. In those days, while Mordecai sat in the king's gate, two of the king's chamberlains, Bigthan and Teresh, of those which kept the door, were wroth, and sought to lay hand on the king Ahasuerus. And the thing was known to Mordecai, who told it unto Esther the queen; and Esther certified the king thereof in Mordecai's name. And when inquisition was made of the matter, it was found out; therefore they were both hanged on a tree: and it was written in the book of the chronicles before the king. Although we belong to God, enemies would still rise up. Weapons would be formed against us. Shadows of death would surround us. But the war is won. The enemy has already been defeated. The weapons, though formed, cannot hurt us. And certainly no shadow can ever kill us. When we are in Jesus, we are always protected and already victorious. The devil cannot touch us directly.

The devil knows all of this too. But he still goes around like an old, roaring lion trying his best to frighten people away from God. Young lions do not roar, but are stealthy when catching prey. The devil roars his loudest so we would switch our focus away from Jesus to self. The devil loves self-adulation, the flesh, and self-works. He wants the best seat in the palace. He wants to be admired and praised for his position. He represented the law which required all to bow down before it. He came in the form of Haman.

We read in *Esther 3:1-12, After these things did king Ahasuerus promote Haman the son of Hammedatha the Agagite, and advanced him, and set his seat above all the princes that were with him. And all the king's servants, that were in the king's gate, bowed, and reverenced Haman: for the king had so commanded concerning him. But Mordecai bowed not, nor did him reverence. Then the king's servants, which were in the king's gate, said unto Mordecai, Why transgressest thou the king's commandment? Now it came to pass, when they spake daily unto him, and he hearkened not unto them, that they told Haman, to see whether Mordecai's matters would stand: for he had told them that he was a Jew. And when Haman saw that Mordecai bowed not, nor did him reverence, then was Haman full of wrath. And he thought scorn to lay hands on Mordecai alone; for they had shewed him the people of Mordecai: wherefore Haman sought to destroy all the Jews that were throughout the whole kingdom of Ahasuerus, even the people of Mordecai. In the first month, that is, the month Nisan, in the twelfth year of king Ahasuerus, they cast Pur, that is, the lot, before Haman from day to day, and from month to month, to the twelfth month, that is, the month Adar. And Haman said unto king Ahasuerus, There is a certain people scattered abroad and dispersed among the people in all the provinces of thy kingdom; and their laws are diverse from all people; neither keep they the king's laws: therefore it is not for the king's profit to suffer them. If it please the king, let it be written that they may be destroyed: and I will pay ten thousand talents of silver to the hands of those that have the charge of the business, to bring it into the king's treasuries. And the king took his ring from his hand, and gave it unto Haman the son of Hammedatha the Agagite, the Jews' enemy. And the king said unto Haman, The silver is given to thee, the people also, to do with them as it seemeth good to thee. Then were the king's scribes called on the thirteenth day of the first month, and there was written according to all that Haman had commanded unto the king's lieutenants, and to the governors that were over every province, and to the rulers of every people of every province according to the writing thereof, and to every people after their language; in the name of king Ahasuerus was it written, and sealed with the king's ring.*

Haman was an Agagite, a descendant from Agag, king of the Amalekites. The Amalekites had fought consistently with the Israelites, from the time the Israelites left Egypt. They attacked and burnt Israel repeatedly through the years. Even the name Agag meant 'burnt'. King Saul was commanded to annihilate them but he kept Agag alive. We saw this in *1 Samuel 15:8-9, And he took Agag the king of the Amalekites alive, and utterly destroyed all the people with the edge of the sword. But Saul and the people spared Agag, and the best of the sheep, and of the oxen, and of the fatlings, and the lambs, and all that was good, and would not utterly destroy them: but every thing that was vile and refuse, that they destroyed utterly.* Haman came from that Agag lineage and continued seeking out Jews in order to destroy them. He obtained the written law, sealed with the king's seal, to obliterate the Jews. He was even willing to pay to have the Jews killed off. His action sounded so correct and praiseworthy. He exalted himself. In fact, since Haman also represented the law, none would be able to stand before him. Haman enforced the law based on performance and obedience. Anyone transgressing against the law made Haman wrathful. *Romans 4:15* states, *Because the law worketh wrath: for where no law is, there is no transgression.* If there was no law, there would have been no transgression. Since everyone transgressed, all bowed down before the law. Except Modecai, a prefigure of Jesus! Grace does not bow down to the law.

Modecai heard about the law and told it to Hadassah. The decree to kill all the Jews in the kingdom was tragic news. And it could not be revoked as it had the king's seal upon it! We knew this from *Daniel 6:8, Now, O king, establish the decree, and sign the writing, that it be not changed, according to the law of the Medes and Persians, which altereth not.* Modecai asked Hadassah to go before the king and to appeal to him. Hadassah replied that all who approached Ahaseurus, unless called, would be put to death. But she would go before the king even though it was not according to the law. Before she did it though, she fasted three days and nights. She knew that she would perish otherwise.

We read of this account in *Esther 4:-17, Then called Esther for Hatach, one of the king's chamberlains, whom he had appointed to attend upon her, and gave him a commandment to Mordecai, to know what it was, and why it was. So Hatach went forth to Mordecai unto the street of the city, which was before the king's gate. And Mordecai told him of all that had happened unto him, and of the sum of the money that Haman had promised to pay to the king's treasuries for the Jews, to destroy them. Also he gave him the copy of the writing of the decree that was given at Shushan to destroy them, to shew it unto Esther, and to declare it unto her, and to charge her that she should go in unto the king, to make supplication unto him, and to make request before him for her people. And Hatach came and told Esther the words of Mordecai. Again Esther spake unto Hatach, and gave him commandment unto Mordecai; All the king's servants, and the people of the king's provinces, do know, that whosoever, whether man or woman, shall come unto the king into the inner court, who is not called, there is one law of his to put him to death, except such to whom the king shall hold out the golden sceptre, that he may live: but I have not been called to come in unto the king these thirty days. And they told to Mordecai Esther's words. Then Mordecai commanded to answer Esther, Think not with thyself that thou shalt escape in the king's house, more than all the Jews. For if thou altogether holdest thy peace at this time, then shall there enlargement and deliverance arise to the Jews from another place; but thou and thy father's house shall be destroyed: and who knoweth whether thou art come to the kingdom for such a time as this? Then Esther bade them return Mordecai this answer, Go, gather together all the Jews that are present in Shushan, and fast ye for me, and neither eat nor drink three days, night or day: I also and my maidens will fast likewise; and so will I go in unto the king, which is not according to the law: and if I perish, I perish. So Mordecai went his way, and did according to all that Esther had commanded him.*

Continuing on in *Esther 5:1-14, Now it came to pass on the third day, that Esther put on her royal apparel, and stood in the inner court of the king's house, over against the king's house: and the king sat upon his royal throne in the royal house, over against the gate of the house. And it was so, when the king saw Esther the queen standing in the court, that she obtained favour in his sight: and the king held out to Esther the golden sceptre that was in his hand. So Esther drew near, and touched the top of the sceptre. Then said the king unto her, What wilt thou, queen Esther? and what is thy request? it shall be even given thee to the half of the kingdom. And Esther answered, If it seem good unto the king, let the king and Haman come this day unto the banquet that I have prepared for him. Then the king said, Cause Haman to make haste, that he may do as Esther hath said. So the king and Haman came to the banquet that Esther had prepared. And the king said unto Esther at the banquet of wine, What is thy petition? and it shall be granted thee: and what is thy request? even to the half of the kingdom it shall be performed. Then answered Esther, and said, My petition and my request is; If I have found favour in the sight of the king, and if it please the king to grant my petition, and to perform my request, let the king and Haman come to the banquet that I shall prepare for them, and I will do tomorrow as the king hath said. Then went Haman forth that day joyful and with a glad heart: but when Haman saw Mordecai in the king's gate, that he stood not up, nor moved for him, he was full of indignation against Mordecai. Nevertheless Haman refrained himself: and when he came home, he sent and called for his friends, and Zeresh his wife. And Haman told them of the glory of his riches, and the multitude of his children, and all the things wherein the king had promoted him, and how he had advanced him above the princes and servants of the king. Haman said moreover, Yea, Esther the queen did let no man come in with the king unto the banquet that she had prepared but myself; and to morrow am I invited unto her also with the king. Yet all this availeth me nothing, so long as I see Mordecai the Jew sitting at the king's gate. Then said Zeresh his wife and all his friends unto him, Let a gallows be made of fifty cubits high, and tomorrow speak thou unto the king that Mordecai may be hanged thereon: then go thou in merrily with the king unto the banquet. And the thing pleased Haman; and he caused the gallows to be made.*

Hadassah could not approach the king. She was not called. Nothing could justify her coming before the king so she did nothing. What about her fasting then, you might ask? Surely that is something. Well, her three days and nights fasting symbolized her death before being resurrected with Christ. She was now the 'new woman' clothed in the regal righteousness of Jesus. She was now true royalty and could approach the throne boldly. When the King saw her, He saw Jesus' righteousness in her. And in us. Without Jesus, we would have been executed promptly. But with Jesus, there is no need to fear death. We are as righteous as Jesus! Hadassah obtained favor in Ahaseurus sight as in *Proverbs 16:15, In the light of the king's countenance is life; and his favour is as a cloud of the latter rain.* The golden scepter that was held out symbolized Jesus as well. We saw this, as Balaam's vision, back in *Numbers 24:17, I shall see him, but not now: I shall behold him, but not nigh: there shall come a Star out of Jacob, and a Sceptre shall rise out of Israel.* He gave life to all who approached the King. The edict to kill all the Jews was given on the thirteenth of Nisan. Hadassah fasted for three days after that. The next day, on the seventeenth of Nisan, she went before the king. Jesus was resurrected on the seventeenth of Nisan. Once again, on the seventeenth, Grace won and death was defeated.

Hadassah then invited the king and Haman to a banquet of wine, to be followed by another banquet the next day. The banquet of wine was a feast to remember what Jesus did for us on the cross. It was His blood that took away all the ugliness of sins. He gave us beauty for ashes. At the feast, the King was captivated by our beauty. Ahaseurus the king, wanted to give half of his extensive kingdom to Hadassah. Our King is much better. He gave us His entire kingdom. Haman was ignored by all. Still, he congratulated himself as he loved self-aggrandizement. But seeing Modecai at the king's gates made him furious. Gates were places of judgment, as in *Deuteronomy 21:18, Judges and officers shalt thou make thee in all thy gates, which the LORD thy God giveth thee, throughout thy tribes: and they shall judge the people with just judgment.* Haman judged Modecai and condemned him to death by hanging.

In the meantime, Ahaseurus wanted to reward the man who had prevented his assassination earlier, as well as Hadassah. Haman, in his fleshly pride, thought that the king wanted to reward him based on his performance. We read in *Esther 6:1-11, On that night could not the king sleep, and he commanded to bring the book of records of the chronicles; and they were read before the king. And it was found written, that Mordecai had told of Bigthana and Teresh, two of the king's chamberlains, the keepers of the door, who sought to lay hand on the king Ahasuerus. And the king said, What honour and dignity hath been done to Mordecai for this? Then said the king's servants that ministered unto him, There is nothing done for him. And the king said, Who is in the court? Now Haman was come into the outward court of the king's house, to speak unto the king to hang Mordecai on the gallows that he had prepared for him. And the king's servants said unto him, Behold, Haman standeth in the court. And the king said, Let him come in. So Haman came in. And the king said unto him, What*

shall be done unto the man whom the king delighteth to honour?
Now Haman thought in his heart, To whom would the king delight
to do honour more than to myself? And Haman answered the king,
For the man whom the king delighteth to honour, Let the royal
apparel be brought which the king useth to wear, and the horse
that the king rideth upon, and the crown royal which is set upon
his head: And let this apparel and horse be delivered to the hand
of one of the king's most noble princes, that they may array the
man withal whom the king delighteth to honour, and bring him on
horseback through the street of the city, and proclaim before him,
Thus shall it be done to the man whom the king delighteth to
honour. Then the king said to Haman, Make haste, and take the
apparel and the horse, as thou hast said, and do even so to
Mordecai the Jew, that sitteth at the king's gate: let nothing fail of
all that thou has spoken. Then took Haman the apparel and the
horse, and arrayed Mordecai, and brought him on horseback
through the street of the city, and proclaimed before him, Thus
shall it be done unto the man whom the king delighteth to honour.

But Ahaseurus rewarded Modecai instead, who sat at the
king's gates. The king rewarded whom he delighted in. The Man
whom God delighted in was Jesus, who sits at His right hand. Jesus
destroyed the enemy of God. God gave Jesus the crown, the royal
apparel, and the horse. He gave Him the keys of the kingdom of
heaven. Similarly, God does not give to us based on our goodness.
He gives to us based on His goodness. Because of Jesus'
obedience, we obtained the reward. He remembers us as He
remembered Noah. At the banquet of wine, Hadassah revealed
Haman's plan to exterminate the Jews. The king found no pleasure
in this as his queen was of Jewish bloodline.

We read of this in *Esther 7:1-10, So the king and Haman*
came to banquet with Esther the queen. And the king said again
unto Esther on the second day at the banquet of wine, What is thy
petition, queen Esther? and it shall be granted thee: and what is
thy request? and it shall be performed, even to the half of the
kingdom. Then Esther the queen answered and said, If I have
found favour in thy sight, O king, and if it please the king, let my
life be given me at my petition, and my people at my request: For

we are sold, I and my people, to be destroyed, to be slain, and to perish. But if we had been sold for bondmen and bondwomen, I had held my tongue, although the enemy could not countervail the king's damage. Then the king Ahasuerus answered and said unto Esther the queen, Who is he, and where is he, that durst presume in his heart to do so? And Esther said, The adversary and enemy is this wicked Haman. Then Haman was afraid before the king and the queen. And the king arising from the banquet of wine in his wrath went into the palace garden: and Haman stood up to make request for his life to Esther the queen; for he saw that there was evil determined against him by the king. Then the king returned out of the palace garden into the place of the banquet of wine; and Haman was fallen upon the bed whereon Esther was. Then said the king, Will he force the queen also before me in the house?

As the word went out of the king's mouth, they covered Haman's face. And Harbonah, one of the chamberlains, said before the king, Behold also, the gallows fifty cubits high, which Haman had made for Mordecai, who had spoken good for the king, standeth in the house of Haman. Then the king said, Hang him thereon. So they hanged Haman on the gallows that he had prepared for Mordecai. Then was the king's wrath pacified. Haman who had desired to be high and lifted up (there is only one 'high and lifted up' mentioned in *Isaiah 57:15*, who inhabits eternity and whose name is Holy) was subsequently hung on the fifty cubits high gallows. The gallows, which was a curse to destroy Modecai first, and the Jews fifty days later, was reversed. What was to be the height of God's shame and defeat became the apex of His glory and victory. Satan was defeated at the cross!

We read in *Ephesians 1:6-7, To the praise of the glory of his grace, wherein he hath made us accepted in the beloved. In whom we have redemption through his blood, the forgiveness of sins, according to the riches of his grace.* Because we are redeemed by His blood, we are now part of Jesus' bloodline. *Matthew 5:17-18* states, *Think not that I am come to destroy the law, or the prophets: I am not come to destroy, but to fulfil. For verily I say unto you, Till heaven and earth pass, one jot or one tittle shall in no wise pass from the law, till all be fulfilled.* **By** itself, the law would have stood forever or until heaven and earth were to pass away. God's law is always good and cannot be destroyed. Not one jot (smallest Hebrew letter) or one tittle (smallest Hebrew stroke) would pass away from the law. Hence, Jesus did not come to destroy or pass away the law, but to fulfill it. The law was good till all was fulfilled. And Jesus fulfilled it all. By His life, blood, and death. Hence, the law was affirmed, fulfilled, and brought to a close by Jesus. It became obsolete.

Continuing on in *Esther 8:1-16, On that day did the king Ahasuerus give the house of Haman the Jews' enemy unto Esther the queen. And Mordecai came before the king; for Esther had told what he was unto her. And the king took off his ring, which he had taken from Haman, and gave it unto Mordecai. And Esther set Mordecai over the house of Haman. And Esther spake yet again before the king, and fell down at his feet, and besought him with tears to put away the mischief of Haman the Agagite, and his device that he had devised against the Jews. Then the king held out the golden sceptre toward Esther. So Esther arose, and stood before the king, And said, If it please the king, and if I have found favour in his sight, and the thing seem right before the king, and I be pleasing in his eyes, let it be written to reverse the letters devised by Haman the son of Hammedatha the Agagite, which he wrote to destroy the Jews which are in all the king's provinces: For how can I endure to see the evil that shall come unto my people? or how can I endure to see the destruction of my kindred? Then the king Ahasuerus said unto Esther the queen and to Mordecai the Jew, Behold, I have given Esther the house of Haman, and him they have hanged upon the gallows, because he laid his hand upon the Jews.*

Write ye also for the Jews, as it liketh you, in the king's name, and seal it with the king's ring: for the writing which is written in the king's name, and sealed with the king's ring, may no man reverse. Then were the king's scribes called at that time in the third month, that is, the month Sivan, on the three and twentieth day thereof; and it was written according to all that Mordecai commanded unto the Jews... And he wrote in the king Ahasuerus' name, and sealed it with the king's ring, and sent letters by posts on horseback, and riders on mules, camels, and young dromedaries: Wherein the king granted the Jews which were in every city to gather themselves together, and to stand for their life, to destroy, to slay, and to cause to perish, all the power of the people and province that would assault them, both little ones and women, and to take the spoil of them for a prey, Upon one day in all the provinces of king Ahasuerus, namely, upon the thirteenth day of the twelfth month, which is the month Adar. The copy of the writing for a commandment to be given in every province was published unto all people, and that the Jews should be ready against that day to avenge themselves on their enemies. So the posts that rode upon mules and camels went out, being hastened and pressed on by the king's commandment. And the decree was given at Shushan the palace. And Mordecai went out from the presence of the king in royal apparel of blue and white, and with a great crown of gold, and with a garment of fine linen and purple: and the city of Shushan rejoiced and was glad. The Jews had light, and gladness, and joy, and honour.

As Haman was now dead, Hadassah pleaded with Ahaserus to reverse the law. But alas, the law to kill all the Jews could not be reversed. It could not be revoked. There was only one way around this. A new higher law had to be written to replace the old one! The king's ring was transferred to Modecai. The new law was written for the Jews by Modecai, as he pleased it to be written. It was a blank check edict! He then sealed it with the king's ring. This higher law allowed the Jews to defend themselves with swords against anyone seeking their destruction. It also allowed them to take possession of their enemies possessions. On top of that, Ahaserus backed the Jews as well. Modecai dressed in royal apparel of blue and white, with a great crown of gold, and a garment of fine linen and purple went out in victory to spread the good news of the new law. There was joy, gladness, and honor among the Jews for light had come. It was a good day for them.

The Mosaic law had authority. It magnified sin. All fell before it. But the Mosaic law was nailed to the cross. Satan lost and Jesus won. A new law came into effect. **Grace was the higher**

law and it replaced the Mosaic law. It was an unconditional guarantee of salvation to all by faith in Jesus. Backed by God's Word, Jesus, we too become dressed in royal garments. This new covenant was sealed with the blood of Jesus. Because of His finished work, we do not go out to victory but from victory. There is joy unspeakable and unending thankfulness, for Grace had come. It is a very good day for all who are in Christ.

Let us continue reading from *Esther 9:1-14,16-17, Now in the twelfth month, that is, the month Adar, on the thirteenth day of the same, when the king's commandment and his decree drew near to be put in execution, in the day that the enemies of the Jews hoped to have power over them, (though it was turned to the contrary, that the Jews had rule over them that hated them;) The Jews gathered themselves together in their cities throughout all the provinces of the king Ahasuerus, to lay hand on such as sought their hurt: and no man could withstand them; for the fear of them fell upon all people. And all the rulers of the provinces, and the lieutenants, and the deputies, and officers of the king, helped the Jews; because the fear of Mordecai fell upon them. For Mordecai was great in the king's house, and his fame went out throughout all the provinces: for this man Mordecai waxed greater and greater. Thus the Jews smote all their enemies with the stroke of the sword, and slaughter, and destruction, and did what they would unto those that hated them. And in Shushan the palace the Jews slew and destroyed five hundred men.*

And Parshandatha (curious-self), *and Dalphon* (self-pity), *and Aspatha* (self-sufficient), *and Poratha* (self-indulgent), *and Adalia* (false self-humility), *and Aridatha* (strong-self), *And Parmashta* (preeminent-self), *and Arisai* (bold-self), *and Aridai* (superior-self), *and Vajezatha* (self-righteousness), *The ten sons of Haman the son of Hammedatha, the enemy of the Jews, slew they; but on the spoil laid they not their hand...Then said Esther, If it please the king, let it be granted to the Jews which are in Shushan to do tomorrow also according unto this day's decree, and let Haman's ten sons be hanged upon the gallows. And the king commanded it so to be done: and the decree was given at Shushan; and they hanged Haman's ten sons. But the other Jews that were in the king's provinces gathered themselves together, and stood for their lives, and had rest from their enemies, and slew of their foes seventy and five thousand, but they laid not their hands on the prey.*

Under the old law, the Jews could not even defend themselves as that would make them outlaws. But under the new law, in the year 473 BC, the Jews took up swords and defeated their enemies. More than 75,000 of their enemies perished. They took none of the spoils, as the favor of God was worth immeasurably more than the spoils of their victory. The Jews were not only saved but promoted to a new higher position. They had great wealth and lasting peace as we see in *Esther 10:3, For Mordecai the Jew was next unto king Ahasuerus, and great among the Jews, and accepted of the multitude of his brethren, seeking the wealth of his people, and speaking peace to all his seed.* There was rest and new life for the Jews in Modecai.

The ten sons of Haman were killed. In Hebrew, each of their names had *self* attached to it. In the *tanakh* or the Hebrew bible, their names are listed separately and each written on a single line of text, in a perpendicular column. Also, the name Vajezatha, the last son on the list, was written with an oversized elongated

alphabet, *vav*. In Hebrew script, *vav* is written like a stake, ‫ו‬. Since the ten sons were hung on the stake, we can conclude that all ten sons were impaled on one long perpendicular stake, instead of ten different stakes. The number ten symbolizes the law. Hence, the law of self-righteousness was hung on the cross. *Colossians 2:14* states, *Blotting out the handwriting of ordinances that was against us, which was contrary to us, and took it out of the way, nailing it to his cross.* The handwriting of ordinances or the law was actually nailed to the cross of Jesus. *Romans 7:6* states, *But now we are delivered from the law, that being dead wherein we were held; that we should serve in newness of spirit, and not in the oldness of the letter.* The new replaced the old. Grace replaced the law. The Jews celebrated that momentous day with feasting and gladness. Instead of death, life came. It is still celebrated today and is called the feast of Purim.

The Israelites entered the Promised Land after Moses died. But when exactly did Moses die? Let us read *Deuteronomy 31:2 and 34:8, And he said unto them, I am an hundred and twenty years old this day; I can no more go out and come in: also the Lord hath said unto me, Thou shalt not go over this Jordan. And the children of Israel wept for Moses in the plains of Moab thirty days: so the days of weeping and mourning for Moses were ended,* and *Joshua 1:11, Pass through the host, and command the people, saying, Prepare you victuals; for within three days ye shall pass over this Jordan, to go in to possess the land, which the Lord your God giveth you to possess it.*

The mourning period for Moses was 30 days. Then it took another 3 days before the Israelites crossed the Jordan. 30+3=33 days in total. We also know that the Israelites finished crossing the Jordan and set up camp in Gilgal on the 10th day of the first calendar month, as in *Joshua 4:19, And the people came up out of Jordan on the tenth day of the first month, and encamped in Gilgal.* Therefore, the 33 days were split up into10 days (Nisan or first month of Jewish new calendar year) and 23days (Adar or last month of old Jewish calendar year). The month of Adar only has 29 days. 29-23=6 days passed in the month of Adar before Moses died. Hence, Moses must have passed away on the 7th day of Adar of the old year. It was also his birthday. He was 120 years old. Of course, what was significant was that the Israelites went into the Promised Land, not in their old year but in their new year. *Deuteronomy 34:5-6* states, *So Moses the servant of the LORD died there in the land of Moab, according to the word of the LORD. And he buried him in a valley in the land of Moab, over against Bethpeor: but no man knoweth of his sepulchre unto this day.* **Moses, as the law, was buried by God in a foreign land so that man would not find it.**

❧ 9 ❧

JESUS AND THE RIGHT-HAND SIDE POSITION

We all know that Jesus sits on the right hand side of the throne of God as found in *Hebrews 12:2, Looking unto Jesus the author and finisher of our faith; who for the joy that was set before him endured the cross, despising the shame, and is set down at the right hand of the throne of God.* But what is the significance of being on the right hand side? And if Jesus is on the right hand side, then who is on the left hand side? Furthermore, we also know that Jesus is our *'paraklétos'*. In English, it means that Jesus is our advocate, our comforter, our intercessor, our mediator, our helper, and our consoler. In our minds, we tend to see Jesus as our lawyer, pleading our cause before a judge. He helps, defends, and intercedes for us. He represents man before God. We read about this in the following verses:

1 John 2:1, And if any man sin, we have an advocate with the Father, Jesus Christ the righteous:

Hebrews 7:25, Wherefore he is able also to save them to the uttermost that come unto God by him, seeing he ever liveth to make intercession for them.

1 Timothy 2:5, For there is one God, and one mediator between God and men, the man Christ Jesus;

When we have an advocate, it follows that we also have an accuser, or a prosecutor. The accuser by definition accuses us of wrongdoing. In *Revelation 12:10*, we read, *And I heard a loud voice saying in heaven, Now is come salvation, and strength, and the kingdom of our God, and the power of his Christ: for the accuser of our brethren is cast down, which accused them before our God day and night.* And who can forget the vivid picture of satan in the book of Job coming before God. We find this in *Job 1:6-7, Now there was a day when the sons of God came to present themselves before the Lord, and Satan came also among them. And the Lord said unto Satan, Whence comest thou? Then Satan answered the Lord, and said, From going to and fro in the earth, and from walking up and down in it.*

We see this again in *1Kings 22:19,21-22, Micaiah continued, Therefore hear the word of the LORD: I saw the LORD sitting on His throne, and all the host of heaven standing by Him on His right and on His left. Then a spirit came forward, stood before the LORD, and said, I will entice him. By what means? asked the LORD. And he replied, I will go out and be a lying spirit in the mouths of all his prophets.* In Micaiah's vision, he saw satan (called the lying spirit here) stepping forward before going out to deceive about 400 prophets. Satan wants to harm us. He walks to and fro on the earth to see whom he may devour. He delights in pointing out our mistakes and sins. We read in *Luke 22:31-32, And the Lord said, Simon, Simon, behold, Satan hath desired to have you, that he may sift you as wheat.* He wants to sift us as wheat, shaking us violently in our faith in Jesus' completed work on the cross. Since satan was in the very presence of God, we tend to think of the throne of God as something like the figure below:

This is the exact picture of the Jewish court system in Jesus' time. Three sets of courts existed at that time. In villages or very small towns, the court was made up of three or seven judges. These courts dealt with civil matters only. In larger towns, the court was made up of twenty-three judges, also called the lesser Sanhedrin. Then there was the Great Sanhedrin which assembled only in the temple in Jerusalem. There were seventy-one judges in this Great Sanhedrin and they met in a room called the 'hall of hewn stones'. This was a chamber built into the north wall of the temple, half inside the sanctuary and half outside. The lesser as well as the great Sanhedrin would handle all cases, although the great Sanhedrin was the supreme court and legislative body when it came to interpreting the Mosaic law.

Sanhedrin means 'sitting together', an 'assembly', or 'council'. Its genesis can be found in *Exodus 18:15-18,21-22, And Moses said unto his father in law, Because the people come unto me to inquire of God: When they have a matter, they come unto me; and I judge between one and another, and I do make them know the statutes of God, and his laws. And Moses' father in law said unto him, The thing that thou doest is not good. Thou wilt surely wear away, both thou, and this people that is with thee: for this thing is too heavy for thee; thou art not able to perform it thyself alone...thou shalt provide out of all the people able men, such as fear God, men of truth, hating covetousness; and place such over them, to be rulers of thousands, and rulers of hundreds, rulers of fifties, and rulers of tens: And let them judge the people.*

Moses needed help in judging the people. His father in law, Jethro Reuel, encouraged him to share this burden of judging with other learned men. These other men had to be competent in the law and to be able to instruct the people on how they must behave and what work they must do, just like Moses did. They must also fear God, be lovers of truth, haters of covetousness, be of good standing in the community, impartial, and possess great wisdom.

Then in *Numbers 11:16-17, And the Lord said unto Moses, Gather unto me seventy men of the elders of Israel, whom thou knowest to be the elders of the people, and officers over them; and bring them unto the tabernacle of the congregation, that they may stand there with thee...and they shall bear the burden of the people with thee, that thou bear it not thyself alone,* we see the formation of the great council. The 70 elders, plus Moses, was the first great assembly. It evolved into the great Sanhedrin consisting of 23 priests, 23 scribes, 23 elders, one vice-president, and one president or high priest (23+23+23+1+1=71). The president was known as *'Rosh HaYeshiva'* or *'Nasi',* meaning prince. The vice-president was *'Av Bet Din'* or father of the court. The great Sanhedrin represented the final authority on Jewish law. However, judgment can only be rendered when all seventy-one members are present.

In the 'hall of hewn stones', the Sanhedrin would sit in a semi-circle so that all members could see each other, as well as all witnesses testifying. Here is an illustration from 1883 of the Sanhedrin from the People's Cyclopedia of Universal Knowledge. In front of this semi-circle, on either side, would sit two clerks.

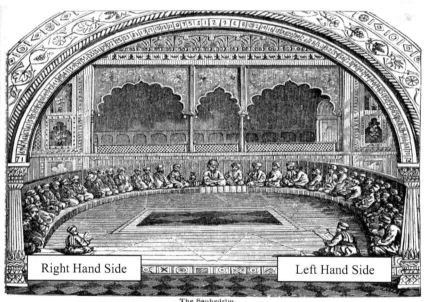

Right Hand Side   Left Hand Side

The Sanhedrim.

One clerk, on the right hand side, would note down everything said by the judges who spoke in favor of acquittal. The other clerk, on the left hand side, would note down everything said by the judges who spoke in favor of condemnation.

We catch a glimpse of the Sanhedrin in action when Jesus was questioned first by Annas, the former high priest of Judaea. In *John 18:12-13,* we read, *Then the band and the captain and officers of the Jews took Jesus, and bound him, And led him away to Annas first; for he was father in law to Caiaphas, which was the high priest that same year.* After being slapped, Jesus was then interrogated and beaten by Caiaphas the high priest. In *Matthew 26:57, And they that had laid hold on Jesus led him away to Caiaphas the high priest, where the scribes and the elders were assembled.* The next day, in the morning, the full Sanhedrin convened and pronounced Jesus guilty. We read this in *Luke 22:66-71, And as soon as it was day, the elders of the people and the chief priests and the scribes came together, and led him into their council, saying, Art thou the Christ? tell us. And he said unto them, If I tell you, ye will not believe: And if I also ask you, ye will not answer me, nor let me go. Hereafter shall the Son of man sit on the right hand of the power of God. Then said they all, Art thou then the Son of God? And he said unto them, Ye say that I am. And they said, What need we any further witness? for we ourselves have heard of his own mouth.* The clerk on the left hand side duly recorded that Jesus was guilty by a unanimous vote of the Sanhedrin.

There is another striking picture of judgment found in *Zechariah 3:1-5, And he shewed me Joshua the high priest standing before the angel of the Lord, and Satan standing at his right hand to resist him. And the Lord said unto Satan,*

***The Lord rebuke thee**, O Satan; even the Lord that hath chosen Jerusalem rebuke thee: is not this a brand plucked out of the fire? Now Joshua was clothed with filthy garments, and stood before the angel. And he answered and spake unto those that stood before him, saying, Take away the filthy garments from him. And unto him*

he said, Behold, I have caused thine iniquity to pass from thee, and I will clothe thee with change of raiment. And I said, Let them set a fair mitre upon his head. So they set a fair mitre upon his head, and clothed him with garments.

The Angel of the Lord is Jesus and He is now the judge. In *John 5:22-23*, it states *For the Father judgeth no man, but hath committed all judgment unto the Son: That all men should honour the Son, even as they honour the Father. He that honoureth not the Son honoureth not the Father which hath sent him.* Joshua was the high priest of Israel at that time and we see satan standing on his right accusing him. Joshua was clothed in filthy garments because all his good works were like filthy rags before Jesus. When satan started accusing him, Jesus rebuked satan and his accusations came to an immediate end. Then Jesus turned towards Joshua and proceeded to remove and replace his filthy garments. He also placed a mitre or a turban of fine linen upon his head. At the front of the turban was a gold inscription, which read 'holiness to the Lord'. We know this from *Leviticus 8:9, And he put the mitre upon his head; also upon the mitre, even upon his forefront, did he put the golden plate, the holy crown.* Only when the high priest was accepted, then the whole nation of Israel was accepted. Hence, Jesus took away Joshua's iniquities, replacing it with His righteousness as symbolized by the fine linen cloth and the turban.

This is not the first time when Jesus rebuked satan. We read in *Jude 9: Yet Michael the archangel, when contending with the devil he disputed about the body of Moses, durst not bring against him a railing accusation, but said, The Lord rebuke thee.* Here, satan wanted the dead body of Moses to be found, for then the Israelites would have worshipped it as an idol. But Michael referred back to Jesus who had all authority and power to rebuke satan! Of course, the body of Moses also stood for the law just as the body of Christ is Grace, as in *Jude 4, For there are certain men crept in unawares, who were before of old ordained to this condemnation, ungodly men, turning the grace of our God into lasciviousness, and denying the only Lord God, and our Lord Jesus Christ.* Law crept into grace and turned passion for Jesus into lust for the law. Satan loves to turn people from Grace to works. That is why Michael said, "The Lord rebukes you!"

We have to contend or fight to bring the gospel back to Grace. The gospel is about Jesus receiving and accepting us and not about us receiving and accepting Him. Salvation by Grace alone has been hijacked by legalists who crept in unawares. With great pride, they shout out *Hebrews 12:14, without holiness no one will see the Lord,* upholding themselves as pure and holy. They completely forget that only two chapters back in *Hebrews 10:10, we have been made holy through the sacrifice of the body of Jesus Christ once for all.* We received from Jesus holiness as well as everything else that is good about us!

Being now familiar with the court system, we believe that when we stand before God one day, Jesus would defend us from all accusations hurled towards us by satan. He would vilify and denigrate us, using the law, but Jesus would counter his every charge. Satan would play a video of our life enumerating all the sins we ever committed. Jesus would say something like, "Yes, he is guilty as you charged, but I paid the price for him, so he is free!" All the while, as heated words are exchanged between prosecutor and defense, we would be stunned by the sheer weight of our sins. We would cringe in embarrassment and hang our heads in shame and guilt. As our sins are called out one after another, even with Jesus counteracting each one, we sink lower and lower into a cesspool of disgrace and embarrassment. Then when our last sin is shouted out in heaven, Jesus says for the umpteenth time, "He is guilty but I paid the price for him." In the Sanhedrin court, the clerk would record an acquittal for us. Whew! We won because of Jesus our advocate. But we lumber like a humiliated hippopotamus bloated with sin into heaven. So, is this picture valid?

In Genesis, we know that all authority was given to Adam. *Psalm 8:6* states, *Thou madest him to have dominion over the works of thy hands; thou hast put all things under his feet.* This authority included being in the presence of God. But satan, though he was thrown out of heaven, managed to fool Adam and Eve. We read about satan's fall in *Isaiah 14:12, How art thou fallen from heaven, O Lucifer, son of the morning! how art thou cut down to the ground, which didst weaken the nations!* and again in *Luke 10:18, And he said unto them, I beheld Satan as lightning fall from heaven.* Adam and Eve, having sinned, lost their authority to satan. Satan could once again appear before the throne of God. This was how satan managed to be in God's presence in the book of Job.

But Jesus' finished work on the cross won this authority back. He is the one who has ALL things under His feet. We see this again in *Colossians 2:15, And having spoiled principalities and powers, he made a shew of them openly, triumphing over them in it.* After the cross, satan lost all authority and is now cast out of heaven definitively. We read about this in *Revelation 12:7-12, And there was war in heaven: Michael and his angels fought against the dragon; and the dragon fought and his angels, And prevailed not; neither was their place found any more in heaven. And the great dragon was cast out, that old serpent, called the Devil, and Satan, which deceiveth the whole world: he was cast out into the earth, and his angels were cast out with him. And I heard a loud voice saying in heaven, **Now is come salvation**, and strength, and the kingdom of our God, and the power of his Christ: for the accuser of our brethren is cast down, which accused them before our God day and night. And they overcame him by the **blood of the Lamb, and by the word of their testimony**; and they loved not their lives unto the death. Therefore rejoice, ye heavens, and ye that dwell in them. Woe to the inhabiters of the earth and of the sea! for the devil is come down unto you, having great wrath, because he knoweth that he hath but a short time.*

When Salvation or Jesus went back to heaven (now is Salvation come), the accuser of all believers is cast out forever. Satan was defeated by 'the blood of the Lamb and the word of their testimony'. What other word can there be to testify other than Jesus? Satan, utterly defeated, has no more access to heaven. We read this in *John 12:31, Now is the judgment of this world: now shall the prince of this world be cast out.* In fact, why would God put Jesus (Truth) and satan (Not Truth) on equal positions before His court? Why would God listen to satan who is a liar and a murderer? *John 8:44,* states, *He was a murderer from the beginning, and abode not in the truth, because there is no truth in him. When he speaketh a lie, he speaketh of his own: for he is a liar, and the father of it.*

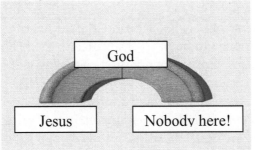

There is no longer an accuser in heaven because of the finished work of Jesus! Jesus went back to be with His Father and sat down at His right hand. We see this in *Hebrews 10:12-14, But this man, after he had offered one sacrifice for sins forever, sat down on the right hand of God; From henceforth expecting till his enemies be made his footstool. For by one offering he hath perfected for ever them that are sanctified,* and again in *Psalm 110:1, The LORD said unto my Lord, Sit thou at my right hand, until I make thine enemies thy footstool.* Before God, we are perfect even as Jesus is perfect. Before God, we are righteous even as Jesus is righteous. Jesus fulfilled the law which the devil used to accuse us. Jesus even replaced the 70 elders of Moses with His own 70, as we read in *Luke 10:1, After these things the Lord appointed other seventy also, and sent them two and two before his face into every city and place, whither he himself would come.* Jesus' 70 would bring Peace not judgment wherever they go, even to Gentile cities! Jesus acquitted all of us at the cross. Jesus sits on the right hand side of the Father just like the clerk who recorded the acquittal verdict. The clerk of the Sanhedrin, on the right hand side, was just a shadow of Jesus. For Jesus is the brightness, the *apaugasma,* or Shekinah Glory of God. He acquits us permanently.

Hebrews 2:14-16 states, *Forasmuch then as the children are partakers of flesh and blood, he also himself likewise took part of the same; that through death he might destroy him that had the power of death, that is, the devil; And deliver them who through fear of death were all their lifetime subject to bondage. For verily he took not on him the nature of angels; but he took on him the seed of Abraham. Wherefore in all things it behoved him to be made like unto his brethren, that he might be a merciful and faithful high priest in things pertaining to God, to make reconciliation for the sins of the people.* Jesus's death destroyed satan who had power over death through the law. Jesus fulfilled the law, canceled death, and absolved us from the death sentence of sin. We no longer need to fear death nor be under its bondage. Jesus was not born an angel to die for fallen angels. He was born a man to die for us. Unlike Adam who tried to become like god and so died, Jesus became one with us, to redeem, reconcile us back to God, and to give us life everlasting.

As such, it is grossly incorrect for us to think of God as a very angry rage-filled God who demands retributive justice. He wants to beat and kick the shit out of us but because Jesus stepped in for us, He beat and kicked the shit out of Jesus! Only then did God calm down. And only until we sin again, Then God gets all riled up with us yet again. Ready to beat and kick the shit out of us again. So Jesus has to take the beating and the kicking from His abusive Father all over again! Again and again and again! Satan wants us to think of God this way. Who would want intimacy with such a sadistic, cruel, and vicious God? Satan would never want us to know the true nature of God who loved us so much that he gave us His only begotten Son, Jesus, to die for us while we were yet sinners. God is NEVER angry with us. Only at sin. So Jesus came not to take a beating from His Father but to defeat sin permanently. In doing so, He lovingly reconciled us back to God!

And not only that. In *Hebrews 4:14-16* we read, *Seeing then that we have a great high priest, that is passed into the heavens, Jesus the Son of God, let us hold fast our profession. For we have not an high priest which cannot be touched with the feeling of our infirmities; but was in all points tempted like as we are, yet without sin. Let us therefore come boldly unto the throne of grace, that we may obtain mercy, and find grace to help in time of need.* **Jesus took on flesh and became one of us. Then He became one with us. He bore sicknesses and diseases with us,**

suffered through agonizing physical and mental pains with us, went through life's storms and accusations with us, suffered the devastation of heartbreaks and failures with us, lived wrecked and broken lives with us, faced ruined futures and loneliness with us, wept through grieves and despairs with us, bowed His head and died for us, and was placed in the grave for us. He went through it all with us so He could redeem us from it all. He literally went through hell with and for us, to take us with Him to heaven. He now sits at the right hand of God as one of us! There is now a glorified human body sitting next to God! This is glorified Humanity. Jesus, as humanity, that is you and I, enthroned. Because of what Jesus went through, there is no law, no accusations, no video playback, no humiliation, no disgrace, no record of our wrongs, no death, no remembrance of sins, and no devil. We can now come boldly before the throne of Grace, not punishment.

Jesus does not keep account of our sins as in *Psalm 130:3, If you, LORD, kept a record of sins, Lord, who could stand?* Then we read in *Jeremiah 31:34, for I will forgive their iniquity, and I will remember their sin no more.* Because of Jesus' finished work, we are no longer sinners! Jesus, as the all-seeing Stone, removed all sins in a single day in *Zechariah 3:9, See, the stone I have set in front of Joshua! There are seven eyes on that one stone, and I will engrave an inscription on it, says the LORD Almighty, and I will remove the sin of this land in a single day.* As there is no condemnation in heaven for believers, there is no need for a clerk to record condemnation verdicts. **There is no accuser on the left hand side of God! That is why the Bible is silent on who sits on the left hand side of God. On the right hand side sits one of us, Jesus as us, to declare us righteous by His blood. He perfected us forever!** Because of Jesus, we walk into heaven as sons and daughters. We enter heaven to meet Abba Father with heads held high, as in *Psalm 3:3, you are my glory, the one who holds my head high.* We are vindicated, absolved, exonerated, and redeemed. Jesus is always on our side because He is one of us! We get to sit with our resurrected Jesus who is God!

❧ 10 ❧

JESUS AND JOB

The book of Job is probably one of the most misinterpreted books in the whole bible. Many verses from the book are quoted and applied in peoples' lives to great detriment. These hogwash teachings usually show God as being schizophrenic, Job as being a saint for his obedience through intense suffering (given by God), and satan as being equal to God.

Let us begin in *Job 1:1-22, There was a man in the land of Uz, whose name was Job; and that man was perfect and upright, and one that feared God, and eschewed evil. And there were born unto him seven sons and three daughters. His substance also was seven thousand sheep, and three thousand camels, and five hundred yoke of oxen, and five hundred she asses, and a very great household; so that this man was the greatest of all the men of the east. And his sons went and feasted in their houses, every one his day; and sent and called for their three sisters to eat and to drink with them. And it was so, when the days of their feasting were gone about, that Job sent and sanctified them, and rose up early in the morning, and offered burnt offerings according to the number of them all: for Job said, It may be that my sons have sinned, and cursed God in their hearts. Thus did Job continually.*

Now there was a day when the sons of God came to present themselves before the Lord, and Satan came also among them. And the Lord said unto Satan, Whence comest thou? Then Satan answered the Lord, and said, From going to and fro in the earth, and from walking up and down in it. And the Lord said unto Satan,

*Hast thou **considered** my servant Job, that there is none like him in
the earth, a perfect and an upright man, one that feareth God, and
escheweth evil? Then Satan answered the Lord, and said, Doth Job
fear God for nought? Hast not thou made an hedge about him, and
about his house, and about all that he hath on every side? thou
hast blessed the work of his hands, and his substance is increased
in the land. But put forth thine hand now, and touch all that he
hath, and he will curse thee to thy face. And the Lord said unto
Satan, Behold, all that he hath is **in thy power**; only upon himself
put not forth thine hand. So Satan went forth from the presence of
the Lord.*

*And there was a day when his sons and his daughters were
eating and drinking wine in their eldest brother's house: And there
came a messenger unto Job, and said, The oxen were plowing, and
the asses feeding beside them: And the Sabeans fell upon them, and
took them away; yea, they have slain the servants with the edge of
the sword; and I only am escaped alone to tell thee. While he was
yet speaking, there came also another, and said, The fire of God is
fallen from heaven, and hath burned up the sheep, and the
servants, and consumed them; and I only am escaped alone to tell
thee. While he was yet speaking, there came also another, and
said, The Chaldeans made out three bands, and fell upon the
camels, and have carried them away, yea, and slain the servants
with the edge of the sword; and I only am escaped alone to tell
thee. While he was yet speaking, there came also another, and
said, Thy sons and thy daughters were eating and drinking wine in
their eldest brother's house: And, behold, there came a great wind
from the wilderness, and smote the four corners of the house, and
it fell upon the young men, and they are dead; and I only am
escaped alone to tell thee. Then Job arose, and rent his mantle,
and shaved his head, and fell down upon the ground, and
worshipped, And said, Naked came I out of my mother's womb, and
naked shall I return thither: the Lord gave, and the Lord hath
taken away; blessed be the name of the Lord. In all this Job sinned
not, nor charged God foolishly.*

The traditional explanation is straightforward. Job was a
very good person. He was perfect and upright, he feared God, and

eschewed evil. God was very pleased with all that Job did so He rewarded him abundantly with family, livestock, and material possessions. Job was so good that he offered sacrifices to God for sins that his family might have been committed inadvertently. But because Job was perfect, he did not have to offer up any sacrifices for himself. One day, when God was talking to satan, God challenged the devil to a dare. God presented Job to satan and dared him to defy Job's integrity, uprightness, and perfection. Satan jumped at the opportunity to test Job's obedience and faith. He replied to God that should God remove His protection and blessings upon Job's life, Job would do a U-turn and start to curse God instead. God smirked because He knew the righteousness of Job. God then gave permission to satan to go ahead and begin the destruction upon His blessings. Satan happily obliged and demolished all of Job's houses, expunged his livestock, killed his servants, and annihilated his family. Job, upon hearing the cataclysmic events that had occurred, fell on his knees and worshipped God.

The story continues In *Job 2:4-11, And Satan answered the Lord, and said, Skin for skin, yea, all that a man hath will he give for his life. But put forth thine hand now, and touch his bone and his flesh, and he will curse thee to thy face. And the Lord said unto Satan, Behold, he is in thine hand; but save his life. So went Satan forth from the presence of the Lord, and smote Job with sore boils from the sole of his foot unto his crown. And he took him a potsherd to scrape himself withal; and he sat down among the ashes. Then said his wife unto him, Dost thou still retain thine integrity? curse God, and die. But he said unto her, Thou speakest as one of the foolish women speaketh. What? shall we receive good at the hand of God, and shall we not receive evil? In all this did not Job sin with his lips. Now when Job's three friends heard of all this evil that was come upon him, they came every one from his own place; Eliphaz the Temanite, and Bildad the Shuhite, and Zophar the Naamathite: for they had made an appointment together to come to mourn with him and to comfort him.*

The next time God met satan, God smiled and prodded satan, "Did you see what Job did? All of his blessings were gone but he still did not curse me. I told you so." Satan scratched the horns on his head, thought for a moment, then replied, "You did not allow me to harm him personally. If you do that, then he will curse you." God wanting to prove His point that Job's obedience would triumph any suffering that came his way, agreed with satan. So once again, with God's permission, satan poured boils and sores upon Job, from the top of his head to the bottom of his feet. When the boils ruptured and oozed, Job covered his broken skin, even on his head, with ashes and dust. Unable to wear normal clothes because of the pus and worms, he put on coarse sackcloth which stuck and cleaved to his infectious seeping boils like it was sown unto him. He could feel his bones and sinews piercing through his torn and purulent skin. We read of this in the following scriptures:

Job 7:5, My flesh is clothed with worms and clods of dust; my skin is broken, and become loathsome.

Job 16:15, I have sewed sackcloth upon my skin, and defiled my horn in the dust.

Job 30:17-19, My bones are pierced in me in the night season: and my sinews take no rest. By the great force of my disease is my garment changed: it bindeth me about as the collar of my coat. He hath cast me into the mire, and I am become like dust and ashes.

But through the anguish and pain, Job did not sin with his lips. He castigated his wife for speaking foolishly about God and he ignored his friends who had come to comfort him. Through his suppurations, he secreted self-righteous integrity. He was a martyr. He came into this world naked, he would return naked. God gave and God took away. God blessed and God punished. God gives both good and evil. Who can understand the mind of God? After all, His ways are not our ways and His thoughts are not our thoughts. Such is life! C'est la vie! Que sera sera! Whatever will be, will be!

The moral of the story is very simple. God's will for us is that we suffer as that is the way our faith is tested. He purifies us by suffering. Like an all-consuming fire, He will burn the impurities from us. The more intense the heat and the more intense the pain, the purer we will become. It is because He loves us that he allows this pain to come unto us. We become more humble. We repent more. That is why He permits satan to torture us. In the end, we become more perfect. It is His will that we, as His sons and daughters, stand obedient and strong through this period of excruciation. We will come out as fine gold. Even though God gave us the pain yet He will bring us through the pain. We trust in God's goodness even as He tortures us. That is how we learn to love Him back. It is God's will that all believers are tested to prove how good they are. The test strengthens us. We earn points for our faithfulness, our trustworthiness, our righteousness, our obedience, and our commitment to God. At the end, God sees how good we are and rewards us abundantly. If we die from the pain before we receive our rewards, then our rewards will be carried forward into heaven. That is why Job was rewarded bountifully at the end of the book. Good job, Job!

While the explanation above sounds pious and holy, we conveniently forget that if we can be refined by fire such that we have no impurities left, then we have no need for a Savior! Also, if it is true that God had given permission to satan to steal, then satan is no longer a thief. Furthermore, God agreeing with satan to steal from Job established a criminal agreement between God and satan. If satan is a thief, then God is the mastermind behind the thief! Did God agree to such a deal with the devil or is there another better interpretation?

The book of Job is a very old book. It was written after Babel, but predates Abraham and Moses. Hence, it was written before both the Abrahamic and the Mosaic Covenant. We get a first glimpse of Job's self-righteousness when he offered sacrifices for his family but not for himself. He thought himself so good, so perfect, and so upright that he was exempt. Because he feared God and purposefully avoided evil, God must love him back. God owed him!

We are then brought into a scene in heaven where God was addressing satan. We know that satan was cast out before the creation of man. But because he tricked Adam, he won the authority to once again appear before God. It was Adam's prerogative, now lost to satan, until Jesus took it back after the cross. Satan answered God by stating that he had been walking to and fro the whole earth. There is a single purpose for his walking, and we read it in *1 Peter 5:8, Be sober, be vigilant; because your adversary the devil, as a roaring lion, walketh about, seeking whom he may devour:* Satan walks about seeking whom he may destroy. The 'whom' in this case was Job. Satan set his sight upon Job. God said, *Hast thou considered my servant Job?* The Hebrew word for 'hast thou considered' here is *'hăśamtā'* or 'set face toward'. Satan had set his face and sights towards Job already! And God knew of it! A proper reading would be more like this: God said, "Have you not already set your face on Job?" At that time, satan had complete authority over the earth. Today, he no longer has that authority over believers. *1 John 5:18-19, We know that whosoever is born of God sinneth not; but he that is begotten of God keepeth himself, and that wicked one toucheth him not. And we know that we are of God, and the whole world lieth in wickedness.* Believers are not open for devouring because they belong to Jesus. What happened to Job cannot happen to believers.

We read further in *2 Corinthians 4:4, In whom the god of this world hath blinded the minds of them which believe not, lest the light of the glorious gospel of Christ, who is the image of God, should shine unto them* and again in *Ephesians 2:2, Wherein in time past ye walked according to the course of this world, according to the prince of the power of the air, the spirit that now worketh in the children of disobedience:* When Jesus won the victory at the cross, satan's direct influence over believers came to an end.

Colossians 2:15 states, *And having spoiled principalities and powers, he made a shew of them openly, triumphing over them in it.* We also see this in *Ephesians 1:19-23, And what is the exceeding greatness of his power to usward who believe, according to the working of his mighty power, Which he wrought in Christ, when he raised him from the dead, and set him at his own right hand in the heavenly places, Far above all principality, and power, and might, and dominion, and every name that is named, not only in this world, but also in that which is to come: And hath put all things under his feet, and gave him to be the head over all things to the church, Which is his body, the fulness of him that filleth all in all.* Because of the finished work of Jesus, everything, including satan, is under Jesus' feet. Satan is not on an equal level with God. *1 John 4:4* states, *Ye are of God, little children, and have overcome them: because greater is he that is in you, than he that is in the world.* Jesus is far, far greater.

When Jesus returned home to heaven, Satan was cast out forever. He no longer has an audience with God nor does he has access to God. We read this in *John 12:31, Now is the judgment of this world: now shall the prince of this world be cast out* and in *Revelation 12:8-9, neither was their place found any more in heaven. And the great dragon was cast out, that old serpent, called the Devil, and Satan, which deceiveth the whole world: he was cast out into the earth, and his angels were cast out with him.*

God confirmed satan as the ruler of the world, at that time, by acknowledging that everything Job had was in the hand of satan. Satan had the power to take away what God had blessed Job with. The conversation that God had with satan was not a challenge to test Job's goodness. It was not a test of how obedient Job is or could be under suffering. Satan had set his sights on destroying Job and as prince of the world, he was going to do it. Therefore, satan by his own hand, not God's hand, demolished and destroyed all that was dear to Job, including his health.

Job, upon hearing the destruction of his houses, his livestock, his servants, and his family fell upon his knees, turned his face towards God, and worshipped his own self-righteousness! In his mind, these types of extirpation only happened to bad people. But he was good. Bad people, who did evil, deserve to be extirpated but good people like him, deserve to be rewarded. He could not understand the reason for this unjust punishment. He cried out in self-pity, *Naked came I out of my mother's womb, and naked shall I return thither: the Lord gave, and the Lord hath taken away; blessed be the name of the Lord.* This saying is quoted verbatim at many funerals and at other disasters.

Job was severely wrong and ignorant about God. While it is true that we be-came naked because of sin, we return fully clothed in Christ righteousness. We are never naked again. And yes, it is true that God gives, but it is satan that took away.

The only things that God takes away from us are our nakedness, our shame, our guilt, our condemnation, our poverty, our pains, our diseases, our defeats, and all our sins. All of these He hung on His cross!

James 1:17 states that *Every good gift and every perfect gift is from above, and cometh down from the Father of lights, with whom is no variableness, neither shadow of turning.* All good and perfect gifts are blessings from God and since He has no variableness, He never turns around and confiscates what He gave in the first place. We all know from *Romans 11:29, For the gifts and calling of God are without repentance*, that whatever God gave to us is irrevocably ours, even if we misuse His perfect gifts! Of course, the perfectly good gift from above is Jesus! Then in *Romans 8:28, And we know that all things work together for good to them that love God, to them who are the called according to his purpose,* we are assured that because of Jesus, all things work together for good, not bad.

It is clear that it was an ignorant Job, not God, that said *the Lord gave, and the Lord hath taken away.* Towards the end of the book, Job admitted that he had not known God and had not understood Him. He had spoken foolishly much like his wife whom he had berated. We read in *Job 42:3, therefore have I uttered that I understood not; things too wonderful for me, which I knew not,* This is similar to Hannah's prayer in *1 Samuel 2:6-7, The LORD killeth, and maketh alive: he bringeth down to the grave, and bringeth up. The LORD maketh poor, and maketh rich: he bringeth low, and lifteth up.* Hannah who lived under the law and had a sorrowful spirit, could not have known Grace fully. Let us not use their foolish statements as noteworthy biblical quotations. It comforts nobody and it further implies that God is schizophrenic, His kingdom divided against itself, and His mind varying from day to day. Who can trust in a schizoid God, who cannot even make up His mind? Or two minds?

The three friends of Job mentioned here are Eliphaz, Bildad, and Zophar. Together with Job, they had a huge sin-blaming, mud-flinging, and self-justifying circus.

Eliphaz slung the first volley. Job deserved all of his problems and suffering as he was great in wickedness and infinite in his iniquities and sins. He should be happy in his suffering. *Job 4:7-9, Remember, I pray thee, who ever perished, being innocent? or where were the righteous cut off? Even as I have seen, they that plow iniquity, and sow wickedness, reap the same. By the blast of God they perish, and by the breath of his nostrils are they consumed. Job 5:17, Behold, happy is the man whom God correcteth: therefore despise not thou the chastening of the Almighty: Job 22:3-5, Is it any pleasure to the Almighty, that thou art righteous? or is it gain to him that thou makest thy ways perfect? Will he reprove thee for fear of thee? will he enter with thee into judgment? Is not thy wickedness great? and thine iniquities infinite?*

Bildad then chimed in and accused Job of hidden sins. Can rushes grow without swampy ground? Job must be sinning as evidenced by God's judgment upon him. But if Job would show humility and repentance, then he could earn God's blessings back. *Job 8:3-6, Doth God pervert judgment? or doth the Almighty pervert justice? If thy children have sinned against him, and he have cast them away for their transgression; If thou wouldest seek unto God betimes, and make thy supplication to the Almighty; If thou wert pure and upright; surely now he would awake for thee, and make the habitation of thy righteousness prosperous. Job 8:11-13, Can the rush grow up without mire? can the flag grow without water? Whilst it is yet in his greenness, and not cut down, it withereth before any other herb. So are the paths of all that forget God; and the hypocrite's hope shall perish: Job 18:5-8, Yea, the light of the wicked shall be put out, and the spark of his fire shall not shine. The light shall be dark in his tabernacle, and his candle shall be put out with him. The steps of his strength shall be straitened, and his own counsel shall cast him down. For he is cast into a net by his own feet, and he walketh upon a snare.*

His third friend, Zophar, full of legalism, advised Job to get right with God. If only Job would listen and just do right, everything would come up roses. If not, then he would just inherit more portions of suffering.

Job 11:13-17, If thou prepare thine heart, and stretch out thine hands toward him; If iniquity be in thine hand, put it far away, and let not wickedness dwell in thy tabernacles. For then shalt thou lift up thy face without spot; yea, thou shalt be stedfast, and shalt not fear: Because thou shalt forget thy misery, and remember it as waters that pass away: And thine age shall be clearer than the noonday; thou shalt shine forth, thou shalt be as the morning.

Job 20:29, This is the portion of a wicked man from God, and the heritage appointed unto him by God.

Job recoiled at the accusations of his friends. He went on a self-justifying harangue of how righteous he was. It was indeed a soliloquy masterpiece on self-righteousness. It was all about 'I' and nothing to do with God.

Job 31:3-10, Is not destruction to the wicked? and a strange punishment to the workers of iniquity? Doth not he see my ways, and count all my steps? If I have walked with vanity, or if my foot hath hasted to deceit; Let me be weighed in an even balance, that God may know mine integrity. If my step hath turned out of the way, and mine heart walked after mine eyes, and if any blot hath cleaved to mine hands; Then let me sow, and let another eat; yea, let my offspring be rooted out. If mine heart have been deceived by a woman, or if I have laid wait at my neighbour's door; Then let my wife grind unto another, and let others bow down upon her.

Job 31:13, If I did despise the cause of my manservant or of my maidservant, when they contended with me;

Job 31:16-17, If I have withheld the poor from their desire, or have caused the eyes of the widow to fail; Or have eaten my morsel myself alone, and the fatherless hath not eaten thereof;

Job 31:19, If I have seen any perish for want of clothing, or any poor without covering;

Job 31:21, If I have lifted up my hand against the fatherless, when I saw my help in the gate:

Job 31:24-25, If I have made gold my hope, or have said to the fine gold, Thou art my confidence; If I rejoiced because my wealth was great, and because mine hand had gotten much;

Job 31:29, If I rejoiced at the destruction of him that hated me, or lifted up myself when evil found him:
Job 31:33, If I covered my transgressions as Adam, by hiding mine iniquity in my bosom:

In fact, Job believed that if he were to call upon God and present his case of righteousness before the courtroom of God, he would be found shining as pure gold. That would prove that his friends were a pack of liars and their reproach of him baseless. God would be on his side because of his goodness and obedience.

Job 13:3-5, Surely I would speak to the Almighty, and I desire to reason with God. But ye are forgers of lies, ye are all physicians of no value. O that ye would altogether hold your peace! and it should be your wisdom.
Job 23:3-7, Oh that I knew where I might find him! that I might come even to his seat! I would order my cause before him, and fill my mouth with arguments. I would know the words which he would answer me, and understand what he would say unto me. Will he plead against me with his great power? No; but he would put strength in me. There the righteous might dispute with him; so should I be delivered for ever from my judge.
Job 13:18, Behold now, I have ordered my cause; I know that I shall be justified.
Job 23:10-12, But he knoweth the way that I take: when he hath tried me, I shall come forth as gold. My foot hath held his steps, his way have I kept, and not declined. Neither have I gone back from the commandment of his lips; I have esteemed the words of his mouth more than my necessary food.
Job 27:6, My righteousness I hold fast, and will not let it go: my heart shall not reproach me so long as I live.
Job 31:35-37,Oh that one would hear me! behold, my desire is, that the Almighty would answer me, and that mine adversary had written a book. Surely I would take it upon my shoulder, and bind it as a crown to me. I would declare unto him the number of my steps; as a prince would I go near unto him.

When God did not run to answer him, Job got all confused. Punishment was for the wicked. He was righteous. God punished the wrong person. God made a big mistake! If not, then God must want to punish everybody, both wicked and perfect. Of course, he was in the perfect category as his conduct had been exemplary. Maybe God will correct Himself from His mistake of slaying him.

Job 10:15, If I be wicked, woe unto me; and if I be righteous, yet will I not lift up my head. I am full of confusion; therefore see thou mine affliction;

Job 21:27, Behold, I know your thoughts, and the devices which ye wrongfully imagine against me.

Job 9:22, This is one thing, therefore I said it, He destroyeth the perfect and the wicked.

Job 13:15, Though he slay me, yet will I trust in him: but I will maintain mine own ways before him.

When God did not correct Himself, Job cried bitterly and wanted to die. In Job's reasoning, he had not done any injustice to anyone and his prayers to God had been pure. God was so unfair as to ignore his righteousness. God had not judged correctly. God had not come running when he had called. What was wrong with God?

Job 16:11-17, God hath delivered me to the ungodly, and turned me over into the hands of the wicked. I was at ease, but he hath broken me asunder: he hath also taken me by my neck, and shaken me to pieces, and set me up for his mark. His archers compass me round about, he cleaveth my reins asunder, and doth not spare; he poureth out my gall upon the ground. He breaketh me with breach upon breach, he runneth upon me like a giant. I have sewed sackcloth upon my skin, and defiled my horn in the dust. My face is foul with weeping, and my eyelids is the shadow of death; Not for any injustice in mine hands: also my prayer is pure.

Job 3:11-13, Why died I not from the womb? why did I not give up the ghost when I came out of the belly? Why did the knees prevent me? or why the breasts that I should suck? For now should I have lain still and been quiet, I should have slept: then had I been at rest,

Job 6:4, For the arrows of the Almighty are within me, the poison whereof drinketh up my spirit: the terrors of God do set themselves in array against me.

Job 9:15-18, Whom, though I were righteous, yet would I not answer, but I would make supplication to my judge. If I had called,

*and he had answered me; yet would I not believe that he had
hearkened unto my voice. For he breaketh me with a tempest, and
multiplieth my wounds without cause. He will not suffer me to take
my breath, but filleth me with bitterness.*
*Job 19:7-9, Behold, I cry out of wrong, but I am not heard: I cry
aloud, but there is no judgment. He hath fenced up my way that I
cannot pass, and he hath set darkness in my paths. He hath
stripped me of my glory, and taken the crown from my head.*

In Job's misery, his heart cried out for a man that would
plead with God. Job, stuck in the quagmire of self-righteousness,
realized his need for a mediator. That mediator was none other
than Jesus Himself. Job knew that His Redeemer, Jesus, lives but
was too full of sanctimonious self to admit that he needed Jesus.
*Job 16:20-21, My friends scorn me: but mine eye poureth out tears
unto God. O that oe might plead for a man with God, as a man
pleadeth for his neighbour!*
*Job 19:25-26, For I know that my redeemer liveth, and that he
shall stand at the latter day upon the earth: And though after my
skin worms destroy this body, yet in my flesh shall I see God:*

Then out of nowhere, a fourth friend by the name of Elihu
spoke up. When Elihu spoke, Job's words ended. Elihu, to a large
extent, spoke for God as he reprimanded Job for his exceeding
self-righteousness, and his vanity. Job, because of the tree of
knowledge of good and evil, thought his conscience could guide
him. But he was reproved and chided for speaking without
knowledge nor wisdom.
*Job 32:2-3, Then was kindled the wrath of Elihu the son of
Barachel the Buzite, of the kindred of Ram: against Job was his
wrath kindled, because he justified himself rather than God. Also
against his three friends was his wrath kindled, because they had
found no answer, and yet had condemned Job.*
*Job 34:35-37, Job hath spoken without knowledge, and his words
were without wisdom. My desire is that Job may be tried unto the
end because of his answers for wicked men. For he addeth
rebellion unto his sin, he clappeth his hands among us, and
multiplieth his words against God.*

Job 35:1-2, Elihu spake moreover, and said, Thinkest thou this to be right, that thou saidst, My righteousness is more than God's? Job 35:13, Surely God will not hear vanity, neither will the Almighty regard it.
Job 35:16, Therefore doth Job open his mouth in vain; he multiplieth words without knowledge.

Elihu began to speak of Jesus. While Job was all vanity, Jesus is all verity! Only Jesus is righteous and is able to save man from going into the pit. Only Jesus can make man righteous before God. Only Jesus can make a man youthful again. Only Jesus takes away all sin. Only Jesus gives light and all who know Jesus are enlightened with the Light of the Living. Jesus is Life and all those who have faith in Him are alive. Only Jesus sanctifies and redeems. Jesus is also all wisdom and all knowledge as we read in *Colossians 2:3, In whom are hid all the treasures of wisdom and knowledge.* **Only the Wisdom of God, Jesus, gives us wisdom from God!**

Jesus is literally Wisdom in *Proverbs 8:1,22-31, Doth not wisdom cry? The LORD possessed me in the beginning* (in Hebrew, *reshith*) *of his way, before his works of old. I was set up from everlasting, from the beginning, or ever the earth was. When there were no depths, I was brought forth; when there were no fountains abounding with water. Before the mountains were settled, before the hills was I brought forth: While as yet he had not made the earth, nor the fields, nor the highest part of the dust of the world. When he prepared the heavens, I was there. Then I was by him, as one brought up with him: and I was daily his delight, rejoicing always before him; Rejoicing in the habitable part of his earth; and my delights were with the sons of men.* The same word, *b'reshith* (in the beginning) was used in *Genesis 1:1*. '*B'reshith*' is not a time label but Wisdom or Jesus! Hence, the very first word of the bible referred to Jesus! Jesus was with God during creation, rejoicing in it. Hence, only Jesus as Wisdom, can restore Job fully and freely.

Job 33:23-30, If there be a messenger with him, an interpreter, one among a thousand, to shew unto man his uprightness: Then he is gracious unto him, and saith, Deliver him from going down to the

pit: I have found a ransom. His flesh shall be fresher than a child's: he shall return to the days of his youth: He shall pray unto God, and he will be favourable unto him: and he shall see his face with joy: for he will render unto man his righteousness. He looketh upon men, and if any say, I have sinned, and perverted that which was right, and it profited me not; He will deliver his soul from going into the pit, and his life shall see the light. Lo, all these things worketh God oftentimes with man, To bring back his soul from the pit, to be enlightened with the light of the living.
1 Corinthians 1:24,30, But unto them which are called, both Jews and Greeks, Christ the power of God, and the wisdom of God. But of him are ye in Christ Jesus, who of God is made unto us wisdom, and righteousness, and sanctification, and redemption. Ephesians 1:17, That the God of our Lord Jesus Christ, the Father of glory, may give unto you the spirit of wisdom and revelation in the knowledge of him.

When Job heard that God's solution for sin was Jesus, not punishment in the pit, he acknowledged that he was obnoxious in his self-righteousness. He had spoken of things which he did not understand nor knew. He spoke as though he knew God, but he only knew about God. He did not have a relationship with God. He had spoken from his knowledge and so had his friends. He only had man's wisdom. They were all wrong. Job repented from his wrong thinking and brought it back in line with God's Wisdom.
Job 40:3-4, Then Job answered the Lord, and said, Behold, I am vile; what shall I answer thee? I will lay mine hand upon my mouth.
Job 42:1-6, Then Job answered the Lord, and said, I know that thou canst do everything, and that no thought can be withholden from thee. Who is he that hideth counsel without knowledge? therefore have I uttered that I understood not; things too wonderful for me, which I knew not. Hear, I beseech thee, and I will speak: I will demand of thee, and declare thou unto me. I have heard of thee by the hearing of the ear: but now mine eye seeth thee. Wherefore I abhor myself, and repent in dust and ashes.

Unmerited Grace was given to Job and his friends despite their utter blindness to the goodness of God before. Despite Job's undeserving position, he was given the position to pray and to offer up sacrifices for his friends. Seven bullocks and seven rams, signifying the perfection of Jesus, was offered as a burnt offering. Jesus was more than enough to remove their folly of self-works and self-justification.

Job 42:7-9 states, *And it was so, that after the Lord had spoken these words unto Job, the Lord said to Eliphaz the Temanite, My wrath is kindled against thee, and against thy two friends: for ye have not spoken of me the thing that is right, as my servant Job hath. Therefore take unto you now seven bullocks and seven rams, and go to my servant Job, and offer up for yourselves a burnt offering; and my servant Job shall pray for you: for him will I accept: lest I deal with you after your folly, in that ye have not spoken of me the thing which is right, like my servant Job. So Eliphaz the Temanite and Bildad the Shuhite and Zophar the Naamathite went, and did according as the Lord commanded them: the Lord also accepted Job.*

Now that Job had nothing and was unable to better his position by himself, God could supply him anew. The bullocks and rams were provided by God through Eliphaz, as Job had no animals left. Because of God's goodness, He turned Job's captivity by satan around. He also forgave Job's three friends from their foolishness. Because of God's riches, He gave Job twice what he had before. Job became very, very rich. All of Job's hypocritical friends and family who had abandoned him before, now seeing God's double portion blessings upon his life, sidled up to his side, to each give him a piece of money and an earring of gold. They hissed in his ear their 's-s-sympathies' for his recent misfortune, as they coiled around his table of blessings.

Job 19:13-19, *He hath put my brethren far from me, and mine acquaintance are verily estranged from me. My kinsfolk have failed, and my familiar friends have forgotten me. They that dwell in mine house, and my maids, count me for a stranger: I am an alien in their sight. I called my servant, and he gave me no answer; I intreated him with my mouth. My breath is strange to my wife, though I intreated for the children's sake of mine own body. Yea, young children despised me; I arose, and they spake against me.*

All my inward friends abhorred me: and they whom I loved are turned against me.
Job 42:10-17 And the Lord turned the captivity of Job, when he prayed for his friends: also the Lord gave Job twice as much as he had before. Then came there unto him all his brethren, and all his sisters, and all they that had been of his acquaintance before, and did eat bread with him in his house: and they bemoaned him, and comforted him over all the evil that the Lord had brought upon him: every man also gave him a piece of money, and everyone an earring of gold. So the Lord blessed the latter end of Job more than his beginning: for he had fourteen thousand sheep, and six thousand camels, and a thousand yoke of oxen, and a thousand she asses. He had also seven sons and three daughters. And he called the name of the first, Jemima; and the name of the second, Kezia; and the name of the third, Keren-happuch. And in all the land were no women found so fair as the daughters of Job: and their father gave them inheritance among their brethren. After this lived Job an hundred and forty years, and saw his sons, and his sons' sons, even four generations. So Job died, being old and full of days.

Just as Jesus always overpays the debt owed, all of Job's livestock and material possessions were overpaid back. Everything that was lost was doubled back. But God only gave him the same number of sons and daughters as he had before. This is because his previous seven sons and three daughters are with God in heaven. God did not count them as 'lost'. They were never destroyed as did the livestock and other possessions. Altogether, Job still had fourteen sons and six daughters, albeit, half of them were with God.

The three daughters of Job were named Jemima meaning 'dove or beautiful in song'; Kezia meaning 'cinnamon or beautiful in smell'; and Kerrenhappuch meaning 'cosmetic box or beautiful in sight'. The focus on the daughters and their inheritance signified our inheritance as the bride of Christ. We, the church, like the daughters of Job are beautiful in song, beautiful in smell, and beautiful in sight. All because Jesus cleansed us and made us beautiful.

❧ 11 ❧

JESUS AND GOMER

No, we are not talking about Gomer Pyle, that countrified, wide eyed and slack jawed employee at Wally's filling station in the old black and white Andy Griffith TV show. Gomer here is a much more colorful character. In fact, the Gomer that we are talking about here is a prostitute, an adulteress, a slave, a worshipper of the devil, and a bride of Jesus!

We read of Gomer in *Hosea 1:1-4,6,8, And the Lord said to Hosea, Go, take unto thee a wife of whoredoms and children of whoredoms: for the land hath committed great whoredom, departing from the Lord. So he went and took Gomer the daughter of Diblaim; which conceived, and bare him a son. And the Lord said unto him, Call his name Jezreel...And she conceived again, and bare a daughter. And God said unto him, Call her name Lo-ruhamah... Now when she had weaned Lo-ruhamah, she conceived, and bare a son. Then said God, Call his name Lo-ammi.* In that period of time when Hosea prophesied, the Jewish nation was divided into two kingdoms. Hosea lived in the northern kingdom called Israel or Ephraim. The southern kingdom was known as Judah. The whole nation was rich but neglected the law which they were obliged to follow. There was much sin and the law magnified their sin. As such, both northern and southern kingdoms came under the curse of punishment and death. But God, despite the law, showed His amazing Grace upon them.

Hosea meaning 'salvation or savior' is a type of Jesus. He was sent by God to a fallen world, to a red light district, to take for himself a bride which was a prostitute. *Romans 3:23* states, *For all have sinned, and come short of the glory of God.* The bride's name was Gomer, the daughter of Diblaim. Gomer meant 'consumption or consumed by sin' and Diblaim meant 'dried or dead'. We read in *Ephesians 2:1, And you hath he quickened, who were dead in trespasses and sins.* We like both Israel and Judah were indeed dead, consumed by our own sins. But even though we were dead in our sins, Jesus still loved us, married us, and took us home with Him.

Gomer had three children with Hosea. The first was called *Jezreel* (God sows and scatters), the second *Lo-ruhamah* (Not-loved), and the third *Lo-ammi* (Not-a-people). Their names indicated their conditions. Because of the peoples' sins, God would scatter them. They would be unloved and not be a people of God. But something was to come whereby all their names would be changed. They would become planted, loved, and become His people. They would become sons and daughters.

Gomer was not content with her married life and continued in sin (she did not yet have *Philippians 4:13, I can do all things through Christ which strengtheneth me,* where Jesus is to be our contentment in every circumstance). She rejected her husband's love for her and went back to being a prostitute. She loved men between her breasts and men that she thought would take care of her needs and wants. We read this in *Hosea 2:1-13, Say ye unto your brethren, Ammi; and to your sisters, Ru-hamah. Plead with your mother, plead: for she is not my wife, neither am I her husband: let her therefore put away her whoredoms out of her sight, and her adulteries from between her breasts; Lest I strip her naked, and set her as in the day that she was born, and make her as a wilderness, and set her like a dry land, and slay her with thirst. And I will not have mercy upon her children; for they be the children of whoredoms. For their mother hath played the harlot: she that conceived them hath done shamefully: for she said, I will go after my lovers, that give me my bread and my water, my wool and my flax, mine oil and my drink. Therefore, behold, I will hedge up thy way with thorns, and make a wall, that she shall not find her paths. And she shall follow after her lovers, but she shall not overtake them; and she shall seek them, but shall not find them: then shall she say, I will go and return to my first husband; for then was it better with me than now. For she did not know that I gave her corn, and wine, and oil, and multiplied her silver and gold, which they prepared for Baal. Therefore will I return, and take away my corn in the time thereof, and my wine in the season thereof, and will recover my wool and my flax given to cover her nakedness. And now will I discover her lewdness in the sight of her lovers, and* **none shall deliver her out of mine hand.** *I will also cause all her mirth to cease, her feast days, her new moons, and her sabbaths, and all her solemn feasts. And I will destroy her vines and her fig trees, whereof she hath said, These are my rewards that my lovers have given me: and I will make them a forest, and the beasts of the field shall eat them. And I will visit upon her the days of Baalim, wherein she burned incense to them, and she decked herself with her earrings and her jewels, and she went after her lovers, and forgat me, saith the Lord.*

In her adultery, Jesus as Hosea, still provided for her secretly. Corn, wine, oil, wool, flax, figs, silver and gold and other blessings were provided unconditionally. All the while, Gomer thought it was other men that had provided for her. She merited stoning but received unmerited bounty. She wasted her provision, yet was provided for. Just like Gomer, even though God knew that we will waste some of His provision, yet He provided for us bountifully. It was all unmerited. Gomer even received unmerited protection. A hedge and a wall were put up to surround her from her destructive lovers but she bypassed them and continued her feast with death.

We see 'Gomer' also in *Ezekiel 16:4-6, 8-12, On the day of your birth your cord was not cut, nor were you washed with water for cleansing. You were not rubbed with salt or wrapped in cloths. No one cared enough for you to do even one of these things out of compassion for you. Instead, you were thrown out into the open field, because you were despised on the day of your birth. Then I passed by and saw you wallowing in your blood, and as you lay there in your blood I said to you, 'Live!' So I spread My cloak over you and covered your nakedness. I pledged Myself to you,*

entered into a covenant with you, and you became Mine, declares
the Lord GOD. Then I bathed you with water, rinsed off your
blood, and anointed you with oil. I clothed you in embroidered
cloth and gave you sandals of fine leather. I wrapped you in fine
linen and covered you with silk. I adorned you with jewelry, and I
put bracelets on your wrists and a chain around your neck. I put a
ring in your nose, earrings on your ears, and a beautiful crown
upon your head. No one took care of them but God. He supplied
all for them, But both Israel and Judah betrayed God. They took
the jewelry, the fine cloths and made phallic idols out of them. Not
only that but they prostituted themselves with the Assyrians and
the Chaldeans/Babylonians. For their transgressions, they were
exiled, yet we read in *verse 60, But I will remember the covenant I*
made with you in the days of your youth, and I will establish an
everlasting covenant with you. Despite the punishments from the
Mosaic law, God remembered His covenant with Abraham. God
Himself would atone for all the evil that they did.

Hence, despite Gomer's multiple transgressions, Jesus still
loved her with a love that would never let her go. Continuing in
Hosea 2:14-23, Therefore, behold, I will allure her, and bring her
into the wilderness, and speak comfortably unto her. And I will
give her her vineyards from thence, and the valley of Achor for a
door of hope: and she shall sing there, as in the days of her youth,
and as in the day when she came up out of the land of Egypt. And it
shall be at that day, saith the Lord, that thou shalt call me Ishi;
and shalt call me no more Baali. For I will take away the names of
Baalim out of her mouth, and they shall no more be remembered
by their name. And in that day will I make a covenant for them
with the beasts of the field, and with the fowls of heaven, and with
the creeping things of the ground: and I will break the bow and the
sword and the battle out of the earth, and will make them to lie
down safely. And I will betroth thee unto me forever; yea, I will
betroth thee unto me in righteousness, and in judgment, and in
lovingkindness, and in mercies. I will even betroth thee unto me in
faithfulness: and thou shalt know the Lord. And it shall come to
pass in that day, I will hear, saith the Lord, I will hear the heavens,
and they shall hear the earth; And the earth shall hear the corn,

and the wine, and the oil; and they shall hear Jezreel. And I will sow her unto me in the earth; and I will have mercy upon her that had not obtained mercy; and I will say to them which were not my people, Thou art my people; and they shall say, Thou art my God.

Regardless of all, Jesus loved Gomer with an immutable love. A love that cannot and will not change. He would entice her to a quiet, peaceful desert place and speak comforting words to her. He would transform her valley of Achor (valley of troubles, where Achan was stoned to death) into a Door of Hope where she would sing with gladness and joy. Jesus reversed Achor to become a place of Rest, as in the dual fulfillment prophecy of *Isaiah 65:10, Sharon will become a pasture for flocks, and the Valley of Achor a resting place for herds, for my people who seek me.* No matter the evil that the Israelites did, God would restore them just as Gomer would be restored like when she was a youth. Jesus would not be her *Baali* or Master, but her *Ishi* or Husband. Jesus married Gomer and gave her covenantal rights to His righteousness, faithfulness, and lovingkindness/Grace. Gomer deserved nothing but received everything. Because of Jesus, even the childrens' names were changed. Jezreel would no longer mean scattered, but planted. Lo-ruhamah would become Ruhamah. The 'Not' from Not-loved would be stricken. Not-loved became loved. Lo-ammi became Ammi. Not-a-people became a people, just as in *Romans 9:25-26, I will call them my people, which were not my people; and her beloved, which was not beloved. And it shall come to pass, that in the place where it was said unto them, Ye are not my people; there shall they be called the children of the living God.* Here, Gentiles which were not God's people became God's people too.

In the meantime, the many sins of Gomer had caught up with her. She had become a slave. Naked and shivering in her shame, she was put up for sale. It was as written in *Deuteronomy 28:68, And the LORD shall bring thee into Egypt again with ships, by the way whereof I spake unto thee, Thou shalt see it no more again: and there ye shall be sold unto your enemies for bondmen and bondwomen, and no man shall buy you.* The Israelites would offer themselves up for sale as slaves to their enemies but none would buy them. But at Gomer's sale, Jesus showed up! There was no reproach and no condemnation as He over paid the full ransom price for her. We see this in *Hosea 3:1-3, Then said the Lord unto me, Go yet, love a woman beloved of her friend, yet an adulteress, according to the love of the Lord toward the children of Israel, who look to other gods, and love flagons of wine. So I bought her to me for fifteen pieces of silver, and for an homer of barley, and an half homer of barley: And I said unto her, Thou shalt abide for me many days; thou shalt not play the harlot, and thou shalt not be for another man: so will I also be for thee.*

Another man possessed Gomer - one who enslaved her. The full price for a slave was thirty shekels of silver as in *Exodus 21:32, If the ox shall push a manservant or a maidservant; he shall give unto their master thirty shekels of silver, and the ox shall be stoned* and in *Leviticus 27:4, And if it be a female, then thy estimation shall be thirty shekels.* For a woman suspected of adultery, barley could also be used and accepted as payment. In *Numbers 5:15,* we read, *Then shall the man bring his wife unto the priest, and he shall bring her offering for her, the tenth part of an ephah of barley meal.* How much was barley worth? We find the answer in *Leviticus 27:16, And if a man shall sanctify unto the Lord some part of a field of his possession, then thy estimation shall be according to the seed thereof: an homer of barley seed shall be valued at fifty shekels of silver.* A homer of barley was worth fifty shekels of silver. Since Hosea or Jesus paid 15 shekels of silver and 1½ homers of barley for Gomer, the total price paid was 15+50+25 = 90 pieces of silver.

Once again, Jesus overpaid for us. We may not be worth much to others but we are very worthy in His estimation. The number 3, stands for completeness or perfection. While our value is only thirty, He triples that amount because we are perfection to Him. Many times we feel that we are not worth much. Just like Gomer, we feel like trash. We feel like a piece of rusted metal that has long lost its sheen of brightness. We feel broken inside and cracked at the edges. When people look at us, they scoff at our corroded appearance. They label us as useless junk. We feel worse than a slave. We feel that our value is much less than thirty pieces of silver. Then Jesus comes along and pays triple for us. We cannot fathom His extravagance. Jesus values us the way He sees us and to Him we are perfection. He purifies our adulterated state. He mends our deterioration. He wants us to abide with Him as a wife and not as a harlot. We shall not be for any other man because we are for Jesus. *1 Corinthians 7:23* states, *Ye are bought with a price; be not ye the servants of men.* Gomer deserved stoning for being an adulteress but received unmerited Grace and love instead. As in *Lamentations 3:22-23, It is of the Lord's mercies that we are not consumed, because his compassions fail not. They are new every morning: great is thy faithfulness,* and *Psalm 52:8, I trust in God's unfailing love forever and ever.* Jesus' love for us never comes to an end!

Similarly, God continued to love an unfaithful, and adulterous Israel and Judah. Both the kingdoms backslid, meaning that they broke law after law of the Mosaic covenant. They thought they could please God by offering up burnt offerings and sacrifices, after making offerings to idols such as the queen of heaven (possibly the naked Asherah/Ashterte worshipped as the consort of Yahweh) in *Jeremiah 7:18, The children gather wood, and the fathers kindle the fire, and the women knead their dough, to make cakes to the queen of heaven, and to pour out drink offerings unto other gods.* Hence, their works to please God were likened to a morning cloud and as dew drops upon the ground. It was as nothing. We read of this in the following verses:

Hosea 4:16-17, For Israel slideth back as a backsliding heifer: now the Lord will feed them as a lamb in a large place. Ephraim is joined to idols: let him alone.

Hosea 5:5, therefore shall Israel and Ephraim fall in their iniquity; Judah also shall fall with them.

Hosea 6:4-7, O Ephraim, what shall I do unto thee? O Judah, what shall I do unto thee? for your goodness is as a morning cloud, and as the early dew it goeth away...For I desired mercy, and not sacrifice; and the knowledge of God more than burnt offerings. But they like men have transgressed the covenant: there have they dealt treacherously against me.

According to the law, the kingdoms of Israel or Ephraim and Judah deserved punishment and death. Hosea's contemporary,

Isaiah wrote in *Isaiah 1:3-4, The ox knoweth his owner, and the ass his master's crib: but Israel doth not know, my people doth not consider. Ah sinful nation, a people laden with iniquity, a seed of evildoers, children that are corrupters: they have forsaken the LORD, they have provoked the Holy One of Israel unto anger, they are gone away backward...the whole head is sick, and the whole heart faint. From the sole of the foot even unto the head there is no soundness in it.* They forgot God and became dumber than donkeys and oxen. They were sick from the head to the heart to the soles of their feet. Another contemporary, Micah wrote in *Micah 3:12, Therefore because of you, Zion will be plowed like a field, Jerusalem will become a heap of rubble, the temple hill a mound overgrown with thickets.* And coming back to Hosea:

Hosea 5:9-10, Ephraim will be laid waste...Judah's leaders are like those who move boundary stones. I will pour out my wrath on them like a flood of water.

Hosea 9:16-17, Ephraim is smitten, their root is dried up, they shall bear no fruit: yea, though they bring forth, yet will I slay even the beloved fruit of their womb. My God will cast them away, because they did not hearken unto him: and they shall be wanderers among the nations.

Israel's or Ephraim leaders worshipped idols while Judah's leaders stole land by moving boundary stones. The law would punish them both, making Ephraim a desolation and Jerusalem a heap of rubble. Eye for eye, stone for stone! But at the end, Jesus as Grace would still rescue them. **In the contest between law and Grace, Grace wins every time. Law loses not because of its weakness but because of Grace overwhelming strength. Grace is indestructible as it has no works in it. It is unfailing as it does not depend on our performance. And it is unchangeable as Grace is Jesus and He does not change.** *Malachi 3:6* states, *For I am the Lord, I change not;* No matter what whoredom the nations of Israel and Judah did, God said that He still loved them and will carry them as in *Isaiah 46:3-4, Listen to me, you descendants of Jacob, all the remnant of the people of Israel, you whom I have upheld since your birth, and have carried since you were born. Even to your old age and gray hairs I am he, I am he who will* *sustain you. I have made you and I will carry you; I will sustain you and I will rescue you.*

We read in *Matthew 21:31, Jesus saith unto them, Verily I say unto you, That the publicans and the harlots go into the kingdom of God before you.* It was not that the tax collectors and prostitutes were good. They both sold their bodies to the Romans for money. But they also believed in John the Baptist who pointed to Jesus! It was this belief in Jesus that mattered. The goodness of Jesus prodigiously engulfed their badness, bringing them into the kingdom of God. Law made them slaves but Grace bought them back. We see in *Hosea 6:1-3, Come, and let us return unto the Lord: for he hath torn, and he will heal us; he hath smitten, and he will bind us up. After two days will he revive us: in the third day he will raise us up, and we shall live in his sight. Then shall we know, if we follow on to know the Lord: his going forth is prepared as the morning; and he shall come unto us as the rain, as the latter and former rain unto the earth.* The former rains, a symbol of the law, only pointed to Jesus. But the law itself smote and tore Gomer. However, the latter rains as Jesus, spoke gently to a torn and smitten Gomer, "No matter what you have done, I still love you! Come, let us go back home together!" Because of Jesus, both Israel and Judah would be healed, revived and brought up. Their wounds would be bound up. They would be resurrected and raised up on the third day. as the land did from the seas on the third day in *Genesis 1:9*! They would be refreshed and restored by Jesus. He came and He would certainly come again. Not to deal with sin as in *Hebrews 9:28, He will come again, not to deal with our sins, but to bring salvation to all who are eagerly waiting for him.* God desired us to know Him as God of Grace! This was confirmed by Jesus, when he rebuked the Pharisees in *Matthew 9:13, for I am not come to call the righteous, but sinners to repentance.*

We continue to see this love in the following scriptures: *Hosea 11:4, I drew them with cords of a man, with bands of love: and I was to them as they that take off the yoke on their jaws. Hosea 13:9,14, O Israel, thou hast destroyed thyself; but in me is thine help. I will ransom them from the power of the grave; I will redeem them from death.*

Hosea 14:4-7, I will heal their backsliding, I will love them freely: for mine anger is turned away from him. I will be as the dew unto Israel: he shall grow as the lily, and cast forth his roots as Lebanon. His branches shall spread, and his beauty shall be as the olive tree, and his smell as Lebanon. They that dwell under his shadow shall return; they shall revive as the corn, and grow as the vine: the scent thereof shall be as the wine of Lebanon. Jesus cut off the chains of slavery from us and then He drew us to Himself with bands and cords of unconditional love. He took the yoke off from us and fed us Grace. He overpaid the ransom for us. He is our Savior from death. *1 Corinthians 15:55-57, O death, where is thy sting? O grave, where is thy victory? The sting of death is sin; and the strength of sin is the law. But thanks be to God, which giveth us the victory through our Lord Jesus Christ.* We do not writhe in guilt, chained by sin, and gnawed by worms. Jesus broke every bar of the grave and set us free, as in *Psalm 49:15, But God will redeem my soul from the power of the grave: for he shall receive me.* We let go of the works of our hands and rest in what Jesus did as in *Romans 4:4-5, Now to him that worketh is the reward not reckoned of grace, but of debt. But to him that worketh not, but believeth on him that justifieth the ungodly, his faith is counted for righteousness.* In Him, by faith, without works, we are righteous. **A believer in Jesus can never backslide for he was justified without any works on his part. He did not work for his justification and therefore, cannot backslide from his justification. That is why the word 'backsliding' cannot be found under the new covenant of Grace. Only people living under the law can backslide, from doing the law to not doing the law.**

In Jesus, we cannot help but grow in the knowledge of His love for us. Even when we do not know all the answers, Jesus still says of us as in *Song of Solomon 1:8* and *4:1, If you yourself do not know, Most beautiful among women. How beautiful you are, my darling - how very beautiful!* In Jesus, we end up ever more beautiful in our appearance and ever more fragrant in our scent. We are and always will be the most beautiful and most fragrant to Him! We are His forevermore!

❧ 12 ❦

JESUS AND THE CONCUBINE

To commemorate the first Passover whereby God saved all the firstborn sons and animals of the Israelites; the firstborn, both of people and animals, were sanctified back to God. We read of this in *Exodus 13:12-13, That thou shalt set apart unto the Lord all that openeth the matrix, and every firstling that cometh of a beast which thou hast; the males shall be the Lord's. And every firstling of an ass thou shalt redeem with a lamb; and if thou wilt not redeem it, then thou shalt break his neck: and all the firstborn of man among thy children shalt thou redeem* and again in *Exodus 22:29, Thou shalt not delay to offer the first of thy ripe fruits, and of thy liquors: the firstborn of thy sons shalt thou give unto me.* The firstborn male 'clean' animal was set aside for God just as the firstborn male child was sanctified for service to God. They would be special. However, after the law was given, the Israelites were found worshipping the golden calf. This disqualified them all but the Levites, from becoming the future priests that would serve in the tabernacle. The Levites were the ones who stood with Moses in *Exodus 32:26, Then Moses stood in the gate of the camp, and said, Who is on the Lord's side? let him come unto me. And all the sons of Levi gathered themselves together unto him.* The Levites were not somehow a better tribe. They were just chosen by God

We read further about this replacement in *Numbers 3:40-51, And the Lord said unto Moses, Number all the firstborn of the males of the children of Israel from a month old and upward, and take the number of their names. And thou shalt take the Levites for me (I am the Lord) instead of all the firstborn among the children of Israel; and the cattle of the Levites instead of all the firstlings among the cattle of the children of Israel. And Moses numbered, as the Lord commanded him, all the firstborn among the children of Israel. And all the firstborn males by the number of names, from a month old and upward, of those that were numbered of them, were twenty and two thousand two hundred and threescore and thirteen. And the Lord spake unto Moses, saying, Take the Levites instead of all the firstborn among the children of Israel, and the cattle of the Levites instead of their cattle; and the Levites shall be mine: I am the Lord. And for those that are to be redeemed of the two hundred and threescore and thirteen of the firstborn of the children of Israel, which are more than the Levites; Thou shalt even take five shekels apiece by the poll, after the shekel of the sanctuary shalt thou take them: (the shekel is twenty gerahs:) And thou shalt give the money, wherewith the odd number of them is to be redeemed, unto Aaron and to his sons. And Moses took the redemption money of them that were over and above them that were redeemed by the Levites: Of the firstborn of the children of Israel took he the money; a thousand three hundred and threescore and five shekels, after the shekel of the sanctuary: And Moses gave the money of them that were redeemed unto Aaron and to his sons, according to the word of the Lord, as the Lord commanded Moses.*

When counted, there were 22,273 firstborn sons, 273 more than there were Levites. These 273 firstborn sons were then redeemed by paying for them five shekels of silver each (273x5=1365). We know their value from *Leviticus 27:6, And if it be from a month old even unto five years old, then thy estimation shall be of the male five shekels of silver.* Once redeemed, they no longer had to work in the tabernacle. Hence, we now know that the first Passover directly and specifically saved all the firstborns sons, aged from one month up till five years old; and then indirectly all the other Israelites as well. They were all redeemed.

Many people wonder if the Levites have special status considering that they replaced the firstborn sons. Maybe God made them holier than the other Jews as they served in the temple of God in lieu of the firstborn sons? Moses was a Levite. Aaron, the first high priest of Israel, was also from the tribe of Levi. Maybe, somehow, they are the only ones who could follow the law?

Of course, we know that nobody could follow the law. No flesh could be justified by the law. After the law was given, the Israelites found it impossible to keep it. Attempting to follow the law brought death. The whole country degenerated into chaos and depravity as every man did that which was right in his own eyes. 'Every man' included the Levites.

This culminated in *Judges 19:1-9, And it came to pass in those days, when there was no king in Israel, that there was a certain Levite sojourning on the side of mount Ephraim, who took to him a concubine out of Bethlehem Judah. And his concubine played the whore against him, and went away from him unto her father's house to Bethlehem Judah, and was there four whole months. And her husband arose, and went after her, to speak friendly unto her, and to bring her again, having his servant with him, and a couple of asses: and she brought him into her father's house: and when the father of the damsel saw him, he rejoiced to meet him. And his father in law, the damsel's father, retained him; and he abode with him three days: so they did eat and drink, and lodged there. And it came to pass on the fourth day, when they arose early in the morning, that he rose up to depart: and the damsel's father said unto his son in law, Comfort thine heart with a morsel of bread, and afterward go your way. And they sat down, and did eat and drink both of them together: for the damsel's father had said unto the man, Be content, I pray thee, and tarry all night, and let thine heart be merry. And when the man rose up to depart, his father in law urged him: therefore he lodged there again. And he arose early in the morning on the fifth day to depart: and the damsel's father said, Comfort thine heart, I pray thee. And they tarried until afternoon, and they did eat both of them. And when the man rose up to depart, he, and his concubine, and his servant, his father in law, the damsel's father, said unto him, Behold, now the day draweth toward evening, I pray you tarry all night: behold, the day groweth to an end, lodge here, that thine heart may be merry; and to morrow get you early on your way, that thou mayest go home.*

Let us first interpret this story on its surface meaning. Because of the corruption the country had sank to, all the people in this story are nameless. There was a Levite who married again. But his concubine cheated on him, then ran away back to her father's house. The Levite went after her to bring her back. The law dictated death to an adulteress. But the Levite was kind and wanted to 'speak friendly' to her. He was an example of how a husband should behave in confronting an adulterous wife. She dishonored him yet he still wanted to bring her back home. The Levite ended up spending five days in her father's house. Instead of berating the father of the concubine, the Levite spent time eating and drinking with him.

We continue the story in *Judges 19:10-21, But the man would not tarry that night, but he rose up and departed, and came over against Jebus, which is Jerusalem; and there were with him two asses saddled, his concubine also was with him. And when they were by Jebus, the day was far spent; and the servant said unto his master, Come, I pray thee, and let us turn in into this city of the Jebusites, and lodge in it. And his master said unto him, We will not turn aside hither into the city of a stranger, that is not of the children of Israel; we will pass over to Gibeah. And he said unto his servant, Come, and let us draw near to one of these places to lodge all night, in Gibeah, or in Ramah. And they passed on and went their way; and the sun went down upon them when they were by Gibeah, which belongeth to Benjamin. And they turned aside thither, to go in and to lodge in Gibeah: and when he went in, he sat him down in a street of the city: for there was no man that took them into his house to lodging. And, behold, there came an old man from his work out of the field at even, which was also of mount Ephraim; and he sojourned in Gibeah: but the men of the place were Benjamites. And when he had lifted up his eyes, he saw a wayfaring man in the street of the city: and the old man said, Whither goest thou? and whence comest thou? And he said unto him, We are passing from Bethlehem Judah toward the side of mount Ephraim; from thence am I: and I went to Bethlehem Judah, but I am now going to the house of the Lord; and there is no man that receiveth me to house. Yet there is both straw and provender for our asses; and there is bread and wine also for me, and for thy handmaid, and for the young man which is with thy servants: there is no want of any thing. And the old man said, Peace be with thee; howsoever let all thy wants lie upon me; only lodge not in the street. So he brought him into his house, and gave provender unto the asses: and they washed their feet, and did eat and drink.*

When the Levite finally left, it was late in the day. He arrived in Jebus (old name for Jerusalem) by nightfall. The Levite, a holy man who was chosen by God to serve in the tabernacle, did not want to stay in the city of the Jebusites. The Jebusites were not family, so to speak. They were pagans. So he traveled tenaciously on to the city of Gibeah, where the Benjamites dwelled. Now, this was family, for the Benjamites were one of the original twelve tribes of Israel. But nobody in the city offered him any hospitality, until an old man took him in. The Levite declared proudly that he was going to the house of the Lord yet nobody entertained him. Shame on all for treating a righteous man of God in this callous manner!

Judges 19:22-30, Now as they were making their hearts merry, behold, the men of the city, certain sons of Belial, beset the house round about, and beat at the door, and spake to the master of the house, the old man, saying, Bring forth the man that came into thine house, that we may know him. And the man, the master of the house, went out unto them, Nay, my brethren, nay, I pray you, do not so wickedly; seeing that this man is come into mine house, do not this folly. Behold, here is my daughter a maiden, and his concubine; them I will bring out now, and humble ye them, and do with them what seemeth good unto you: but unto this man do not so vile a thing. But the men would not hearken to him: so the man took his concubine, and brought her forth unto them; and they knew her, and abused her all the night until the morning: and when the day began to spring, they let her go. Then came the woman in the dawning of the day, and fell down at the door of the man's house where her lord was, till it was light. And her lord rose up in the morning, and opened the doors of the house, and went out to go his way: and, behold, the woman his concubine was fallen down at the door of the house, and her hands were upon the threshold. And he said unto her, Up, and let us be going. But none answered. Then the man took her up upon an ass, and the man rose up, and gat him unto his place. And when he was come into his house, he took a knife, and laid hold on his concubine, and divided her, together with her bones, into twelve pieces, and sent her into all the coasts of Israel. And it was so, that all that saw it said, There was no such deed done nor seen from the day that the children of Israel came up out of the land of Egypt unto this day: consider of it, take advice, and speak your minds.

Just as they were about to eat and drink, some Benjamites came and harassed the old man for giving accommodation to the Levite. They wanted to rape the Levite. The old man refused and offered them his daughter and the Levite's concubine instead. Kudos to the old man! When the Benjamites started arguing, the concubine was thrust out of the house. The men caught her and gang raped her all night. Half dead, she still managed to stumble her way back to the old man's house only to collapse on the doorstep. When the Levite finally awoke the next morning to continue on with his journey, he found his concubine on the threshold of the house. He spoke to her but she did not reply back. He knew the law in *Leviticus 20:10* which stated, *And the man that committeth adultery with another man's wife, even he that committeth adultery with his neighbour's wife, the adulterer and the adulteress shall surely be put to death* and again in *Deuteronomy 22:22, If a man be found lying with a woman married to an husband, then they shall both of them die, both the man that lay with the woman, and the woman: so shalt thou put away evil from Israel.*

The concubine deserved death. The Benjamites who had raped his concubine deserved death too. He would make everything right under the law. When they finally got home, the concubine was butchered up like one of the tabernacle offerings. The Levite had butchered many animals before and had no problem in dividing up the concubine into twelve pieces which he sent to all the other tribes of Israel. By this sacrificial action, the Levite, a holy man, thought that he had once again kept evil away from all of Israel. Only the Benjamites would be punished. A national judgment would fall on them. Righteousness would prevail as civil war broke out between the Benjamites and the other tribes of Israel. The Levite saved the day by obeying the law.

But is there another deeper meaning behind this deplorable story? Apart from the initial explanation as to how spiritually low the nation of Israel had sunk, the rest of the explanation reeks of self-righteousness, sexism, sex-crazed homosexual mobs, and chopped up body parts FedEx-ed by the mafia-like Levite.

The Levite in the story stood for the Jews or the law. He was inflexible and abusive. He married another wife but he refused to call her a wife, choosing to call her a concubine instead. The concubine came from Bethlehem Judah, where Jesus was born. She was a virgin when she married him but he treated her as a harlot and abused her. *Leviticus 21:13-15* states, *And he shall take a wife in her virginity. A widow, or a divorced woman, or profane, or an harlot, these shall he not take: but he shall take a virgin of his own people to wife. Neither shall he profane his seed among his people: for I the Lord do sanctify him.* The concubine represented Grace. Jews were to be blessed unconditionally as Jesus would be the Promised Seed to Abraham. But they rejected Him choosing to call Him a false Messiah. Instead of welcoming Him, they abused Him. Law cannot live with Grace. Law rapes, then condemns Grace as the rapist. Grace was treated as a harlot. So Grace left and went back to her Father's house.

The concubine was not a whore or an adulteress, as she would have been stoned to death. Under any other circumstance, she would have been given a divorce as in *Deuteronomy 24:1-2, When a man hath taken a wife, and married her, and it come to pass that she find no favour in his eyes, because he hath found some uncleanness in her: then let him write her a bill of divorcement, and give it in her hand, and send her out of his house. And when she is departed out of his house, she may go and be another man's wife.* Under the law, the Levite could not stone her because she was not guilty of adultery and he could not give her a bill of divorcement because he found no uncleanness in her.

A mixture of law and Grace is impossible. *Romans 11:6* states, *And if by grace, then is it no more of works: otherwise grace is no more grace. But if it be of works, then is it no more grace: otherwise work is no more work.* Grace was welcomed back at her Father's home. When the law came, the Father was delighted to see him too. Those who practice the law are equally loved by God. By law, the father had to return her daughter. But He delayed her departure as much as possible. For the next five days, the Father blessed and supplied His best to the Levite. The abusive Levite deserved nothing but received nonetheless. The Father comforted the Levite's heart with drink and food. This was symbolic of the Lord's supper. The Jews were reminded of Jesus but they continued to reject Him. After five days of Grace, the Levite unequivocally rejected unmerited favor. He chose instead to continue his abuse of his concubine. Law has never stopped persecuting Grace. We read this in *Galatians 4:29, But as then he that was born after the flesh persecuted him that was born after the Spirit, even so it is now.* As Ishmael persecuted Isaac, law continues to persecute Grace, even till today.

As the Levite traveled back home, his self-righteousness rejected the city of the Jebusites. Jebusite comes from the Hebrew verb, '*bus*', meaning 'to tread or to trample down'. The Levite believed he was not like those sinners, those Jebusites. He saw himself as too holy to stay in their polluted city. Therefore, he passed by. He went on to the city of Gibeah. When asked by the old man, the Levite proudly replied that he had enough provision for his donkeys and himself. He completely ignored his concubine. He placed his donkeys above his concubine. Law condemns and never nourishes the person.

In the Benjamite city, the law had multiplied sin as everybody did what was right in his eyes. The Levite was about to be punished for his many sins. It took the form of a gang who came to rape him. The old man offered his daughter but that was rejected. Nobody could save the Levite. Nobody except his concubine! The one whom he rejected and despised saved him. She took his place. Grace was mocked, beaten, raped, ravished, and left to die. In the meantime, after a good night's sleep, the Levite awoke to find his half-dead concubine at the doorstep. Speaking perfunctorily and without care, he stepped over her before taking her back home on his donkey. The Levite knew the story about Lot and the city of Sodom very well. Sodomy or having sex with a person of the same gender was punishable by death as we read in *Leviticus 20:13, If a man also lie with mankind, as he lieth with a woman, both of them have committed an abomination: they shall surely be put to death; their blood shall be upon them.* Although he was not sodomized, he wanted to punish the Benjamites. For his pride had been hurt. It was certainly not love for his concubine that he butchered her into twelve parts.

In death, Grace was divided up and given to all the twelve branches of the Jewish tree. *Leviticus1:6* states, *And he shall flay the burnt offering, and cut it into his pieces.* Grace is the burnt offering, stripped of its skin, and cut into pieces. But the twelve tribes did not understand the gift. The tribes only saw the law. *Exodus 21:23-25* states, *And if any mischief follow, then thou shalt give life for life, Eye for eye, tooth for tooth, hand for hand, foot for foot, burning for burning, wound for wound, stripe for stripe.* The body parts so infuriated the Israelites that they went to war with the Benjamites. In the end, after many deaths, God defeated the Benjamites as in *Judges 20:35, And the LORD struck Benjamin before Israel.* Because of the law, death came to all the twelve tribes.

The Levitical priesthood of Aaron was faulty. It was faulty before it started as the Levites killed 3000 of their own brothers in defending the law, as in *Exodus 32:28, And the children of Levi did according to the word of Moses: and there fell of the people that day about three thousand men.* Everything had to change, starting from the High Priest. Therefore, Jesus became our new High Priest after the order of Melchisedec. He came out of the tribe of Judah, not Levi. Through Aaron, people received the law. But through Jesus, people received Grace. We read this in *Hebrews 7:11-17, If therefore perfection were by the Levitical priesthood, (for under it the people received the law,) what further need was there that another priest should rise after the order of Melchisedec, and not be called after the order of Aaron? For the priesthood being changed, there is made of necessity a change also of the law. For he of whom these things* *are spoken pertaineth to another tribe, of which no man gave attendance at the altar. For it is evident that our Lord sprang out of Juda; of which tribe Moses spake nothing concerning priesthood. And it is yet far more evident: for that after the similitude of Melchisedec there ariseth another priest, Who is made, not after the law of a carnal commandment, but after the power of an endless life. For he testifieth, Thou art a priest for ever after the order of Melchisedec.*

And again in *Hebrews 7:22-28, By so much was Jesus made a surety of a better testament. And they truly were many priests, because they were not suffered to continue by reason of death: But this man, because he continueth ever, hath an unchangeable priesthood. Wherefore he is able also to save them to the uttermost that come unto God by him, seeing he ever liveth to make intercession for them. For such an high priest became us, who is holy, harmless, undefiled, separate from sinners, and made higher than the heavens; Who needeth not daily, as those high priests, to offer up sacrifice, first for his own sins, and then for the people's: for this he did once, when he offered up himself. For the law maketh men high priests which have infirmity; but the word of the oath, which was since the law, maketh the Son, who is consecrated for evermore.* The law made the Levites priests. It was for a period of time. But the promise made Jesus the High Priest forevermore. It was an unchangeable promise. For those who come to Jesus, He would save them to the uttermost. In Greek, uttermost is '*panteles*' meaning 'wholly and completely, through all time'. Jesus saved us wholly and completely through all time. Salvation through Jesus is irreversible as it is good for all time!

David caught a glimpse of this marvelous Grace too in *2 Samuel 12:13-24, And David said unto Nathan, I have sinned against the Lord. And Nathan said unto David, The Lord also hath put away thy sin; thou shalt not die. Howbeit, because by this deed thou hast given great occasion to the enemies of the Lord to blaspheme, the child also that is born unto thee shall surely die. And Nathan departed unto his house. And the Lord struck the child that Uriah's wife bare unto David, and it was very sick. David therefore besought God for the child; and David fasted, and went in, and lay all night upon the earth. And the elders of his house arose, and went to him, to raise him up from the earth: but he would not, neither did he eat bread with them. And it came to pass on the seventh day, that the child died. And the servants of David feared to tell him that the child was dead: for they said, Behold, while the child was yet alive, we spake unto him, and he would not hearken unto our voice: how will he then vex himself, if we tell him that the child is dead? But when David saw that his servants whispered, David perceived that the child was dead: therefore David said unto his servants, Is the child dead? And they said, He is dead.*

Then David arose from the earth, and washed, and anointed himself, and changed his apparel, and came into the house of the Lord, and worshipped: then he came to his own house; and when he required, they set bread before him, and he did eat. Then said his servants unto him, What thing is this that thou hast done? thou didst fast and weep for the child, while it was alive; but when the child was dead, thou didst rise and eat bread. And he said, While the child was yet alive, I fasted and wept: for I said, Who can tell whether God will be gracious to me, that the child may live? But now he is dead, wherefore should I fast? can I bring him back again? I shall go to him, but he shall not return to me. And David comforted Bath-sheba his wife, and went in unto her, and lay with her: and she bare a son, and he called his name Solomon: and the Lord loved him.

Because of David's sins, he was liable for the death penalty. Instead of loving his neighbor, he sent his literal 'neighbor' to die. Uriah died because of David. David himself acknowledged this in *2 Samuel 12:5, As the LORD liveth, the man that hath done this thing shall surely die.* Also, the punishment for adultery with Bathsheba was death. David deserved death twice over but got life. All because of his child who died in his place. This unnamed but innocent child paid the full price for the crimes of his father, David. David saw unmerited Grace as described in *Romans 4:6-8, Even as David also describeth the blessedness of the man, unto whom God imputeth righteousness without works, Saying, Blessed are they whose iniquities are forgiven, and whose sins are covered. Blessed is the man to whom the Lord will not impute sin.* By works, David could never have been called righteous. But because of Grace, righteousness was imputed unto him. His iniquities were forgiven and his sins covered. David was restored by Grace and was given another son by the name of Solomon or Jedidiah, meaning 'beloved friend of God'. Who but Jesus would call David a beloved friend of God through his son's name? And because of Grace, David was shown that a Greater Son of his would one day pay the full price for all of mankind. This Son would be Jesus! With Jesus, our sins are not just covered but taken away forever and for all time.

David was not the only man who merited death but got life. We see in *Mark 15:7,15, And there was one named Barabbas, which lay bound with them that had made insurrection with him, who had committed murder in the insurrection. And so Pilate, willing to content the people, released Barabbas unto them, and delivered Jesus, when he had scourged him, to be crucified.* Barabbas, a murderer, was set free as Jesus, an innocent man, was ignominiously crucified. Jesus went through Gethsemane (where He was pressed for us), to Gabbatha (where He was trialed, mocked, and scourged for us), and ultimately to Golgotha (where He was made sin for us). Solely because of Jesus, righteousness was imputed to us. Sin is not imputed to us even when we sin because all sin had already been imputed upon Jesus. We are blessed because of what Jesus did on the cross. We are saved because of what Jesus did on the cross. We are now bound to Freedom. We are now bound to Life. Because of Jesus, we have the irreversible guarantee that both salvation and blessings are good to the uttermost! What a guarantee we have in Jesus!

❧ 13 ❧

JESUS AND CLEANLINESS

"Cleanliness is next to godliness!" That is what many people learned while they were children. As usual, the world would like us to think that the act of cleaning ourselves up would also make us clean before God. So is that true? Let us examine what God says about cleanliness and un-cleanliness.

Deuteronomy 23:9-14 states, *When the host goeth forth against thine enemies, then keep thee from every wicked thing. If there be among you any man, that is not clean by reason of uncleanness that chanceth him by night, then shall he go abroad out of the camp, he shall not come within the camp: But it shall be, when evening cometh on, he shall wash himself with water: and when the sun is down, he shall come into the camp again. Thou shalt have a place also without the camp, whither thou shalt go forth abroad: And thou shalt have a paddle upon thy weapon; and it shall be, when thou wilt ease thyself abroad, thou shalt dig therewith, and shalt turn back and cover that which cometh from thee: For the LORD thy God walketh in the midst of thy camp, to deliver thee, and to give up thine enemies before thee; therefore shall thy camp be holy: that he see no unclean thing in thee, and turn away from thee.* Under the law, any soldier having a wet dream must bathe his whole body for he is considered unclean until the evening. From the front, the law now turns to the backside. Any soldier who wanted to defecate must do so outside the camp. With a designated trowel, he must dig and cover up the excrement. Failure to do so would be considered unclean.

Under the law, any person that has a blemish cannot offer up sacrifices before God. This is because they were considered unclean. *Leviticus 21:16-21,23* states, *And the Lord spake unto Moses, saying, Speak unto Aaron, saying, Whosoever he be of thy seed in their generations that hath any blemish, let him not approach to offer the bread of his God. For whatsoever man he be that hath a blemish, he shall not approach: a blind man, or a lame, or he that hath a flat nose, or any thing superfluous, Or a man that is brokenfooted, or brokenhanded, Or crookbackt, or a dwarf, or that hath a blemish in his eye, or be scurvy, or scabbed, or hath his stones broken; No man that hath a blemish of the seed of Aaron the priest shall come nigh to offer the offerings of the Lord made by fire. Only he shall not go in unto the vail, nor come nigh unto the altar, because he hath a blemish; that he profane not my sanctuaries: for I the Lord do sanctify them.*

*A*and again in *Deuteronomy 23:1-3,17-18, He that is wounded in the stones, or hath his privy member cut off, shall not enter into the congregation of the Lord. A bastard shall not enter into the congregation of the Lord; even to his tenth generation shall he not enter into the congregation of the Lord. An Ammonite or Moabite shall not enter into the congregation of the Lord; even to their tenth generation shall they not enter into the congregation of the Lord forever. There shall be no whore of the daughters of Israel, nor a sodomite of the sons of Israel. Thou shalt not bring the hire of a whore, or the price of a dog, into the house of the LORD thy God for any vow: for even both these are abomination unto the LORD thy God.* Therefore, under the law, a blind man, a lame man, a man that has a broken nose, foot, or hand, a hunchback, a stunted man, an eunuch, a castrated man, a bastard, male and female temple prostitutes and their earnings, as well as cursed nations were all unclean.

But, of course, the worst blemish of all was none other than leprosy. The law regarding leprosy of the skin, hair, and scalp can be found in *Leviticus 13:42-46,50-52, Then the priest shall look upon it: and, behold, if the rising of the sore be white reddish in his bald head, or in his bald forehead, as the leprosy appeareth in the skin of the flesh; He is a leprous man, he is unclean: the priest shall pronounce him utterly unclean; his plague is in his head. And the leper in whom the plague is, his clothes shall be rent, and his head bare, and he shall put a covering upon his upper lip, and shall cry, Unclean, unclean. All the days wherein the plague shall be in him he shall be defiled; he is unclean: he shall dwell alone; without the camp shall his habitation be.   And the priest shall look upon the plague, and shut up it that hath the plague seven days: And he shall look on the plague on the seventh day: if the plague be spread in the garment, either in the warp, or in the woof, or in a skin, or in any work that is made of skin; the plague is a fretting leprosy; it is unclean. He shall therefore burn that garment, whether warp or woof, in woollen or in linen, or any thing of skin, wherein the plague is: for it is a fretting leprosy; it shall be burnt in the fire.*

If a white reddish sore has penetrated the dermis of a man's scalp, that man is declared by a priest as a leprous man. He is not just unclean, but utterly unclean. His clothes would be removed from him and burnt. A covering would be put upon his upper lip, and he shall cry 'unclean, unclean' all day long. He will be a reject of society. He will live by himself for the rest of his life outside the city walls. The priest who pronounced him unclean does nothing to help or cure him.

But healing may be achieved by self-works, namely by prayers and supplications. *1 Kings 8:37-39*, states that *If there be in the land famine, if there be pestilence, blasting, mildew, locust, or if there be caterpiller; if their enemy besiege them in the land of their cities; whatsoever plague, whatsoever sickness there be; What prayer and supplication soever be made by any man, or by all thy people Israel, which shall know every man the plague of his own heart, and spread forth his hands toward this house: Then hear thou in heaven thy dwelling place, and forgive, and do, and give to every man according to his ways, whose heart thou knowest; (for thou, even thou only, knowest the hearts of all the children of men;)* The leper had to earn God's favor in order to be healed. Under the law, he had to deserve his healing or continue in the curse of leprosy. Since God knows the hearts of all men, which

were continuously evil, there was no hope to earn this favor by
self-works. We cannot manipulate God by our good works.

A leper's skin is a mixture of white and raw flesh. This
mixture of healthy flesh with diseased flesh is unclean. A mixture
of works and Grace is always unclean. We read this in *Leviticus
13:9-14, When the plague of leprosy is in a man, then he shall be
brought unto the priest; And the priest shall see him: and, behold,
if the rising be white in the skin, and it have turned the hair white,
and there be quick raw flesh in the rising; It is an old leprosy in
the skin of his flesh, and the priest shall pronounce him unclean,
and shall not shut him up: for he is unclean. And if a leprosy break
out abroad in the skin, and the leprosy cover all the skin of him
that hath the plague from his head even to his foot, wheresoever
the priest looketh; Then the priest shall consider: and, behold, if
the leprosy have covered all his flesh, he shall pronounce him
clean that hath the plague: it is all turned white: he is clean. But
when raw flesh appeareth in him, he shall be unclean.*

The man is unclean as long as he has diseased flesh on him.
But when the disease overtakes the man completely the priest will
pronounce the man clean! But how can a man who has no healthy
flesh left be pronounced clean? Should he not be pronounced
totally unclean? It goes against logic. The answer is found in
*Galatians 3:27, For as many of you as have been baptized into
Christ have put on Christ.* **When a man has no hope left in
himself, when he comes to the end of himself, then Jesus takes
over and cleanses him completely. His old skin is no more. His
new skin and covering is Jesus! He is clothed, wrapped,
swathed, enveloped in Christ. To be clean, the man must have
no mixture of skins. The moment raw flesh appears, the man is
considered unclean again. The works of the flesh cannot be
added to Grace.**

Isaiah 1:18, states, *Come now, and let us reason together,
saith the Lord: though your sins be as scarlet, they shall be as
white as snow; though they be red like crimson, they shall be as
wool.* Actually, Jesus cleanses us whiter than snow when we were
completely crimson in our sins, as in *Psalm 51:7, wash me, and I
shall be whiter than snow.* When we are wholly scarlet then Jesus

takes over. We see this again in *Revelation 3:15-16, I know thy works, that thou art neither cold nor hot: I would thou wert cold or hot. So then because thou art lukewarm, and neither cold nor hot, I will spue thee out of my mouth.* If hot is good and cold is bad, then lukewarm must be better than cold. But God prefers hot or cold, not lukewarm! This mixture of hot and cold, healthy and diseased flesh, white and red spots is what God will spew out of His mouth. A mixture is unclean to God. A man with no leprosy at all is considered 'hot' while a man completely covered from head to toe with leprosy is 'cold'. And we all know that the person who is cold has need for a Savior! A person living one hundred percent under the law would cry out for Jesus. Only people who live under mixtures may fall into the erroneous thinking that their works merit them salvation or keep them saved.

The ceremony for the healing of lepers is found in *Leviticus 14:4-14, Then shall the priest command to take for him that is to be cleansed two birds alive and clean, and cedar wood, and scarlet, and hyssop: And the priest shall command that one of the birds be killed in an earthen vessel over running water: As for the living bird, he shall take it, and the cedar wood, and the scarlet, and the hyssop, and shall dip them and the living bird in the blood of the bird that was killed over the running water: And he shall sprinkle upon him that is to be cleansed from the leprosy seven times, and shall pronounce him clean, and shall let the living bird loose into the open field. And he that is to be cleansed shall wash his clothes, and shave off all his hair, and wash himself in water, that he may be clean: and after that he shall come into the camp, and shall tarry abroad out of his tent seven days. But it shall be on the seventh day, that he shall shave all his hair off his head and his beard and his eyebrows, even all his hair he shall shave off: and he shall wash his clothes, also he shall wash his flesh in water, and he shall be clean.*

And on the eighth day he shall take two he lambs without blemish, and one ewe lamb of the first year without blemish, and three tenth deals of fine flour for a meat offering, mingled with oil, and one log of oil. And the priest that maketh him clean shall present the man that is to be made clean, and those things, before

the Lord, at the door of the tabernacle of the congregation: And
the priest shall take one he lamb, and offer him for a trespass
offering, and the log of oil, and wave them for a wave offering
before the Lord: And he shall slay the lamb in the place where he
shall kill the sin offering and the burnt offering, in the holy place:
for as the sin offering is the priest's, so is the trespass offering: it is
most holy: And the priest shall take some of the blood of the
trespass offering, and the priest shall put it upon the tip of the right
ear of him that is to be cleansed, and upon the thumb of his right
hand, and upon the great toe of his right foot:

When the healing is unmerited, the leper does not search
for the priest. Instead, the priest goes out of his way to search for
the leper. He goes outside the city walls to the leper colony. Jesus
still goes out of His way to look for us. In fact, He left heaven to
come and look for us all! We are that precious to Him! Two clean
birds were chosen. One of them was sacrificed in an earthen vessel
over running water. Jesus was sacrificed as sin for us in the flesh.
He was never sin in the Spirit. The hyssop represented the whip,
the cedar wood the cross, and the scarlet the blood. His blood
saved us, not the water. The running water, or the word of God, is
necessary to continuously cleanse us from wrong thoughts and
other pollutions from the world we live in. The second bird
represented us, brushed scarlet by sin but transformed by the blood
of Jesus. We are set free by the blood. The second bird flies off
covered in the blood of the first bird. All our sins are remembered
no more. It is Jesus' blood that cleansed us, saved us, and will
resurrect us. When we believe that about Jesus' blood, our Father
counts that as faith from our part. **It is not our faith that saved us,**
but the belief in what Jesus has done that saved us.

The leper, another symbol of us, was sprinkled with the
blood seven times. The leper did nothing to deserve the healing.
The number seven stood for perfection. Only after the leper was
sprinkled with the blood of perfection or Jesus, was he pronounced
clean. He is a now a new creation as symbolized by his washing of
himself, his clothes, and his shaving off of all his hair. He is both
ceremonially clean as well as physically clean. This born again,
hairless man then makes an offering of lamb and oil, once again

typifying Jesus. The blood from one of the lambs would be put upon the man's right ear, right hand thumb, and the great toe of his right foot. The man is now forgiven for his trespasses from his head down to his toes.

That was also the reason why the Canaanite king, Adonibezek, not covered by the blood, had his sinful thumbs and toes cut off in *Judges 1: 6-7, But Adonibezek fled; and they pursued after him, and caught him, and cut off his thumbs and his great toes. And Adonibezek said, Threescore and ten kings, having their thumbs and their great toes cut off, gathered their meat under my table: as I have done, so God hath requited me. And they brought him to Jerusalem, and there he died.* But he had heard about God. That was why his ears were not cut off. He deserved death but was brought to Jerusalem, where he lived until he died.

Nothing but Jesus can make the undeserved deserving and the unclean clean. We read in *Haggai 2:12-14, Then said Haggai, If one that is unclean by a dead body touch any of these, shall it be unclean? And the priests answered and said, It shall be unclean. Then answered Haggai, and said, So is this people, and so is this nation before me, saith the Lord; and so is every work of their hands; and that which they offer there is unclean.* Under the law, the unclean thing actually makes the priest unclean.

But in *Mark 1:40-45* we read, *And there came a leper to him, beseeching him, and kneeling down to him, and saying unto him, If thou wilt, thou canst make me clean. And Jesus, moved with compassion, put forth his hand, and touched him, and saith unto him, I will; be thou clean. And as soon as he had spoken, immediately the leprosy departed from him, and he was cleansed, And he straitly charged him, and forthwith sent him away; And saith unto him, See thou say nothing to any man: but go thy way, shew thyself to the priest, and offer for thy cleansing those things which Moses commanded, for a testimony unto them. But he went out, and began to publish it much, and to blaze abroad the matter, insomuch that Jesus could no more openly enter into the city, but was without in desert places: and they came to him from every quarter.* Under the law, the leper was not to be touched. With Jesus, they deserved to be touched. And with compassion as well.

Under the law, the clean would become unclean. But under Grace, the unclean would become clean. When the leper began to walk and to freely publicize what the Lord had done for him throughout the city, Jesus could no longer walk freely throughout the same city! He took on our infirmities and gave us His strength. He bore our sicknesses and He gave us His health. He took our 'un-cleanliness' and gave us His cleanliness. He took on our shame and He gave us His glory. He bore our sins and He gave us His righteousness.

Because of what Jesus did, let us not insult Him by not agreeing with Him about what He did for us. *Amos 3:3 states, Can two walk together, except they be agreed?* Under the law, God and His prophets walked and agreed together. More so, under Grace, let us walk and agree with Jesus. If He said that we are clean, let us agree with Him and say that we are clean. If He paid back the debt we could not pay, let us agree with Him that the debt is fully paid. If He said that we are healed by His stripes, let us agree with Him that we are indeed healed already. If He said that He will restore all to us, let us agree with Him and receive His restoration. If He said that He will provide for us abundantly, let us agree with Him and receive the abundance. If He said that He died for **all** our sins, let us agree with Him and be no longer sin conscious. If He called us saints, let us agree with Him and call ourselves saints (not sinners) as well. If He gave us His righteousness, let us agree with Him and thank Him for His gift of righteousness. If He said that He loves us, let us agree with Him and revel in it. If He said that He perfected us, let us agree and celebrate that His perfection perfected us. Let us walk together with Jesus and agree with what He says about us!

It is all about Jesus! *Numbers 19:1-9 states, And the Lord spake unto Moses and unto Aaron, saying, This is the ordinance of the law which the Lord hath commanded, saying, Speak unto the children of Israel, that they bring thee a red heifer without spot, wherein is no blemish, and upon which never came yoke: And ye shall give her unto Eleazar the priest, that he may bring her forth without the camp, and one shall slay her before his face: And Eleazar the priest shall take of her blood with his finger, and sprinkle of her blood directly before the tabernacle of the congregation seven times: And one shall burn the heifer in his sight; her skin, and her flesh, and her blood, with her dung, shall he burn: And the priest shall take cedar wood, and hyssop, and scarlet, and cast it into the midst of the burning of the heifer. Then the priest shall wash his clothes, and he shall bathe his flesh in water, and afterward he shall come into the camp, and the priest shall be unclean until the even. And he that burneth her shall wash his clothes in water, and bathe his flesh in water, and shall be unclean until the even. And a man that is clean shall gather up the ashes of the heifer, and lay them up without the camp in a clean place, and it shall be kept for the congregation of the children of Israel for a water of separation: it is a purification for sin.*

The Jews have a parable that connects the Red Heifer to the sin of the golden calf - *A handmaiden's son soiled the king's palace with his filth. The king commanded, 'Let the mother come, and clean up the child's filth',* i.e. the red heifer atoned for the sin of the golden calf. But the mother heifer is just as 'sinful' as the child calf! Only Jesus as the red heifer, the ash in the water, and the waters of separation can separate us from the filth of sin and death. Nothing else would do. Jesus is also the cedar and the hyssop. Cedar is strong while hyssop is weak. Jesus encompasses strong to weak, Aleph to Tav, A to Z, alpha to omega. Jesus is also the scarlet in the fire. He took the fire for us. He burnt for us. That is why we can never be burnt after Him for there is nothing left to burn. There will never be a fiery death for us because of Jesus.

Jesus was reduced to ash for us. That was the only way. For only when we are covered with the 'ashes' of Jesus, can we be made clean. As Jesus is the water of separation and there is none other, rejecting Him meant rejecting the only solution to becoming clean. Without Jesus, we remain unclean. We cannot be made clean until Jesus finished His work. That is why the priest, the one who burnt the red heifer, and the one who collected the ashes all remained unclean until the even. Jesus finished His work on the cross, on the even. When He said, "It is finished!" it was even time or around 3pm. Jesus finished the work in making us clean. We are made clean and we remain clean forever because of His blood.

Note that though we are made clean in Jesus, we still need the running water to purify our thoughts every day. The world system based on meritocracy has to be washed away and replaced by Jesus' words based on Grace every day.

There will come a day in the future when Jesus will return to rule in this world. We call this day the Second Coming of Christ. Jesus will rule for a period of 1000 years. For the Jews, this period will be the fulfillment of the Abrahamic Covenant. The specific boundaries of the land that God promised Abraham in *Genesis* will finally be fulfilled. The Jews will finally worship Jesus, as in *Ezekiel 36:28, And ye shall dwell in the land that I gave to your fathers; and ye shall be my people, and I will be your God.* Jesus, the promised Davidic King, will be their King. He will rule from Jerusalem.

God promised Jesus a kingdom that He would rule in *Daniel 7:13-14, behold, one like the Son of man came with the clouds of heaven, and came to the Ancient of days, and they brought him near before him. And there was given him dominion, and glory, and a kingdom, that all people, nations, and languages, should serve him: his dominion is an everlasting dominion, which shall not pass away, and his kingdom that which shall not be destroyed.* Jesus 'came back' to heaven and received this kingdom from His Father. And just as He 'came up' to heaven He will 'come back down' to earth one day, to reign in the worldly kingdom which was given to Him, as in *Matthew 24:30, they shall see the Son of man coming in the clouds of heaven with power and great glory.* In this future 1000 year rule by Jesus, there will be no curse, no sickness, all animals will live in peace, and the earth will be restored. All believers of Jesus make up the people, nations, and languages mentioned here. They will also rule with Christ. The present world system will be no more. Finally, there will be world peace. The nations will live together with and under Jesus in righteousness, prosperity, joy, and comfort. His kingdom cannot be destroyed, will never pass away like smoke, for it is an everlasting kingdom!

❧ 14 ❧

JESUS AND BELOVED NINEVEH

We first meet Jonah as a great prophet in the reign of King Jeroboam II in *2 Kings 14:25, He restored the coast of Israel from the entering of Hamath unto the sea of the plain, according to the word of the Lord God of Israel, which he spake by the hand of his servant Jonah.* The word of the Lord had been spoken by Jonah. He had prophesied correctly that Israel's lands would be restored. Their enemy, the Assyrians, would be pushed back. Jonah became a very famous prophet after that. So famous that he would now answer only to the sound of his own voice!

We begin with *Jonah 1:1-3, Now the word of the Lord came unto Jonah the son of Amittai, saying, Arise, go to Nineveh, that great city, and cry against it; for their wickedness is come up before me. But Jonah rose up to flee unto Tarshish from the presence of the Lord, and went down to Joppa; and he found a ship going to Tarshish: so he paid the fare thereof, and went down into it, to go with them unto Tarshish from the presence of the Lord.*

Nineveh, the great and wicked city, was to one day become the capital of the whole Assyrian empire under king Sennacherib. For now, Jonah was told by God to go, warn, and save this enemy city of impending doom. But Jonah did not like the sound of God's voice. After all, he was the famous prophet who prophesied against, not for, the Assyrians. In Jonah's mind, Nineveh did not deserve to be saved because of her wickedness towards Israel. Nineveh merited destruction, not salvation! He knew better than God! Jonah full of self-righteous indignation ran to Joppa, heading for Tarshish, or in the opposite direction of Nineveh. As it was his own work, he paid his own fare. God did not pay for his self-righteous act.

We continue in *Jonah1:4-6, 9-17, But the Lord sent out a great wind into the sea, and there was a mighty tempest in the sea, so that the ship was like to be broken. Then the mariners were afraid, and cried every man unto his god, and cast forth the wares that were in the ship into the sea, to lighten it of them. But Jonah was gone down into the sides of the ship; and he lay, and was fast asleep. So the shipmaster came to him, and said unto him, What meanest thou, O sleeper? arise, call upon thy God, if so be that God will think upon us, that we perish not.*

And he said unto them, I am an Hebrew; and I fear the Lord, the God of heaven, which hath made the sea and the dry land. Then were the men exceedingly afraid, and said unto him, Why hast thou done this? For the men knew that he fled from the presence of the Lord, because he had told them. Then said they unto him, What shall we do unto thee, that the sea may be calm unto us? for the sea wrought, and was tempestuous. And he said unto them, Take me up, and cast me forth into the sea; so shall the sea be calm unto you: for I know that for my sake this great tempest is upon you. Nevertheless the men rowed hard to bring it to the land; but they could not: for the sea wrought, and was tempestuous against them. Wherefore they cried unto the Lord, and said, We beseech thee, O Lord, we beseech thee, let us not perish for this man's life, and lay not upon us innocent blood: for thou, O Lord, hast done as it pleased thee. So they took up Jonah, and cast him forth into the sea: and the sea ceased from her raging. Then the men feared the Lord exceedingly, and offered a sacrifice unto the Lord, and made vows. Now the Lord had prepared a great fish to swallow up Jonah. And Jonah was in the belly of the fish three days and three nights.

Jonah, who lived under the law, was punished severely for not doing what God had called him to do. A mighty storm overtook the ship he was in. As the pagan mariners cried out with fear, they began casting their goods and then their gods overboard. When that proved insufficient, they rowed as hard as they could, in their own strength, but that got them nowhere too. As their self-works availed nothing, they abandoned their own strength and cried out to God for their salvation. They became believers and even offered a sacrifice to the Lord.

All this while, Jonah the prophet, rested on his past performance. He was a one-prophecy prophet but so full of himself that he could not see his downward spiral - down to Joppa, down into the bowels of the ship, down to sleep, and very soon, down into the sea, then down into the belly of the fish. When questioned by the mariners, he answered haughtily and in pride that he was a Hebrew who feared the Lord. God would save him because he was a great prophet. It was his idea to get into the boat and it was his wisdom to not warn Nineveh. And if the mariners were to cast him into the sea, he would calm the storm. God would save him for sure. And because of his goodness and self-sacrifice, God would even save the undeserving pagan mariners. It was all about himself and his self-righteousness. Jonah was a great prophet in his own mind.

God had to finally separate Jonah from the mariners. He separated works from Grace. Works was thrown into the sea and swallowed up by a great fish. To Jonah, it was like being a prisoner in the bottom of the mountain. When he could open his eyes, he saw bars above him. But that still did not change Jonah. From inside the belly of fish-Nemo, his pride continued unabated. He offered up verbatim prayers, all the while congratulating himself on his own sacrifice, on his own payment, and on his own ability to look towards the temple. This is symbolic of the self-righteous Jews who were thrown out of God's family into the sea of Gentile nations, swallowed by the ministry of death. But though cast out and dispersed yet they never drowned, albeit in the belly of a fish. The bars that Jonah saw, from time to time, were the teeth of the fish. Jonah suffered like Jeremiah suffered, in *Lamentations 3:5-9, He has besieged me and surrounded me with bitterness and hardship. He has made me dwell in darkness like those dead for ages. He has walled me in so I cannot escape; He has weighed me down with chains. Even when I cry out and plead for help, He shuts out my prayer. He has barred my ways with cut stones; He has made my paths crooked.* Covered with seaweed and buffeted by eddying pools of water mixed with corroding enzymatic fluids, God kept Jonah alive by providing him with enough oxygen from the open mouth of the fish.

We read this in *Jonah 2:1- 10, Then Jonah prayed unto the Lord his God out of the fish's belly, And said, I cried by reason of mine affliction unto the Lord, and he heard me; out of the belly of hell cried I, and thou heardest my voice. For thou hadst cast me into the deep, in the midst of the seas; and the floods compassed me about: all thy billows and thy waves passed over me. Then I said, I am cast out of thy sight; yet I will look again toward thy holy temple. The waters compassed me about, even to the soul: the depth closed me round about, the weeds were wrapped about my head. I went down to the bottoms of the mountains; the earth with her bars was about me forever: yet hast thou brought up my life from corruption, O Lord my God. When my soul fainted within me I remembered the Lord: and my prayer came in unto thee, into thine holy temple. They that observe lying vanities forsake their own mercy. But I will sacrifice unto thee with the voice of thanksgiving; I will pay that that I have vowed. Salvation is of the Lord. And the Lord spake unto the fish, and it vomited out Jonah upon the dry land.*

When God could not stand Jonah's self-righteous attitude any longer, he spoke to the fish which listened and promptly vomited Jonah out onto dry land. Together with partially digested fish and squid! By then, Jonah had spent three days and three nights in the belly of the fish. In that time, he should have died to the old man and be resurrected as the new man. But he was not resurrected. Just regurgitated! He was still the old man, reeking of stink, self-indignation, vomit, enzymes, ooze, and puke. And of course, none of fish-Nemo fish family believed his fish story!

Proverbs 26:11-12, states that *As a dog returneth to his vomit, so a fool returneth to his folly. Seest thou a man wise in his own conceit? there is more hope of a fool than of him.* We also see in *Isaiah 28:8, For all tables are full of vomit and filthiness, so that there is no place clean.* Jonah was a conceited man who stumbled in his judgment. The number 3 usually stands for a new resurrected life but not for Jonah. He was foolish and was still wallowing in the vomit and filthiness of self-centeredness.

When God called Jonah to go and warn Nineveh again, he went, but more so to evade punishment, then as a changed and resurrected man willingly answering a call from God. He still disdained Nineveh and all its ill-deserving, undeserving inhabitants. To him, they deserved hell fire. Hell referred to the valley of Hinnom, Ge-hinnom or Ge-henna, a cursed garbage burning place. Later, it became known as the valley of Slaughter in *Jeremiah 19:5-6, They have built also the high places of Baal, to burn their sons with fire for burnt offerings unto Baal, which I commanded not, nor spake it, neither came it into my mind: Therefore, behold, the days come, saith the LORD, that this place shall no more be called Tophet, nor The valley of the son of Hinnom, but The valley of slaughter.* To Jonah, the Assyrians deserved to be burned to a charred crisp just as the children of the kings of Judah were burned in this valley of burning hell. In *Mark 9:43*, hell/Ge-henna is the place *where the fire never goes out.*

But something unexpectedly happened. We see this in *Jonah 3:1-10, And the word of the Lord came unto Jonah the second time, saying, Arise, go unto Nineveh, that great city, and preach unto it the preaching that I bid thee. So Jonah arose, and went unto Nineveh, according to the word of the Lord. Now Nineveh was an exceeding great city of three days' journey. And Jonah began to enter into the city a day's journey, and he cried, and said, Yet forty days, and Nineveh shall be overthrown. So the people of Nineveh believed God, and proclaimed a fast, and put on sackcloth, from the greatest of them even to the least of them. For word came unto the king of Nineveh, and he arose from his throne, and he laid his robe from him, and covered him with sackcloth, and sat in ashes. And he caused it to be proclaimed and published through Nineveh by the decree of the king and his nobles, saying, Let neither man nor beast, herd nor flock, taste any thing: let them not feed, nor drink water: But let man and beast be covered with sackcloth, and cry mightily unto God: yea, let them turn everyone from his evil way, and from the violence that is in their hands. Who can tell if God will turn and repent, and turn away from his fierce anger, that we perish not? And God saw their works, that they turned from their evil way; and God repented of the evil, that he had said that he would do unto them; and he did it not.*

To Jonah's amazement, the whole city of Nineveh, from the king to the animals in the city, repented. Just like the mariners in the boat, the whole city turned back to God. This made Jonah hopping mad for he did not want them to be saved. A changed and resurrected Jonah would not have been mad with anger. He would have been exceedingly glad! But a self-righteous Jonah thought otherwise. How dared God save them? What right did God have to show grace to such an evil and wicked population? Outrageous, this Grace stuff! Saving Assyrians was like saving rabid dogs. You just cannot trust God to do the right thing anymore!

We continue in *Jonah 4:1-11, But it displeased Jonah exceedingly, and he was very angry. And he prayed unto the Lord, and said, I pray thee, O Lord, was not this my saying, when I was yet in my country? Therefore I fled before unto Tarshish: for I knew that thou art a gracious God, and merciful, slow to anger, and of great kindness, and repentest thee of the evil. Therefore now, O Lord, take, I beseech thee, my life from me; for it is better for me to die than to live. Then said the Lord, Doest thou well to be angry? So Jonah went out of the city, and sat on the east side of the city, and there made him a booth, and sat under it in the shadow, till he might see what would become of the city. And the Lord God prepared a gourd, and made it to come up over Jonah, that it might be a shadow over his head, to deliver him from his grief. So Jonah was exceeding glad of the gourd. But God prepared a worm when the morning rose the next day, and it smote the gourd that it withered. And it came to pass, when the sun did arise, that God prepared a vehement east wind; and the sun beat upon the head of Jonah, that he fainted, and wished in himself to die, and said, It is better for me to die than to live. And God said to Jonah, Doest thou well to be angry for the gourd? And he said, I do well to be angry, even unto death. Then said the Lord, Thou hast had pity on the gourd, for the which thou hast not laboured, neither madest it grow; which came up in a night, and perished in a night: And should not I spare Nineveh, that great city, wherein are more than six score thousand persons that cannot discern between their right hand and their left hand; and also much cattle?*

In fact, he did not believe that God would spare the city, so he made a little leafy shelter just outside of Nineveh, sat under it, and waited for the hellfire and brimstone drones to rain down upon the accursed city. He was a type of the elder son in the parable of the three prodigals who refused to enter the celebratory party thrown by the father. And As Jonah waited, a gourd plant with broad leaves sprang up and gave him even more shade from the hot sun. He felt mollified in his anger. His goodness and obedience had been rewarded. He deserved the shade the plant provided from the fiery sun. But he could not see that the veil over his own eyes overshadowed the shade from the gourd plant. Behind his veil, he believed that Nineveh deserved death from the fiery holocaust that God would send.

But the gourd died instead. And the hellfire missiles from heaven never came! **Finally, Jonah admitted the reason why he had fled from God. It was because he knew that God was Grace, loving people when they did not deserve it and showing kindness to them that merited none. Jonah did not deserve the shade from the broad leaves of the gourd but got it anyways. Nineveh merited death but found favor instead.** Jonah, seething with anger and self-righteousness at God, thought it better to die than to see the Assyrians live. However, God, brimming with Grace thought it better that the Assyrians live rather than die. There were 120,000 small babies or children who could not discern their right from their left hands in Nineveh. This number would be significantly higher had it included the whole populace. There was also much livestock in the city. While Jonah shouted 'unclean', God whispered 'clean'. While Jonah demanded that some sins be called out, God gave Grace that took ALL sins away.

This repentant city of Nineveh went on to become one of the greatest cities in the ancient world, and the capital city of the Assyrian empire. We read of their future in *2 Kings 17:5-6, Then the king of Assyria came up throughout all the land, and went up to Samaria, and besieged it three years. In the ninth year of Hoshea the king of Assyria took Samaria, and carried Israel away into*

Assyria. The Assyrians even captured Samaria, a city in northern Israel. Because of Grace, the Assyrians kept on winning while the Israelites kept on losing. However, newer generations of Assyrians abandoned God and were in turn conquered by the Medians, Scythians, and Cimmerians, fulfilling *Nahum 1:14, Your name will no longer be perpetuated. I will eliminate the carved image and the cast metal image from the house of your gods. I will prepare your grave, for you are contemptible.*

And what happened to Jonah? Well, we are not told the details but we know that he wrote the book of Jonah telling us about God's Amazing Grace. And as the ending of the book is all about God and nothing about Jonah, we can presume that Jonah's flight was overtaken by God's reach. Jonah's great fall was reversed by God's greater lift. Jonah's stink was replaced by His fragrance. Jonah's many sins were blotted out by His unbounded Grace. Jonah was emptied to be refilled with Grace. He entered the party thrown by His Father. For only a fully restored Jonah could understand fully what unmerited Grace is. And then write about it. It is for us, eternal beings living a temporal life, to choose Life over death, to believe in Jesus over the devil.

That is why Jesus answered the scribes and Pharisees in *Matthew 12:39-40, An evil and adulterous generation seeketh after a sign; and there shall no sign be given to it, but the sign of the prophet Jonas: For as Jonas was three days and three nights in the whale's belly; so shall the Son of man be three days and three nights in the heart of the earth.* The sign of Jonah is the unmistakable sign that Jesus is who He is. Jesus would die and then three days later He would be resurrected. For Jonah! For the scribes and Pharisees! For you and me! For the whole world! He pursues us fervently even as we fervently reject Him. *Lamentations 3:22-23* states*, It is of the LORD'S mercies that we are not consumed, because his compassions fail not. They are new every morning: great is thy faithfulness.* From death, suffering, and hopelessness to life, compassion, and hope. Hell to heaven. Darkness to light. Jesus as Grace rises anew, consistently, and faithfully every morning, as the Bright Morning Star (*Revelations 22:16*) for us!

❧ 15 ❧

JESUS AND THE ARMOR OF GOD

Every morning, many people wake up and proceed to put on their spiritual armor. They remember the exhortation from *2 Timothy 2:3, Thou therefore endure hardness, as a good soldier of Jesus Christ.* They believe that they belong to the army of God. As a good soldier, and in order to stand up to the wiles and attacks of satan, they dutifully suit up. They would put on their breastplate of righteousness, gird their loins with truth, shod their feet with the gospel of peace, take up their shield of faith, don their helmet of salvation, and lastly, heave up their sword of the Spirit.

This procedure is found in *Ephesians 6:10-17, Finally, my brethren, be strong in the Lord, and in the power of his might. Put on the whole armour of God, that ye may be able to stand against the wiles of the devil. For we wrestle not against flesh and blood, but against principalities, against powers, against the rulers of the darkness of this world, against spiritual wickedness in high places. Wherefore take unto you the whole armour of God, that ye may be able to withstand in the evil day, and having done all, to stand. Stand therefore, having your loins girt about with truth, and having on the breastplate of righteousness; And your feet shod with the preparation of the gospel of peace; Above all, taking the shield of faith, wherewith ye shall be able to quench all the fiery darts of the wicked. And take the helmet of salvation, and the sword of the Spirit, which is the word of God:*

This whole army of God sounds very good until we discover that nowhere in the Bible has God called us to be an army for Him. God already has an army and it is made up of angels. We see this in *2 Kings 6:17, And Elisha prayed, and said, Lord, I pray thee, open his eyes, that he may see. And the Lord opened the eyes of the young man; and he saw: and, behold, the mountain was full of horses and chariots of fire round about Elisha.*

The reason God has not called us to be in any army is very simple. He wants us to know that He is our Protector and that He will fight our battles for us. He is Jehovah- Sabaoth. In English, He is God-Protector, the Lord of hosts, the Lord of all the armies. And His army is always more than enough to win any battle. *Psalm 24:10* asks, *Who is this King of glory? The Lord of hosts, he is the King of glory.* God Himself is our deliverer and our salvation from all our enemies, spiritual and physical. *Psalm 18:2-3,* states *The Lord is my rock, and my fortress, and my deliverer; my God, my strength, in whom I will trust; my buckler, and the horn of my salvation, and my high tower. I will call upon the Lord, who is worthy to be praised: so shall I be saved from mine enemies.*

Jeremiah the prophet found this out when he prophesied against the priests and other prophets in the house of the Lord. We read in *Jeremiah 26:4-9, And thou shalt say unto them, Thus saith the Lord; If ye will not hearken to me, to walk in my law, which I have set before you, To hearken to the words of my servants the prophets, whom I sent unto you, both rising up early, and sending them, but ye have not hearkened; Then will I make this house like Shiloh, and will make this city a curse to all the nations of the earth. So the priests and the prophets and all the people heard Jeremiah speaking these words in the house of the Lord. Now it came to pass, when Jeremiah had made an end of speaking all that the Lord had commanded him to speak unto all the people, that the priests and the prophets and all the people took him, saying, Thou shalt surely die. Why hast thou prophesied in the name of the Lord, saying, This house shall be like Shiloh, and this city shall be desolate without an inhabitant? And all the people were gathered against Jeremiah in the house of the Lord.*

The spiritual leaders wanted to kill Jeremiah because of his prophecy against them. At the same time, another prophet by the name of Urijah prophesied the exact same thing as Jeremiah. "You will both die!" the priests said. We read this in *Jeremiah 26:20-24, And there was also a man that prophesied in the name of the Lord, Urijah the son of Shemaiah of Kirjath-jearim, who prophesied against this city and against this land according to all the words of Jeremiah: And when Jehoiakim the king, with all his mighty men, and all the princes, heard his words, the king sought to put him to death: but when Urijah heard it, he was afraid, and fled, and went into Egypt; And Jehoiakim the king sent men into Egypt, namely, Elnathan the son of Achbor, and certain men with him into Egypt. And they fetched forth Urijah out of Egypt, and brought him unto Jehoiakim the king; who slew him with the sword, and cast his dead body into the graves of the common people. Nevertheless the hand of Ahikam the son of Shaphan was with Jeremiah, that they should not give him into the hand of the people to put him to death.*

Urijah, upon hearing the death sentence, fled to Egypt for safety but was caught, killed and his body thrown into the graves of the common people. Jeremiah, hearing the same death sentence, sought safety in the hands of Ahikam. The name Ahikam means 'my Brother has arisen'. My Brother, Jesus, is my protector and He fights my battles for me. *Isaiah 54:17* states, *No weapon that is formed against thee shall prosper; and every tongue that shall rise against thee in judgment thou shalt condemn. This is the heritage of the servants of the Lord, and their righteousness is of me, saith the Lord.* Every tongue that said Jeremiah was to die was condemned. Every weapon that was already formed against Jeremiah to kill him did not prosper. Why? Because Jeremiah's righteousness was in Jesus and Jesus has arisen and has saved him.

If we are the army and we fight and win our own battles, then we have no further need for God as our Protector. We become self-sufficient in our works. *Exodus 14:14* states, *The Lord shall fight for you, and ye shall hold your peace.* Our part is to do nothing but to rest and observe Him fighting for us!

When the Israelites came out of Egypt, God hovered over them and protected them like an eagle protecting her young. God alone bore them on wings and took them to high places. No enemies could reach them there. They would be protected and provided for. We see this in *Deuteronomy 32:11-13, As an eagle stirreth up her nest, fluttereth over her young, spreadeth abroad her wings, taketh them, beareth them on her wings: So the Lord alone did lead him, and there was no strange god with him. He made him ride on the high places of the earth, that he might eat the increase of the fields; and he made him to suck honey out of the rock, and oil out of the flinty rock;* We ride high as we watch our Savior, Jesus, do battle for us.

Psalm 91, 1-7,15-16 says it all, *He that dwelleth (yashab) in the secret place of the most High shall abide under the shadow of the Almighty. I will say of the Lord, He is my refuge and my fortress: my God; in him will I trust. Surely he shall deliver thee from the snare of the fowler, and from the noisome pestilence. He shall cover thee with his feathers, and under his wings shalt thou trust: his truth shall be thy shield and buckler. Thou shalt not be afraid for the terror by night; nor for the arrow that flieth by day; Nor for the pestilence that walketh in darkness; nor for the destruction that wasteth at noonday. A thousand shall fall at thy side, and ten thousand at thy right hand; but it shall not come nigh thee. He shall call upon me, and I will answer him: I will be with him in trouble; I will deliver him, and honour him. With long life will I satisfy him, and shew him **my salvation.***

Under the law, the Israelites had cities of refuge. We read this in *Joshua 20:2-3,6, Speak to the children of Israel, saying, Appoint out for you cities of refuge, whereof I spake unto you by the hand of Moses: That the slayer that killeth any person unawares and unwittingly may flee thither, and they shall be your refuge from the avenger of blood. And he shall dwell in that city, until he stand before the congregation for judgment, and until the death of the high priest that shall be in those days: then shall the slayer return, and come unto his own city.* Once a person enters a city of refuge, he is safe there from the avenger of blood (*gaal dam*). He will be granted protection and a trial to see if his murderous act was negligent or intentional. If found guilty of intentional murder, he would be turned over to the avenger kinsman and be put to death. But even if not guilty, he still could not leave the city for the avenger kinsman could kill him and not be guilty. An example of this was Abner who had killed another man in self-defense but when he left Hebron, the city of refuge he was in, was killed by Joab the brother of the man he killed. We read this in *2 Samuel 3:27, And when Abner was returned to Hebron, Joab took him aside in the gate to speak with him quietly, and smote him there under the fifth rib, that he died, for the blood of Asahel his brother.* There is only one instance where every person is free to leave without having to suffer any consequence at all. That is when the high priest dies! Under the law, the Israelites had six cities of refuge. Under Grace, we have the seventh and the true City of Refuge, Jesus! No matter the guilt, we are judged 'not guilty' because all judgment fell on our High Priest, Jesus. Jesus is also our Blood Avenger. However not on us but on sin!

Hebrews 6:18 states, *That by two immutable things, in which it was impossible for God to lie, we might have a strong consolation, who have fled for refuge to lay hold upon the hope set before us.* The certain Hope set before us is Jesus! It is impossible for God to lie and His promise for us in Jesus is unshakeable. Jesus is much more than just a place of refuge. He is our fortress, shield, buckler (small shield), deliverer, and protector as well. With outstretched wings He covers and protects us from diseases, snares, arrows, and destruction as we dwell (*yashab* meaning to sit) in the secret place of the most High. We are honored as we sit under Grace and enjoy a rich, rewarding, long life. We will be shown 'my salvation' (in Hebrew, *Yeshua*) or JESUS! He is the High Priest that never dies. We are forever safe and saved in Jesus.

Not only is God our protector but He also fights for us. The bible is replete with examples where God fought for His people. We see in *Deuteronomy 3:22, Ye shall not fear them: for the Lord your God he shall fight for you.* And in *2 Chronicles 20:17, Ye shall not need to fight in this battle: set yourselves, stand ye still, and see the salvation of the Lord with you.* God showed this clearly in *Judges 7:2-6, And the Lord said unto Gideon, The people that are with thee are too many for me to give the Midianites into their hands, lest Israel vaunt themselves against me, saying, Mine own hand hath saved me. Now therefore go to, proclaim in the ears of the people, saying, Whosoever is fearful and afraid, let him return and depart early from mount Gilead. And there returned of the*

*people twenty and two thousand; and there remained ten thousand.
And the Lord said unto Gideon, The people are yet too many;
bring them down unto the water.   So he brought down the people
unto the water: and the Lord said unto Gideon, Every one that
lappeth of the water with his tongue, as a dog lappeth, him shalt
thou set by himself; likewise every one that boweth down upon his
knees to drink. And the number of them that lapped, putting their
hand to their mouth, were three hundred men: but all the rest of
the people bowed down upon their knees to drink water.*

The Midianites were too numerous to count while Gideon's
army only numbered 32,000. Yet God said it was too many. From
32,000 it was whittled down to 300. Why was this so? The answer
was lest they proclaimed that it was their own hands that saved
them. The last selection was all about the Master. Dogs lap water
while looking at their Master. The men who lapped like dogs kept
their eyes on their Master or Jesus. Thus, they were chosen. The
others, who kneeled down to drink, saw their own reflection and
strength in the water. They were disqualified for they did not look
to Jesus.

Jesus was also the barley cake that defeated the whole host
of Midianites in *Judges 7:13, And when Gideon was come, behold,
there was a man that told a dream unto his fellow, and said,
Behold, I dreamed a dream, and, lo, a cake of barley bread
tumbled into the host of Midian, and came unto a tent, and smote it
that it fell, and overturned it, that the tent lay along.* Jesus
wrought a great victory as He smote the Midianites and overturned
them that same night. The Midianites fell solely because of Jesus.
Before Gideon went to face the Midianites, he met Jesus, in *Judges
6:20-21,23, Then the angel of the LORD put forth the end of the
staff that was in his hand, and touched the flesh and the
unleavened cakes; and there rose up fire out of the rock, and
consumed the flesh and the unleavened cakes. And the LORD said
unto him, Peace be unto thee; fear not: thou shalt not die.* Jesus as
the angel of the Lord acknowledged the flesh and unleavened
cakes as His body. Jesus would cover Gideon physically so he
would not die in the battle as we read in *Judges 6:34, So the Spirit
of the LORD covered Gideon like clothing.*

We read of the attack on the Midianites camp in *Judges 7:16,20-22, And he divided the three hundred men into three companies, and he put a trumpet in every man's hand, with empty pitchers, and lamps within the pitchers, And the three companies blew the trumpets, and brake the pitchers, and held the lamps in their left hands, and the trumpets in their right hands to blow withal: and they cried, The sword of the LORD and of Gideon. And they stood every man in his place round about the camp: and all the host ran, and cried, and fled. And the three hundred blew the trumpets, and the LORD set every man's sword against his fellow, even throughout all the host.* They were to blow on their shofars first. Then they were to break their pitchers so that the light from the torches within would shine into the darkness. It was the strangest battle plan for it was Jesus' fight, not Gideon. In the ensuing confusion, Midian killed Midian.

But then we read in *Isaiah 9:2,4,6, The people that walked in darkness have seen a great light: they that dwell in the land of the shadow of death, upon them hath the light shined. For thou hast broken the yoke of his burden, and the staff of his shoulder, the rod of his oppressor, as in the day of Midian. For unto us a child is born, unto us a son is given.* **Just as Gideon defeated the enemy with light, Jesus would defeat the final enemy, death, by bursting into death's darkness as the Great Light! The Great Light that would never flame out! His death killed death! It gave us life - permanently! Light killed darkness. Let the shofar sound the name of Jesus! Jesus broke the yoke, the staff, and the rod of death by His resurrection.**

So if we are not called to be soldiers and to fight our battles, then why are we told to put on the armor of God? The answer is that the whole armor is symbolic of Jesus and His righteousness. We caught a glimpse of this in the Passover back in *Exodus 12:13, when I see the blood, I will pass over you.* The Israelites were told that the blood of the lamb would save them. **When God sees the blood, He will pass over them.** Jesus' blood was the only covering they needed. Hence, we read in *Romans 13:12, 14, let us therefore cast off the works of darkness, and let us put on the armour of light. But put ye on the Lord Jesus Christ.*

Let us put on Jesus, our Armor of Light and Righteousness, as in *2 Corinthians 6:7, By the word of truth, by the power of God, by the armour of righteousness on the right hand and on the left.* The righteousness of God is Jesus and it stretches from the right to the left hand. **The whole armor of God is Jesus. Paul is telling us to put on Jesus!** *Galatians 3:27* **states,** *For as many of you as have been baptized into Christ have put on Christ.* **With Jesus, we have righteousness, length of days, riches, and honor. Jesus is the only covering we need. We died when we put on Jesus. When the devil comes as a Pharisee of the law to steal, kill, and destroy (*John 10:10*), he sees Jesus and has to flee.**

We read in the following scriptures that Jesus is indeed the full armor of God. He fights for us! It is His work, not ours! *Isaiah 11:5, And* **righteousness shall be the girdle of his loins,** *and* **faithfulness the girdle of his reins.**
Isaiah 59:17, For he put on **righteousness as a breastplate,** *and an* **helmet of salvation** *upon his head.*
Isaiah 52:7, How beautiful upon the mountains are the **feet of him that bringeth good tidings, that publisheth peace; that bringeth good tidings of good, that publisheth salvation.**
2 Samuel 22:36, Thou hast also given me **the shield of thy salvation***: and thy gentleness hath made me great.*
Isaiah 49:2, And he hath made my **mouth like a sharp sword.**

When we have faith in Jesus as the Son of God, we overcome the world. *1 John 5:5* states, *Who is he that overcometh the world, but he that believeth that Jesus is the Son of God?* We read too in *Revelation 3:21, To him that overcometh will I grant to sit with me in my throne, even as I also overcame, and am set down with my Father in his throne.* Because He overcame the world, so do we, as in *Colossians 2:15, And having spoiled principalities and powers, he made a shew of them openly, triumphing over them in it.* We get to sit with Him because of Him! Jesus granted us that right. All our works do not seat us there nor do all our failures unseat us. We are overcomers in this world solely because we are clad with Jesus, our Righteous Armor. The night and darkness of self-works is far gone. The day of Light and Grace is at hand. So put on Jesus Christ!

❧ 16 ❧

JESUS AND FIVE SMOOTH STONES

The armor of God comes alive in the well known story of David and Goliath. We read of this in *1 Samuel 17:1-11, Now the Philistines gathered together their armies to battle, and were gathered together at Shochoh, which belongeth to Judah, and pitched between Shochoh and Azekah, in Ephes-dammim. And Saul and the men of Israel were gathered together, and pitched by the valley of Elah, and set the battle in array against the Philistines. And the Philistines stood on a mountain on the one side, and Israel stood on a mountain on the other side: and there was a valley between them. And there went out a champion out of the camp of the Philistines, named Goliath, of Gath, whose height was six cubits and a span. And he had an helmet of brass upon his head, and he was armed with a coat of mail; and the weight of the coat was five thousand shekels of brass. And he had greaves of brass upon his legs, and a target of brass between his shoulders. And the staff of his spear was like a weaver's beam; and his spear's head weighed six hundred shekels of iron: and one bearing a shield went before him. And he stood and cried unto the armies of Israel, and said unto them, Why are ye come out to set your battle in array? am not I a Philistine, and ye servants to Saul? choose you a man for you, and let him come down to me. If he be able to fight with me, and to kill me, then will we be your servants: but if I prevail against him, and kill him, then shall ye be our servants, and serve us. And the Philistine said, I defy the armies of Israel this day; give me a man, that we may fight together. When Saul and all Israel heard those words of the Philistine, they were dismayed, and greatly afraid.*

Saul and his armies stood on one mountain while Goliath and his Philistine armies stood on another. Saul is our flesh facing the mountain of law, called Goliath. The name Goliath or *gālǝyāt* comes from the root words *gala* (reveal), *gola* (captive), and *gillayon* (tablet). Goliath reveals our captivity to the tablets of the law. Every part of Goliath's armor was made of brass. Brass stood for judgment. Each accoutrement upon him was an indictment against the sins of Israel. It is interesting to note that his spear's head weighed 600 shekels of iron, he had on 6 pieces of armor and his height was 6 cubits (666)! When Goliath, numbered 666 and clad in brass, stood up, all flesh trembled before it. Goliath taunted the Israelites quivering flesh for forty days, a shadow of satan tempting Jesus with works in the desert. Then David appeared.

We read this in *1 Samuel 17:23-27, And as he talked with them, behold, there came up the champion, the Philistine of Gath, Goliath by name, out of the armies of the Philistines, and spake according to the same words: and David heard them. And all the men of Israel, when they saw the man, fled from him, and were sore afraid. And the men of Israel said, Have ye seen this man that is come up? surely to defy Israel is he come up: and it shall be, that the man who killeth him, the king will enrich him with great riches, and will give him his daughter, and make his father's house free in Israel. And David spake to the men that stood by him, saying, What shall be done to the man that killeth this Philistine, and taketh away the reproach from Israel? for who is this uncircumcised Philistine, that he should defy the armies of the living God? And the people answered him after this manner, saying, So shall it be done to the man that killeth him.*

David, coming unto the battlefied, heard the taunts of Goliath and wondered why everyone was so afraid. Why was the Philistine allowed to defy God? In *Leviticus 24:16* we read, *And he that blasphemeth the name of the Lord, he shall surely be put to death, and all the congregation shall certainly stone him: as well the stranger, as he that is born in the land, when he blasphemeth the name of the Lord, shall be put to death.* For forty days now,

Goliath had been blaspheming the name of the Lord and nobody had stoned him to death, as dictated by the law. They broke the law and deserved punishment but God sent David to them instead. Grace was sent to an undeserving king, a symbol of us. David, who had experienced Grace in *1 Samuel 16:13, Then Samuel took the horn of oil, and anointed him in the midst of his brethren: and the Spirit of the LORD came upon David from that day forward,* volunteered to go against Goliath. The horn of oil, symbolizing Jesus, had delivered David from the bear and the lion. Now Jesus would remove the reproach of Goliath from Israel.

We continue in *1 Samuel 17:32-39, And David said to Saul, Let no man's heart fail because of him; thy servant will go and fight with this Philistine. And Saul said to David, Thou art not able to go against this Philistine to fight with him: for thou art but a youth, and he a man of war from his youth. And David said unto Saul, Thy servant kept his father's sheep, and there came a lion, and a bear, and took a lamb out of the flock: And I went out after him, and smote him, and delivered it out of his mouth: and when he arose against me, I caught him by his beard, and smote him, and slew him. Thy servant slew both the lion and the bear: and this uncircumcised Philistine shall be as one of them, seeing he hath defied the armies of the living God. David said moreover, The Lord that delivered me out of the paw of the lion, and out of the paw of the bear, he will deliver me out of the hand of this Philistine. And Saul said unto David, Go, and the Lord be with thee. And Saul armed David with his armour, and he put an helmet of brass upon his head; also he armed him with a coat of mail. And David girded his sword upon his armour, and he assayed to go; for he had not proved it. And David said unto Saul, I cannot go with these; for I have not proved them. And David put them off him.*

But before David went to face Goliath, King Saul tried to put his own armor on David. As it was the king's armor, it must have been the best that hands could have wrought. **Yet, the best self-works cannot stand against the law. For the best is still sin! All of man's works for all time still falls far short. The best sinner still goes to hell.** We know that King Saul was a man of works as he tried to please both God and men. Because of his failures, he became neurotic and started fearing both God and men. His rigid and stone cold armor of self-works would have severely constricted David. Its weight alone would have been self defeating. David recognized this and put the armor away from him. This allowed him to flow in the goodness and unmerited favor from God.

So in *1 Samuel 17:40 And he took his staff in his hand, and chose him five smooth stones out of the brook, and put them in a shepherd's bag which he had, even in a scrip; and his sling was in his hand: and he drew near to the Philistine.* Sling in Hebrew is *qela'* (spelled Qof, Lamed, Ayin or numerically 100, 30, 70). The numeric total of 200 (100+30+70) signified the insufficiency of man. So David took five smooth stones from a brook! There were many rough stones in the valley and atop the mountain but these stones were smooth and flawless. The Hebrew word for stone here is *eh'ben* and is written like this: אֶבֶן The word for father in Hebrew is אַב (reading right to left) and is pronounced *ab*. The word for son in Hebrew is בֵּן and is pronounced *ben*. Hence, stone in Hebrew here means the Father and the Son. *Isaiah 57:6* states, *Among the smooth stones of the stream is thy portion;* Five stands for Grace. David's portion is Grace. In Jesus is David's inheritance. Only Jesus can fulfill the law. He ended the law. We read in *Romans 10:4, For Christ is the end of the law for righteousness to everyone that believeth.*

Jesus is the continuous Living Water that washes away the law that was etched on stone. Even though only one smooth stone was needed to defeat Goliath, five stones were given as a symbol of Jesus' overpayment. Man's sling was insufficient but each stone of Grace is more than sufficient. The other four stones were for the defeat of Goliath's four brothers (or sons) later on. We read of Ishbi-benob, Saph, Lahmi, and the fourth brother with six fingers and six toes defeat in *2 Samuel 21:22, These four were born to the giant in Gath, and fell by the hand of David, and by the hand of his servants.* Grace always overpays the law. For where sin abounds, Grace super-abounds. No matter how deep the pit of our sin, the hand of Grace reaches deeper still. No matter how high the mountain of our sin, the living waters of Grace extend higher. In fact, if our sin was a plastic cup, His Grace would be all the oceans of the world poured upon it.

We continue in *1 Samuel 17:41-50, And the Philistine came on and drew near unto David; and the man that bare the shield went before him. And when the Philistine looked about, and saw David, he disdained him: for he was but a youth, and ruddy, and of a fair countenance. And the Philistine said unto David, Am I a dog, that thou comest to me with staves? And the Philistine cursed David by his gods. And the Philistine said to David, Come to me, and I will give thy flesh unto the fowls of the air, and to the beasts of the field. Then said David to the Philistine, Thou comest to me with a sword, and with a spear, and with a shield: but I come to thee in the name of the Lord of hosts, the God of the armies of Israel, whom thou hast defied. This day will the Lord deliver thee into mine hand; and I will smite thee, and take thine head from thee; and I will give the carcases of the host of the Philistines this day unto the fowls of the air, and to the wild beasts of the earth; that all the earth may know that there is a God in Israel. And all this assembly shall know that the Lord saveth not with sword and spear: for the battle is the Lord's, and he will give you into our hands. And it came to pass, when the Philistine arose, and came and drew nigh to meet David, that David hasted, and ran toward the army to meet the philistine. And David put his hand in his bag, and took thence a stone, and slang it, and smote the Philistine in his forehead, that the stone sunk into his forehead; and he fell upon his face to the earth. So David prevailed over the Philistine with a sling and with a stone, and smote the Philistine, and slew him; but there was no sword in the hand of David. Therefore David ran, and stood upon the Philistine, and took his sword, and drew it out of the sheath thereof, and slew him, and cut off his head therewith.*

Goliath was defeated by Grace and Grace alone. If David had had any armor or sword with him, he would have lost the battle. **There is a God in Israel. Only God can deliver the people from the law by providing a Savior. The staff, symbolic of the cross, and the smooth stone of Father and Son defeated**

the giant. Jesus as the Lord of hosts defeated Goliath, a symbol of satan, sin, and death. Satan defeated. Sin obliterated. Death died. The battle belonged to the Lord. It was never our battle. We see in *Psalm 5:12, For thou, Lord, wilt bless the righteous; with favour wilt thou compass him as with a shield.* Jesus is our shield of favor and He is always more than enough.

That is why David had no use for Goliath's armor as well. So he put it away as we read in *1 Samuel 17:54, And David took the head of the Philistine, and brought it to Jerusalem; but he put his armour in his tent.* Goliath's head, severed with his own sword, was taken back to Jerusalem. In Hebrew, the word skull, as in severed from the body, is *gulgoleth.* We all know that Jesus was crucified on a hill known as Golgotha, as we see in *John 19:17-18, And he bearing his cross went forth into a place called the place of a skull, which is called in the Hebrew Golgotha: Where they crucified him, and two other with him, on either side one, and Jesus in the midst.* Golgotha is Greek for skull. We do not know for sure but it seems likely that Goliath's head was buried in the area where Jesus was crucified. Jesus crushed satan's head, the crooked serpent, upon Golgotha or Calvary and replaced the law with Grace!

On a side note, we know that the descendants of Ishmael (son of Hagar, second wife of Abraham) and the other sons of Abraham through Keturah (third wife of Abraham) were given the east country. We read of Ishmael in *Genesis 16:11-13, The angel of the LORD also said to her: You are now pregnant and you will give birth to a son. You shall name him Ishmael, for the LORD has heard of your misery. He will be a wild donkey of a man; his hand will be against everyone and everyone's hand against him, and he will live in hostility toward all his brothers, And she called the name of the LORD that spake unto her, Thou God seest me (El Roi),* and again in *Genesis 21:16-20,* when Hagar, after Abraham had sent her away, *said, Let me not see the death of the child. And she sat over against him, and lift up her voice, and wept. And God heard the voice of the lad; and the angel of God called Hagar out of heaven, and said unto her, What aileth thee, Hagar? fear not; for God hath heard the voice of the lad where he is. Arise, lift up the lad, and hold him in thine hand; for I will make him a great nation. And God opened her eyes, and she saw a well of water; and she went, and filled the bottle with water, and gave the lad drink. And God was with the lad; and he grew, and dwelt in the wilderness, and became an archer.* Jesus, as Messenger, said that Ishmael would be a wild donkey of a man who will war against many people with his own hands and many people will war against him. He will be a great nation and great with bow and arrows. Hagar knew God as *El Roi*, the God who Sees, but she was not a party to the Abrahamic covenant. So when she cried to Him, God saw Hagar but heard Ishmael. Ishmael was heard because he was Abraham's seed, and was given Life giving water. For Jesus loved Ishmael and his descendants as well.

A later prophecy by Zechariah showed us that the rugged and independent descendants of Ishmael would indeed only be defeated by a King who will ride upon that wild donkey and cut off his battle bow. *Zechariah 9:9-10* states, *Rejoice greatly, O daughter of Zion; shout, O daughter of Jerusalem: behold, thy King cometh unto thee: he is just, and having salvation; lowly, and riding upon an ass, and upon a colt the foal of an ass. And I will cut off the chariot from Ephraim, and the horse from Jerusalem, and the battle bow shall be cut off: and he shall speak peace unto the heathen: and his dominion shall be from sea even to sea, and from the river even to the ends of the earth.* Of course, we know that Jesus was that King who rode upon that wild donkey. Not any donkey but a wild one that nobody had sat on before. In *Mark 11:2,7, And saith unto them, Go your way into the village over against you: and as soon as ye be entered into it, ye shall find a colt tied, whereon never man sat; loose him, and bring him. And they brought the colt to Jesus, and cast their garments on him; and he sat upon him.* When Jesus has authority over them, the descendants of Ishmael will have peace!

Grace always wins. In Jesus, we are well able to overcome every circumstance. We see this back in *Numbers 13:30-33, And Caleb stilled the people before Moses, and said, Let us go up at once, and possess it; for we are well able to overcome it. But the men that went up with him said, We be not able to go up against the people; for they are stronger than we. And they brought up an evil report of the land which they had searched unto the children of Israel, saying, The land, through which we have gone to search it, is a land that eateth up the inhabitants thereof; and all the people that we saw in it are men of a great stature. And there we saw the giants, the sons of Anak, which come of the giants: and we were in our own sight as grasshoppers, and so we were in their sight.* Caleb, trusting in Grace, told the people that they were well able to overcome the giant enemies living in their Promised Land. Not because they were so strong, but because Mammoth Grace would trample over everything! The battle belonged to God and He had won the war. But the other ten spies looked at their own strength and works. It seemed that every time we take our eyes off God and focus on our-selves, we lose vision of who we really are. Starting from Adam and Eve who saw them-selves naked and were afraid, to these ten spies who contradicted Caleb and brought forth an evil report. They saw themselves as grasshoppers and cowed before the stature of their enemies. They conceded the battle before it began.

But not David! We read in *1 Chronicles 14: 9-11, And the Philistines came and spread themselves in the valley of Rephaim. And David inquired of God, saying, Shall I go up against the Philistines? and wilt thou deliver them into mine hand? And the LORD said unto him, Go up; for I will deliver them into thine hand. So they came up to Baalperazim; and David smote them there. Then David said, God hath broken in upon mine enemies by mine hand like the breaking forth of waters: therefore they called the name of that place Baalperazim.* Once again, the Philistines spread themselves out to do battle with David in the valley of Rephaim or giants. However, God broke in among the Philistines yet again like water breaking forth. Baalperazim meant 'possessor of breaches'. David won as he trusted in the Possessor of Breaches, or Breakthroughs, Jesus! God would breakthrough and save David every time. That was how God saved David when Ishbibenob, son of a giant, in *2 Samuel 21:16*, cornered him and was about to kill him. God broke through as Abishai, meaning 'Father of Gifts' and killed the giant instead! God wanted David to not just be a giant killer but a king!

Goliath's sword was eventually wrapped in cloth and put behind the ephod. We read this in *1 Samuel 21:9, And the priest said, The sword of Goliath the Philistine, whom thou slewest in the valley of Elah, behold, it is here wrapped in a cloth behind the ephod.* The ephod (or apron) was one part of the high priest garments. It is described in *Exodus 39:2,4-7, And he made the ephod of gold, blue, and purple, and scarlet, and fine twined linen. They made shoulder pieces for it, to couple it together: by the two edges was it coupled together. And the curious girdle of his ephod, that was upon it, was of the same, according to the work thereof; of gold, blue, and purple, and scarlet, and fine twined linen; as the Lord commanded Moses. And they wrought onyx stones inclosed in ouches of gold, graven, as signets are graven, with the names of the children of Israel. And he put them on the shoulders of the ephod, that they should be stones for a memorial to the children of Israel; as the Lord commanded Moses.*

The ephod is not to be worshipped as Gideon found out in *Judges 8:27, and all Israel went thither a whoring after it.* It was but a symbol of Jesus. It was made of gold, blue, purple, and scarlet threads, intertwined with fine white linen. Gold signified divinity, blue signified heaven, purple indicated royalty, red represented man, and white linen the righteousness of Jesus. He was divinity, from heaven, became the Son of man, and imputed to us His royalty and righteousness. Blue mixed with red becomes purple. **We become royalty or purple forever because of Jesus.** He is our golden girdle of truth. And on His shoulders are onyx stones, set in gold, with the names of all His children graven therein. Jesus lifts and upholds us on His resurrected shoulders. *Isaiah 9:6* states, *For unto us a child is born, unto us a son is given: and the government shall be **upon his shoulder**: and his name shall be called Wonderful, Counsellor, The mighty God, The everlasting Father, The Prince of Peace.* My name is on Jesus' shoulder. Your name is on Jesus' shoulder. Our names are not just written down but engraved, signifying permanency and eternity with Him. The sword of self-works is behind Jesus because it is He that will lead and fight our battles, as we ride upon His resurrected shoulders.

❧ 17 ❧

JESUS AND THE PRODIGAL MANAGER

Throughout His ministry, Jesus kept going after the lost sheep. But many sheep, though lost, were rebellious. In *Luke 9:59-62* we read, *And he said unto another, Follow me. But he said, Lord, suffer me first to go and bury my father. Jesus said unto him, Let the dead bury their dead: but go thou and preach the kingdom of God. And another also said, Lord, I will follow thee; but let me first go bid them farewell, which are at home at my house. And Jesus said unto him, No man, having put his hand to the plough, and looking back, is fit for the kingdom of God.* At first glance, it seemed that Jesus wanted His people to plow with Him. Not only plow but those who would never glance backwards. Looking backwards would result in a crooked line. Are we not to show how great, mighty, and straight our efforts are? Are we not as oxen with side blinders, trudging onwards endlessly for Jesus? But a careful examination of the two men in the story showed us that they never followed Jesus. They were non-believers. Jesus came for them but they repudiated Him. They were rebellious sheep with good excuses. One demurred to bury his father while the other excused himself to say goodbyes. They never put their hands to the plow. They were not fit for the kingdom as they were never in the kingdom. The only plower who never looked back was Jesus. Jesus came plowing for them but they did not accept Him.

This incident resulted in a full blown parable that we read in *Luke 14:12-23, Then said he also to him that bade him, When thou makest a dinner or a supper, call not thy friends, nor thy*

*brethren, neither thy kinsmen, nor thy rich neighbours; lest they
also bid thee again, and a recompence be made thee. But when
thou makest a feast, call the poor, the maimed, the lame, the blind:
And thou shalt be blessed; for they cannot recompense thee...A
certain man made a great supper, and bade many: And sent his
servant at supper time to say to them that were bidden, Come; for
all things are now ready. And they all with one consent began to
make excuse. The first said unto him, I have bought a piece of
ground, and I must needs go and see it: I pray thee have me
excused. And another said, I have bought five yoke of oxen, and I
go to prove them: I pray thee have me excused. And another said, I
have married a wife, and therefore I cannot come. So that servant
came, and shewed his lord these things. Then the master of the
house being angry said to his servant, Go out quickly into the
streets and lanes of the city, and bring in hither the poor, and the
maimed, and the halt, and the blind. And the servant said, Lord, it
is done as thou hast commanded, and yet there is room. And the
lord said unto the servant, Go out into the highways and hedges,
and compel them to come in, that my house may be filled.*

Jesus has prepared a huge feast for all Jews. Every blessing
of God was provided for at the feast. All were invited except those
who would recompense Jesus for His invitation. These were the
Jews who were rich in their works. An eye for an eye and a feast
for a feast. Fair and square. These Jews refused to accept that the
feast was free and hence, were not invited. However, even among
those invited, many rejected the invitation. They had bought land
which they had not seen and oxen which they had not proved!
Being married to the law, they gave excuses,. However, the poor,
maimed, lame, and the blind were delighted with the invitation.
They could not recompense, they had nothing to give back, and
they did not make any excuses either. They could not walk without
help. They were devoid of works and depended entirely on Grace
to bring them in. They came by the thousands but there was still
more room at the feast. Gentiles were then brought in from the
hedges, the streets, and the highways. **Billions came because
Jesus said they could come. And the house of God was finally
filled!**

Accepting unworthy people to the feast drew the ire of the elite Pharisees and scribes. We read in *Luke 15:1-9, Then drew near unto him all the publicans and sinners for to hear him. And the Pharisees and scribes murmured, saying, This man receiveth sinners, and eateth with them. And he spake this parable unto them, saying, What man of you, having an hundred sheep, if he lose one of them, doth not leave the ninety and nine in the wilderness, and go after that which is lost, until he find it? And when he hath found it, he layeth it on his shoulders, rejoicing. And when he cometh home, he calleth together his friends and neighbours, saying unto them, Rejoice with me; for I have found my sheep which was lost. I say unto you, that likewise joy shall be in heaven over one sinner that repenteth, more than over ninety and nine just persons, which need no repentance. Either what woman having ten pieces of silver, if she lose one piece, doth not light a candle, and sweep the house, and seek diligently till she find it? And when she hath found it, she calleth her friends and her neighbours together, saying, Rejoice with me; for I have found the piece which I had lost.*

This parable was for both Pharisees and sinners (they were called sinners as Jesus had not died for them yet) to hear. Jesus was both the man and the woman who actively came looking for sinners, His lost sheep and His lost silver piece. The sheep was gone. The silver coin was lost. There was nothing the sheep or the coin could do by itself to wander back home. So Jesus initiated the find. In *John 1:43-45,48, The day following Jesus would go forth into Galilee, and findeth Philip, and saith unto him, Follow me. Now Philip was of Bethsaida, the city of Andrew and Peter. Philip findeth Nathanael, and saith unto him, We have found him, of whom Moses in the law, and the prophets, did write, Jesus of Nazareth, the son of Joseph. Nathanael saith unto him, Whence knowest thou me? Jesus answered and said unto him, Before that Philip called thee, when thou wast under the fig tree, I saw thee.* Jesus found Philip and Nathanael first before they followed Him.

And He will not rest until He finds us as well. Jesus came to seek and save those who are lost. For we can only be lost if we had belonged to Him first. The lost are those who cannot, by their own strength, find their way back home. We who are lost need not fear to be found by Him. He does not seek us out to correct us. It has nothing to do with our mistakes, disobedience, or sins. We, the lost sheep, are found because of His love, grace, and care for us. The 'further lost' we are, the 'further more' He will pursue us. We are picked up and then carried back on Jesus' shoulder to underscore that it was by Grace that we are brought back home, not by our own walk. The coin could not roll its way back. It was found after Jesus shone His light into the darkness, searched and swept for it. Now we are secure in the palm of His hand. We are assured of our salvation, resting on His resurrected shoulders. **Jesus rejoiced in finding us!** We belong to Jesus and He will never let us go. Guaranteed! We read about this in *Romans 8:38-39, For I am persuaded, that neither death, nor life, nor angels, nor principalities, nor powers, nor things present, nor things to come, Nor height, nor depth, nor any other creature, shall be able to separate us from the love of God, which is in Christ Jesus our Lord.* **God had joined us to Jesus, as in *1 Corinthians 6:17, But he that is joined unto the Lord is one spirit.* Then we read in *Mark 10:9, What therefore God hath joined together, let not man put asunder.* No man can break apart or tear Jesus away from us!**

The other 99 sheep which were left in the wilderness symbolized the Jews who believed that they needed no repentance. They did not believe they were lost as they trusted in their self-righteousness, piety, and pretense. There was great rejoicing in heaven for the one lost sheep, now found! There was no rejoicing for the 99 sheep who got left behind in the wilderness!

Silver coins in Jesus' time carried an image. Whether it was Caesar Augustus, Tiberius, Pontius Pilate or Herod, Jesus was interested only in the coin that had 'lost' this image. The re-found coin would bear the Image, His image, namely the image of Jesus. The coins which bore the old image were ignored. In both cases, the Master rejoiced when the lost sheep and the lost silver piece was found and brought home.

Similarly, in *Matthew 18:10,14*, we read *Take heed that ye despise not one of these little ones…Even so it is not the will of your Father which is in heaven, that one of these little ones should perish.* We are told not to despise children for their helplessness. For it is their very powerlessness, or those that are helpless like children, that activated Jesus' radical grace. As we all belong to Him, It is not the will of the Father that any should perish.

Jesus then told the famous parable of the three prodigals. No matter what mistakes we have done, He will still love us and welcome us home. *Isaiah 63:16* states, *Surely you are still our Father! Even if Abraham and Jacob would disown us, LORD, you would still be our Father. You are our Redeemer from ages past.* For the Jews, even if Abraham were to disown them which is a physical impossibility as they were from his loins, God would still be their Father and their Redeemer.

After he finished that parable, He began another parable that stumped the Pharisees. It was a parable that accentuated His love for sinners. It is found in *Luke 16:1-14, And he said also unto his disciples, There was a certain rich man, which had a steward; and the same was accused unto him that he had wasted his goods. And he called him, and said unto him, How is it that I hear this of thee? give an account of thy stewardship; for thou mayest be no longer steward. Then the steward said within himself, What shall I do? for my lord taketh away from me the stewardship: I cannot dig; to beg I am ashamed. I am resolved what to do, that, when I am put out of the stewardship, they may receive me into their houses. So he called every one of his lord's debtors unto him, and said unto the first, How much owest thou unto my lord? And he said, An hundred measures of oil. And he said unto him, Take thy bill, and sit down quickly, and write fifty. Then said he to another, And how much owest thou? And he said, An hundred measures of wheat. And he said unto him, Take thy bill, and write fourscore. And the lord commended the unjust steward, because he had done wisely: for the children of this world are in their generation wiser than the children of light. And I say unto you, Make to yourselves friends of the mammon of unrighteousness; that, when ye fail, they may receive you into everlasting habitations. He that is faithful in that which is least is faithful also in much: and he that is unjust in the least is unjust also in much. If therefore ye have not been*

faithful in the unrighteous mammon, who will commit to your trust
the true riches? And if ye have not been faithful in that which is
another man's, who shall give you that which is your own? No
servant can serve two masters: for either he will hate the one, and
love the other; or else he will hold to the one, and despise the
other. Ye cannot serve God and mammon. And the Pharisees also,
who were covetous, heard all these things: and they derided him.

First of all, the manager wasted his master's goods. By any
performance measure, he was a bad manager. When called out that
he was wasteful, he became even more wasteful. He was now
prodigious or extravagant in the wastefulness of His master's
goods. He called every one of his master's debtors in and
proceeded to rescind and forgive them their debts. It was not his oil
nor his wheat, but he was prodigal in reducing their debts. When it
was noised in the town that the manager was reducing debts, all the
debtors showed up. The man slashed, curtailed, and reduced debts,
left and right. When the master finally showed up…at this point,
all the Pharisees leaned in closer to Jesus. They waited with bated
breath to hear the punishment for the prodigal manager. Would it
be stoning, scourging, whipping, imprisonment or chains? A
hanging perhaps? But Jesus dropped a bombshell on them. The
manager was commended and praised for his actions! The
Pharisees who were covetous, gasped, then laughed themselves
silly at the ridiculous ending. They derided and mocked Jesus for
the stupid parable.

But was it stupid? The manager in the parable is us. We
made many mistakes. If we were to be judged after our works, we
would be severely reprimanded. So our only hope rests in the
goodness of our Master. Our Master is Jesus. His Grace is endless
and super-abundant. It covered all our mistakes. Though we erred,
our Master forgave us. Yes, we are God's stewards but God's
accounts are not about balancing numbers, or of debits and credits.
We do not deposit good works so as to withdraw forgiveness when
we need it. For the Master forgave us without any good works on
our part. He took the loss for our blunders. By His sacrifice, He
tore up our ledgers. We cannot ever, no never, out-sin Grace.

When we are managers or stewards of God, we represent Him and act on His behalf. So as managers for God, who had received Grace, we can now show Grace to others. **Our job is to show our Master's willingness to forgive debt.** Hence, we call in all the debtors. It did not matter whether the debts were big or small. Paul underscored that he was the biggest sinner in *1 Timothy 1:14-15, And the grace of our Lord was exceeding abundant with faith and love which is in Christ Jesus. This is a faithful saying, and worthy of all acceptation, that Christ Jesus came into the world to save sinners; of whom I am chief.* But even the biggest sin was exceeding abundantly removed by Grace. All debtors are to be shown radical Grace. That is why we are to make ourselves friends to the unrighteous mammon so that we can tell them about the righteousness of Jesus. When they understand and believe that their debts or sins have already been forgiven by the finished work of Jesus, they join us in everlasting habitations. We should show them Jesus' willingness and ability to write off their debts. As children of the Light, we should understand this much more than children of the world. As we are acting on behalf of Jesus, all forgiveness is actually from Jesus, not from us or the church.

It is very important to understand that Jesus forgave the debt that we owed to the law, not to God. We are debtors to the law because of our inability to become righteous under it, as explained in *Galatians 5:3, For I testify again to every man that is circumcised, that he is a debtor to do the whole law.* **God, through Jesus, forgave us this debt that we owed to the law. He accomplished what we could not do. God never made us debtors to Him. As such, we were never debtors to God Himself. Jesus did not pay back the debt we owed to God but to the law.** That is why the master commended the prodigal servant. For he did what he saw his master had done for him. His master won him. He won others. Just as Paul in *1 Corinthians 9:19, to win as many as possible.* Similarly, we can also do what our Master, Jesus, has done for us! As Jesus showed us His unbridled love, let us share this unbridled love with others.

❧ 18 ❧

JESUS, JEWS, AND GENTILES part 1

Jews and Gentiles alike, need to have faith in Jesus. Yet many Jews, even to this day, reject Jesus. We know that from *John 1:11, He came unto his own, and his own received him not.* To the Jews, there is only one God. There is no Son of God as that would mean two Gods. And if we bring in the Holy Spirit, that would make three Gods! To them, only pagans believe in many gods. They do not consider that God is spirit and is three in one, as in *Genesis 1:26, Let **us** make man in our image, after **our** likeness.* Also, the Jews reject Jesus because the Jewish Messiah would be a leader who would reunite the Jewish nation. He would also rebuild the temple, establish moral perfection, peace, and justice to the whole world (*Jerusalem Talmud Berakhot 2*). Jesus Christ did none of that! He was crucified and died ignominiously instead!

Also, only Yahweh covenanted with them and gave them the law which is 'the way'. Jesus have no covenant with them and does not add one iota to the strength of the law! The Jews actually consider Jesus as a traitor to Judaism. They blame Him for having started a sect. We know this from the Roman procurator Antonius Felix questioning of Paul in *Acts 24:5, For we have found this man a public menace and one who stirs up dissensions among all the Jews throughout the world, and a ringleader of the sect of the Nazarenes.* Jesus' followers were called Nazarenes or Nazoreans. It was a contemptible label from Jesus of Nazareth. Nazareth was so disgusting that even Nathanael asked, *Can anything good come out of Nazareth?* in *John 1:46.* We all know that in *Acts 11:26 the*

disciples were called Christians first in Antioch. The word
'Christian' was another derogatory word as the disciples followed
'Christ'. Of course, in *midrashic* texts, both Christians and Rome
were associated with Esau who received no covenantal inheritance
from God. The Jews believe that God only has a covenantal
relationship with Jacob or Israel!

To the Jews, Jesus is contemptible. And blasphemous. At
best, He means absolutely nothing to them! Jews do not need to be
'saved'. They just have to follow the law. Forgiveness to the Jews
meant forgiveness from breaking the law. In the Torah, this
forgiveness or atonement is by animal sacrifices. But as present
day Jews do not have a temple to offer these sacrifices, they earn
their forgiveness by prayers, repentance, and good deeds. From
mono-theism (one God) they became mono-Me-ism (one Me)!

Hence, in light of their rejection of Jesus, did God reject the
Jews back, in favor of the Gentiles? The answer can be found in
*Romans 11:12, 17-29, Now if the fall of them be the riches of the
world, and the diminishing of them the riches of the Gentiles...And
if some of the branches be broken off, and thou, being a wild olive
tree, wert graffed in among them, and with them partakest of the
root and fatness* (we are talking about 'fatness' or riches/blessings,
not salvation) *of the olive tree...because of unbelief they were
broken off, and thou standest by faith. Be not highminded, but fear:
For if God spared not the natural branches, take heed lest he also
spare not thee. Behold therefore the goodness and severity of God:
on them which fell, severity; but toward thee, goodness, if thou
continue in his goodness: otherwise thou also shalt be* **cut off***. And
they also, if they abide not still in unbelief, shall be graffed in: for
God is able to graff them in again. For if thou wert cut out of the
olive tree which is wild by nature, and wert graffed contrary to
nature into a good olive tree: how much more shall these, which be
the natural branches, be graffed into their own olive tree?...that
blindness in part is happened to Israel, until the fulness of the
Gentiles be come in. And so all Israel shall be saved* (now we are
talking about salvation)*: as it is written, There shall come out of
Sion the Deliverer, and shall turn away ungodliness from Jacob:
For this is my covenant unto them, when I shall take away their*

sins. As concerning the gospel, they are enemies for your sakes: but as touching the election, they are beloved for the fathers' sakes. For the gifts and calling of God are without repentance.

Because of their unbelief in Jesus, the Jews were as branches broken off the tree. But the tree is still an olive tree with an Abrahamic covenant root! God's promises to Abraham are still good, as in *Galatians 3:17-18, the Law, which came 430 years later, does not invalidate a covenant previously ratified by God, so as to nullify the promise. For if the inheritance is based on law, it is no longer based on a promise; but God has granted it to Abraham by means of a promise.* Just as the promise of Jesus was not based on the law, God promised that He would graft the Jews one day back again into their own olive tree. The Gentiles were grafted into the blessings of God. Gentiles *never* replace Jews for the natural branches of the olive tree were the Jews. Although they rejected Jesus, they were never rejected back. God's gifts and blessings for the Jews were without repentance, meaning that it will never be rescinded or revoked. However, both Gentiles and Jews can be **cut off** from the fatness or blessings (not salvation) of God if they branch away from the root, who is always Jesus.

While the Jews were never rejected, they were displaced. We saw a shadow of this back in *Genesis 48:13-14* and *18-20, And Joseph took them both, Ephraim in his right hand toward Israel's left hand, and Manasseh in his left hand toward Israel's right hand, and brought them near unto him. And Israel stretched out his right hand, and laid it upon Ephraim's head, who was the younger, and his left hand upon Manasseh's head, guiding his hands wittingly; for Manasseh was the firstborn. And Joseph said unto his father, Not so, my father: for this is the firstborn; put thy right hand upon his head. And his father refused, and said, I know it, my son, I know it: he also shall become a people, and he also shall be great: but truly his younger brother shall be greater than he, and his seed shall become a multitude of nations.*

Joseph brought out his two sons for his father, Jacob (also known as Israel) to bless. Manasseh, the older, was before Jacob's right hand and was to receive the greater blessing. Manasseh, symbolizing the Jews, was supposed to receive the greater or the first born blessing. The first born blessing was a double portion blessing! *Deuteronomy 21:17* states, *for the firstborn, by giving him a double portion of all that he hath.* It did not matter from which wife or whether one is loved and the other not. The firstborn child has the right to a double portion.

Because the Jews rejected Jesus, as in *Isaiah 50:2, Wherefore, when I came, was there no man? when I called, was there none to answer?* they were displaced from their first born position! That is why Jacob crossed his hands as he stretched out his hands to bless his grandsons. Jacob's right hand reached for Ephraim's head instead. The younger grandson thus got the greater blessing! Here, Ephraim symbolized the Gentiles, the multitude of nations. **Jacob's inexplicable action of cross-ing his hands can now be easily understood. Because of the cross, the Gentiles received the greater blessing! Hence, the Gentiles became greater than the Jews. The Gentiles received the double portion blessing meant for the Jews!**

But for now, the Jews would be abased, as we see in *Luke 14:7-11, And he put forth a parable to those which were bidden, when he marked how they chose out the chief rooms; saying unto them, When thou art bidden of any man to a wedding, sit not down in the highest room; lest a more honourable man than thou be bidden of him; And he that bade thee and him come and say to thee, Give this man place; and thou begin with shame to take the lowest room. But when thou art bidden, go and sit down in the lowest room; that when he that bade thee cometh, he may say unto thee, Friend, go up higher: then shalt thou have worship in the presence of them that sit at meat with thee. For whosoever exalteth himself shall be abased; and he that humbleth himself shall be exalted.* The Host is Jesus Himself. Everyone had seats and everybody came by invitation. No presents or gifts were required. But when Jesus saw the Jews jostling to get the best seats, He commented that those who thought they deserved the best seats would be set aside for those who deserved less. In the end, the Gentiles whom the Jews thought were unworthy would occupy the best and highest seats, while the Jews would fill the lower benches. Jesus exalts, positions, and seats His guests the way He wants. By the position of their seats, the Gentiles would now point the Jews back to Jesus. This was of course untenable for the Jews as they believed that they and only they were chosen by God. The first remain the first. In the Jewish mind, God cannot displace them because of their ethnicity. They had a covenant with God. The Gentiles had none. But Jesus unequivocally challenged them and said in *Luke 19:10, For the Son of Man came to seek and to save the lost.* All were lost. Everyone. It included both Jews and Gentiles. They both needed the New Covenant of Grace!

Another depiction of this was in *Acts 20:7-12, Paul preached unto them, ready to depart on the morrow and continued his speech until midnight. And there were many lights in the upper chamber, where they were gathered together. And there sat in a window a certain young man named Eutychus, being fallen into a deep sleep: and as Paul was long preaching, he sunk down with sleep, and fell down from the third loft, and was taken up dead. And Paul went down, and fell on him, and embracing him said, Trouble not yourselves; for his life is in him. When he therefore was come up again, and had broken bread, and eaten, and talked a long while, even till break of day, so he departed. And they brought the young man alive, and were not a little comforted.*

Eutychus was a symbol of the Jews. He was a young Jew probably related to one of the seven men (Tychicus has the same meaning as Eutychus) who traveled with Paul through Macedonia and Greece and now were at Troas. There were many lights in this upper chamber reflecting the many lights in the upper room in Jerusalem. But Eutychus ignored it all, sat precariously on the window, and fell into a deep sleep. Most Jews closed their eyes to Jesus after Pentecost, as explained in *Acts 28:27-28* states, *For the heart of this people is waxed gross, and their ears are dull of hearing, and their eyes have they closed; lest they should see with their eyes, and hear with their ears, and understand with their heart, and should be converted, and I should heal them. Be it known therefore unto you, that the salvation of God is sent unto the Gentiles, and that they will hear it.* Then Eutychus fell from the third floor window. Initially, the Jews had a vantage position with a vantage view of God. But they fell into the darkness (rejected Jesus) and in their fall, light (accepted Jesus) came to the Gentiles.

We read in *Romans 11:8,11, (According as it is written, God hath given them the spirit of slumber, eyes that they should not see, and ears that they should not hear;) unto this day. I say then, Have they stumbled that they should fall? God forbid: but rather through their fall salvation is come unto the Gentiles, for to provoke them to jealousy.*

But that was not the end of the story. Luke the doctor who wrote *Acts* said that Eutychus died. But Paul went down and resurrected Eutychus dead body. Even though Eutychus was now resurrected, he was set aside while Paul continued his preaching and teaching of Grace. Similarly, the Jews would be set aside while the Gentiles continue to share, preach, teach and remember Jesus. The last would be first. But the Jews would be brought back to their fullness or 'first-ness' in Christ one day. They would be provoked when they see the many blessings of God on the Gentiles. The Jews fell, died, but will be resurrected. Their casting away was for the reconciling of the world. This would last for a season. Then the Jews would be brought back again, from death into life, with Jesus. Because of the Abrahamic covenant, all Jews are beloved to God even though many of them consider the gospel of Jesus to be their enemy. **The blindness of the Jews will last for a season until the fullness of the Gentiles, meaning salvation of the Gentiles be complete. Then the Jews will be grafted back into their rightful place in the tree.**

Let us read from *Luke 19:12-26, He said therefore, A certain nobleman went into a far country to receive for himself a kingdom, and to return. And he called his ten servants, and delivered them ten pounds, and said unto them, Occupy till I come. But his citizens hated him, and sent a message after him, saying, We will not have this man to reign over us. And it came to pass, that when he was returned, having received the kingdom, then he commanded these servants to be called unto him, to whom he had given the money, that he might know how much every man had gained by trading. Then came the first, saying, Lord, thy pound hath gained ten pounds. And he said unto him, Well, thou good*

servant: because thou hast been faithful in a very little, have thou
authority over ten cities. And the second came, saying, Lord, thy
pound hath gained five pounds. And he said likewise to him, Be
thou also over five cities. And another came, saying, Lord, behold,
here is thy pound, which I have kept laid up in a napkin: For I
feared thee, because thou art an austere man: thou takest up that
thou layedst not down, and reapest that thou didst not sow. And he
saith unto him, Out of thine own mouth will I judge thee, thou
wicked servant...Wherefore then gavest not thou my money into the
bank, that at my coming I might have required mine own with
usury? And he said unto them that stood by, Take from him the
pound, and give it to him that hath ten pounds...For I say unto you,
That unto every one which hath shall be given; and from him that
hath not, even that he hath shall be taken away from him.

At first glance, this simple parable reeks simply of work
and productivity. Each servant of the Lord had been given one
pound for investment purposes. When the Lord returned, one of the
good servants had multiplied what he originally had ten times over.
He now had ten pounds. Another managed to leverage one pound
into five. Then came a lazy servant who had not done anything
productive with what he had been given. He had not even invested
his one pound so as to earn some interest. The ones who had been
responsible and had worked hard were commended, told that they
were good and faithful, and finally rewarded exponentially. The
good servant who had ten pounds was rewarded with authority
over ten cities, the one with five over five cities. However, the lazy
servant was chastised by His master and called wicked and lazy.
His one pound was forcefully taken from him and given to the one
who had ten!

We see the same parable in *Matthew 25:14-30*. Here, we
gain further insight into the plight of the lazy servant. We read In
verse 30, And cast ye the unprofitable servant into outer darkness:
there shall be weeping and gnashing of teeth. Hence, the moral of
this parable from a 'works' perspective is to be faithful and to
multiply our God-given talents; reproduce diligently; grow and
enlarge our empires. God loves and rewards all those who are
accountable, responsible, faithful, and investment savvy! We

should all be good managers of God's money, talents, skills, and gifts because that is His expectation. Our performance and achievement matters very much. Woe to anyone who fails to multiply what God has given to them! At the end, God rewards those who are deserving while He casts away and punishes those who are undeserving.

However, this parable was actually written for the Jews going through the Tribulation. We know that the dual fulfillment prophecy of *Matthew 24* dealt with the desolation of Jerusalem in AD70 and again during the Tribulation. Jesus is the nobleman who went abroad to receive His kingdom from His Father. He would be returning again to reign in His kingdom after the Tribulation. However, during the Tribulation, Jews as symbolized by the number ten, would be called to evangelize not only other Jews but Gentiles as well. They would be given Grace yet again. The difference this time is that many Jews would accept the free gift! Eutychus symbolized these Jews who were once dead but would now accept Jesus and rise again!

We read in *Romans 1:16, For I am not ashamed of the gospel of Christ: for it is the power of God unto salvation to everyone that believeth; to the Jew first, and also to the Greek.* Jesus, the dynamic *dunamis* power of God, was given to the Jewish nation first. This is what we call covenantal priority. *Romans 15:8* states, *Now I say that Jesus Christ was a minister of the circumcision for the truth of God, to confirm the promises made unto the fathers:* Jesus was a minister to the circumcision or the Jews. God promised Jesus to Abraham and God kept His promise. Jesus was the promised 'Seed' and 'King' to Abraham. If the Jews had accepted Jesus then, they would have become the most blessed and favored nation in the world. Eutychus meant fortunate. God's original plan was for the Jews to be so fortunate, so blessed, that they would be the fishbowl for all the Gentile nations.

Israel was to be a fishbowl nation so that all Gentile nations would see the blessedness of the Jews. The Gentiles would become jealous and turn to Jesus. The Jews were chosen for this. If they had accepted Jesus, there would have been no diseases, no hunger nor thirst, no pains, no defeats, no poverty, no wrongs, and no deaths. Only Jesus can annul sin and its effects. We read in *Matthew 11:5, The blind receive their sight, and the lame walk, the lepers are cleansed, and the deaf hear, the dead are raised up, and the poor have the gospel preached to them.* Jesus fulfilled *Isaiah 35:5-6, Then the eyes of the blind shall be opened, and the ears of the deaf shall be unstopped. Then shall the lame man leap as an hart, and the tongue of the dumb sing.* But they rejected Jesus, the nobleman, who would have provided all. Hence, the blessings which the Jews were to enjoy went to the Gentiles who would then provoke them back to Jesus, as Paul wrote in *Romans 10:19, 11:14, I will make you envious by those who are not a nation; I will make you angry by a nation that has no understanding… if somehow I may move my own people to jealousy and save some of them.* But they refused to be 'moved' as they continued to spurn and reject Jesus.

Sad to say, but the Jews would by and large only come back to Jesus during the worst suffering they and all humanity would ever see i.e. during the Tribulation. At the end of the Tribulation, Jesus will return to rule His kingdom, This parable gives us insight as to what the Jews would be doing during the Tribulation. Jesus asked the first two Jewish servants (the two witnesses in *Revelation*?) what they had done with their free gift of Grace. One servant replied that his 'pound' had gained ten pounds. Note that it was not his work but his pound that had worked. The first servant shared Jesus during the Tribulation which resulted in ten other Jews coming to know Jesus. The second with five. And so on. Jesus defined good and faithful servants as those who received Grace then shared it with others. Just as before the Tribulation, the gospel of Christ is the power of God unto salvation! The power is in Jesus Himself. Never in us. Neither in the Jews. We cannot add anything to God's power. We redeem none. Only the finished work of Jesus redeemed and multiplied.

However, a self-righteous servant came up before Jesus. He thought God was like him, as in *Psalm 50:21, you thought I was just like you.* As he had not worked for the free gift, he returned it. "Lord, behold, here is your pound back". He did not see the value in the gift. Just as Adam was afraid and wrapped himself with fig leaves, this servant was afraid and wrapped Grace in a piece of cloth. When Jesus was born he was wrapped in linen signifying His death. But when He was resurrected, He left the napkin that covered His face and the linen that wrapped His body back in the tomb. Unlike the law which wore a veil, Jesus wants to be fully revealed.

Because the servant was of the law, he claimed that Jesus reaped where He had not sown and took what He had not laid down. In his law soaked mind, Jesus was unworthy to collect the harvest as He had not worked for it. He could not see that Jesus had sown and had laid down His life even before creation. *John 4:37-38 states, And herein is that saying true, One soweth, and another reapeth. I sent you to reap that whereon ye bestowed no labour: other men laboured, and ye are entered into their labours.* The One who sowed first was Jesus. Grace always supplied first. Jesus labored and we reaped the benefits of His labor. The self-righteous fearful servant rejected Jesus. Hence, the benefits of Grace was 'taken away from him'. Only after he had rejected Grace were the benefits passed on to others who received it with great joy. Those who have Grace will be supplied with even more. Grace upon Grace. Those who reject Grace would be thrown out into the darkness where they would weep and gnash their teeth. We can now understand *Matthew 24:39-41, until the flood came, and took them all away...two be in the field...Two women shall be grinding at the mill; the one shall be taken, and the other left.* Those taken would weep with frustration, not remorse. They would gnash their teeth with anger, not pain. They thought their self-righteous works were sufficient but it was not.

A crucial exchange took place that has often been missed. The nobleman, Jesus, inquired of the servant as to why he had not put the pound into the bank and hence, minimally, the pound would have earned some interest. But charging interest or usury on loans to a brother Jew is prohibited under the law. We read in *Deuteronomy 23:19-20, Thou shalt not lend upon usury to thy brother; usury of money...Unto a stranger thou mayest lend upon usury; but unto thy brother thou shalt not lend upon usury.* However, it is permissible to charge interest to non-Jews! The pound was to be used and to be multiplied until it reached the Gentiles! In a sense, Jesus asked the Jews to invest in Gentile 'banks' during the Tribulation. Their interest would be Gentile believers. Jesus confirmed this in *Isaiah 42:6, give thee for a covenant of the people, for a light of the Gentiles.* The rewards for the Jewish servants who shared Jesus, were many cities full of Gentiles! Rewards in heaven usually refer to people. The Gentiles, together with the Jews, would be co-heirs to all the blessings of God because of Jesus. They would reign together. *Galatians 3:26-27* states, *For ye are all the children of God by faith in Christ Jesus. For as many of you as have been baptized into Christ have put on Christ. There is neither Jew nor Greek...for ye are all one in Christ Jesus.* Just as before the Tribulation, Gentiles will be one family with the Jews.

It is not that Jews have never shared the gospel with Gentiles before. We read in *Matthew 12:38-42, The men of Nineveh shall rise in judgment with this generation, and shall condemn it: because they repented at the preaching of Jonas; and, behold, a greater than Jonas is here. The queen of the south shall rise up in the judgment with this generation, and shall condemn it: for she came from the uttermost parts of the earth to hear the wisdom of Solomon; and, behold, a greater than Solomon is here.* Jonah (or Jonas) went to the Ninevites, who were Gentiles, and they repented and believed. The queen of the south, a Gentile by the name of Sheba, came to believe in God after hearing about Him from Solomon. Hence, whole Gentile cities and kingdoms came to believe in God because the Jews shared Grace. Jesus is much greater than either Jonah or Solomon . Only Jesus as Grace is to be shared to the uttermost parts of the earth. In fact, many Jewish priests shared Jesus too as we read *Acts 6:7, So the word of God spread. The number of disciples in Jerusalem increased rapidly, and a large number of priests became obedient to the faith.*

Ephesians 2:11-22 states, *Wherefore remember, that ye being in time past Gentiles in the flesh, who are called Uncircumcision by that which is called the Circumcision in the flesh made by hands; That at that time ye were without Christ,*

being aliens from the commonwealth of Israel, and strangers from
the covenants of promise, having no hope, and without God in the
world: But now in Christ Jesus ye who sometimes were far off are
made nigh by the blood of Christ. For he is our peace, who hath
made both one, and hath broken down the middle wall of partition
between us... And that he might reconcile both unto God in one
body by the cross...Now therefore ye are no more strangers and
foreigners, but fellowcitizens with the saints, and of the household
of God; And are built upon the foundation of the apostles and
prophets, Jesus Christ himself being the chief corner stone; In
whom all the building fitly framed together groweth unto an holy
temple in the Lord.

Gentiles were once aliens, strangers, and without hope.
They were the 'far off' ones, having no covenant with God. The
Jews had a covenant, a rulebook, which would point them to Jesus.
But they fell in love with the rulebook instead. Only Jesus could
remove the partition, the fence, the boundary, the label, between
Jews and Gentiles. He reconciled both unto God with His blood on
the cross. **The blood line of Jesus washed away the color line.**
Jews and Gentiles, circumcised and uncircumcised,
serpents/vipers and dogs, became one. We are fellowcitizens,
the fitly framed building that is the holy temple of God, built
together upon the same foundation - Jesus Himself!

The rewards for sharing Grace are always people. Jesus
told Peter in *Mark 10:29-30, There is no man that hath left house,*
or brethren, or sisters, or father, or mother, or wife, or children, or
lands, for my sake, and the gospel's, But he shall receive an
hundredfold now in this time, houses, and brethren, and sisters,
and mothers, and children, and lands, with persecutions; and in
the world to come eternal life. The reward in sharing Grace would
be a hundredfold of brothers, sisters, mothers, and children. Note
that those who left wives for long periods of time while
ministering the gospel do not get rewarded with a hundred wives!
Similarly with fathers. There is only one Father and He is more
than sufficient for us - disciples who gloriously wear the name
'Nazarene' and 'Christian'.

❧ 19 ❧

JESUS, JEWS, AND GENTILES part 2

We receive everything by unmerited Grace. We read in *Matthew 20:1-14, For the kingdom of heaven is like unto a man that is an householder, which went out early in the morning to hire labourers into his vineyard. And when he had agreed with the labourers for a penny a day, he sent them into his vineyard. And he went out about the third hour, and saw others standing idle in the marketplace, And said unto them; Go ye also into the vineyard, and whatsoever is right I will give you. And they went their way. Again he went out about the sixth and ninth hour, and did likewise. And about the eleventh hour he went out, and found others standing idle, and saith unto them, Why stand ye here all the day idle? They say unto him, Because no man hath hired us. He saith unto them, Go ye also into the vineyard; and whatsoever is right, that shall ye receive. So when even was come, the lord of the vineyard saith unto his steward, Call the labourers, and give them their hire, beginning from the last unto the first. And when they came that were hired about the eleventh hour, they received every man a penny. But when the first came, they supposed that they should have received more; and they likewise received every man a penny. And when they had received it, they murmured against the goodman of the house, Saying, These last have wrought but one hour, and thou hast made them equal unto us, which have borne the burden and heat of the day. But he answered one of them, and said, Friend, I do thee no wrong: didst not thou agree with me for a penny? Take that thine is, and go thy way: I will give unto this last, even as unto thee.*

Here, Jesus was answering a question posed by Peter at the end of *Matthew19, See, we have left all and followed You. Therefore what shall we have?* This parable is about God blessing us based upon His riches and grace, not on our hard work. Otherwise we would say that we had earned it. God is the Goodman of the house and He has invited all of us into His vineyard so we can become attached to His Vine, Jesus. The times mentioned; the early morning, the third, sixth, ninth, and eleventh hour all corresponded to the day when Jesus was crucified. It began when He was delivered to Pilate early in the morning and it ended when He was buried at the eleventh hour. Jesus was the only laborer in the vineyard. He did all the work. The Jews were invited in first, then the Gentiles. Everyone who is attached to the Vine, Jesus, is saved and blessed. But because of the Jewish attachment to the Mosaic law, the Gentiles have now become first. The last to come, the Gentiles, were the first to be paid. They received 'whatsoever is right' which is the righteousness of Jesus.

The first who came, the Jews, who bore the burden and heat, were now the last to be paid. They received 'what they had agreed' as their blessings came from the law. By the law, they 'supposed that they should have received more' so they murmured. They like Peter, brought up their long list of works. So Jesus gently reminded them that while blessings could be earned by the law, salvation was only through Him! Salvation is not a business transaction nor a business partnership. For He did all the work of salvation. Hence, Jesus would treat Jews and Gentiles as equals. Later in *Matthew 13:52* we read, *Then said he unto them, Therefore every scribe which is instructed unto the kingdom of heaven is like unto a man that is an householder, which bringeth forth out of his treasure things new and old.* The Goodman of the house or householder, sees us all as treasures, both new and old; Gentiles and Jews; last and first. We are His, no matter when or how Jesus came to us and called us into His vineyard. It is all Grace, never works.

This demarcation between Jews and Gentiles is carried on into *Matthew 21:33-44, Hear another parable: There was a certain householder, which planted a vineyard, and hedged it round about, and digged a winepress in it, and built a tower, and let it out to husbandmen, and went into a far country: And when the time of the fruit drew near, he sent his servants to the husbandmen, that they might receive the fruits of it. And the husbandmen took his servants, and beat one, and killed another, and stoned another. Again, he sent other servants more than the first: and they did unto them likewise. But last of all he sent unto them his son, saying, They will reverence my son. But when the husbandmen saw the son, they said among themselves, This is the heir; come, let us kill him, and let us seize on his inheritance. And they caught him, and cast him out of the vineyard, and slew him. When the lord therefore of the vineyard cometh, what will he do unto those husbandmen? They say unto him, He will miserably destroy those wicked men, and will let out his vineyard unto other husbandmen, which shall render him the fruits in their seasons. Jesus saith unto them, Did ye never read in the scriptures, The stone which the builders rejected, the same is become the head of the corner: this is the Lord's doing, and it is marvellous in our eyes? Therefore say I unto you, The kingdom of God shall be taken from you, and given to a nation bringing forth the fruits thereof. And whosoever shall fall on this stone shall be broken: but on whomsoever it shall fall, it will grind him to powder.*

The vineyard belongs to God as all the land belongs to Him, as in *Leviticus 25:23, for the land is mine.* In fact, in *Psalm 24:1, A Psalm of David. The earth is the LORD'S, and the fulness thereof; the world, and they that dwell therein.* The first cultivators or husbandmen of this particular land were the Jews. They rejected His prophets and killed His Son, Jesus. And cast Him out of the vineyard or outside the walls of Jerusalem. Because of their rejection of the Son of God, their vineyard would be handed over to new husbandmen, the Gentiles. Just as there were two groups of husbandmen, there were two sets of stones. Each group had their own 'stone'. The Jews cherished the law of stone. By their own walk, they tripped and fell on the stony law which broke them.

Meanwhile, another stone fell on the Gentiles. This stone was Jesus. Jesus is the brilliant bright white stone in *Revelation 2:17, I will give him a white stone, and a new name written on the stone which no one knows except the one who receives it.* Jesus' name is on the stone and we who believed in Him see His name in the stone. This stone grinded all into powder before re-making them into His image. He would work through them to produce abundant fruit blessings from His vineyard.

However, the veil of the stony law masked Jesus. As such, the Jews could not see Jesus. When Jesus walked among them, they rejected Him. Even after He was resurrected, they rejected Him. When Peter preached to them, they rejected Him by and large. Then when Paul went to the Jewish diaspora in Rome, to persuade them with the same message of Jesus, they rejected Him yet again. *Acts 28:22-24* states, *But we desire to hear of thee what thou thinkest: for as concerning this sect, we know that every where it is spoken against. And when they had appointed him a day, there came many to him into his lodging; to whom he expounded and testified the kingdom of God, persuading them concerning Jesus, both out of the law of Moses, and out of the prophets, from morning till evening. And some believed the things which were spoken, and some believed not.* The Jewish leaders of the diaspora called believers of Jesus a sect! They spoke against these believers everywhere they were. So after they listened to Paul, they argued among themselves. Some believed and some did not. At the end, they decided to reject Jesus. We learned of this in *Acts 28:27, For the heart of this people is waxed gross, and their ears are dull of hearing, and their eyes have they closed; lest they should see with their eyes, and hear with their ears, and understand with their heart, and should be converted.*

Till this present day, most Jews continue to reject Jesus. Meanwhile, the Gentiles came to Jesus in droves. We read this first in *Acts 13:42-44, And when the Jews were gone out of the synagogue, the Gentiles besought that these words might be preached to them the next sabbath. Now when the congregation was broken up, many of the Jews and religious proselytes followed Paul and Barnabas: who, speaking to them, persuaded them to* continue in the grace of God. And the next sabbath day came almost the whole city together to hear the word of God. The Gentiles besought the message of Jesus as Grace. Jesus was such good news that whole Gentile cities besought Jesus! In *Acts 28*, just before Rome, Paul was shipwrecked on Malta or Melita meaning honey, where the Gentile inhabitants welcomed the sweet message of Jesus! For three months, the island dripped with Grace honey. Many became saved and healed. What a sweet time they had before sending Paul on his way again.

We foresaw this back in *Matthew 22:1-14, And Jesus answered and spake unto them again by parables, and said, The kingdom of heaven is like unto a certain king, which made a marriage for his son, And sent forth his servants to call them that were bidden to the wedding: and they would not come. Again, he sent forth other servants, saying, Tell them which are bidden, Behold, I have prepared my dinner: my oxen and my fatlings are killed, and all things are ready: come unto the marriage. But they made light of it, and went their ways, one to his farm, another to his merchandise: And the remnant took his servants, and entreated them spitefully, and slew them. But when the king heard thereof, he was wroth: and he sent forth his armies, and destroyed those murderers, and burned up their city. Then saith he to his servants, The wedding is ready, but they which were bidden were not worthy. Go ye therefore into the highways, and as many as ye shall find, bid to the marriage. So those servants went out into the highways, and gathered together all as many as they found, both bad and good: and the wedding was furnished with guests. And when the king came in to see the guests, he saw there a man which had not on a wedding garment: And he saith unto him, Friend, how camest thou in hither not having a wedding garment? And he was speechless. Then said the king to the servants, Bind him hand and foot, and take him away, and cast him into outer darkness; there shall be weeping and gnashing of teeth. For many are called, but few are chosen.*

The king's son is Jesus. All Jews were invited to the wedding. They did not have to do a single thing or work. Everything that needed to be done was done. They just had to come. But Jesus was repudiated and spurned by His own people. The Gentiles were then grafted in by Grace. Just like the Jews, they did not have to do a single work to merit their invitation. All people, bad and good, were invited. The only requirement was that they had to have a wedding garment called Jesus. Without Jesus, the 'good' cannot be a guest. As stated before, those who thought they could get in by their works were left speechless as they weep with anger. But with Jesus, even the 'bad' are guests.

Luke 4:22,24-27 states, *And they said, Is not this Joseph's son? And he said, Verily I say unto you, No prophet is accepted in his own country. But I tell you of a truth, many widows were in Israel in the days of Elias, when the heaven was shut up three years and six months, when great famine was throughout all the land; But unto none of them was Elias sent, save unto Sarepta, a city of Sidon, unto a woman that was a widow. And many lepers were in Israel in the time of Eliseus the prophet; and none of them was cleansed, saving Naaman the Syrian. And all they in the synagogue, when they heard these things, were filled with wrath.*

When the people asked in amazement, "Is not this Joseph's son?", we automatically assume that the people were speaking about Joseph the carpenter. But Jesus' answer seems to indicate otherwise. Jesus told the people that a prophet is not accepted in his own country. That is why Elijah went to the widow in Sarepta/Zarephath and Elisha went to Naaman the Syrian. Both the widow and Naaman were Gentiles. When the Jews rejected Jesus, He went to the Gentiles, who became His bride. The widow symbolized the Gentiles who were not part of the Abrahamic covenant. Without God, the Gentiles would have nothing but Jesus came to them. He became a Husband to the widow. He even brought her dead son back to life in the upper room, a place symbolic of Jesus. That is why we are alive too.

On the subject of Joseph the carpenter, and Jesus being his son, we would assume that Jesus was probably skilled in carpentry too, So we would think that of His many parables, at least some would allude to carpentry. But there were none. This is because the carpenter in *Isaiah 44:9,15, graven image are all of them go(tohu)...he maketh a god, even his graven image: he falleth*

*down unto it, and worshippeth it, and prayeth unto it, and saith,
Deliver me; for thou art my god,* ended up worshipping his own
work! Our idols are formless *tohu* and void *bohu* just as the world
was before God spoke and created light. God creates. We make.
And carpentry is all about 'making' with our own hands while
Grace is all about 'receiving' from His hands what He created.

But there was another Joseph who was a prophet, who
dreamt and interpreted dreams. He was likewise rejected by his
brothers. He was then taken to Potiphar and ultimately, to Pharaoh.
Once again, both Potiphar and Pharaoh were Gentiles. This Joseph
rose to become the prime-minister of Egypt and saved all of Israel
from the famine. In a sense, all of Israel would die if not for
Joseph. *Psalm 77:15* states, *Thou hast with thine arm redeemed thy
people, the sons of Jacob and Joseph.* The sons of Joseph do not
refer only to his biological sons but to all of Israel sons. And of all
his 'sons', the greatest one had come! "Is not this Joseph's son,
Jesus?" the people asked. Indeed He was. The greatest Son had
come. The Jews believed that they were the only people who were
worthy of God's blessings. Definitely not the Gentiles. But Jesus'
arm would redeem ALL people, as in *Isaiah 52:10, The LORD
hath made bare his holy arm in the eyes of all the nations; and all
the ends of the earth shall see the salvation of our God.* Jesus'
response so infuriated the Jews that they caught Jesus and tried to
kill Him. But He escaped their grasp.

It is also interesting to note that just before Elijah went to
the widow, he was fed meat and bread by ravens. We read this in *1
Kings 17:5-6, for he went and dwelt by the brook Cherith, that is
before Jordan. And the ravens brought him bread and flesh in the
morning, and bread and flesh in the evening; and he drank of the
brook.* In the drought and famine, Elijah drank sweet living water
from the brook Cherith. Cherith was located east of the Jordan, the
boundary of the Israelite nation. Cherith means 'cutting off'.
Hence, Elijah was cut off from the Jews. For a short time, he was
drinking Grace and eating meat and bread fed to him by ravens.
Ravens are unclean birds for the Jews (*Leviticus 11:15*). They feed
on carrion or decaying flesh. But Grace makes the unclean clean

and the dead alive. Jesus was the Meat and Bread which sustained Elijah, day and night, while he was hiding from King Ahab.

Jesus actually spoke of this 'bread' in *Mark 8:17-21, Why reason ye, because ye have no bread? perceive ye not yet, neither understand? have ye your heart yet hardened? Having eyes, see ye not? and having ears, hear ye not? and do ye not remember? When I brake the five loaves among five thousand, how many baskets full of fragments took ye up? They say unto him, Twelve. And when the seven among four thousand, how many baskets full of fragments took ye up? And they said, Seven. And he said unto them, How is it that ye do not understand?*

When Jesus fed the five thousand there remained twelve baskets of leftovers. The word used for basket here is *'kophinous'* meaning a small basket. Jesus came for Israel first as symbolized by the twelve *kophinous* of leftovers. Also, the leftover bread was barley which was always the first harvest. But when Jesus fed the four thousand there were seven baskets left over. The word used for basket here is *'spyridas'* or large basket. This was the same type of basket that Paul hid in, and was lowered from the wall by the disciples, to escape the Jews who wanted to kill him in *Acts 9:25*. Following the small baskets would come large baskets of harvest. These would be the Gentiles. Paul in a Gentile basket would bring the Bread of Life to them! The number seven signified that Jesus' Gentile bride would be perfect as He would make them perfect. But whether Jews or Gentiles, Jesus would be broken and be fed to all. Jesus is always more than sufficient for all of us. Elijah first, then Elisha.

This was seen back in *2 Kings 4:42-44, And there came a man from Baal-shalisha, and brought the man of God bread of the firstfruits, twenty loaves of barley, and full ears of corn in the husk thereof. And he said, Give unto the people, that they may eat. And his servitor said, What, should I set this before an hundred men? He said again, Give the people, that they may eat: for thus saith the Lord, They shall eat, and shall leave thereof. So he set it before them, and they did eat, and left thereof, according to the word of the Lord.* In a time of famine, a man from the city of Baal-shalisha brought Elisha his firstfruits, consisting of twenty loaves of bread and some corn. This food was given to a hundred men to eat, yet there were plenty of leftovers. Jesus was the firstfruit offering and He is always greater than any famine, physical or spiritual.

The miracle of the loaves was meant to teach Jesus' disciples about Grace. We read this in *Mark 6:45-52, And straightway he constrained his disciples to get into the ship, and to go to the other side before unto Bethsaida, while he sent away the people. And when he had sent them away, he departed into a mountain to pray. And when even was come, the ship was in the midst of the sea, and he alone on the land. And he saw them toiling in rowing; for the wind was contrary unto them: and about the fourth watch of the night he cometh unto them, walking upon the sea, and would have passed by them. But when they saw him walking upon the sea, they supposed it had been a spirit, and cried out: For they all saw him, and were troubled. And immediately he talked with them, and saith unto them, Be of good cheer: it is I; be not afraid. And he went up unto them into the ship; and the wind ceased: and they were sore amazed in themselves beyond measure, and wondered. For they considered not the miracle of the loaves: for their heart was hardened* and the conclusion in *John 6:21, and immediately the ship was at the land whither they went.*

Jesus sent His disciples to Bethsaida but they decided to go toward Capernaum instead. After all they thought they knew better. We tend to think the same way as well. After many hours of toiling and rowing in their own self-works against the contrarian wind, they saw Jesus walking on the sea. They cried out with fear for they thought they had seen a spirit. They all knew Jesus, yet thought He was a spirit! This was because they were busy trying to save themselves. Their eyes were on themselves. They were troubled and afraid. Only after Jesus talked with them, and they willingly received Him, did He enter their boat. Otherwise, He would have passed them by. When Jesus entered the boat, the contrarian wind stopped and they were miraculously transported to their destination. Jesus then made a curious comment that they had not considered the miracle of the loaves.

The boat symbolized the Jewish nation or the church which had chosen to go its own way. Jesus is on the mountain praying for that church. For us. Without Jesus, the nation or church would be buffeted by the law. It would require them to push harder, row harder, and try harder. And there would be no guarantee of ever arriving. *Ephesians 4:14-15* states, *That we henceforth be no more children, tossed to and fro, and carried about with every wind of doctrine, by the sleight of men, and cunning craftiness, whereby they lie in wait to deceive.* The church had been tossed to and fro by the law for a long time. It had fallen for the sleight of men, who with crafty formulas, sold the church grace on credit. Buy now pay later. Now that you are in the boat, let me tell you the cost of staying in the boat. The people became like described in *Haggai 1:5-6, You have planted much, but harvested little. You eat, but never have enough. You drink, but never have your fill. You put on clothes, but are not warm. You earn wages, only to put them in a purse with holes in it.* No matter what we do to remain in the boat, it is never good enough!

Just like the disciples in the boat, many churches are so caught up with self-works that they do not realize that Jesus is no longer even in the church (boat)! Jesus has to stand at the door of the church and knock, as in *Revelation 3:20, Behold, I stand at the door, and knock: if any man hear my voice, and open the door, I will come in to him, and will sup with him, and he with me.* This verse is not for unbelievers but for the 'blind' church in Laodicea. In fact, many churches are indeed greatly afraid of Jesus. They do not want to hear His voice nor open the door for Him to come in. Because when Jesus comes into the boat, He will remove their oars, and bring them to His destination! All their years of hard work of bobbing and swirling around would then be for nothing! Just like the Israelites eddying around in the wilderness until He stepped into the Jordan and brought them safely to the other side.

The miracle of the loaves was Jesus Himself. The people were told to sit down and receive the loaves. Jesus is the Bread of Life. They were not to labor for it. *John 6:26-27* states, *Jesus answered them and said, Verily, verily, I say unto you, Ye seek me, not because ye saw the miracles, but because ye did eat of the* *loaves, and were filled. Labour not for the meat which perisheth, but for that meat which endureth unto everlasting life, which the Son of man shall give unto you: for him hath God the Father sealed.* The people in the desert near Bethsaida, the people in the city of Bethsaida, the people in Capernaum, and the people of Gennesaret where the boat eventually landed; they all needed the Bread of Life or the Meat which gives everlasting life. However, many of us tend to eat the wrong meat as described in *Exodus 22:31, neither shall ye eat any flesh that is torn of beasts in the field; ye shall cast it to the dogs.* Instead of eating Jesus, we eat torn works-based meat from satan! Jesus is the Meat and the Bread that we did not labor for but received by Grace!

As the Jews rejected Jesus, they inadvertently rejected unmerited protection. We all know that the Jewish city of Jerusalem and its temple fell to the Romans, who burned up their city in AD70. The fall of the Jewish nation was prophesied in *Isaiah 40:7-8, The grass withereth, the flower fadeth: because the spirit of the Lord bloweth upon it: surely the people is grass. The grass withereth, the flower fadeth: but the word of our God shall stand forever.* God loved the grass and the flowers. He adorned them richly even though He knew that they would wither and fade away quickly. How much more He loved His people and would bless them but the Jews continued to reject Jesus, and so they withered and faded away too. Only Jesus, the Word, stands forever. Jesus would be revealed as the Glory of the Lord and every Jew would see Him. This was symbolized beautifully in *2 Samuel 3:1, Now there was long war between the house of Saul and the house of David: but David waxed stronger and stronger, and the house of Saul waxed weaker and weaker.* Saul, representing the law, became weaker and weaker while David, representing Grace, became stronger and stronger. Then one day, Saul was replaced.

Let us invite Jesus as Grace in! Do not let Him pass by. Without Him, we will head in the wrong direction. End up at the wrong destination. But with Jesus, there will be rest from our own works and we will be transported immediately to the right destination. And what a destination it will be!

ༀ 20 ༀ

JESUS AND THE BRIDESMAIDS

Many people may not be familiar with the customs of a Jewish wedding. So let us go over some of the main points. First, a spouse has to be acquired. This comes in the form of a marriage contract (*ketubah*), where the redemptive price (*mohar*) for the bride is specified. The *ketubah* also spells out the husband's obligations to the wife. If the conditions are agreeable to the bride, they will drink a glass of wine together. They are now considered as betrothed. The bride would then take a *mikveh* or cleansing bath. Hence, the bride is consecrated or set apart for the groom. Even though the woman is now legally the wife of the man, this betrothal (*kiddushin*) period can be as long as 1-2 years. During this time, the marriage is not consummated (much like Joseph and Mary). Besides the redemptive price, the husband would supply the wife with many gifts (*mattan*) too. These gifts would remind her of his love for her.

Meanwhile, the bridegroom would go back to his father's house to build a wedding chamber (*chador*) on his father's property. The chamber must be fitting for the bride. The wedding chamber is only ready if and when the father approves of it. Nobody knows when this day will be, only the father. After a period of time, the approval will be granted. The bridegroom can now go and fetch his bride for the wedding ceremony (*nesu'in*). He approaches the bride's house like a thief in the night. As he nears the house, he will suddenly burst into shouting and blow his shofar. The bride, unaware of the date and hour, will quickly get herself ready to leave. The groom would then lift up his bride and go back to the wedding chamber where they would spend the next seven days, or bridal week, together. During this bridal week, a feast would be organized, not only to show his love, but where the bride would be introduced to all the guests. Exuberant music and dancing would ensue.

    We recognize that the steps in the Jewish wedding is highly symbolic. The spouse is us. We are chosen by Jesus to be His bride. We read in *2 Corinthians 11:2, For I am jealous over you with godly jealousy: for I have espoused you to one husband, that I may present you as a chaste virgin to Christ.* He paid the redemptive price for us. *1 Corinthians 6:20* states *For ye are bought with a price: therefore glorify God in your body, and in your spirit, which are God's.* We could not be bought with silver and gold as we were more precious than that. The price to buy us was Jesus Himself. *1 Peter 1:18-19, Forasmuch as ye know that ye were not redeemed with corruptible things, as silver and gold, from your vain conversation received by tradition from your fathers; But with the precious blood of Christ.* We see in *Isaiah 62:5, For as a young man marrieth a virgin, so shall thy sons marry thee: and as the bridegroom rejoiceth over the bride, so shall thy God rejoice over thee,* that Jesus is madly in love with us! He rejoices over us after paying the ultimate price for us.

    We, the bride, drank from His cup. *Matthew 26:27-28, And he took the cup, and gave thanks, and gave it to them, saying, Drink ye all of it; For this is my blood of the new testament, which is shed for many for the remission of sins.* The wine is symbolic of His blood. It is His blood that sealed the contract. We are now betrothed to Him. In *Hosea 2:19-20, And I will betroth thee unto me forever; yea, I will betroth thee unto me in righteousness, and in judgment, and in lovingkindness, and in mercies. I will even betroth thee unto me in faithfulness: and thou shalt know the Lord.* We now get baptized, both by water and by the Holy Spirit. Before Jesus goes away, He gives us many gifts by the Holy Spirit.

    Meanwhile Jesus, who came for us, goes back home to prepare a place for us. *John 14:2-3* states that *In My Father's house are many rooms; if that were not so, I would have told you, because I am going there to prepare a place for you. And if I go and prepare a place for you, I am coming again and will take you to Myself, so that where I am, there you also will be.* Jesus has prepared this place for us. Those who are already 'in Him' get to be 'with Him' forever. It is this place where He will receive us unto Himself, for where He is there we will be also, as in *Isaiah 26:19-20, Your dead will live; their bodies will rise. Awake and sing, you who dwell in the dust! Come, my people, enter your rooms and close your doors behind you.* We will sing with joy, for with Jesus there are pleasures forevermore. We may even find the rooms 'familiar' for Jesus will be there! There is no darkness behind the doors for Jesus is Light.

Only the Father knows the exact day when Jesus will come back again for His bride as in *Mark 13:32, But of that day and that hour knoweth no man, no, not the angels which are in heaven, neither the Son, but the Father.* As the Son of Man He did not know but as the Son of God, He knew perfectly. Jesus is our husband and He will come back for us. *Isaiah 54:5, For thy Maker is thine husband; the Lord of hosts is his name; and thy Redeemer the Holy One of Israel; The God of the whole earth shall he be called.* That day is described in *1 Thessalonians 4:16-17, For the Lord himself shall descend from heaven with a shout, with the voice of the archangel, and with the trump of God: and the dead in Christ shall rise first: Then we which are alive and remain shall be caught up (harpazó) together with them in the clouds, to meet the Lord in the air: and so shall we ever be with the Lord* and in *1 Corinthians 15:52-53, In a moment, in the twinkling of an eye, at the last trump: for the trumpet shall sound, and the dead shall be raised incorruptible, and we shall be changed.* This event, *harpazó*, is commonly called the rapture of the church or bride. With a loud shout and a trumpet blast, Jesus Himself comes to lift/take us away in the air/clouds. Jesus would probably shout what is written in *Revelation 11:12, And they heard a loud voice from heaven saying to them, **Come up (anabainó) here**.* Just as Zacchaeus *anabainó* the tree, we *anabainó* to heaven! After the rapture, there will be seven years of tribulation on earth. For believers, this period is bridal week with feasting in heaven.

Being now familiar with the Jewish wedding, we can better understand a well known parable found in *Matthew 25:1-13, Then shall the kingdom of heaven be likened unto ten virgins, which took their lamps, and went forth to meet the bridegroom. And five of them were wise, and five were foolish. They that were foolish took their lamps, and took no oil with them: But the wise took oil in their vessels with their lamps. While the bridegroom tarried, they all slumbered and slept. And at midnight there was a cry made, Behold, the bridegroom cometh; go ye out to meet him. Then all those virgins arose, and trimmed their lamps. And the foolish said unto the wise, Give us of your oil; for our lamps are gone out. But the wise answered, saying, Not so; lest there be not enough for us and you: but go ye rather to them that sell, and buy for yourselves. And while they went to buy, the bridegroom came; and they that were ready went in with him to the marriage: and the door was shut. Afterward came also the other virgins, saying, Lord, Lord, open to us. But he answered and said, Verily I say unto you, I know you not. Watch therefore, for ye know neither the day nor the hour wherein the Son of man cometh.*

The traditional explanation for this parable goes something like this. At the start, all the virgins or bridesmaids were saved. Oil represented the Holy Spirit and they all had it. As none of them knew when the groom would come back, they all waited eagerly. Much time passed and some of the bridesmaids began to get lazy. Their oil supply began to run out. When Jesus showed up unexpectedly, the wise and the ready still had oil left in their lamps. They ran out to meet Him and then joined Him in the marriage feast. Meantime, the foolish bridesmaids could not light their lamps as they had ran out of oil. They now had to go out and buy some more oil. Hence, they missed the wedding party as they were locked out. They were all invited but because of their unpreparedness, were ultimately left out. This meant that they lost their salvation due to their own negligence. A full fifty percent of all believers would lose their salvation as symbolized by the five foolish virgins. God is not mocked by people's laziness, so be very vigilant for nobody knows when Jesus will come back again.

However, the explanation does not explain the fact that all the bridesmaids, not some, slumbered and slept. None were more watchful than the others. Also, a believer cannot have more or less of the Holy Spirit. The Holy Spirit is a Person of the Trinity, also called the Spirit of Christ, and cannot be divided up. He is not like water which can be divided and can exist only as a solid, liquid, or gas at any time. God is one, existing as three, at the same time! Either one has Him or one does not have Him. We cannot leak the Holy Spirit. He is not an inflatable doll inside of us with a small puncture. The Holy Spirit cannot be 'not enough for us' as He is, like Jesus, always more than enough for us. The foolish bridesmaids were told to go out and buy some more oil or Holy Spirit. If we can buy the Holy Spirit, then He cannot be a free gift. But the chief weakness of this 'self-works' explanation is that Jesus came back for His bride, not the bridesmaids!

The book of Matthew was written for the Jews. In fact, Jesus specifically prohibited His disciples to share with the Gentiles! We read this in *Matthew 10:5-6, These twelve Jesus sent forth, and commanded them, saying, Go not into the way of the Gentiles, and into any city of the Samaritans enter ye not: But go rather to the lost sheep of the house of Israel.* The Jews had covenantal priority, as we know from *Romans 1:16, For I am not ashamed of the gospel of Christ: for it is the power of God unto salvation to everyone that believeth; to the Jew first, and also to the Greek.* It was to the Jew 'first' that Salvation came, not only in time but in priority. The Jews saw Him. Salvation came to them. Jesus was one of them. But they rejected Him. They were ashamed of Him! *John 1:11-12,* stated that *He came unto his own, and his own received him not. But as many as received him, to them gave he power to become the sons of God, even to them that believe on his name.* Jesus subsequently left with his bride.

The bridesmaids of *Matthew 25* were those Jews who rejected Jesus. There were ten virgins (*parthenos*, in Greek), the number ten reminding us that they followed the Mosaic law. These unbelieving Jews are described here as those who slumbered. *Romans 11:8* states, *(According as it is written, God hath given them the spirit of slumber, eyes that they should not see, and ears that they should not hear;) unto this day.* They were left behind at the rapture, but during the ensuing seven year tribulation period, many of them would come to know Jesus, signified by the oil. In *Revelation*, the bridesmaids were described with the same word, *parthenos* (virgins). We read in *Revelation 14:1,4, And I looked, and, lo, a Lamb stood on the mount Sion, and with him an hundred forty and four thousand, having his Father's name written in their foreheads. These are they which were not defiled with women; for they are virgins.* There were 144,000 of them, from all the tribes of Israel (except Dan and Ephraim), witnessing for Christ during that time. However, only five of the ten had the Holy Spirit in them. Five always stands for Grace in the bible. These tribulation saints were still saved by Grace, not works. The five virgins without oil were false believers. They did not lose their salvation. Note that all their lamps lighted at the start but five of the lamps burnt out. All of the lamps had oil in their wicks but only five had oil in the vessel. They looked the same from the outside but only those who had Jesus entered in. This was prophesied back in *Daniel 12:2-3, And many of those who sleep in the dust of the ground will awake, these to everlasting life, but the others to disgrace and everlasting contempt. And those who have insight will shine like the glow of the expanse of heaven, and those who lead the many to righteousness, like the stars forever and ever.* Daniel's vision was for his people, the Jews. At the end of the tribulation, not all Jews would awake or be resurrected to life. But those who do are likened to shining stars.

The vendors who purport to sell the Holy Spirit are the law keepers who deny the Lord Jesus. They make merchandise of the people and they are known as false prophets and false teachers. They pervert the way of truth which is Jesus and only Jesus. They teach people to slumber but their damnation slumbereth not. We read this in *2 Peter 2:1-3, But there were false prophets also among the people, even as there shall be false teachers among you, who privily shall bring in damnable heresies, even denying the Lord that bought them, and bring upon themselves swift destruction. And many shall follow their pernicious ways; by reason of whom the way of truth shall be evil spoken of. And through covetousness shall they with feigned words make merchandise of you: whose judgment now of a long time lingereth not, and their damnation slumbereth not.* Despite unspeakable horrors and persecutions during the Tribulation, as many as fifty percent of all Jews would remain blind to Jesus! Why is that so?

The answer is found in *2 Thessalonians 2:7-8, For the mystery of iniquity doth already work: only he who now letteth will let, until he be taken out of the way. And then shall that Wicked be revealed, whom the Lord shall consume with the spirit of his mouth, and shall destroy with the brightness of his coming:* The Holy Spirit is not taken away during the Tribulation. He still points to Jesus as the only way. But His work in restraining the wicked one or satan is taken out of the way. An unrestrained satan will bring unimaginable ruin, havoc, and death upon the world.

But because of the Abrahamic covenant, all Jews can rest in the prophecy of *Isaiah 62:1-5, For Zion's sake will I not hold my peace, and for Jerusalem's sake I will not rest, until the righteousness thereof go forth as brightness, and the salvation thereof as a lamp that burneth. And the Gentiles shall see thy righteousness, and all kings thy glory: and thou shalt be called by a new name, which the mouth of the Lord shall name. Thou shalt also be a crown of glory in the hand of the Lord, and a royal diadem in the hand of thy God. Thou shalt no more be termed Forsaken; neither shall thy land any more be termed Desolate: but thou shalt be called Hephzi-bah, and thy land Beulah: for the Lord delighteth in thee, and thy land shall be married...and as the bridegroom rejoiceth over the bride, so shall thy God rejoice over thee.* Jerusalem, a symbol for all Jews, will be restored in righteousness and glory. Jesus who is in *Isaiah 28:5, In that day the LORD of hosts will be a crown of glory, and a diadem of beauty,* will give His crown of glory and His royal diadem (jeweled headdress) to His people. They will no longer be called Forsaken nor Desolate but Delight (*Hephzi-bah*) and Married (*Beulah*). They would realize their sin of rejecting Jesus, as prophesied in *Zechariah 12:10, And I will pour upon the house of David, and upon the inhabitants of Jerusalem, the spirit of grace and of supplications: and they shall look upon me whom they have pierced.* They would look and recognize that Jesus' blood as the Fountain that had always been available for them since *Zechariah 13:1, In that day* (Jesus crucified) *there shall be a fountain opened to the house of David and to the inhabitants of Jerusalem for sin and for uncleanness.* One day, God will delight that the Jews will also be married to Jesus. Jesus is still their only hope for salvation.

It is incontrovertible that there will come a day when the Jews would acknowledge Jesus as Savior. We see this in *Jeremiah 31:31-34, Behold, the days come, saith the Lord, that I will make a new covenant with the house of Israel, and with the house of Judah... But this shall be the covenant that I will make with the house of Israel; After those days, saith the Lord, I will put my law in their inward parts, and write it in their hearts; and will be their God, and they shall be my people. And they shall teach no more every man his neighbour, and every man his brother, saying, Know the LORD: for they shall all know me... I will forgive their iniquity, and I will remember their sin no more.* The Mosaic law which they asked for and received, would be no more. In its place, a new law written in their hearts (not on stone). They will know Jesus as the Son of God as well. 'Know' means 'to be in union with'. Once again, God will be their God and they will be His people but this time through union with Jesus. And only because of Jesus, their sins would be remembered no more.

It is interesting to note that God the Father told the same thing to His Son, Jesus, in *Psalm 102:25-28, In the beginning you laid the foundations of the earth, and the heavens are the work of your hands. They will perish, but you remain; they will all wear out like a garment. Like clothing you will change them and they will be discarded. But you remain the same, and your years will never end. The children of your servants will live in your presence; their descendants will be established before you.* Jesus by whom all things were made would become the perfect Sacrifice. He would die young but His life would never end. Even the earth and the heavens will perish, but by Jesus' sacrifice, all of God's children, and their children; Jews and Gentiles; bridesmaids and the bride; all believers would be alive forever and live with Jesus in His presence and be established before Him!

❧ 21 ❧

JESUS AND A GOOD WHIPPING

The Olympic motto is made up of three Latin words, namely: *Citius, Altius*, and *Fortius*. In English, it means Faster, Higher, and Stronger. While excellent for competitive sports, this motto has somehow leapt its way into the church and turned the Gospel into a performance race for the best and the fittest. If you are not the best then you must be a loser!

We read in *1 Corinthians 9:24-26, Know ye not that they which run in a race run all, but one receiveth the prize? So run, that ye may obtain. And every man that striveth for the mastery is temperate in all things. Now they do it to obtain a corruptible crown; but we an incorruptible. I therefore so run, not as uncertainly; so fight I, not as one that beateth the air.* From a sportive perspective, the interpretation is as follows. Paul is saying that we are all in a race but only one of us will receive the prize. So train up your body and bring it into subjection. Work out, keep fit, have a disciplined lifestyle, get that lazy body pumping out, do your spiritual exercise drills, and educate your mind to have a winning attitude. On race day, run as fast as you can to beat all your competitors. You and you alone will win the prize! Your prize will be crowns in heaven. All those who did not win are castaways, has-beens, and wannabes. They are good for nothing but to be cast away and thrown into hell. What good is a silver medalist? Who remembers the second place finisher?

Based on this interpretation, many preachers mistakenly try to help their congregants by giving them long lists of self-improvement works. If they improve themselves, then the assumption is that they will become better Christian athletes. Fix up your life, try harder, do not give up, get up, get up again, suck it up, rededicate, recommit, do more, do better, achieve! Only you can control and be in charge of your destiny! So we charge ahead and fix ourselves, fix our families, our health, our workplaces, our communities, our politics, our planet. We will see to it that justice is done. An eye for an eye. We will eradicate world hunger, viruses, and human trafficking. We will be accountable, disciplined, promise keepers. We will dig deep down into ourselves, earn our stripes, become holy. But eventually, we will encounter situations that make it impossible for us to continue on. At that point, because it is beyond our power, and we are exhausted, we quit. We quit on ourselves and we quit on God. We are just not good enough. We do not realize that what we fought so hard to attain was already attained for us by the finished work of Jesus. The key is to be found in *verse 26* where Paul says that he does not run with uncertainty. He does not beat the air with futility. **He is certain of his prize because Jesus entered the race, won the race, and procured him the prize. He does not run to obtain the prize. He received the prize *before* he began the race. He was a Promise Receiver. That is why he ran the race.**

We see this clearly in *Philippians 3:13-16, Brethren, I count not myself to have apprehended: but this one thing I do, forgetting those things which are behind, and reaching forth unto those things which are before, I press toward the mark for the prize of the high calling of God in Christ Jesus. Let us therefore, as many as be perfect, be thus minded: and if in anything ye be otherwise minded, God shall reveal even this unto you. Nevertheless, whereto we have already attained, let us walk by the same rule, let us mind the same thing.* Paul stated clearly that he had already attained the prize which is Jesus. And that is also why he can press toward the mark and to reach forward continuously. If we forget that we already have the prize (other-minded), the Holy Spirit will remind us of our righteousness in Christ so that we will be like-minded again. The Holy Spirit reminds us all of the same thing - that Jesus entered and finished the race and won the crown for us. We do not start the race to gain victory. We start the race from victory.

We read in *Acts 20:24, But none of these things move me, neither count I my life dear unto myself, so that I might finish my course with joy, and the ministry, which I have received of the Lord Jesus, to testify the gospel of the grace of God.* Paul partakes in the race to preach the gospel of Grace because of the incorruptible prize given freely to him, who is Jesus Himself. Jesus won the race for us and presented us with Himself! So because we have the prize, we now can go out and run the race too. We too can share Grace! *Hebrews 12:1-2* states, *Wherefore seeing we also are compassed about with so **great a cloud** of witnesses, let us lay aside every weight, and the sin which doth so easily beset us, and let us run with patience the race that is set before us, Looking unto Jesus the author and finisher of our faith.* Both great (*tosoutos*) and cloud (*nephos*) here refer to 'a multitude' and not how morally great the heroes of faith were. They were actually a bunch of liars, drunks, cheaters, murderers, doubters, adulterers, absentee fathers i.e. they were just like us. And just like all these deeply flawed people, let us look to Jesus only!

But there is a parable that seems to suggest that Jesus would beat us if we do not perform according to His standards. The parable is Jesus' answer to *Luke 11:53,* where *the Pharisees and the teachers of the law began to oppose him fiercely and to besiege him with questions.* We read in *Luke 12:35-48, Let your loins be girded about, and your lights burning; And ye yourselves like unto men that wait for their lord, when he will return from the wedding; that when he cometh and knocketh, they may open unto him immediately. Blessed are those servants, whom the lord when he cometh shall find watching: verily I say unto you, that he shall gird himself, and make them to sit down to meat, and will come forth and serve them. And if he shall come in the second watch, or come in the third watch, and find them so, blessed are those servants. And this know, that if the goodman of the house had known what hour the thief would come, he would have watched, and not have suffered his house to be broken through. Be ye therefore ready also: for the Son of man cometh at an hour when ye think not. Then Peter said unto him, Lord, speakest thou this parable unto us, or even to all? And the Lord said, Who then is that faithful and wise steward, whom his lord shall make ruler over his household, to give them their portion of meat in due season? Blessed is that servant, whom his lord when he cometh shall find so doing. Of a truth I say unto you, that he will make him ruler over all that he hath. But and if that servant say in his heart, My lord delayeth his coming; and shall begin to beat the menservants and maidens, and to eat and drink, and to be drunken; The lord of that servant will come in a day when he looketh not for him, and at an hour when he is not aware, and will cut him in sunder, and will appoint him his portion with the unbelievers. And that servant, which knew his lord's will, and prepared not himself, neither did according to his will, shall be beaten with many stripes. But he that knew not, and did commit things worthy of stripes, shall be beaten with few stripes. For unto whomsoever much is given, of him shall be much required: and to whom men have committed much, of him they will ask the more.*

The traditional understanding of this parable is as follows. The faithful and wise servant is the servant who has disciplined himself to be always in a watching, waiting, and ready mode. When Jesus returns, the servant would spring up and swing the door open on the very first knock. Actually, if the servant was really watching, he would have seen Jesus from afar and would have the door open before Jesus even got there. For his due diligence and faithfulness, Jesus would take on the role of a servant, gird Himself, and serve him back. Blessed is the servant who is found 'doing'. The other servant who was not coiled-up, ready-to-bounce-into-action, will be beaten for his languor. Because he did not watch attentively, he will be whipped. Believers who are sluggish, who lower their standard of holiness and neglect the moral duties of their positions will be whipped. In accordance with the law, if he sinned willfully then he will be whipped with many stripes. If he sinned ignorantly then he will be whipped with fewer stripes. Finally, those who heard of Jesus but did not convert and those who converted but did nothing, their houses not filled with prayer and good deeds, would be cut in two (in Greek, *dichotomeó*) by Jesus, the chainsaw killer from heaven, before being thrown into hell! Accountability, accountability, accountability! Indolence will make us lose our salvation. Sloth will earn us a place in hell together with all other unbelievers. Frighten all, especially FOMOs, with torment and hell!

Degrees of punishment were based on the Mosaic law. Depending on how serious the sin was, there would be differing levels of punishment and restitutions (many stripes or fewer stripes). Under the law, the guiding principle is *Exodus 21:23-25,* which states, *thou shalt give life for life, Eye for eye, tooth for tooth, hand for hand, foot for foot, Burning for burning, wound for wound, stripe for stripe.* We see this many times in the scriptures: *Ezekiel 18:30, Therefore I will judge you, O house of Israel, every one according to his ways, saith the Lord God.*
Jeremiah 25:14, I will recompense them according to their deeds, and according to the works of their own hands.
Matthew 5:22, That whosoever is angry with his brother without a cause shall be in danger of the judgment: and whosoever shall say to his brother, Raca, shall be in danger of the council: but whosoever shall say, Thou fool, shall be in danger of hell fire.

Before Jesus died on the cross, He also referred to differing levels of sin in *John 19:11, Jesus answered...therefore he that delivered me unto thee hath the greater sin.* If there were greater sins then there must be lesser sins. But when Jesus died on the cross as the perfect and complete payment, both greater and lesser sins were obliterated for all mankind, and for all time. We read in *Ecclesiastes 7:20, Indeed, there is not a righteous person on earth who always does good and does not ever sin,* and *Romans 3:23-24, For all have sinned, and come short of the glory of God; Being justified freely by his grace through the redemption that is in Christ Jesus:* All sinned. But all justified freely by Grace! The varied categories of sins disappeared. So while people can still sin, there are no longer categories of sin. One sin is not more serious than another. Sin is sin.

This parable is actually about Jesus' return one day. While He was gone, abusive servants who claimed to be His, used the strictness of the law to profit for themselves as well as to control the people. The law was used to beat and condemn the people. These abusive servants were the Pharisees. They used the law to amass great wealth as we see in *James 5:2-4, Your riches are corrupted, and your garments are motheaten. Your gold and silver is cankered; and the rust of them shall be a witness against you, and shall eat your flesh as it were fire. Ye have heaped treasure together for the last days. Behold, the hire of the labourers who have reaped down your fields, which is of you kept back by fraud, crieth: and the cries of them which have reaped are entered into the ears of the Lord of sabaoth.* They were corrupted and had dealt unjustly with their laborers. They also controlled the exchange of money at the temples and the sale of sacrificial animals.

So, are all worldly blessings to be avoided then? Many people use the scripture above from *James*, to reject everything in this world. They also use another scripture found in *1 John 2:15-16, Love not the world, neither the things that are in the world. If any man love the world, the love of the Father is not in him. For all that is in the world, the lust of the flesh, and the lust of the eyes, and the pride of life, is not of the Father, but is of the world.* However, both scriptures do not refer to rejection of worldly blessings. We should be grateful for the blessings that God has provided for us in this world. Note that the scripture does not say the love *for* the Father but the love *of* the Father. **The worldly person is a person who does not have the love *of* the Father, who is Jesus, in him or her.** Without Jesus, the worldly person loves the world and lust after worldly things, just as the Pharisees. But a person who hates the world and rejects all worldly things as the ascetics do, also do not have the love of the Father in them! It is all about having or not having Jesus, not riches.

Man often believes that he can save himself because of his innate goodness even to the point of extending a hand out to God so that He can participate in man's act of self-salvation. This type of warped thinking typified the Pharisees who could not enter into the kingdom of heaven because of their self-righteousness, just as a heavily burdened camel could not go through the eye of a needle. We read in *Matthew 19:23-26, Then said Jesus unto his disciples, Verily I say unto you, That a rich man shall hardly enter into the kingdom of heaven. And again I say unto you, It is easier for a camel to go through the eye of a needle, than for a rich man to enter into the kingdom of God. When his disciples heard it, they were exceedingly amazed, saying, Who then can be saved? But Jesus beheld them, and said unto them, With men this is impossible; but with God all things are possible.* The rich man here was symbolic of the Pharisees. The exaggerated contrast was deliberate to point out the impossibility for men to enter in by his rich burden of self-works. Impossibility comes when men bulge with self-righteousness, are puffed up because they earned their wings, when their moral bank accounts are overloaded with pious deeds, when weighed down with so much holiness that it cascade from their self-made halos. But with Jesus, what was impossible became possible. *Genesis 18:14*, states *Is anything too hard for the Lord?* We enter the kingdom of God with no burdens at all as Jesus had taken it all away by His finished work on the cross.

Romans 2:12-14 states, *For as many as have sinned without law shall also perish without law: and as many as have sinned in the law shall be judged by the law. For not the hearers of the law are just before God, but the doers of the law shall be justified. For when the Gentiles, which have not the law, do by nature the things contained in the law, these, having not the law, are a law unto themselves.* Sinners without the law perish. But sinners under the law perish too as nobody can do the law in its entirety. All are disqualified. The law was given to the Jews but many Gentiles put themselves under it. It thus became a law unto them and they come under its curse. *Galatians 5:4* states, *Christ is become of no effect unto you, whosoever of you are justified by the law; ye are fallen from grace.* **Hence, those with the law (Jews) and those without the law (Gentiles) - both are unsaved! It is NEVER about the law. For nobody can be saved apart from JESUS! He is the only way!**

The Pharisees used the law as an iron hand to control, manipulate, and persecute the people. The law was used by the Pharisees to persecute Jesus' disciples to the point of death. Beatings and imprisonments were common. But there will come a time when all of them would stand before Jesus. Their judgment would be swift and simple. Through the law is the knowledge of sin. Their sins, whether intentional or ignorant, would be exposed. As they rejected Grace, the law would show them their respective punishments according to their sins. For as many laws as the religious leaders gave, the same would be required back from them. According to the law, they would be beaten with many or few stripes. Ignorance of the law is not an excuse, as we read in *Leviticus 5:17, And if a soul sin, and commit any of these things which are forbidden to be done by the commandments of the Lord; though he wist it not, yet is he guilty, and shall bear his iniquity.* But they would not get what they deserve. None of them would be punished for their sins. Why? Because Jesus died for their sins too. However, they would still be cut asunder from the presence of God. But only because they were unbelievers, not sinners.

Hence, as the price for all sins have already been paid, judgment would only be based on whether a person is a believer or an unbeliever in Jesus Christ. Condemnation never comes from Jesus. The world was wrecked, ruined, and hopeless in sin. Condemned already! The reason Jesus came was to un-condemn the condemned! To save sinners, whom He loved, as in *John 3:16-18, For God so loved the world, that he gave his only begotten Son, that whosoever believeth in him should not perish, but have everlasting life. For God sent not his Son into the world to condemn the world; but that the world through him might be saved. He that believeth on him is not condemned: but he that believeth not is condemned already, because he hath not believed in the name of the only begotten Son of God.* The watchful servants are the believers. Jesus is the One whom they have committed themselves to and they can continue to ask from Him, until they meet Him one day. Then they would be sat down and served by Jesus Himself. This is a direct reference to the Marriage Feast of the Lamb and the Judgment/Bema Seat of Christ. Believers are joint-heirs with Jesus. All believers would sit and feast with Jesus, our Promise Keeper, as in *Psalm 105:8, He remembers his covenant forever, the promise he made, for a thousand generations.*

❧ 22 ❧

JESUS AND THE MAD CITY

While it is easy to spot madness in individuals, it is remarkably harder to spot madness in whole groups or societies. Let us read from *Mark 4:35-41, And the same day, when the even was come, he saith unto them, Let us pass over unto the other side. And when they had sent away the multitude, they took him even as he was in the ship. And there were also with him other little ships. And there arose a great storm of wind, and the waves beat into the ship, so that it was now full. And he was in the hinder part of the ship, asleep on a pillow: and they awake him, and say unto him, Master, carest thou not that we perish? And he arose, and rebuked the wind, and said unto the sea, Peace, be still* (in Greek *phimoó*). *And the wind ceased, and there was a great calm. And he said unto them, Why are ye so fearful? how is it that ye have no faith? And they feared exceedingly, and said one to another, What manner of man is this, that even the wind and the sea obey him?* We continue in *Mark 5:1-20, And they came over unto the other side of the sea, into the country of the Gadarenes. And when he was come out of the ship, immediately there met him out of the tombs a man with an unclean spirit, Who had his dwelling among the tombs; and no man could bind him, no, not with chains: Because that he had been often bound with fetters and chains, and the chains had been plucked asunder by him, and the fetters broken in pieces: neither could any man tame him. And always, night and day, he was in the mountains, and in the tombs, crying, and cutting himself with stones. But when he saw Jesus afar off, he ran and worshipped him, And cried with a loud voice, and said, What have I to do with thee, Jesus, thou Son of the most high God? I adjure thee by God, that thou torment me not. For he said unto him, Come out of the man, thou unclean spirit. And he asked him, What is thy name? And he answered, saying, My name is Legion: for we are many. And he besought him much that he would not send them away out of the country. Now there was there nigh unto the mountains a great herd of swine feeding. And all the devils besought him, saying, Send us into the swine, that we may enter into them. And forthwith Jesus gave them leave. And the unclean spirits went out, and entered into the swine: and the herd ran violently down a steep place into the sea, (they were about two thousand;) and were choked in the sea. And they that fed the swine fled, and told it in the city, and in the country. And they went out to see what it was that was done. And they come to Jesus, and see him that was possessed with the devil, and had the legion, sitting, and clothed, and in his right mind: and they were afraid. And they that saw it told them how it befell to him that was possessed with the devil, and also concerning the swine. And they began to pray him to depart out of their coasts. And when he was come into the ship, he that had been possessed with the devil prayed him that he might be with him. Howbeit Jesus suffered him not, but saith unto him, Go home to thy friends, and tell them how great things the Lord hath done for thee, and hath had compassion on thee. And he departed, and began to publish in Decapolis how great things Jesus had done for him: and all men did marvel.*

The traditional explanation for this story is very simple. Jesus and His disciples were setting off to the other side of the sea. As they sailed, a severe storm arose. The storm came from God as a test of their faith. The disciples failed and had to depend upon Jesus to calm the storm down. Jesus rebuked them and asked them where their faith was in the midst of the storm or trial. They needed more faith as they should not have been afraid during the test. We do not know when the storms of life will come. So we should be prepared and grow our faith to withstand the trials which would surely come our way. When they finally landed, the disciples saw why their faith had been tested.

An insane man, with a legion of demons in him, met them. Because of Jesus' faith, the demons fell down before Him. He commanded the demons to come out of the man and into a herd of swine, which subsequently stampeded off a promontory and drowned in the sea. A befitting end for demons. The insane man, captured by fetters of sin, stood as a symbol for mankind caught in sin. All of us need faith to be set free. If not, then we need more faith like the kind Jesus' had.

The citizens of the city, seeing the insane man made sane and thousands of drowned, bloated, and demon possessed pigs, were afraid. They blamed the whole ruckus squarely on Jesus. They had no faith in Jesus so they ran Him out of their city. As Jesus sailed away, He left an entire city population quagmired in unbelief. In the meantime, the disciples learned the importance of having great faith. Great faith, not just faith, was the key to casting out demons and conquering fear and unbelief.

It is quite a good explanation, but it does not explain why Jesus calmed the storm which His Father had sent. It does not explain why they needed great faith because Jesus had just told them that all they needed was faith the size of a mustard seed. It does not explain why Jews were taking care of pigs, maybe even for consumption, when the law specifically stated that pigs were unclean animals. It does not explain why He traveled across the lake to meet a single man and it does not explain why the people in the city were afraid of this man, even after he was healed.

The crossing over of Jesus and His disciples to the country of the Gadarenes and Gergesenes occured just after He had explained to them the parable of the mustard seed. The mustard seed was supposed to grow into a bush, but had been perverted into a very big tree full of branches where the law-keepers could line up and sit. The law had by now run amuck, bringing about *Isaiah 65:4, Which remain among the graves, and lodge in the monuments, which eat swine's flesh.* That is why Jesus said to His disciples, 'Let us pass over onto the other side'. It was necessary to leave the law for a better covenant, a covenant of Grace. But when the disciples followed Jesus into the boat of Grace, the horrendous waves and wind of the law struck them, bow first, seeking to sink it. The disciples tried valiantly to save the boat with their own wisdom and self works but to no avail. When their self-works failed and they realized they were going to perish in the storm of the law, they stumbled towards the rear or stern part of the boat where Jesus was sleeping. Because Jesus is Grace, He was to be found in a restful position, on a pillow, farthest removed from the onslaught of the waves of the law. The chaos of the storm arose only after Jesus, whose peace passes all understanding, had fallen asleep. Where Grace is absent, the law will rise up. The disciples, who had left Jesus alone, could not save themselves.

But then Grace spoke as prophesied in *Psalm 107:26-29, their soul melts because of troubles. They are troubled, they stagger as a drunkard, and all their wisdom is swallowed up. Then they cry to the Lord in their affliction, and he brings them out of their distresses. And he commands the storm, and it is calmed into a gentle breeze, and its waves are still.* The howling wind calmed into a gentle breeze. The screaming requirements of the law were stilled, *phimoó* meaning muzzled, by Jesus. With Jesus, nobody goes under. Jesus fulfilled the law. He accomplished it all. What was required was faith in Him. Not more faith but faith in Jesus' works. The storm was not sent by the Father and then quelled by Jesus because that would imply a schizoid divided Trinity. It was a storm of false theology which brought troubles, afflictions, and distresses but now rebuked (in Hebrew *gaar*, as He *gaar* the sea in *Nahum 1:4* and as He *gaar* satan in *Zechariah 3:2*) by Jesus. He is with us as He takes us out of the law and into Grace. Only He could *gaar* and *phimoó* the storm that the law brought. Through Jesus, all those who believe in Him are saved.

There were two cities on the other side of the lake by the names of Gardara and Gergesa. Both were wealthy cities. They had important people living there. The country of the Gadarenes and Gergesenes could have been the original settlement for the tribe of Gad, Gad being one of the twelve sons of Jacob. Of course, the original Gadites had passed away by now, to be replaced by a mixture of Gentiles and Jews. Paganism and the law stood side by side. This was evidenced by the inhabitants of the land rearing pigs in large numbers which were considered unclean by the Jews.

We know that Jesus was sent to reach the Jews. In *Matthew 15:24, But he answered and said, I am not sent but unto the lost sheep of the house of Israel.* Although Jesus did minister to the Gentiles, His chief ministry was to the Jews. We see this again in *Mark 7:25-30, For a certain woman, whose young daughter had an unclean spirit, heard of him, and came and fell at his feet: The woman was a Greek, a Syrophenician by nation; and she besought him that he would cast forth the devil out of her daughter. But Jesus said unto her, Let the children first be filled: for it is not meet to take the children's bread, and to cast it unto the dogs. And she answered and said unto him, Yes, Lord: yet the dogs under the table eat of the children's crumbs. And he said unto her, For this saying go thy way; the devil is gone out of thy daughter. And when she was come to her house, she found the devil gone out, and her daughter laid upon the bed.*

The Gentile woman sought healing for her daughter who had an unclean spirit. Jesus told her that His ministry was primarily for the children of Israel and not for the 'dogs' or Gentiles. Under the law, the woman was disqualified. But the woman replied that as a 'dog' she would eat the crumbs of Jesus that fell off the table. The children's bread referred to the body of Jesus. **Even the crumbs of Jesus' body would heal anyone, anytime.** The woman did not realize that under Grace, she was fully qualified. Because of her faith in Jesus' perfect faith, her daughter became fully healed. Her daughter found her rest upon the bed of Jesus' finished work. It truly is as stated in *Psalm 84:10, Better is one day in your courts than a thousand elsewhere; I would rather be a doorkeeper in the house of my God than dwell in the tents of the wicked.* One day of God's favor is better than a thousand days of men's favor. One crumb of Jesus is more than sufficient healing for our entire body! One drop of Jesus' blood is more than sufficient to cleanse us from a lifetime of sin and wickedness. Even the outside of Grace is far better than the insides of the law! God's least is far better than the world's best! And God only gave us His best!

Another example can be found in *Matthew 8:5-8,10,13, And when Jesus was entered into Capernaum, there came unto him a centurion, beseeching him, And saying, Lord, my servant lieth at home sick of the palsy, grievously tormented. And Jesus saith unto him, I will come and heal him. The centurion answered and said, Lord, I am not worthy that thou shouldest come under my roof: but* **speak the word** *only, and my servant shall be healed. When Jesus heard it, he marvelled, and said to them that followed, Verily I say unto you, I have not found so great faith, no, not in Israel. And Jesus said unto the centurion, Go thy way; and as thou hast believed, so be it done unto thee. And his servant was healed in the selfsame hour.* The centurion was a man with authority but he knew that he was not worthy. Under the law, a Gentile was never good enough, no matter his worldly position. He was disqualified under the law. He could not earn his way into God's blessings. But under Grace, he became qualified. He did not have to earn the blessings as it was given to him freely. **And just like the Greek woman, Jesus told him that he had great faith because both of them put their faith in Jesus who had perfect faith. After all, Jesus was Faith as He is the substance of things hoped for and the evidence of things not seen. Jesus is the only necessary spoken Word!**

So the reason Jesus went across the lake was to rescue another lost sheep of the house of Israel, possibly a Gadite descendant. In this country of the Gadarenes, we find whole cities filled with spiritually naked and wretched people. They believed they were clean but were really wretched. They were captives, chained to their wisdom of right and wrong. They were filled with a mixture of law, paganism, and a belief in demons.

This mixture was enough to drive people mad. Two of the Jews became insane and possessed. So the people of the city threw them out to live in the tombs. This whitewashed tombs would be their home. We see in *Matthew 8:28, And when he was come to the other side into the country of the Gergesenes, there met him two possessed with devils, coming out of the tombs, exceeding fierce, so that no man might pass by that way.* But one was much fiercer than the other and so, the focus of the scripture was on this one particular person. Nothing could bind this man nor tame him. His mixture of beliefs allowed him to live among the tombs, even though that was forbidden under the law. Over the years, he had broken many chains of the law by his own strength but not all. This was evidenced by the fact that he was still cutting himself with the stony law, and would then cry bitterly, night and day. The law exposed his spiritual and physical nakedness and his madness at trying to follow it. No matter what he did, it was never enough.

When Jesus came, the naked man who had tried to be free for so many years ran to Him and worshipped Him. People living under the law sooner or later see their utter inability to save themselves. The sole objective of the law was to show people that they needed a Savior. And so Grace came. The helpless man had done everything in his own strength and had achieved naught, so he was ready to just receive from Jesus. The demons that had tormented the man recoiled at the sight of Jesus. They begged Him to not send them to the abyss or Tartarus. We know Tartarus from *2 Peter 2:4, For if God didn't spare angels when they sinned, but cast them down to Tartarus, and committed them to pits of darkness, to be reserved for judgment* and again in *Jude 6, The angels too, who did not keep to their own domain but deserted their proper dwelling, he has kept in eternal chains, in gloom, for the judgment of the great day.* There were many of them. Hence, their name, legion! Fearing Tartarus, the legion of demons asked Jesus' permission to enter into the pigs. As there were around two thousand pigs, there must have been at least two thousand demons. Their first action was one of destruction as they thrust and tumbled over each other, off the embankment, and into the sea.

When the citizens of the country heard of this event, they came out in force to see for themselves what had transpired. When they reached Jesus, they saw the insane 'sitting, clothed, and in his right mind' at the feet of Jesus. He sat because Jesus had finished the work. He was clothed in the pillow of clothes that Jesus had purposefully brought for him. He was now clothed by and with Jesus. The storm in him had been calmed down. He was now in his right mind because he had the mind of Christ. Just as the storm, he was now still and at peace, as in *Isaiah 26:3, Thou wilt keep him in perfect peace, whose mind is stayed on thee.*

Interestingly enough, there was a prophecy back in *Genesis 49:18-19, I have waited for thy salvation, O Lord. Gad, a troop shall overcome him: but he shall overcome at the last.* The Gadites were good warriors but were ultimately conquered by the Assyrians. They never overcame that defeat but dispersed into other lands. So they never 'overcome at the last'. A better explanation for the fulfillment of this prophecy was that this was the Gadite (representing the tribe) whom the troop or marauding band of demons overcame. He was waiting for somebody to save him. Then Jesus came. Jesus shall overcome at the last! The original Hebrew words meant 'but He will attack them at their heels'. That explained why the pigs violently shoved and tumbled over each other because Jesus was attacking them at their heels. **No legion of demons could ever stand against He who came. Similarly, the Roman legion/cohort in the garden of Gethsemane found this out too! At His name, they all fell!**

The inhabitants were afraid. Just like the Pharisees, they probably believed that Jesus casted out the demons through satan. In *Matthew 12:24, But when the Pharisees heard it, they said, This fellow doth not cast out devils, but by Beelzebub the prince of the devils.* They still had the old mind. They saw the man healed and clothed in Jesus' righteousness but could not comprehend it. What had the man done to deserve this miraculous turnaround? The inhabitants could not see that Grace was standing right in front of them. It was never about what the man had done but about what Jesus had done.

Then the inhabitants saw the sea dotted with their dead pigs. What had Jesus done to their pigs? Just like the Pharisees who wondered what had happened to their overturned tables, their oxen, sheep, and doves which flew the coop and were crapping everywhere. Overwhelmed with anger at the loss of their pigs and fearful of Jesus and the healed 'mad' man, they forced Jesus out of their coast. They reasoned that Jesus was mad. Furthermore, Jesus could also be working for or with the devil. Beware of Jesus!

What happened to the inhabitants thereof? We read in *Matthew 12:43-45, When the unclean spirit is gone out of a man, he walketh through dry places, seeking rest, and findeth none. Then he saith, I will return into my house from whence I came out; and when he is come, he findeth it empty, swept, and garnished.*

Then goeth he, and taketh with himself seven other spirits more wicked than himself, and they enter in and dwell there: and the last state of that man is worse than the first. Even so shall it be also unto this wicked generation. These verses referred to the Israelites captivity in Babylon, where they walked through dry places. But in these foreign lands, they were prohibited as well as incapacitated to follow the Mosaic law. They did not have a temple or tabernacle in their exile and were thus, unable to continuously offer up sacrifices to God. Hence, the unclean spirit of works left them for a period of time. When the Israelites were finally allowed by King Cyrus of Persia (as prophesied by name in *Isaiah 45:1* one hundred and fifty years before he was born) to return to Jerusalem, they found that Jerusalem, the house from which they came from, empty, swept and spruced up. But instead of reinstating God as their center, they broke into sects. From one unclean spirit they now took in seven and their state became worse off than before. The seven sects/spirits were the Pharisees (teachers of the law), Sadducees (priests in the temple), Herodians (affiliated with Herod), Zealots (violent resistance group), Sicarii (extremists dagger men), Essenes (ascetic monastic group who wrote the Dead Sea Scrolls), and all the Hellenistic (Greek mixed) Jews. They were altogether a wicked generation. All of them were blind to Jesus! Note that John the Baptist probably came from the Essenes community but was booted out for his 'seeing' Jesus!

The inhabitants in the cities were the actual crazies. The lunatics ran the asylum. They chased Jesus away from their coast. Without Jesus, their state became seven times worse off than before. Seven stands for perfection. In this case, they were perfectly insane as they chased their Savior away. But were they condemned for their deranged action? When the former 'mad' man wanted to depart with Jesus, he was sent back into Gadara, one of the league of ten Greek/Hellenistic cities (Deca-polis meaning 10 cities).The number ten also signified the law. Jesus did not condemn but had compassion for them. The sane man was charged with the Great Commission to share with them what great things Jesus had done for him. He obeyed, as in *Matthew 28:20,* and started sharing the good news of Jesus as Grace!

❧ 23 ❧

JESUS AND RESTORATION

Jesus restores all things. *Acts 3:20-21 states, And he shall send Jesus Christ, which before was preached unto you: Whom the heaven must receive until the times of restitution of all things, which God hath spoken by the mouth of all his holy prophets since the world began.* **In Jesus, everything is set right, as though man had not fallen.** Jesus loves restoring people back to their rightful positions. The rightful position of a man or woman is to be as Jesus is. *1 John 4:15-17, states that Whosoever shall confess that Jesus is the Son of God, God dwelleth in him, and he in God. And we have known and believed the love that God hath to us. God is love; and he that dwelleth in love dwelleth in God, and God in him. Herein is our love made perfect, that we may have boldness in the day of judgment: because as he is, so are we in this world.* As Jesus is, so are we in this world. Because Jesus occupies an exalted position in Heaven, our natural position here on earth is similarly exalted. If we fall short of our position, then Jesus restores us back to where we are supposed to be.

One of the first people restored by God was the high priest, Aaron. We read in *Exodus 32:1-5, And when the people saw that Moses delayed to come down out of the mount, the people gathered themselves together unto Aaron, and said unto him, Up, make us gods, which shall go before us; for as for this Moses, the man that brought us up out of the land of Egypt, we wot not what is become of him. And Aaron said unto them, Break off the golden earrings, which are in the ears of your wives, of your sons, and of your daughters, and bring them unto me. And all the people brake off the golden earrings which were in their ears, and brought them unto Aaron. And he received them at their hand, and fashioned it with a graving tool, after he had made it a molten calf: and they said, These be thy gods, O Israel, which brought thee up out of the land of Egypt. And when Aaron saw it, he built an altar before it; and Aaron made proclamation, and said, Tomorrow is a feast to the Lord.* When Moses was up on mount Sinai, the Israelites demanded from Aaron a god who would lead them. One whom they could see. But Aaron did not make them a god. He literally made them God, which was represented by the golden calf or in Hebrew '*egel*'. He proclaimed that the next day would be a feast to the Lord or the golden *egel*. The Israelites promised to do everything the Lord asked them but could not fulfill even the first commandment. Death ensued.

Then we read in *Leviticus 4:3-4, If the priest that is anointed do sin according to the sin of the people; then let him bring for his sin, which he hath sinned, a young bullock without blemish unto the Lord for a sin offering. And he shall bring the bullock unto the door of the tabernacle of the congregation before the Lord; and shall lay his hand upon the bullock's head, and kill the bullock before the Lord.* Aaron, having sinned before God, could now atone for his sin by offering a bullock to God. But Aaron never offered a bullock for his sin. Instead, he was told to offer an *egel.* This was in direct contrast to the law for a priest's sin offering! We see this in *Leviticus 9:1-2, 8, And it came to pass on the eighth day, that Moses called Aaron and his sons, and the elders of Israel; And he said unto Aaron, Take thee a young calf for a sin offering, and a ram for a burnt offering, without blemish, and offer them before the Lord. Aaron therefore went unto the altar, and slew the calf of the sin offering, which was for himself.* The first *egel* that Aaron fashioned was made of gold and was demonic. But this second *egel* was a shadow of Jesus. With Jesus, Aaron who deserved death was restored to his rightful priestly position. A restored Aaron, decked in his priestly garments, wore a golden mitre upon his head symbolizing Jesus. **As Jesus' thoughts**

are always pure and holy, Aaron's thoughts became pure and holy as well. He was restored.

Another well known restoration account can be found in *Matthew 26:31-34, Then saith Jesus unto them, All ye shall be offended because of me this night: for it is written, I will smite the shepherd, and the sheep of the flock shall be scattered abroad. But after I am risen again, I will go before you into Galilee. Peter answered and said unto him, Though all men shall be offended because of thee, yet will I never be offended. Jesus said unto him, Verily I say unto thee, That this night, before the cock crow, thou shalt deny me thrice.* And again in *Luke 22:33-34, And he said unto him, Lord, I am ready to go with thee, both into prison, and to death. And he said, I tell thee, Peter, the cock shall not crow this day, before that thou shalt thrice deny that thou knowest me.*

We all know what happened next. In *John 18:17-18, 25-27, Then saith the damsel that kept the door unto Peter, Art not thou also one of this man's disciples? He saith, I am not. And the servants and officers stood there, who had made a fire of coals; for it was cold: and they warmed themselves: and Peter stood with them, and warmed himself. And Simon Peter stood and warmed himself. They said therefore unto him, Art not thou also one of his disciples? He denied it, and said, I am not. One of the servants of the high priest, being his kinsman whose ear Peter cut off, saith, Did not I see thee in the garden with him? Peter then denied again: and immediately the cock crew.*

Peter boasted and staunchly proclaimed his loyalty for Jesus. He boasted that he would never be offended by men, that he would go to prison and even die for Jesus. That is the wisdom of the flesh. It always sounds so good and palatial. What we did for Jesus instead of what Jesus did for us! So haughty and highfalutin' until he ended up denying Jesus three times, by the man-made fire. For all his blustery braggadocio talk, Peter ended up like the rest of us, failing bitterly. He was not even at the cross when Jesus was hung. We weep bitterly at our weakness, for failing to do what we said we will do.

We get a little bit more information from *Luke 22:60-61, And immediately, while he yet spake, the cock crew. And* **the Lord** *turned, and looked upon Peter. And Peter remembered the word of the Lord, how he had said unto him, Before the cock crow, thou shalt deny me thrice.* The Lord turned and looked at Peter! Not Jesus, but the Lord! The Greek word for Lord here is *'Kyrios'* meaning master and owner. No matter what mistakes Peter made and said, he still belonged to Jesus. Jesus looked at Peter with a look that said, "No matter your mistakes, you are still Mine!" It was the look of unconditional love for and acceptance of Peter.

Later, after His resurrection, Jesus met with Peter separately in an event described in *Luke 24:33-34, And they rose up the same hour, and returned to Jerusalem, and found the eleven gathered together, and them that were with them, Saying, The Lord is risen indeed, and hath appeared to Simon.* Jesus had already met with Peter. While the details of this meeting were not recorded in the bible, I am sure it had to do with Jesus reassuring Peter that there would be no condemnation of him for not being present, like John, at the foot of the cross.

This is reinforced in *John 21:2-14, There were together Simon Peter, and Thomas called Didymus, and Nathanael of Cana in Galilee, and the sons of Zebedee, and two other of his disciples. Simon Peter saith unto them, I go a fishing. They say unto him, We also go with thee. They went forth, and entered into a ship immediately; and that night they caught nothing. But when the morning was now come, Jesus stood on the shore: but the disciples knew not that it was Jesus. Then Jesus saith unto them, Children, have ye any meat? They answered him, No. And he said unto them, Cast the net on the right side of the ship, and ye shall find. They cast therefore, and now they were not able to draw it for the multitude of fishes. Therefore that disciple whom Jesus loved saith unto Peter, It is the Lord. Now when Simon Peter heard that it was the Lord, he girt his fisher's coat unto him, (for he was naked,) and did cast himself into the sea. And the other disciples came in a little ship; (for they were not far from land, but as it were two hundred cubits,) dragging the net with fishes. As soon then as they were come to land, they saw a fire of coals there, and fish laid thereon, and bread. Jesus saith unto them, Bring of the fish which ye have now caught. Simon Peter went up, and drew the net to land full of great fishes, and hundred and fifty and three: and for all there were so many, yet was not the net broken. Jesus saith unto them, Come and dine.* Once again, Peter and the other disciples stepped into their boat of self-works. They knew that in that sea, fish bite at night. So they went fishing. But their self-works caught them nothing. Not until Jesus came along. This was after His resurrection. It was now morning and the chance of catching fish was slim. Yet, Jesus provided. They caught so much fish that they could not haul it in. Yet their net did not break. The number 153 is found in *2 Kings 1:1-17.* Only the third captain out of the 3 sets of captains with their fifties (51x3=153) was saved. He and his army lived solely because Jesus appeared to Elijah, as in *2 Kings 1:15, Then the angel of the LORD said to Elijah, Go down with him. Do not be afraid of him.* What a breakfast lesson for the disciples! Grace would supplant the law, and turn the world upside down. The nets were changed from port side to starboard side. The Gentiles would now become part of the catch. They would likewise, live!

Before the cross, we read in *Luke 5:4-6, Simon, Launch out into the deep, and let down your nets for a draught. And Simon answering said unto him, Master, we have toiled all the night, and have taken nothing: nevertheless at thy word I will let down the net. And when they had this done, they inclosed a great multitude of fishes: and their net brake.* Jesus asked Peter to let down his nets but Peter only let down one net! There was also a multitude of fish, symbolizing the Jews. But the net broke! **After the cross, their net did not break!** The fish caught after the cross symbolized the Gentile nations that would be reached for Jesus. The net could not break because Grace is now the net. **Grace is unbreakable!**

The resurrected Christ will draw all to Him. Everything caught in the deep belongs to Him. We read this in *John 12:32, And I, if I be lifted up from the earth, will draw all_ unto me.* The word 'men' is not in the original Greek. He drew ALL, anyone and everything, including judgment for all sins, to Himself. *Jeremiah 31:3* states, *The Lord hath appeared of old unto me, saying, Yea, I have loved thee with an everlasting love: therefore with lovingkindness have I drawn thee.* Jesus is all in all. There is no pulling nor pushing. Only a drawing. There are no threats nor demands. Only an unconditional supply of everlasting love, forgiveness, and lovingkindness (*checed* or Grace).

Jesus had already cooked them breakfast by the time they landed. Peter who had swam in first was greeted by Jesus with fish over a fire of coals and bread. God always provides for us first. Way before we could haul in our catch of fish, Jesus had already provided fish. As Peter warmed himself by the Jesus-made fire, it reminded him of the man-made fire that he had warmed himself with, on the night he denied Jesus. What he could not have known was that the whole setup was to restore him fully. We continue reading in *John 21:15-17, So when they had dined, Jesus saith to Simon Peter, Simon, son of Jonas, lovest thou me more than these?... Feed my lambs...He saith to him again the second time, Simon, son of Jonas, lovest thou me?...Feed my sheep...He saith unto him the third time, Simon, son of Jonas, lovest thou me?...Feed my sheep.*

After Peter had eaten and warmed himself, Jesus turned to Peter and questioned him. But it was not about the mistakes that he had done. For Jesus knew the mistakes that Peter would make before he was born. Instead, He asked Peter three times whether he loved Him. The original Greek words for love, as used here, are *'phileo'* and *'agape'* which are used interchangeably in the bible. One is not a lower form of love than the other to mean different levels of love Peter had for Jesus. The explanation for this conversation is actually very simple. Peter denied Jesus three times before, by the man-made fire of self-works. Jesus now affirms Peter three times, by His fire of finished works. The number 3 stands for perfection. Perfect failure to perfect reinstatement and restoration. Peter, because of his denial of Jesus felt unworthy to share the gospel. So he had to be restored by Grace. Jesus as Grace would always be with Peter, as in *John 21:18-19, when you are old you will stretch out your hands, and someone else will dress you and lead you where you do not want to go. Jesus said this to indicate the kind of death by which Peter would glorify God.* Peter would feed His sheep until he too was hung on the cross in Rome.

One of the best known statements on restoration is in the dual fulfillment prophecy of *Joel 2:23-26, Be glad then, ye children of Zion, and rejoice in the Lord your God: for he hath given you the former rain moderately, and he will cause to come down for you the rain, the former rain, and the latter rain (Teacher for righteousness* in Young's translation) *in the first month. And the floors shall be full of wheat, and the fats shall overflow with wine and oil. And I will restore to you the years that the locust hath eaten, the cankerworm, and the caterpiller, and the palmerworm, my great army which I sent among you. And ye shall eat in plenty, and be satisfied, and praise the name of the Lord your God, that hath dealt wondrously with you: and my people shall never be ashamed.* The former rains brought blessings. But the blessings were stolen away by satan as the locust and the worm as in *Deuteronomy 28:38-39, Thou shalt carry much seed out into the field, and shalt gather but little in; for the locust shall consume it. Thou shalt plant vineyards, and dress them, but shalt neither drink of the wine, nor gather the grapes; for the worms shall eat them.* The former rains or the Mosaic covenant brought both blessings and curses.

Psalm 69:4 states, They that hate me without a cause are more than the hairs of mine head: they that would destroy me, being mine enemies wrongfully, are mighty: then I restored that which I took not away. Jesus' chief enemy was not the people but satan. But Jesus said that He Himself would restore what He did not take away! He would restore our sinless nature. For he is the Teacher *for* our righteousness. Jesus as Grace is the latter rain as in *Zechariah 10:1, Ask ye of the LORD rain in the time of the latter rain; so the LORD shall make bright clouds, and give them showers of rain, to everyone grass in the field.* Not only would He would restore our position just as before the fall, but He would restore the land. The harvest would be plenteous. The barn floors would be full of wheat and the vats would overflow with wine and oil. We shall eat of this wheat and drink of this wine, symbolic of the bread and wine of the Lord's supper. When we eat of this Bread, years of life would be restored to us. What the devil took away and wasted, Jesus would restore and multiply.

❧ 24 ❧

JESUS AND ONESIMUS

As Jesus did, so did Paul. As Jesus restored, so did Paul. In ancient times, masters had many servants (`ebed`). Servants work for a wage. Others sell themselves by their own accord into servitude to pay off debts. Paul addressed some of these servants in his writings:

Ephesians 6:5-9, Servants, be obedient to them that are your masters according to the flesh, with fear and trembling, in singleness of your heart, as unto Christ; Not with eyeservice, as menpleasers; but as the servants of Christ, doing the will of God from the heart; With good will doing service, as to the Lord, and not to men: Knowing that whatsoever good thing any man doeth, the same shall he receive of the Lord, whether he be bond or free. And, ye masters, do the same things unto them, forbearing threatening: knowing that your Master also is in heaven; neither is there respect of persons with him.

Colossians 4:1, Masters, give unto your servants that which is just and equal; knowing that ye also have a Master in heaven.

1 Timothy 6:1-2, Let as many servants as are under the yoke count their own masters worthy of all honour, that the name of God and his doctrine be not blasphemed. And they that have believing masters, let them not despise them, because they are brethren; but rather do them service, because they are faithful and beloved, partakers of the benefit. These things teach and exhort.

Titus 2:9-11, Exhort servants to be obedient unto their own masters, and to please them well in all things; not answering again; Not purloining, but shewing all good fidelity; that they may adorn the doctrine of God our Saviour in all things. For the grace of God that bringeth salvation hath appeared to all men.

Paul's message to servants who were believers, was simple. Even though they were under the yoke, they were to do everything as to the Lord, and not unto men. That way, their master will come to know the Lord Jesus because of their righteous behavior. When masters became believers, then they would treat their servants justly and equally, considering that they are now brothers in Christ. This way, Grace would be shown to all. But not all servants behave in that exemplary manner. Some spoke bad about their masters, stole from them, and ran away. We read of one such case in the book of Colossians and Philemon. Is restoration possible for a runaway servant? Is restoration possible for a victimized master?

We begin in *Colossians 4:7-9, All my state shall Tychicus declare unto you, who is a beloved brother, and a faithful minister and fellowservant in the Lord: Whom I have sent unto you for the same purpose, that he might know your estate, and comfort your hearts; With Onesimus, a faithful and beloved brother, who is one of you. They shall make known unto you all things which are done here.* Paul, who was in prison in Rome, was sending two men out. Their names were Tychicus and Onesimus.

The story continues in *Philemon 1-9, Paul, a prisoner of Jesus Christ, and Timothy our brother, unto Philemon our dearly beloved, and fellowlabourer, And to our beloved Apphia, and Archippus our fellowsoldier, and to the church in thy house: Grace to you, and peace, from God our Father and the Lord Jesus Christ. I thank my God, making mention of thee always in my prayers, Hearing of thy love and faith, which thou hast toward the Lord Jesus, and toward all saints; That the communication of thy faith may become effectual by the acknowledging of every good thing which is in you in Christ Jesus. For we have great joy and consolation in thy love, because the bowels of the saints are refreshed by thee, brother. Wherefore, though I might be much bold in Christ to enjoin thee that which is convenient, Yet for love's sake I rather beseech thee, being such an one as Paul the aged, and now also a prisoner of Jesus Christ.*

We get more information now. The two men were going to the house of a rich man, Philemon. Philemon was described as a beloved brother, a co-laborer, a man full of love and faith that the bowels of the saints were refreshed by him. He also had a church in his house, signifying a rather large domicile. After this thorough buttering up of Philemon, Paul proceeded to drop a bombshell on him. Onesimus, one of the two men, seemed to be not a goody two-shoes disciple at all. In fact, he was a former servant in the house of Philemon. Onesimus did not like to be a servant, so he complained, spoke bad, stole, and then eventually ran away from Philemon. However, somewhere along the way, Onesimus met Paul, probably in Rome, heard the radical gospel of Grace, and became a believer. His whole life turned around. From being unprofitable, he became profitable. From being useless he became useful. He was a servant *of* sin set free by Jesus. He was redeemed and restored by Grace. We read in *John 8:34-36, Jesus answered them, Verily, verily, I say unto you, Whosoever committeth sin is the servant of sin. And the servant abideth not in the house for ever: but the Son abideth ever. If the Son therefore shall make you free, ye shall be free indeed.*

Onesimus became free indeed from sin. He would never be a servant again as he was now a son. If he sinned, he would still not be a servant *to* sin as he had been set free from being a servant *of* sin! We read that Tychicus was sent to Philemon in Colossae, accompanied by Paul's son, Onesimus! He left Colossae as a servant but he returned as a son. Paul requested Philemon to receive his son, Onesimus, as he would himself. *Philemon 10-17, I beseech thee for my son Onesimus...Which in time past was to thee unprofitable, but now profitable to thee and to me: Whom I have sent again: thou therefore receive him, that is, mine own bowels...For perhaps he therefore departed for a season, that thou shouldest receive him forever; Not now as a servant, but above a servant, a brother beloved, specially to me, but how much more unto thee, both in the flesh, and in the Lord? If thou count me therefore a partner, receive him as myself.* Onesimus, as a servant, did not abide in Philemon's house forever. But Onesimus, as a son, would abide in Paul and Philemon's house forever.

Paul, knowing that Onesimus stole from Philemon before, then made a radical Grace statement. *Philemon 18-19, If he hath wronged thee, or oweth thee ought, put that on mine account; I Paul have written it with mine own hand, I will repay it: albeit I do not say to thee how thou owest unto me even thine own self besides.* Whatever debt that Onesimus owed to Philemon, Paul would pay it back. **Put that on my account and I will repay it!** Charge it to me! I will pay it all back with my own hand! The dirt on the son was wiped clean by the unrestrained hand of the father. *Ephesians 1:6-7, To the praise of the glory of his grace, wherein he hath made us accepted in the beloved. In whom we have redemption through his blood, the forgiveness of sins, according to the riches of his grace;* Similarly, we are accepted forever because He redeemed us. Not by our accomplishments and achievements but through His blood according to the riches of His Grace.

Philemon 20, Yea, brother, let me have joy of thee in the Lord: refresh my bowels in the Lord. Having confidence in thy obedience I wrote unto thee, knowing that thou wilt also do more than I say. But withal prepare me also a lodging: for I trust that through your prayers I shall be given unto you. There salute thee Epaphras, my fellowprisoner in Christ Jesus; Marcus, Aristarchus, Demas, Lucas, my fellowlabourers. The grace of our Lord Jesus Christ be with your spirit. Amen. In the end, Paul urged Philemon to do even 'more' for Onesimus. More than just providing a bed but a home; more than just for a period of time but forever; more than just a brother but as a son. Whatever we lost, the restoration amount is always more. *Exodus 22:1* states, *If a man shall steal an ox, or a sheep, and kill it, or sell it; he shall restore five oxen for an ox, and four sheep for a sheep.* And again in *Exodus 22:9, For all manner of trespass, whether it be for ox, for ass, for sheep, for raiment, or for any manner of lost thing, which another challengeth to be his, the cause of both parties shall come before the judges; and whom the judges shall condemn, he shall pay double unto his neighbor,* or in *Proverbs 6:31, But if he be found, he shall restore sevenfold.* Jesus is the judge but He also took the thieving neighbor's place and paid more for us.

In addition, Paul requested Philemon to prepare for him a bed as well. Even though Paul was still a prisoner in Rome and may never be released, he knew he was free in Jesus. He was free just like Onesimus. We do not know how much more was given to Onesimus but in *Galatians 4:1-7*, we read, *Now I say, That the heir, as long as he is a child, differeth nothing from a servant, though he be lord of all; But is under tutors and governors until the time appointed of the father. Even so we, when we were children, were in bondage under the elements of the world: But when the fulness of the time was come, God sent forth his Son, made of a woman, made under the law, To redeem them that were under the law, that we might receive the adoption of sons. And because ye are sons, God hath sent forth the Spirit of his Son into your hearts, crying, Abba, Father. Wherefore thou art no more a servant, but a son; and if a son, then an heir of God through Christ.* Under the law, Onesimus would be treated as a servant. The law treated all as servants. It put us all under bondage. We can never be sons and daughters under the law. But Onesimus is now redeemed and restored by Grace. He became a son. And as a son to Philemon, Onesimus came into his inheritance! From servant to heir! From must-serve to get-to-serve!

We were similarly redeemed from the law. Jesus, born under the law, fulfilled all its obligations and then removed it. We are heirs to all that God has for us but we cannot claim the inheritance as long as we are 'children' or 'servants'. The children were the Jews who were breastfed with the milk of the law and had to be weaned from it. The servants were the Gentiles who could never earn their position to become sons or daughters. But by Jesus' finished work, children were weaned and servants were adopted. Both Jews and Gentiles become sons and daughters of God, to receive their full inheritance. We now eat 'meat' and are no longer servants (why would God the Creator of all want servants anyhow). It is all because of Jesus.

❧ 25 ❧

JESUS AND OUR SENSES

We spoke about a spirit of slumber in an earlier chapter. This spirit is produced by the law and it veils our sight and our hearing. We saw this slumbering spirit way back in *1 Samuel 1:11-13, And she vowed a vow, and said, O Lord of hosts, if thou wilt indeed look on the affliction of thine handmaid, and remember me, and not forget thine handmaid, but wilt give unto thine handmaid a man child, then I will give him unto the Lord all the days of his life, and there shall no razor come upon his head. And it came to pass, as she continued praying before the Lord, that Eli marked her mouth. Now Hannah, she spake in her heart; only her lips moved, but her voice was not heard: therefore Eli thought she had been drunken.* God remembered Hannah. He did not make a deal with Hannah. When God remembers, it is done! As it was done, Hannah dedicated the yet un-conceived Samuel to the Lord.

Eli the high priest accused Hannah of being drunk. Eli, having the spirit of slumber in him, wanted to hear audible words while Hannah, meaning Grace, had spoken from her heart. The law produced deafness as stated in *Jeremiah 6:10, To whom shall I speak, and give warning, that they may hear? behold, their ear is uncircumcised, and they cannot hearken.* Eli had two sons, Hophni and Phinehas, both officiating priests in the temple. Like their father, they too were of uncircumcised ears. They could not hear the Word of God or Jesus. Hophni's name came from the word *chophen* which meant 'the hollow of the hand'. Phinehas' name derived from two words, *peh* and *nachash* meaning 'mouth of a serpent'. Taken together, we can see that Eli's two sons abused the people by beating and lying to them. They stole sacrifices and had sexual relations with the women who served in the temple, as in *1 Samuel 2*. Together with their father, they controlled the people with the law and beat them up with it.

The law produced spiritual blindness and deafness, as in *1 Samuel 3:1-5, And the child Samuel ministered unto the LORD before Eli. And the word of the LORD was precious in those days; there was no open vision. And it came to pass at that time, when Eli was laid down in his place, and his eyes began to wax dim, that he could not see; And ere the lamp of God went out in the temple of the LORD, where the ark of God was, and Samuel was laid down to sleep, That the LORD called Samuel: and he answered, Here am I. And he ran unto Eli, and said, Here am I; for thou calledst me. And he said, I called not; lie down again.* The name Samuel meant 'heard of God'. Grace produced hearing. Samuel heard Jesus and became a great prophet and judge! Eli heard nothing. His eyes did not see too. *Romans 10:17* states, *So then faith cometh by hearing, and hearing by the word of God.* Our faith came because we heard Jesus! The Galatians were similarly rebuked by Paul in *Galatians 3:1-2, O foolish Galatians, who hath bewitched you, that ye should not obey the truth, before whose eyes Jesus Christ hath been evidently set forth, crucified among you? This only would I learn of you, Received ye the Spirit by the works of the law, or by the hearing of faith?* To hear any other teaching besides Jesus, to see the law after seeing Jesus, is to be bewitched by the law. As the moronic Galatians! The Holy Spirit never resides in people with witchcraft teaching. He only resides in people who hear by faith, Jesus!

Believers in Jesus can see, hear and speak without the veil. We read in *Acts 2:1-6, 12-13, And when the day of Pentecost was fully come, they were all with one accord in one place. And suddenly there came a sound from heaven as of a rushing mighty wind, and it filled all the house where they were sitting. And there appeared unto them cloven tongues like as of fire, and it sat upon each of them. And they were all filled with the Holy Ghost, and began to speak with other tongues, as the Spirit gave them utterance. And there were dwelling at Jerusalem Jews, devout men, out of every nation under heaven. Now when this was noised abroad, the multitude came together, and were confounded, because that every man heard them speak in his own language. And they were all amazed, and were in doubt, saying one to another, What meaneth this? Others mocking said, These men are full of new wine.* The 120 disciples who waited in the upper room is the fulfillment of the 120 priests who blew on their trumpets, awaiting the glory of the Lord to fall in the newly built Solomon's temple from *2 Chronicles 5:12.*

The 120 waited expectantly. None left until the sign came. In this case, the Holy Spirit came rushing in and sat upon them. It was as though the Holy Spirit had been waiting a long time for this momentous event to arrive! While they could not see the Holy Spirit sitting upon their own heads, they could see the Holy Spirit sitting upon their friends heads. At this resurrection sign that God would always be with them, the exodus into the streets of Jerusalem happened. The voice of God spoke through them and Jesus was widely shared to the Gentiles who were living in Jerusalem at that time. In their own tongues. Jubilee and freedom for all. At the same time, the Pharisaical Jews who were spiritually deaf and blind accused the disciples of being drunk. They were ironically 'correct' for the disciples were filled with new wine or Jesus. This was just a presage to the Marriage Feast of the Lamb where all would be filled with Jesus!

The law blinds us as we read in *John 9:1-16,24,28,34, And as Jesus passed by, he saw a man which was blind from his birth. And his disciples asked him, saying, Master, who did sin, this man, or his parents, that he was born blind? Jesus answered, Neither hath this man sinned, nor his parents: but that the works of God should be made manifest in him. I must work the works of him that sent me, while it is day: the night cometh, when no man can work. As long as I am in the world, I am the light of the world. When he had thus spoken, he spat on the ground, and made clay of the spittle, and he anointed the eyes of the blind man with the clay, And said unto him, Go, wash in the pool of Siloam, (which is by interpretation, Sent.) He went his way therefore, and washed, and came seeing. The neighbours therefore, and they which before had seen him that he was blind, said, Is not this he that sat and begged? Some said, This is he: others said, He is like him: but he said, I am he. Therefore said they unto him, How were thine eyes opened? He answered and said, A man that is called Jesus made clay, and anointed mine eyes, and said unto me, Go to the pool of Siloam, and wash: and I went and washed, and I received sight. Then said they unto him, Where is he? He said, I know not. They brought to the Pharisees him that aforetime was blind. And it was the sabbath day when Jesus made the clay, and opened his eyes. Then again the Pharisees also asked him how he had received his sight. He said unto them, He put clay upon mine eyes, and I washed, and do see. Therefore said some of the Pharisees, This man is not of God, because he keepeth not the sabbath day. Others said, How can a man that is a sinner do such miracles?.. Then again called they the man that was blind, and said unto him, Give God the praise: we know that this man is a sinner. Then they reviled him, and said, Thou art his disciple; but we are Moses' disciples. And they cast him out.*

Even Jesus' disciples were blinded by the law. They believed that doing bad brought bad things into peoples' lives (just as Job's friends or what we call karma). Therefore when they saw Jesus noticing the blind man, they asked Jesus about the sin the blind man did *before* he was born! That sin which he must have done in the womb which led him to being born blind! Or at the very least, his parents sinned leading God to punish them with a blind son. The disciples had a sin mentality which Jesus corrected immediately. Spiritual blindness was worse than physical blindness. We are to look at Jesus, not sin!

In *John 6:28-29* we read, *Then said they unto him, What shall we do, that we might work the works of God? Jesus answered and said unto them, This is the work of God, that ye believe on him whom he hath sent.* **The disciples thought they had to do the works of God. But Jesus said that there was only one work to be done and that was to believe in Him!** Therefore, the works of God would be made manifest in this blind man. People would believe in Jesus because of this blind man. *I must work the works* *of him that sent me, while it is day: the night cometh, when no man can work,* is Jesus finishing up the work of redemption that God sent Him to do. Jesus worked during the day and finished His work before the night came. No man can add to Jesus' completed work!

Siloam meant sent. Jesus was the Sent One. But the physically blind man could not see that. He did not ask for healing. He did not even know about Jesus. But the Healer came to him. He was to receive from the Sent One. Once healed, he did not have to beg anymore. Meanwhile, the neighbors of the healed man brought him to where the spiritually blind Pharisees sat. Jesus made clay for man to see that He made man from clay. He knew the man would be presented before the Pharisees. Jesus wanted the Pharisees to see the heavy clay over their eyes! So with much clay of the law upon their eyes, the Pharisees questioned the man who had no clay over his eyes. They accused him of being a disciple of Jesus. They boasted numerous times as to what they knew, culminating in the boast that they knew they were disciples of Moses, not realizing that they were actually boasting of their great spiritual blindness. *2 Corinthians 3:15* states, *But even unto this day, when Moses is read, the vail is upon their heart.*

They were perfectly represented by Elymas the sorcerer whom Paul addressed in *Acts 13:10-11, And said, O full of all subtilty and all mischief, thou child of the devil, thou enemy of all righteousness, wilt thou not cease to pervert the right ways of the Lord? And now, behold, the hand of the Lord is upon thee, and thou shalt be blind, not seeing the sun for a season. And immediately there fell on him a mist and a darkness; and he went about seeking some to lead him by the hand.* The Pharisees even 'knew' that Jesus was a sinner as He had kneaded clay with spit, had anointed, and had healed on a Sabbath. The Son of God, His disciples, the former blind man, and all who believed in Jesus were cast out. Hence, the Pharisees casted out the only One who could have washed the clay of the law off their slumbering eyes. Without the Son, they sit in darkness, not seeing the sun for a season!

We continue reading in *John 9:35-41, Jesus heard that they had cast him out; and when he had found him, he said unto him, Dost thou believe on the Son of God? He answered and said, Who is he, Lord, that I might believe on him? And Jesus said unto him, Thou hast both seen him, and it is he that talketh with thee. And he said, Lord, I believe. And he worshipped him. And Jesus said, For judgment I am come into this world, that they which see not might see; and that they which see might be made blind. And some of the Pharisees which were with him heard these words, and said unto him, Are we blind also? Jesus said unto them, If ye were blind, ye should have no sin: but now ye say, We see; therefore your sin remaineth.* The man who received from Jesus was originally blind, like the Pharisees. All of them had clay over their eyes. But unlike the Pharisees who rejected the Light that was sent to them, he received the Light. Jesus was that Light. Not only was he healed of his blindness but his spiritual eyes were opened. The man became completely restored. He was 're-created' by the One who said 'Let there be light'. He believed on Jesus while the Pharisees believed on Moses or the law. **Those who were blind to the law saw Grace while those who saw the law were blind to Grace.**

In Genesis, Adam and Eve's eyes were opened and they saw their nakedness. But with Jesus, our eyes are opened and we see our righteousness, our hope, our riches, our inheritance, and our power. We know this from *Ephesians 1:18-19, The eyes of your understanding being enlightened; that ye may know what is the hope of his calling, and what the riches of the glory of his inheritance in the saints, And what is the exceeding greatness of his power to us ward who believe, according to the working of his mighty power.* Jesus took the clay of the law off our eyes when His blood mingled with the clay at the foot of the cross. *2 Corinthians 3:18* states, *But we all, with open face beholding as in a glass the glory of the Lord, are changed into the same image from glory to glory, even as by the Spirit of the Lord.* Because of the glory of Grace, we become the image of Jesus! We see Jesus in the glass only because He lifted the veil of the law from us. However, if we see the law, then the veil is upon our hearts and we cannot see Jesus. But when we are blind to the law, we see Jesus, who took away all of our sins. We have no sins because of Jesus!

❧ 26 ❦

JESUS AND PERFECTION

As we continue to walk on water, let us not forget to keep our eyes on Jesus. It is pure radical Grace that enables us to do the impossible. *Psalm 93:3-4* states that *The floods have lifted up, O Lord, the floods have lifted up their voice; the floods lift up their waves. The Lord on high is mightier than the noise of many waters, yea, than the mighty waves of the sea.* If we take our eyes off Jesus, we fall from Grace and start to sink beneath the waves. *Galatians 5:4* states, *Christ is become of no effect unto you, whosoever of you are justified by the law; ye are fallen from grace.* Remember that 'backsliding' was a term used for those under the law. They backslid from 'doing' the law. They relapsed. For example, we say that the Israelites backslid or reverted to idol worship. However, fallen from Grace means falling from a higher level to a lower level. It means falling from relying on the finished work of Jesus (higher level) to relying again on our own works (lower level). Even then, let us continue to keep our eyes on Jesus, as in *1 Peter 1:13, set your hope fully upon the grace being brought to you in the revelation of Jesus Christ.* For only then will we see how many times Grace has rescued us from our falls.

The first symptoms of falling from Grace are spiritual hunger and thirst. We begin to say things like 'we are hungry/thirsty for more of Christ'. We say that we 'leak' and we need 'an infilling' to fill up the leakage. We cry out for 'more of Him' because we are looking at ourselves and not at Him. In *John 6:35* we read, *And Jesus said unto them, I am the bread of life: he* *that cometh to me shall **never hunger**; and he that believeth on me shall **never thirst**.* Clearly, Jesus said that those who are in Him shall never spiritually hunger nor thirst ever again! He is completely sufficient for us; past, present and future. In fact, when He was born He was placed in a manger, or feeding trough. *Luke 2:7* states, *And she brought forth her firstborn son, and wrapped him in swaddling clothes, and laid him in a manger; because there was no room for them in the inn.* **The world, as symbolized by the inn, can never sustain Jesus but Jesus in a manger is more than enough sustenance for the whole world. The world is tiny when compared to Jesus!**

This symbol of Jesus was shown way back in *Judges 6:36-40, And Gideon said unto God, If thou wilt save Israel by mine hand, as thou hast said, Behold, I will put a fleece of wool in the floor; and if the dew be on the fleece only, and it be dry upon all the earth beside, then shall I know that thou wilt save Israel by mine hand, as thou hast said. And it was so: for he rose up early on the morrow, and thrust the fleece together, and wringed the dew out of the fleece, a bowl full of water. And Gideon said unto God, Let not thine anger be hot against me, and I will speak but this once: let me prove, I pray thee, but this once with the fleece; let it now be dry only upon the fleece, and upon all the ground let there be dew. And God did so that night: for it was dry upon the fleece only, and there was dew on all the ground.*

Only one person could literally save the nation of Israel and that person was Jesus, not Gideon. Fleece comes from lambs. Therefore, the fleece symbolized Jesus, the Lamb of God. At the start, the dew was on the fleece only while the whole earth was dry and thirsty. When Gideon wringed out the fleece, the bowl or earth became full of water, as in *Isaiah 44:3, For I will pour water on the thirsty land, and streams on the dry ground.* This was also shown back in *Numbers 11:9, And when the dew fell upon the camp in the night, the manna fell upon it.* The Manna from heaven, Jesus, was in the dew. Jesus is the Living Dew Water and He is always more than sufficient for the whole earth. Jesus poured Himself out for us. At the end, Dew was all around. The Living Water quenched a dying world. Gideon mentioned a tremendously significant phrase that he probably was not aware of. He mentioned 'this once with the fleece'. Gideon had already used the fleece before so this was the second time. It could not have been 'once'. This 'once' could only refer to Jesus, a one-time sacrifice good for all time. With Jesus, nobody can thirst ever again.

John the Baptist ate locusts and wild honey as we read in *Matthew 3:4, And the same John had his raiment of camel's hair, and a leathern girdle about his loins; and his meat was locusts and wild honey.* John ate locusts which swarm and fall as though from heaven. This symbolized the Bread from heaven which was Jesus as in *John 6:50-51, This is the bread which cometh down from heaven, that a man may eat thereof, and not die. I am the living bread which came down from heaven: if any man eat of this bread, he shall live forever: and the bread that I will give is my flesh, which I will give for the life of the world.* Furthermore, John ate honey which signified the sweet blessings of God. Taste and see the sweetness of Jesus. Let Him coat and melt in our mouths.

We also read in *1 Samuel 14:24-27, And the men of Israel were distressed that day: for Saul had adjured the people, saying, Cursed be the man that eateth any food until evening, that I may be avenged on mine enemies. So none of the people tasted any food. And all they of the land came to a wood; and there was honey upon the ground. And when the people were come into the wood, behold, the honey dropped; but no man put his hand to his mouth: for the people feared the oath. But Jonathan heard not when his father charged the people with the oath: wherefore he put forth the end of the rod that was in his hand, and dipped it in an honeycomb, and put his hand to his mouth; and his eyes were enlightened.* Jonathan after tasting the honey, a symbol of Jesus, was enlightened! Jesus is the bread from heaven and He is our sweet honey from God. Jonathan was unlike his father, Saul, who was trying to earn favor from God by not eating.

In *Matthew 5:6*, it states that *Blessed are they which do hunger and thirst after righteousness: for they shall be filled.* As the righteousness of God is Jesus, those who hunger and thirst after Jesus will henceforth, after putting their faith in Jesus, never hunger and thirst again forevermore. They will always be filled and blessed! In Him, there can never be any leakage. Contrary to many teachings, we have no 'hole' in us whereby we leak slowly. There is no puncture in us. We do not drip, dribble, drain or discharge slowly. When we have Jesus, we are continuously blessed. We cannot experience lack in our lives. There is no need for more of Jesus as He is more than enough already.

When Jesus comes into our lives, we instantly have everything. We have all of His fullness and all of His blessings. We read this in *John 1:15-17, John bare witness of him, and cried, saying, This was he of whom I spake, He that cometh after me is preferred before me: for he was before me. And of his fulness have all we received, and **grace for grace**. For the law was given by Moses, but grace and truth came by Jesus Christ,* and again in *Ephesians 1:3, Blessed be the God and Father of our Lord Jesus Christ, who hath blessed us with all spiritual blessings in heavenly places in Christ:* He gave the best to us already. Everything that pertains to life and godliness (no lack) is in us already because of Jesus. There is no need to curry favor with God to get more. There is no need to beg for more. No influence peddling or blackmail. No paying one's dues. No racking up of points. No quid pro quo. We received grace for grace or in Greek, *charis anti charis. Anti* means in exchange for or in return for. We get Grace and then in exchange for that Grace, we get more Grace. Grace heaped upon Grace. Endless Amazing Grace! He gave it all through Jesus as we see in *2 Peter 1:3, According as his divine power hath given unto us all things that pertain unto life and godliness, through the knowledge of him that hath called us to glory and virtue:* Now we have to become aware of what is ours already.

Jesus has the fullness of the Godhead in Him. When we have Him, we have everything. We are complete in Him. Completeness in Him means that we are supplied with provision, protection, safety, favor, wisdom, health, healing, peace, love, righteousness, victory, honor, strength, financial blessings, and long life. We do not need more of God. We do not need more faith, more hope, or more authority. We do not need more of anything as every good thing that we need is already in us through Jesus. That is also why we do not seek after God, look for

God, chase after God, or work for God. God is not hiding, not ignoring us, not running away from us, and God is not our slave master. For Jesus is not only with us but one with us.

Peter wrote about Paul's letters in *2 Peter 3:16-18, which ignorant and unstable people distort, as they do the other Scriptures, to their own destruction. Therefore, dear friends, since you have been forewarned, be on your guard so that you may not be carried away by the error of the lawless and fall from your secure position. But grow in the grace and knowledge of our Lord and Savior Jesus Christ.* Many times, we just as the Jews whom Peter was addressing, seem to be led away into the error of the wicked and to fall away from our secure position in Grace. We need to beware of ignorant, unstable teachers who tell us how bad we are; how lacking we are; how low we are; how unworthy we are; how incomplete we are; and how undeserving we are. These teachers lead us away from Jesus, to focus on self. What we really need is to grow in our understanding of how loved, perfect, complete, and righteous we are in Jesus. We need *Colossians 1:9-10, For this cause we also...desire that ye might be filled with the knowledge of his will in all wisdom and spiritual understanding; ...and increasing in the knowledge of God.* We need to grow in our spiritual knowledge of God, to understand the '*great and precious promises*' already given to us in *2 Peter 1:4,5-9, For this very reason, make every effort to add to your faith goodness; and to goodness, knowledge; and to knowledge, self-control; and to self-control, perseverance; and to perseverance, godliness; and to godliness, mutual affection; and to mutual affection, love. For if you possess these qualities in increasing measure, they will keep you from being ineffective and unproductive in your knowledge of our Lord Jesus Christ. But whoever does not have them is nearsighted and blind, forgetting that they have been cleansed from their past sins.* Let us not forget that all these characteristics mentioned are rightfully ours.

Let no man through philosophy or vain deceit, fool us with another teaching that we are not complete in Christ, who is the Head of all principality and power. We read this in *Colossians 2:8-10, Beware lest any man spoil you through philosophy and vain deceit, after the tradition of men, after the rudiments of the world, and not after Christ. For in him dwelleth all the fulness of the Godhead bodily. And ye are complete in him, which is the head of all principality and power,* and *Philemon 6, That the communication of thy faith may become effectual by the acknowledging of every good thing which is in you in Christ Jesus.* Every spiritual blessing is in us not because we earned it but because of Jesus in us. Nothing good is left out of us because Jesus is in us.

However, when we turn our eyes off Him and back onto ourselves, we begin to lose awareness of who we actually are. Instead of relying on the magnificent rest and water walking abilities given to us by Jesus, we begin to see the impossibility of our circumstances. Whether turbulent or calm, we will sink under the weight of our own performance. Falling from Grace is akin to drowning in our self-works. Our default setting, reinforced by the culture we live in, is self-works. As we lose focus of Jesus, we 'feel' the hunger and thirst returning. The lack and inadequacy returns. The fullness that Jesus purchased for us seems to be less than full. We feel deficient again. We fall into the lie that we need a revival. To be revived. To gain back our initial position of fullness. To be in control again. So we work very hard at becoming what we already are. We plead with God for more of Him. We wait for God to move, to pour Himself into us, to re-visit us. We rededicate our lives, we press in, we seek to encounter Him, when He is already in us. We think the best is around the corner when the Best is within us. Instead of following Him from the inside, we follow after signs and wonders forgetting that the Sign and the Wonder is always inside of us. For we are inhabited not visited. We are like the two Emmaus-bound disciples who in *Luke 24:21* said, *But we were hoping He was the One who would redeem Israel,* when Jesus had already redeemed them! Jesus is never the uncertain future hope but always the certain present Hope!

When we were unbelievers, we thought highly of ourselves. So when we become believers, we think that we should think less of ourselves. We mistakenly think that we have to decrease as John the Baptist said in *John 3:30, He must increase, but I must decrease.* We think we should reduce ourselves till there be 'none of us and all of Him' or 'die-to-self'. But unlike John the Baptist who did not have Jesus or the Holy Spirit in him, we do! We forget that Jesus is in us! He is one with us, as we read in *John 17:22-23, And the glory which thou gavest me I have given them; that they may be one, even as we are one: I in them, and thou in me, that they may be made perfect in one.* Believers are made perfect as they are one with Jesus! They cannot decrease themselves or 'die-to-self' because Jesus has melded Himself into them. Jesus cannot be decreased or killed off. Hence, the only 'decrease' that we can do is to be more Jesus conscious. To 'increase Him', focus on Jesus, not on anyone or anything else. Why? Because only in Jesus is our *sozo* life, the guarantee of perfection and blessings from His finished work on the cross.

The wisdom of this world, often from satan, consistently says that we are far from perfect. In fact, many people boast about how imperfect they are. They look at the flesh and miss the perfection in their spirit and mind. For example, thinking of ourselves still as 'sinners saved by Grace' lead to excuses for sinning! Sinners sin, right? If we replace Jesus with ourselves, then we replace God's wisdom (we are made righteous) with our wisdom (we are still sinners). We advise and counsel people to do right instead of reminding them that they are already fully righteous in Christ. Anything that is not from God cannot last. People cannot do right for long before they start to do wrong again. Many believers just cannot trust Jesus in them to overcome and say no to sin. They would rather trust their own strength. **We should rather trust in the power of Jesus to help and keep us from doing wrong rather than our own strength to do right! But to add to Jesus is to take from Jesus!**

The wisdom of God can be found in *1 Corinthians 2:5-7, 10-16, That your faith should not stand in the wisdom of men, but in the power of God. Howbeit we speak wisdom among them that are perfect: yet not the wisdom of this world, nor of the princes of this world, that come to nought: But we speak the wisdom of God in a mystery, even the hidden wisdom, which God ordained before the world unto our glory: But God hath revealed them unto us by his Spirit: for the Spirit searcheth all things, yea, the deep things of God. For what man knoweth the things of a man, save the spirit of man which is in him?...they are spiritually discerned...But we have the mind of Christ.* Jesus as Grace is revealed to man by the Holy Spirit. But the natural senses of man cannot understand what the Holy Spirit says. The Holy Spirit talks only to our spirit, not our bodily senses. *John 16:12* states, *I have yet many things to say unto you, but ye cannot bear them now.* Because we still live in a fleshly body, we often find ourselves unaware of all that Jesus has for us. When we fall from Grace to the law, we cannot receive more from Jesus because we now trust in the wisdom of men which is of the flesh and in doing so pierce ourselves with many sorrows.

Compare the accounts in *Mark 5:22-23, And, behold, there cometh one of the rulers of the synagogue, Jairus by name; and when he saw him, he fell at his feet, And besought him greatly, saying, My little daughter lieth at the point of death: I pray thee, come and lay thy hands on her, that she may be healed; and she shall live,* to that in *Luke 7:2-7, And a certain centurion's servant, who was dear unto him, was sick, and ready to die. And when he heard of Jesus, he sent unto him the elders of the Jews, beseeching him that he would come and heal his servant. And when they came to Jesus, they besought him instantly, saying, That he was worthy for whom he should do this: For he loveth our nation, and he hath built us a synagogue. Then Jesus went with them. And when he was now not far from the house, the centurion sent friends to him, saying unto him...say in a word, and my servant shall be healed.*

Both Jairus and the centurion had faith that Jesus could and would heal. But Jairus, being the leader of a synagogue, was not aware of the full power of Jesus. He wanted Jesus to come to his house and to lay hands on his daughter. The centurion, having built a synagogue, was more aware of who Jesus was. He believed that Jesus just had to say it and his servant would be healed. **The more aware we are of who Jesus is the more we can receive from Him. We may be sick. That is a fact. But the Truth, who is Jesus, healed us already by the beatings on His body. He went through it for us. So when the fact and the truth does not line up, let us choose truth.** Healed is spelled h-e-a-l-E-D! Past tense.

Done deal. Finished work. Therefore, let us claim and receive the truth that we are indeed healed already by Jesus.

The deep things of God, the things God has prepared for us, the things that God freely gave to us are all revealed to us by the Holy Spirit. We cannot earn these things as they are free. God ordained these things for us before the world was formed. How can we say that we are perfect? Because we know the mind of the Lord as we have been given the mind of Christ! As Jesus is perfect, so are we! We are who God says we are! The Holy Spirit teaches us all things pertaining to who we are in Christ. We are fully anointed as He gave us this anointing, as in *2 Corinthians 1:21, Now he which stablisheth us with you in Christ, and hath anointed us, is God.* There is no need for more or fresh anointing because Christ meaning 'Anointed One' is in us already.

So who is lying to us about who we are in Christ? None other than satan himself and the seducing Pharisaical legalistic teachers who deny Christ and His fullness. We read this in *1 John 2:22-23,27, Who is a liar but he that denieth that Jesus is the Christ? He is antichrist, that denieth the Father and the Son. Whosoever denieth the Son, the same hath not the Father: (but) he that acknowledgeth the Son hath the Father also… as the same anointing teacheth you of all things, and is truth, and is no lie, and even as it hath taught you, ye shall abide in him.*

Present day rabbinical teachers descended from the Pharisees. Fleshly legalistic teachings, be it from the Mosaic law or a body of law which we make, are seductive in that we find it sensually gratifying when we fulfill some or most of it. It gives our flesh great pride and pleasure when we achieve a level of morality and obedience that others cannot attain. The very real danger is that our flesh is very quick to forget Jesus once we have earned a level of respect from man. We revel, lick, and swallow up the adulation and worship from others. As in the garden, satan knows that the flesh always wants to be god. But as believers, we have the Holy Spirit, Jesus, and the Father abiding in us! The Holy Spirit will teach us all things, to correctly reject any and all teachings which add to the finished work of Jesus.

∂ 27 ∽

JESUS AND THE PHARISEES

The word hypocrite (in Greek *hypó* meaning under and *krínō* meaning judge) is usually used for masked actors on the stage as they pretended to be someone whom they were not. They were known as *hypokritēs*. Jesus consistently called the Pharisees hypocrites as they were double faced.

This is clearly illustrated in *Matthew 21:28-30, But what think ye? A certain man had two sons; and he came to the first, and said, Son, go work today in my vineyard. He answered and said, I will not: but afterward he repented, and went. And he came to the second, and said likewise. And he answered and said, I go, sir: and went not.* There were two sons. The first son was a sinner who initially refused Jesus. But he knew that he fell short in every area of his life. So he repented, meaning he changed his mind, and accepted the free gift of Grace. The second son was a hypocrite. He was the one who meticulously followed the law and wanted to appear holy before people. When asked, he was quick to say "Yes, sir!" but it was only an outward show, a mask. The real face under the mask rejected the invitation to enter. That was the Pharisaical hypocrite.

Matthew 23:23-34 states, *Woe unto you, scribes and Pharisees, hypocrites! for ye pay tithe of mint and anise and cummin, and have omitted the weightier matters of the law, judgment, mercy, and faith: these ought ye to have done, and not to leave the other undone. Ye blind guides, which strain at a gnat, and swallow a camel. Woe unto you, scribes and Pharisees, hypocrites! for ye make clean the outside of the cup and of the platter, but within they are full of extortion and excess. Thou blind Pharisee, cleanse first that which is within the cup and platter, that the outside of them may be clean also. Woe unto you, scribes and Pharisees, hypocrites! for ye are like unto whited sepulchres, which indeed appear beautiful outward, but are within full of dead men's bones, and of all uncleanness. Even so ye also outwardly appear righteous unto men, but within ye are full of hypocrisy and iniquity. Woe unto you, scribes and Pharisees, hypocrites! because ye build the tombs of the prophets, and garnish the sepulchres of the righteous, And say, If we had been in the days of our fathers, we would not have been partakers with them in the blood of the prophets...Ye serpents, ye generation of vipers, how can ye escape the damnation of hell? Wherefore, behold, I send unto you prophets, and wise men, and scribes: and some of them ye shall kill and crucify; and some of them shall ye scourge in your synagogues, and persecute them from city to city:*

The Pharisees, in order to appear holy, would steadfastly pay their tithes. They would sieve their wines through a strainer so as to not accidentally swallow a gnat or a tiny fruit fly. Their appearance and their conduct would be laboriously perfect and ponderously righteous. But behind the holy façade, they would extort, steal, persecute, scourge, kill and crucify people. The rot was from the inside. Their judgment was without mercy, pity, or forbearance. For their unjust judgment of the people, Jesus would judge them back. We read this in *Matthew 7:1-5 , Judge not, that ye be not judged. For with what judgment ye judge, ye shall be judged: and with what measure ye mete, it shall be measured to you again. And why beholdest thou the mote that is in thy brother's eye, but considerest not the beam that is in thine own eye? Or how wilt thou say to thy brother, Let me pull out the mote out of thine eye; and, behold, a beam is in thine own eye? Thou hypocrite, first cast out the beam out of thine own eye; and then shalt thou see clearly to cast out the mote out of thy brother's eye.*

The Pharisees were like children playing in the markets. As children, they did not realize that their games with the law were games of death. We read this in *Matthew 11:15-19, He that hath ears to hear, let him hear. But whereunto shall I liken this generation? It is like unto children sitting in the markets, and calling unto their fellows, And saying, We have piped unto you, and ye have not danced; we have mourned unto you, and ye have not lamented. For John came neither eating nor drinking, and they say, He hath a devil. The Son of man came eating and drinking, and they say, Behold a man gluttonous, and a winebibber, a friend of publicans and sinners. But wisdom is justified of her children.* As children, they played a game called weddings and funerals. When the flutes played, they would put on happy faces and would dance for a little while, like at a wedding. But they soon got tired of the game and stopped dancing. Then, a funeral dirge would start and they would all put on long, forlorn faces. After a little while, they got sick of that game too and would not lament any more.

Initially, the Pharisees liked John the Baptist for his stern and austere lifestyle, but then denounced him for having a devil. It was akin to a funeral and they ditched him. Then Jesus came as a bridegroom and invited them a wedding feast, with music and food. That offended them too so they lambasted Jesus for His pleasurable lifestyle and condemned Him as a friend of sinners. **What the Pharisees missed was that John the Baptist represented the old covenant. He was being replaced by Jesus, the new and better covenant. If the Pharisees truly loved the old covenant, they would have mourned, fasted, and lamented its passing. But they did not. And if they had loved the new covenant, they would have danced and feasted with joy that the Son of Man had come, who would transform the sons of men into the sons of God. But they did not do that either.**

Mark 7:13 states, *Making the word of God of none effect through your tradition, which ye have delivered: and many such like things do ye.* The traditions that the Pharisees held onto (here referring to helping parents and hand washing) made the Word of God ineffective. But through these traditions, the Pharisees believed they had the same Father as Jesus. After all, they were Abraham's seeds, just like Jesus was Abraham's seed. But *John 8:37-47* states, *I know that ye are Abraham's seed; but ye seek to kill me, because my word hath no place in you. I speak that which I*

*have seen with my Father: and ye do that which ye have seen with
your father. They answered and said unto him, Abraham is our
father. Jesus saith unto them, If ye were Abraham's children, ye
would do the works of Abraham. But now ye seek to kill me, a man
that hath told you the truth, which I have heard of God: this did
not Abraham. Ye do the deeds of your father. Then said they to
him, We be not born of fornication; we have one Father, even God.
Jesus said unto them, If God were your Father, ye would love me:
for I proceeded forth and came from God; neither came I of
myself, but he sent me. Why do ye not understand my speech? even
because ye cannot hear my word. Ye are of your father the devil,
and the lusts of your father ye will do. He was a murderer from the
beginning, and abode not in the truth, because there is no truth in
him. When he speaketh a lie, he speaketh of his own: for he is a
liar, and the father of it. And because I tell you the truth, ye believe
me not. Which of you convinceth me of sin? And if I say the truth,
why do ye not believe me? He that is of God heareth God's words:
ye therefore hear them not, because ye are not of God.*

    The Pharisees who wanted to kill Jesus contended with
Him first that they had the same father, namely Abraham. Jesus
challenged them that if they were Abraham's children they would
do the works of Abraham. The 'works' of Abraham is stated
clearly in *Romans 4:2-3, For if Abraham were justified by works,
he hath whereof to glory; but not before God. For what saith the
scripture? Abraham believed God, and it was counted unto him for
righteousness.* Abraham believed. That was his work. The
Pharisees did not believe. That was their work. Therefore, Jesus
repudiated their claim of having the same father! Hearing that, the
Pharisees mocked Jesus saying that at least they were not born out
of wedlock, directly accusing Mary and Joseph! Then they claimed
to have another Father, God Himself. Jesus repudiated that too. If
God were their Father, then they would love and accept Jesus, for
God had sent Him. Jesus is God's revelation of Himself! In our
language, Jesus is God's 'selfie' as in *John 14:8: he that hath seen
me hath seen the Father, Colossians 1:15, Who is the image of the
invisible God,* and *Hebrews 1:3, The Son is the radiance of God's
glory and the exact representation of His nature.* **Jesus is the**

exact voice, form, and nature of God. The Pharisees, made *in* God's image, rejected Jesus, *the* exact image of God! Hence, they rejected God the Father. Jesus spoke of unmerited favor because that was what His Father spoke of. The Pharisees did works because that was what their father did. They did not have the revelation of Grace and only did the works of their father, the devil! It began in the garden of Eden when Adam and Eve ate from the tree of good and evil and their eyes and mind became opened to works. Gone were their initial dependence on God alone. Now as self-made gods they began to depend entirely upon tradition and their own self-works. Satan must have laughed hysterically as mankind began to depend on what would kill them!

Similarly, satan showed the Pharisees salvation by zeal for the law which was never meant to save anyone. *Romans 10:2-4* states, *For I bear them record that they have a zeal of God, but not according to knowledge. For they being ignorant of God's righteousness, and going about to establish their own righteousnes have not submitted themselves unto the righteousness of God. For Christ is the end of the law for righteousness to everyone that believeth.* The Pharisees had a zeal for the wrong thing for they could not see *the Zeal of the LORD of armies,* Jesus, in *Isaiah 9:7.* They desired the law instead of the *Desire of all nations,* Jesus, in *Haggai 2:7.* They rejected the righteousness of God, Jesus, and established their own righteousness by the law. As such, they became sons of the devil. Jesus and the Pharisees did not have the same Father! The Pharisees rejected God the Father by rejecting His Son, Jesus. These Pharisees were those whom Jesus would be ashamed of as written in *Mark 8:38, Whosoever therefore shall be ashamed of me and of my words in this adulterous and sinful generation; of him also shall the Son of man be ashamed, when he cometh in the glory of his Father with the holy angels.* Jesus came in the glory of His Father but the Pharisees were ashamed of Him. To be ashamed here meant to reject Grace for fleshly self-works.

Satan does encourage self-works as we read in *2 Corinthians 11:13-15, For such are false apostles, deceitful workers, transforming themselves into the apostles of Christ. And no marvel; for Satan himself is transformed into an angel of light.*

Therefore it is no great thing if his ministers also be transformed as the ministers of righteousness; whose end shall be according to their works. All ministers that minister according to works are called deceitful workers. Satan deceives them into thinking that they are ministers of righteousness. We should not marvel at this as satan is the father of deceit and has blinded many ministers to take up his cause! Since nobody can be righteous by works, satan defeats us by making us exhausted, burnt-out, bitter, and beaten down in chasing after formulas and programs to attain righteousness. All the while, refreshment and fullness is right inside of us. His name is Jesus.

Being fooled by satan, the Pharisees became interpreters and teachers of the law. Using the law, they controlled the population to their advantage. *Matthew 23:2* states, *The scribes and the Pharisees sit in Moses' seat.* They were without compassion, acting like white-washed tombs full of dead men's bones, sucking the life out of the people. We see in *John 7:19, Did not Moses give you the law, and yet none of you keepeth the law?* Not one of them could keep the law, yet they pretended to. The ministry of death, which was the law, not only brought death to the Pharisees but to the people as well. *Matthew 15:7-9* states, *Ye hypocrites, well did Esaias prophesy of you, saying, This people draweth nigh unto me with their mouth, and honoureth me with their lips; but their heart is far from me. But in vain they do worship me, teaching for doctrines the commandments of men.* No law or commandment of men ever saved anyone. Yet it was taught as the truth. Paul warned us of this in *Hebrews 13:9, Be not carried about with divers and strange doctrines. For it is a good thing that the heart be established with grace; not with meats, which have not profited them that have been occupied therein.* The strange doctrine was the law and its need for works and sacrifices. The fruit of the law brings death. Our hearts are to be established and planted in Grace and nothing else. The fruit of Grace is life.

Jesus also warned his disciples continuously to beware of teachers of the law. We see in *Matthew 7:15-18, Beware of false prophets, which come to you in sheep's clothing, but inwardly they are ravening wolves. Ye shall know them by their fruits. Do men gather grapes of thorns, or figs of thistles? Even so every good tree bringeth forth good fruit; but a corrupt tree bringeth forth evil fruit.* The wolves were those who taught salvation by the law. They would grievously attack Grace. They were like corrupt trees which produced evil fruits of self works, cursed with thorns and thistles.

 Acts 20:28-29 states, *Take heed therefore unto yourselves, and to all the flock, over the which the Holy Ghost hath made you overseers, to feed the church of God, which he hath purchased with his own blood. For I know this, that after my departing shall grievous wolves enter in among you, not sparing the flock.* A perversion of the gospel of Grace is the need to maintain salvation by self-works. It is an adulteration of the truth. It is a distortion of salvation by Grace alone. It is cleverly disguised as a teaching of salvation by Jesus at the onset but after that, we *get* to do the law joyfully. We do not *have* to but we *get* to. However, very soon, what we get to do becomes the proof of our salvation. Messianic Jews do the Torah and Christians do self-righteous works. Grace is just a disguise to do the law and to be self-centered again. Have fruits = Saved. No fruits = Not Saved. The fruit becomes much more important than the root, who is Jesus. As time passes, the root is all but forgotten. We forget completely that the Gospel is actually only about Jesus, who is the Root and not a fruit! He is the only proof we will ever need!

 We are all called to preach and teach the gospel or the good news, not good law, of Jesus. *Hebrews 5:12* states, *For when for the time ye ought to be teachers, ye have need that one teach you again which be the first principles of the oracles of God.* We are not called to be Pharisaical teachers who instructed out of the law. The Pharisees laid heavy burdens upon the people and passed judgments upon them. They were teachers in the dark and they were blind guides to the blind. They were foolish instructors to foolish students and they were babe teachers to babes. *Romans 2:16-20* states, that *In the day when God shall judge the secrets of men by Jesus Christ according to my gospel. Behold, thou art called a Jew, and restest in the law, and makest thy boast of God, And knowest his will, and approvest the things that are more excellent, being instructed out of the law; And art confident that thou thyself art a guide of the blind, a light of them which are in darkness, An instructor of the foolish, a teacher of babes, which hast the form of knowledge and of the truth in the law.*

The law had a form of knowledge and truth but was not the real thing. We read in *Matthew 23:13, But woe unto you, scribes and Pharisees, hypocrites! for ye shut up the kingdom of heaven against men: for ye neither go in yourselves, neither suffer ye them that are entering to go in.* Because of the law, the Pharisees could not earn their way into heaven. But because they taught others, they prevented them from entering into heaven as well. They were also the ones who in *1 Thessalonians 2:16, try to keep us from telling the gentiles how they can be saved. As a result, they are constantly adding to the number of sins they have committed. However, wrath has overtaken them at last!* God's wrath on sin came upon these unbelievers who kept preventing others from knowing Grace! They are the ones referred to back in *Matthew 18* who should have their hands and feet cut off and their eyes gouged out for they are enemies of the kingdom of God.

We see in *James 3:1, My brethren, be not many masters, knowing that we shall receive the greater condemnation.* The word 'masters' is *'didáskalos'* in Greek, meaning 'teachers' or one who has mastery in their field of learning. Condemnation were reserved for teachers of the law! This is clear in *Matthew 23:1-8, Then spake Jesus to the multitude, and to his disciples, Saying, The scribes and the Pharisees sit in Moses' seat: All therefore whatsoever they bid you observe, that observe and do; but do not ye after their works: for they say, and do not. For they bind heavy burdens and grievous to be borne, and lay them on men's shoulders; but they themselves will not move them with one of their fingers. But all their works they do for to be seen of men: they make broad their phylacteries, and enlarge the borders of their garments, And love the uppermost rooms at feasts, and the chief seats in the synagogues, And greetings in the markets, and to be called of men, Rabbi, Rabbi. But be not ye called Rabbi: for one is your Master, even Christ; and all ye are brethren.*

The scribes and the Pharisees, as learned teachers, had the power to bind and loose (in Hebrew, *asar we-hittir*), meaning they decided what was forbidden and what was permitted under the law. They enlarged the borders of their own garments by binding heavy burdens and deepened their pockets by loosing parts of the law, on others. We read one such example in *Mark 7:10-13, For Moses said, Honour thy father and thy mother...But ye say, If a man shall say to his father or mother, It is Corban, that is to say, a gift, by whatsoever thou mightest be profited by me; he shall be free. And ye suffer him no more to do ought for his father or his mother; Making the word of God of none effect through your tradition, which ye have delivered.* The law said to honor fathers and mothers, even monetarily. But the Pharisees, loving money more than the law, would say the word '*Corban*' meaning 'gift to God' over the money. The money now cannot be given to fathers and mothers to honor them as it is now a 'gift to god' i.e. themselves. This way, they started a tradition of loosening the law to their advantage. Observe the Pharisaical self-works, traditions, and their law-teaching! Then do what we observed – which is to avoid such self-works, traditions, and law-teaching!

The truth is that there is only one Teacher or Master, and His name is Jesus! We read back in *Matthew 16:18-19, And I say also unto thee, That thou art Peter, and upon this rock I will build my church; and the gates of hell shall not prevail against it. And I will give unto thee the keys of the kingdom of heaven: and whatsoever thou shalt bind on earth shall be bound in heaven: and whatsoever thou shalt loose on earth shall be loosed in heaven.* Binding and loosing has nothing to do with satan and his demonic host. There is no need to fight against a defeated foe. The gates of hell were a place of judgment and condemnation. But it was defeated by the Rock. Jesus lifted up the gates of judgment and hung it on the cross. Law and death cannot win over Grace and Life. Grace is the key to the kingdom of heaven. What the Pharisees loosed, He bound up. Jesus bound up the law and brought it back to its pristine standard. From 'you have heard it said' to 'but I say to you'. Jesus brought the law back to its pure form so that the people would see their need for Him. At the same time, Jesus loosed the whole burden of the law by fulfilling it.

Hebrews 5:13-14 states, *For every one that useth milk is unskilful in the word of righteousness: for he is a babe. But strong meat belongeth to them that are of full age, even those who by reason of use have their senses exercised to discern both good and evil.* Then again in *1 Corinthians 3:1-2, And I, brethren, could not speak unto you as unto spiritual, but as unto carnal, even as unto babes in Christ. I have fed you with milk, and not with meat: for hitherto ye were not able to bear it, neither yet now are ye able.* A baby uses milk. Using milk is defined as being unskillful in the word of righteousness. The Word of Righteousness is Jesus. Therefore, a baby as defined here is a person who knows the law but not Jesus. A baby cannot take meat because he cannot bear it. He is unable to understand Grace as he is still a baby!

We read also in *John 6:27, Labour not for the meat which perisheth, but for that meat which endureth unto everlasting life, which the Son of man shall give unto you: for him hath God the Father sealed.* The meat that perishes are self-works. Self works derive from the knowledge of good and evil. A person who exercises works and labors in it is carnal. By their flesh, they religiously pronounce what is good and what is evil . But a person of full age uses meat because he or she knows Jesus. Because they are connected to Jesus, they can spiritually discern good and evil. The difference is that they work not from their carnal knowledge but from their spiritual discernment. **Hence, milk is the shadow and meat is the reality of Jesus.** Adults in Christ use meat and not milk. Jesus is the meat that never perishes and is given to us without any labor on our part. It endures unto everlasting life. Jesus has complete power over death, both spiritual and physical. That is also why Jesus called for Jairus' daughter to be given meat to eat as we read in *Luke 8:55, And her spirit came again, and she arose straightway: and he commanded to give her meat.* She was only twelve years of age and had died. One would think that Jesus would ask for a glass of milk to be given to her. But milk, or the law, would not do for one raised up by Grace! Only meat would do. Only Grace would do for born again believers. Only Jesus would do!

❧ 28 ❧

JESUS AND FALLING FROM GRACE

Works are pernicious in that it deceives people with a false sense of security. They believe they are secure in something that will ultimately fail them. We read in *Matthew 7:21-27, Not everyone that saith unto me, Lord, Lord, shall enter into the kingdom of heaven; but he that doeth the will of my Father which is in heaven. Many will say to me in that day, Lord, Lord, have we not prophesied in thy name? and in thy name have cast out devils? and in thy name done many wonderful works? And then will I profess unto them, I never knew you: depart from me, ye that work iniquity. Therefore whosoever heareth these sayings of mine, and doeth them, I will liken him unto a wise man, which built his house upon a rock: And the rain descended, and the floods came, and the winds blew, and beat upon that house; and it fell not: for it was founded upon a rock. And every one that heareth these sayings of mine, and doeth them not, shall be likened unto a foolish man, which built his house upon the sand: And the rain descended, and the floods came, and the winds blew, and beat upon that house; and it fell: and great was the fall of it.*

The will of the Father is explained clearly in *John 6:39-40, And this is the Father's will which hath sent me, that of all which he hath given me I should lose nothing, but should raise it up again at the last day. And this is the will of him that sent me, that every one which seeth the Son, and believeth on him, may have everlasting life: and I will raise him up at the last day.* His will is for all people to have faith in Jesus. Those who have faith in Jesus would be eternally secure. In Greek, eternal is *aiónios* not meaning time but 'to be with Jesus'. We cannot be cast out. We cannot lose our salvation. Jesus loses no one! There is only one Rock and that Rock is Jesus. He sustains the house built upon Him. As the Rock is eternal, so is the believer built on it. Sand represents the law. There are many grains of sand corresponding to the many requirements of the law. Those who build upon the granular law will fall. The greater the amount of sand, the greater the fall. More law always equals more sin. We read this in *Romans 5:20, 7:13. Moreover the law entered, that the offence might abound... that sin by the commandment might become exceeding sinful,* and in *1 Corinthians 15:56, and the strength of sin is the law.*

Because of the veil of the law, many Jews cannot see clearly. They cannot see that by the law, sin would become exceedingly sinful because the strength of sin is the law. For example, male Jews would offer up *'shacharit'* or morning prayers every day. There is a portion which goes like this: 'Blessed are you, *HaShem*, King of the universe, for not having made me a Gentile; Blessed are you, *HaShem*, King of the universe, for not having made me a slave; Blessed are you, *HaShem*, King of the universe, for not having made me a woman'. They believed they were blessed because they were allowed by *HaShem* (meaning 'The Name' or God) to perform all the 613 laws. Gentiles, slaves, and women do not have such privileges. Hence, they believed that God was pleased with them because they did more law than the Gentiles, the slaves, and the women! They clean forgot that the reason they were blessed was because God's name was placed on them, as in *Numbers 6:27, So they will put my name on the Israelites, and I will bless them.* It was never works! Present day Jews offer prayers as a substitute for animal sacrifices, as in *Hosea 14:2, Take with you words, and turn to the LORD: say unto him, Take away all iniquity, and receive us graciously: so will we render the calves of our lips.* Daily prayer recitals or 'calves of lips' replaced calf sacrifices. Over time, the total number of these liturgical formulaic prayers grew considerably.

In *Galatians 3:26-29,* we read, *For ye are all the children of God by faith in Christ Jesus. For as many of you as have been baptized into Christ have put on Christ. There is neither Jew nor Greek, there is neither bond nor free, there is neither male nor female: for ye are all one in Christ Jesus. And if ye be Christ's, then are ye Abraham's seed, and heirs according to the promise.* In Jesus, the veil of separation was removed. There is no difference between Jews or Gentiles, bond or free, and male or female. We read in *Galatians 6:15, For in Christ Jesus neither circumcision availeth anything, nor uncircumcision, but a new creature.* At the end, it is the new creation that matters. Nobody becomes new but by Jesus! As believers, we are all children of God because of our faith in Jesus.

We read this in *Romans 3:28, Therefore we conclude that a man is justified by faith without the deeds of the law. Galatians 5:1-4* explains it best, *Stand fast therefore in the liberty wherewith Christ hath made us free, and be not entangled again with the yoke of bondage. Behold, I Paul say unto you, that if ye be circumcised, Christ shall profit you nothing. For I testify again to every man that is circumcised, that he is a debtor to do the whole law. Christ is become of no effect unto you, whosoever of you are justified by the law; ye are fallen from grace.* For the Jews, *Romans 2:28-29* states, *For he is not a Jew, which is one outwardly; neither is that circumcision, which is outward in the flesh: But he is a Jew, which is one inwardly; and circumcision is that of the heart, in the spirit, and not in the letter.* According to Paul, a real Jew is not defined by his ethnicity or by his physical circumcision but by his inward circumcision; that of the heart and not of the flesh. There must be a turning of their hearts or their spirits to Jesus, as in *Galatians 3:7, Therefore know that only those who are of faith are sons of Abraham.* That is why Gentiles who are not from Abraham's loins were considered sons of Abraham because of their faith in Jesus!

Falling from Grace means going back to the law and being entangled in its yoke of bondage again. Circumcision, a work, does absolutely nothing for us. If we stand on circumcision, then we are liable to the whole law. Going back to the law puts us back into a cursed situation whereby we strife, control, manipulate, work, fix, and fight only to reap guilt, pain, envy, hatred, condemnation, and feelings of worthlessness. Our works are never enough. The only way to be free from all of these is to be in Jesus. **The purpose of the law was to lead us to faith in Jesus, not to make us righteous. The very fact that Jesus fulfilled the law established that the law required a Savior. That made the law holy, just, and good!** It is faith in Jesus that mattered, as in *Romans 9:30-31, That the Gentiles, which followed not after righteousness, have attained to righteousness, even the righteousness which is of faith. But Israel, which followed after the law of righteousness, hath not attained to the law of righteousness.* This is a big offense to the Jews who had followed after the law to attain righteousness under it, only to not attain it. It is perturbing to the point of blasphemy to hear that Gentiles, who did not have the law, receive righteousness solely by faith in Jesus as Grace!

But many people do fall from Grace. One of the best examples of this can be found in *Hebrews 6:4-6, For it is impossible for those who were once enlightened, and have tasted of the heavenly gift, and were made partakers of the Holy Ghost, And have tasted the good word of God, and the powers of the world to come, If they shall fall away, to renew them again unto repentance; seeing they crucify to themselves the Son of God afresh, and put him to an open shame.* These verses specifically addressed Jews, not Gentiles, who had fallen away. These were Jews who saw and was with Jesus. They were enlightened by His teachings. They tasted of His miracles. They saw the workings of the Holy Spirit in Jesus' life. Yet they went back to the law.

They escaped the pollution of the flesh and the law, but became entangled again in the many lines and hooks of the law. We read this in *2 Peter 2:20-22, For if after they have escaped the pollutions of the world through the knowledge of the Lord and Saviour Jesus Christ, they are again entangled therein, and overcome, the latter end is worse with them than the beginning. For it had been better for them not to have known the way of righteousness, than, after they have known it, to turn from the holy commandment delivered unto them. But it is happened unto them according to the true proverb, The dog is turned to his own vomit again; and the sow that was washed to her wallowing in the mire.* The people who turned away from Jesus are now worse off than before. They now wallow in their own mire and vomit. They are referred to as swine, as in *Leviticus 11:7, And the swine...he is unclean to you.* The modern word for such people is apostates.

These people knew the way of righteousness, which was Jesus, but turned away from the holy commandment to believe in Him only. The commandments of God can be summarized down to one commandment and that is to believe on the name of Jesus as found in *1 John 3:23-24, And this is his commandment, That we should believe on the name of his Son Jesus Christ, and love one another, as he gave us commandment. And he that keepeth his commandments dwelleth in him, and he in him. And hereby we know that he abideth in us, by the Spirit which he hath given us.* How do we know that we have Jesus in us? Because the Holy Spirit, also called the Spirit of Christ in *Romans 8:9,* will be in us. And how do we know that it is the Holy Spirit in us and not some other spirit? The answer was given in *1 John 4:2, By this you will know the Spirit of God: Every spirit that confesses that Jesus Christ has come in the flesh is from God.* The Holy Spirit confesses Jesus Christ is God who came in the flesh! Jesus is 100% God and 100% man (what scholars call hypostatic union) forever!

But are those who fall from Grace lost? Let us read from *Matthew 14:29-31, And when Peter was come down out of the ship, he walked on the water, to go to Jesus. But when he saw the wind boisterous, he was afraid; and beginning to sink, he cried, saying, Lord, save me. And immediately Jesus stretched forth his hand, and caught him.* The fallen are always lifted up by Jesus! *Isaiah 42:3-4* states that *A bruised (ratsats) reed shall he not break and the smoking (keheh) flax shall he not quench (kabah)... He shall not fail (kahah) nor be discouraged (ratsats), till he have set judgment in the earth.* In Hebrew, Jesus will not *kabah* nor *kahah* the *keheh* and He will not *ratsats* the *ratsats*!

There is no end to Jesus' love for us. He is with us in our shame, our anger, our bitterness, our screams, our tears, our viral stupidity, our mistakes, our sufferings, our losses, our pains, our divorces, our infidelities, and our broken hearts. We read this in *Joshua 1:5, as I was with Moses, so I will be with thee: I will not fail thee, nor forsake thee.* No matter our failures, He will never fail us! No matter our behavior, He will never forsake us! Even if everybody abandon and desert us, He will never ever abandon and desert us. He truly loves us with a love that will never let us go. We realize that we can never be separated from His radical love. We shake with awe at Grace that came as a person - Jesus. We tremble with joy beholding Jesus who gave beauty for ugly ashes, oil of joy for mourning, and garments of praise for the spirit of heaviness (*Isaiah 61:3*). When He told us that we have little faith, it was not a rebuke, but a reminder that He has much more for us. **Let us not doubt but have faith that He has more for us!**

But many people have pointed out a particular verse that seemed to say that Jesus would deny us if we were to deny Him. It is found in *2 Timothy 2:11-13, It is a faithful saying: For if we be dead with him, we shall also live with him: If we suffer, we shall also reign with him: if we deny him, he also will deny us: If we believe not, yet he abideth faithful: he cannot deny himself.* Actually, Paul is emphasizing three times that Jesus is always **with** us as He is one **with** us. Jesus is always faithful and He will always be **with** us. Jesus is **with** us in death and life. Jesus is **with** us in suffering and reigning. Jesus is **with** us when we are faithless (we deny Him) and when we are faithful (we do not deny Him). In Greek, *verse 13* reads, *If we are faithless, he faithful remains, to deny indeed himself not he is able.* **Even when we pull back, appear faithless, and deny Him, yet He will deny our denials of Him because He cannot deny Himself. As He is one with us already,** *to deny indeed Himself not He is able*! So when we deny Him, He is still **with** us. Whether we die, live, suffer, reign, deny, not deny, Jesus is always **with** us! His faith, not our faith, keeps us **with** Him. And that is a faithful saying!

A simple example will suffice. Imagine Jesus holding onto us and us holding onto Him. Then, one day, we let go of Him and choose to go our own way. Does that mean that He has let go of us as well? No, it does not. We can let Him go but He has chosen to never let go of us. Just as in a flying trapeze, it is the Catcher's grip that matters. Jesus caught us. He got what He came for! Why would He let go of you and me, His bride, whom He gave up everything for? *Mark 2:19* states, *And Jesus said unto them, Can the children of the bridechamber fast, while the bridegroom is with them? as long as they have the bridegroom with them, they cannot fast.* The word 'children' as used here is '*huioi*' (in Greek), meaning sons and daughters. As sons and daughters of God, we have Jesus with us forever and ever. That was written into the marriage contract. The bridegroom went away once (hence, the fasting). But because of the Holy Spirit or the Spirit of Christ in us now, Jesus would never go away again. He is the faithful One in *2 Thessalonians 3:3, But the Lord is faithful, who shall stablish you, and keep you from evil.*

We know from *Hebrews 13:5, I will never leave thee, nor forsake thee,* and *Matthew 28:20, lo, I am with you always, even unto the end of the world,* that He is the One who talks to us when our phones and texts stay dark. He is the One who accepts and encourages us when friends skewer us on social media. He is the One who whispers 'I love you' when others tell us to go kill ourselves. He is the One who picks us up from the bathroom floor and wipes the vomit and tears from our faces, after our binges. He is the One whose arm is over our shoulder as we poke, shoot, snort, and overdose ourselves into oblivion. He is the One who calls us His beloved treasure as we manipulate, curse, cheat, lie, and sleep around. He is the One who continues to trust us as we promise for the umpteenth time to work on our mistakes only to end up with even bigger screw-up's . He is the One who cares about us when others use, betray, and leave us to die. He is the One who gets on His knees, hugs, and prays for us as we swear and show Him our middle finger. He is the One who says 'they are alive and with Me' as we scream and blame Him for the loss of our loved ones. And one day, as we lay dying, wondering if we did anything right or enough, He says to us, 'today you will be with Me in Paradise'.

We do our best to spurn and reject Him but He refuses to let us succeed. He will forever be the prodigal Father standing on the highest point of the city every day, looking for us, the prodigal *huioi* to return. He gives us His highest high at our lowest low. Our sin reaches far but His Grace reaches further. We can never be un-loved for His love has been poured out for us on the cross. Even if we are faithless to Jesus, He remains faithful to us.

Ꮼ 29 Ꮼ

JESUS AND ADULTERY

Marriage to Jesus is a very joyful event. However, marriage to Jesus is impossible under the law! We have a sign of this impossibility in *Judges 11:29-40, Then the Spirit of the LORD came upon Jephthah...And Jephthah vowed a vow unto the Lord, and said, If thou shalt without fail deliver the children of Ammon into mine hands, Then it shall be, that whatsoever cometh forth of the doors of my house to meet me, when I return in peace from the children of Ammon, shall surely be the Lord's, and I will offer it up for a burnt offering. So Jephthah passed over unto the children of Ammon to fight against them; and the Lord delivered them into his hands. And he smote them...with a very great slaughter. Thus the children of Ammon were subdued before the children of Israel. And Jephthah came to Mizpeh unto his house, and, behold, his daughter came out to meet him with timbrels and with dances: and she was his only child; beside her he had neither son nor daughter. And it came to pass, when he saw her, that he rent his clothes, and said, Alas, my daughter! thou hast brought me very low, and thou art one of them that trouble me: for I have opened my mouth unto the Lord, and I cannot go back. And she said unto him, My father, if thou hast opened thy mouth unto the Lord, do to me according to that which hath proceeded out of thy mouth; forasmuch as the Lord hath taken vengeance for thee of thine enemies, even of the children of Ammon. And she said unto her father, Let this thing be done for me: let me alone two months, that I may go up and down upon the mountains, and bewail my virginity, I and my fellows.*

And he said, Go. And he sent her away for two months: and she went with her companions, and bewailed her virginity upon the mountains. And it came to pass at the end of two months, that she returned unto her father, who did with her according to his vow which he had vowed: and she knew no man. And it was a custom in Israel, That the daughters of Israel went yearly to lament the daughter of Jephthah the Gileadite four days in a year.

The Spirit of the Lord foretold Jephthah's victory. But Jephthah made a haughty vow to God before leading the Israelites to victory against the Ammonites. Under the law, any vow made to God must be made good. We read this in *Ecclesiastes 5:4-5, When thou vowest a vow unto God, defer not to pay it; for he hath no pleasure in fools: pay that which thou hast vowed. Better is it that thou shouldest not vow, than that thou shouldest vow and not pay;* and again in *Deuteronomy 23:21, When thou shalt vow a vow unto the Lord thy God, thou shalt not slack to pay it: for the Lord thy God will surely require it of thee; and it would be sin in thee.*

The vow was that when he returned home from the battlefield, he would offer up to God as a burnt offering whatever that came out first from the doors of his house. He could not have meant a human sacrifice as that was explicitly forbidden under the law. But to his dismay, his only child, a daughter, came out to meet him first. She would become the burnt offering. However, the offering had to be acceptable under the law. Hence, Jephthah's daughter as a burnt offering was unacceptable as human sacrifices were strictly prohibited under the law. *Deuteronomy 12:31* states, *Thou shalt not do so unto the Lord thy God: for every abomination to the Lord, which he hateth, have they done unto their gods; for even their sons and their daughters they have burnt in the fire to their gods.* It can also be found in *Deuteronomy 18:10, There shall not be found among you any one that maketh his son or his daughter to pass through the fire,* and *Leviticus 18:21, And thou shalt not let any of thy seed pass through the fire to Molech.*

Under the law, vows to God could be redeemed by the person who made the vow in the first place. Jephthah would surely have redeemed his daughter, but she was adamant not to be redeemed! She rejected redemption by Grace. She chose to be a martyr-virgin and fulfilled her father's vow with a lifetime of service in the temple. Just as Hannah did to her son Samuel, in *1 Samuel 1:28, Therefore also I have lent him to the Lord; as long as he liveth he shall be lent to the Lord.* Temple service to the Lord precluded Jephthah's daughter from ever getting married. Hence, she knew no man because she did not know the Son of man.

A person serving under the law cannot live under Grace. Marriage to the law precludes Jesus. Instead of a joyous celebratory marriage to Grace there would only be sadness and lamentations at being married to the law. Jephthah' lineage would end, his daughter would never be a bride, and her companions would never get to be bridesmaids. It became Israel's custom to yearly lament the sad plight of Jephthah's daughter. Little did they know that it would become a daily lamentation. For marriage with the law was graven in stone and could not be broken.

We all know that one of the ten commandments is the command to not commit adultery. It is found in *Exodus 20:14, Thou shalt not commit adultery.* However, when Jesus interpreted this law, it had an even stricter connotation. We read of this in *Matthew 5:27-28, Ye have heard that it was said by them of old time, Thou shalt not commit adultery: But I say unto you, That whosoever looketh on a woman to lust after her hath committed adultery with her already in his **heart**.* Not only must a person not commit adultery, but just the thought of it was considered as guilty as the act. Being married to the law is forever and to even think about anything else, besides the law, is considered as adultery!

So is there any hope for anybody as we have all fallen short of the law? Let us read from *Romans 7:1-6, Know ye not, brethren, (for I speak to them that know the law,) how that the law hath dominion over a man as long as he liveth? For the woman which hath an husband is bound by the law to her husband so long as he liveth; but if the husband be dead, she is loosed from the law of her husband. So then if, while her husband liveth, she be married to another man, she shall be called an adulteress: but if her husband be dead, she is free from that law; so that she is no adulteress, though she be married to another man. Wherefore, my brethren, ye also are become dead to the law by the body of Christ; that ye should be married to another, even to him who is raised from the dead, that we should bring forth fruit unto God. For when we were in the flesh, the motions of sins, which were by the law, did work in our members to bring forth fruit unto death. But now we are delivered from the law, that being dead wherein we were held; that we should serve in newness of spirit, and not in the oldness of the letter.* Paul is not dispensing advice about marital fidelity here, but is stressing the fact that we are all bound to the law as long as we live. The law is the husband and the woman is us. The woman is bound to her husband as long as he lives. As long as her husband lives, she cannot get married to another man, as that would be considered an adulterous act. The only way she can get loose from her husband was if her husband died. If her husband died, then she is released from the law of marriage. Only then does she has a right to marry another man. She would not be considered an adulteress as her husband was now dead. Hence, we are bound together with the law until one party dies. When one party dies, then the obligation ends.

So the only way we can get free from the law is if the law dies. We cannot be under any other covenant/husband as long as the law lives. For that would be adultery! Only if the law dies, then we are released from the law. But the law did not die. It was fulfilled. So the only way left for us to be free from the law was for us to die! And Jesus provided us that way.

Romans 6:3-7 states, *Know ye not, that so many of us as were baptized into Jesus Christ were baptized into his death? Therefore we are buried (sunthaptó) with him by baptism into death: that like as Christ was raised up from the dead by the glory of the Father, even so we also should walk in newness of life. For if we have been planted together in the likeness of his death, we shall be also in the likeness of his resurrection: Knowing this, that our old man is crucified with him, that the body of sin might be destroyed, that henceforth we should not serve sin. For he that is dead is freed from sin.* We who have faith in Christ died with Him and were buried with him. *Sunthaptó* means to bury with. Hence, a double emphasis that we are buried 'with Jesus, with Jesus'! We died 'with Jesus, with Jesus'. *Colossians 3:3* states, *For ye are dead, and your life is hid with Christ in God.* Because we died, all our obligations to the law died as well. We are dead to the law. We become free from the law because we died 'with Jesus, with Jesus' who fulfilled the law.

Jesus died so we could be in His lineage. Jesus is the sole mediator of this new covenant whereby we receive the promise of eternal inheritance. We read this in *Hebrews 9:15-17, And for this cause he is the mediator of the new testament, that by means of death, for the redemption of the transgressions that were under the first testament, they which are called might receive the promise of eternal inheritance. For where a testament is, there must also of necessity be the death of the testator. For a testament is of force after men are dead: otherwise it is of no strength at all while the testator liveth.* And hence, began the New Covenant! At Jesus' death! But what good is this inheritance, the New Covenant, if we remained dead? So Jesus was resurrected so that we would enjoy living in the New Covenant!

We do not have two lives. Our old man died. Together with our old man, sin was nailed to the cross. Sin was ruined. All our sins; past, present, and future, were forgiven. In its place, a new resurrected man with a new **Jesus heart** was born! We walk in newness of life. No new man can serve sin as the new man is freed from sin. The old man sins often but the new man has dominion over sin. Because he is a new man he brings forth good fruit, not 'dead' fruit but 'alive' fruit. The new man can say that he is dead indeed to sin but alive in Christ. We read in *Colossians 2:12-14, Buried with him in baptism, wherein also ye are risen with him through the faith of the operation of God, who hath raised him from the dead. And you, being dead in your sins and the uncircumcision of your flesh, hath he quickened together with him, having forgiven you all trespasses; Blotting out the handwriting of ordinances that was against us, which was contrary to us, and took it out of the way, nailing it to his cross.* We are 'quickened' or made alive with Him! We are bound to Life and Freedom!

As we no longer have any obligation to the law, we can now marry another! So we get married to Jesus! We get to marry Grace! And we get to inherit all that He has for us. We see this in *1*

Corinthians 7:39, The wife is bound by the law as long as her husband liveth; but if her husband be dead, she is at liberty to be married to whom she will; only in the Lord and again in *2 Corinthians 11:2, For I am jealous over you with godly jealousy: for I have espoused you to one husband, that I may present you as a chaste virgin to Christ.* Our one husband is Jesus!

Other scriptures pointing to this can be found in *Galatians 2:19-21, For I through the law am dead to the law, that I might live unto God. I am crucified with Christ: nevertheless I live; yet not I, but Christ liveth in me: and the life which I now live in the flesh I live by the faith of the Son of God, who loved me, and gave himself for me. I do not frustrate the grace of God: for if righteousness come by the law, then Christ is dead in vain* and also in *Ephesians 2:5-6, Even when we were dead in sins, hath quickened us together with Christ, (by grace ye are saved;) And hath raised us up together, and made us sit together in heavenly places in Christ Jesus..*

However, there is a word of caution in this happy marriage. Now that we are married to Jesus, how many of us are still having a relationship on the side, an affair, with the law? How many of us are still flirting and smiling seductively at the law while holding hands with Grace? How many of us are still lusting after the law in our flesh while sleeping with Jesus? How many of us open the door and invite the law to come in thinking that Jesus is not around? How many of us still lust after that thrilling exhilarating sensuous feeling of having nailed a law and the ecstasy of being orgasmically rewarded for it? Grace and law cannot mix. While we may call following the law harmless, even good, God calls it adultery. One of the main reasons for this adulterous affair with the law is because of fear. Fear that Grace would weaken our resolve, our strength of will, to resist sin! Yet God never called us to resist sin but to resist the devil, who wants us to never focus on Jesus!

Jesus is truly Amazing Grace. By His finished work, we get to be with Him forever. Our marriage to Jesus does have a happy ending. Nothing can separate us from His love. No sin, no mistake, no screw-ups, no no-thing can do that. We read in *Romans 8:33-39, Who shall lay anything to the charge of God's elect? It is God that justifieth. Who is he that condemneth? It is Christ that died, yea rather, that is risen again, who is even at the right hand of God, who also maketh intercession for us. Who shall separate us from the love of Christ? shall tribulation, or distress, or persecution, or famine, or nakedness, or peril, or sword? As it is written, For thy sake we are killed all the day long; we are accounted as sheep for the slaughter. Nay, in all these things we are more than conquerors through him that loved us. For I am persuaded, that neither death, nor life, nor angels, nor principalities, nor powers, nor things present, nor things to come, Nor height, nor depth, nor any other creature, shall be able to separate us from the love of God, which is in Christ Jesus our Lord.*

We are more than conquerors or in Greek, *hypernikōmen,* through Jesus who loved us. *Hyper* means overwhelmingly and exceedingly. *Nikōmen* means to overcome, conquer, and be victorious (now you know what Nike means). Hence, nothing in this life can defeat us as we are overwhelmingly and exceedingly victorious over every circumstance. Just like Paul, we overcome persecutions by religious people who believe that they are doing God a service, as in *John 16:2, the time is coming when those who kill you will think they are doing a holy service for God.* We overcome tribulations, cancel cultures within/without the church, and character assassinations. We even overcome death as death brings us permanently into His presence. Our inheritance includes eternal life with Him. And just as Jesus was physically raised up from the place of the dead, Sheol, as in *Psalm 16:10, For You will not abandon my soul to Sheol, nor will You let Your Holy One see decay,* we will also be raised up physically one day in an event called the rapture. Death cannot separate us from Him, as we read in *Romans 2:6, He will judge everyone according to what they have done* (*ergon* meaning one work) and *John 5:28-29* states, *all that are in the graves shall hear his voice, And shall come forth; they that have done good, unto the resurrection of life.* No deep faking here. This is the *ergon,* that one singular work, that guarantees us our resurrection to life. We did good because we believed in that one good person, Jesus, our forever alive husband!

❧ 30 ❧

JESUS AND CONFESSION

In the movie, the Mask of Zorro, there is a confessional booth scene between Antonio Banderas (Zorro) and Catherine Zeta Jones. Zorro was hiding in the dark wooden booth when Catherine started confessing unexpectedly in the next booth, through the perforated screen. It went something like this:

Catherine: *Forgive me father, for I have sinned. It has been three days since my last confession.*

Zorro (taken aback): *Three days? How many sins could you have committed in three days? Come back when you have more time...*

Catherine: *I have broken the fourth commandment, padre.*

Zorro (looking blank but not wanting to sound stupid): *Did you kill somebody?*

Catherine (in shock and disbelief): *No! That's not the fourth commandment!...I dishonored my father.*

Zorro (nonchalantly): *That is not so bad. Maybe your father deserved it!*

Because of the Mosaic law, people who sinned under the law were punished. But God's mercy to His people many times overrode the punishments that the law required. We read of a conversation between God and Moses in *Numbers 14:11-12, 19-20, The Lord: How long will this people provoke me? and how long will it be ere they believe me, for all the signs which I have shewed among them? I will smite them with the pestilence, and disinherit them, and will make of thee a greater nation and mightier than they.*

Moses: Pardon, I beseech thee, the iniquity of this people according unto the greatness of thy mercy, and as thou hast forgiven this people, from Egypt even until now.
The Lord: I have pardoned according to thy word.

Because of the greatness of God's mercy, He forgave the Israelites their iniquities and transgressions. He pardoned them of their sins. But the Israelites were still guilty of wrongdoing. In order to earn forgiveness, they had to continuously offer up sacrifices for their sins. Before the sacrifice was killed, the sinner would lay his hands upon the animal's head as a symbol for transference of sins. At the same time they would confess their litany of sins.

Once a year, the high priest would do the exact same thing for the whole nation of Israel. First, he would confess his own sins upon a bullock's head. For the peoples sins, two goats would be offered. One of the goats would be sacrificed for the sins of all the people. The other goat, called the scapegoat, would be presented alive before God. We see this in *Leviticus 16:21-22, And Aaron shall lay both his hands upon the head of the live goat, and confess over him all the iniquities of the children of Israel, and all their transgressions in all their sins, putting them upon the head of the goat, and shall send him away by the hand of a fit man into the wilderness: And the goat shall **bear** upon him all their iniquities unto a land not inhabited: and he shall let go the goat in the wilderness.* Before the scapegoat was released, the high priest would confess the litany of sins of the children of Israel and put them, with *both* hands, upon the head of the goat. The people would be made clean by the blood of the first sacrificed goat. The second goat, released in the wilderness and never to return, symbolized that all their sins would be remembered no more. Under the law, *both* the blood and the work of confession of sins made the people clean.

But because we live under the new covenant, confession is markedly different. **As our sins are already forgiven because of Jesus' finished work, we no longer need to confess to be forgiven of our sins. God already forgave us. Because of Jesus, our relationship with God is never broken so there is no need**

to confess to restore an unbroken relationship. We are always one with Jesus, never un-one. We see clearly in *Romans 10:9, That if thou shalt confess with thy mouth the Lord Jesus, and shalt believe in thine heart that God hath raised him from the dead, thou shalt be saved.* Our confession is not for God to forgive us because He has already forgiven us. Jesus cleared all of our sins and removed them as far as the east is from the west. He bore ALL our sins. That is why our sins are never seen again, just as the second goat! Hence, our confession, *'homologēsēs'* in Greek, means to agree or say the same thing as God had already said. It means agreeing with what God has declared concerning His Son, Jesus. We agree with God that by the blood of Jesus all our sins are forgiven and never to be seen ever again! We are forever righteous! As Jesus' relationship with God is perfect, so is ours!

We see this prophetically in *Zechariah 6:12-13, Thus speaketh the Lord of hosts, saying, Behold the man whose name is The BRANCH... shall sit and rule upon his throne; and he shall be a priest upon his throne: and the counsel of peace shall be between them both.* The Branch is Jesus. He is both King and Priest bringing peace and harmony to the two offices. But in Hebrew, counsel is *etsah* meaning plan. Hence, 'counsel of peace between them both' also meant that God the Father and God the Son had a definite plan of peace which they foreknew, as in *Acts 2:23, this Jesus, delivered up according to the definite plan and foreknowledge of God, you crucified and killed by the hands of lawless men.* The plan of peace was the New Covenant! Both of them agreed that Jesus would be the price for establishing the New Covenant which would then be given to us as a free gift. Jesus would be our Forever King and Priest of the New Covenant.

We symbolically saw this covenant in *Exodus 21:33-34, And if a man shall open a pit, or if a man shall dig a pit, and not cover it, and an ox or an ass fall therein; The owner of the pit shall make it good, and give money unto the owner of them; and the dead beast shall be his.* While this was part of the law on restitution, it also stood for what God did for us. The man, Adam, dug and opened the pit of sin and subsequently, we all fell in. **Adam, representing man at his best, fell. God, the owner of all,**

made it good and paid the price for sins with His Son, Jesus. Man, at his worst, was lifted out of the pit by Jesus. Our hands were not strong enough to pull ourselves up so His mighty hand reached in. We were dead but now made alive by Him. From that very moment, we belong to Him.

Therefore, confession means 'to agree in our hearts' that Jesus paid the full price for all sins and for all time. He did everything that was needed for us to be saved. Then God raised Him from the dead so that we who were dead now become alive with Him. Our salvation is as good as God's declaration that Jesus died for our sins and was resurrected to give us new life. We confess or *'homo-logos'* or 'same-word', that declaration. We see this in *Matthew 10:32, Whosoever therefore shall confess me before men, him will I confess also before my Father which is in heaven* and in *Philippians 2:11, And that every tongue should confess that Jesus Christ is Lord, to the glory of God the Father.* We confess exuberantly that God has already forgiven us. With Jesus, we are never forgotten, just forgiven. The more we confess about who Jesus is, the more we know who we are in Him. Jesus is our confession as in *Hebrews 3:1, Therefore, holy brothers, you who share in a heavenly calling, consider Jesus, the apostle and high priest of our confession.*

There are many believers who cannot fully confess all about Jesus! We read in *John 12:42-43, Nevertheless among the chief rulers also many believed on him; but because of the Pharisees they did not confess him, lest they should be put out of the synagogue: For they loved the praise of men more than the praise of God.* Because of the desire to be accepted of men, many believers toe the line and conform to their religious traditions rather than ebulliently declaring the finished work of Jesus.

Then there are others, the Gnostics, who cannot confess because they do not believe in sin. But we read in *1 John 1:6-10, and the blood of Jesus Christ his Son cleanseth us from all sin. If we say that we have no sin, we deceive ourselves, and the truth is not in us. If we confess our sins, he is faithful and just to forgive us our sins, and to cleanse us from all unrighteousness. If we say that we have not sinned, we make him a liar, and his word is not in us.*

We can see clearly that John is writing to correct the Gnostics, just as he recorded Jesus correcting the Pharisees in *John 8:24, that ye shall die in your sins: for if ye believe not that **I am**, ye shall die in your sins*. For we are sinners and are in need of **I AM**. When we confess and agree with God, we accept that the blood of **I AM** has cleansed us, or in Greek *katharizó*, from all sins. We were sinners but are now sinners no more! It was done for us and cannot be undone by us. It is also a one time, never to be repeated action (aorist tense).

Gnosticism central teaching is that spirit is entirely good while matter is entirely bad. Jesus only appeared to have a body (Docetic Gnosticism), or the 'spirit Jesus' joined a 'man Jesus' at His baptism but left Him before His crucifixion (Cerinthian Gnosticism). As spirit beings, Gnostics could not be sinners. They were corrected in *1 John 4:2,* and *2 John 1:7, For many deceivers have gone out into the world, those who do not acknowledge Jesus Christ as coming in the flesh. This is the deceiver and the antichrist* (anti meaning to replace Christ). The Gnostics were unbelievers. Some of their popular texts are the gospel of Thomas, the gospel of Philip, and the gospel of Truth. These were among the 52 treatises or texts, found in 1945 near Nag Hammadi in upper Egypt. Note that these Gnostic texts are not the same as the Dead Sea scrolls found in the 12 caves around the Dead Sea neighborhoods from 1946-2021. The Dead Sea scrolls, more than 15,000 fragments of it, are Jewish scrolls, not Gnostic texts.

Jesus cleanses us from all sin, not confession. Legalists who claim that they have successfully confessed all their sins to 'keep the slate clean' before God, forgot that in *James 4:17, Anyone, then, who knows the right thing to do, yet fails to do it, is guilty of sin.* If we know that something is right but do not do it, that is sin! Or in *Romans 14:23 anything that is not of faith is sin,* and *Galatians 3:12, And the law is not of faith.* **Doing the law, which is NOT of faith, is sin!** Then we read *Hebrews 11:6, But without faith it is impossible to please him.* **It is impossible to please God by doing the law, which is NOT of faith!** Why? Because the perfect law would just expose all of man's imperfections! Therefore, Jesus took our slate, stomped on it, ground it to dust, and blew it away. Those whom Jesus cleaned are thoroughly clean. They do not have a slate to keep clean!

Confession does not make us humble. Depending totally on Jesus makes us humble. Similarly, confession does not maintain our salvation. We do not lose intimacy with God when we fall into sin. When we sin, the Holy Spirit immediately reminds us that we are the righteousness of God in Christ. *Romans 5:17* states, *For if by one man's offence death reigned by one; much more they which receive abundance of grace and of the gift of righteousness shall reign in life by one, Jesus Christ.* **As receivers of the gift of righteousness of God in Christ, why are we even tempted by sin? As receivers of an abundance of Grace, why should we have any desire to sin? We should reign over sin in this life! The more Jesus conscious we are, the less sin desire we have. When we reign; sin, satan, and death does not.**

There is another type of confession found in *James 5:16, Confess your faults one to another, and pray one for another, that ye may be healed.* This confession has to do with believers telling their problems to one another, listening, and then praying for each other. This confession has nothing to do with being cleansed by God as believers are already righteous in Christ. Because of the temptations and tribulations in this fallen world, righteous people can encourage each other in Jesus. In *John 16:33*, we read, *In the world ye shall have tribulation: but be of good cheer; I have overcome the world.* Righteous people point and remind each other of the One Man who gave them their righteousness and who forgave them their sins. Because Jesus overcame the world, they too become overcomers. This is the true meaning of *Proverbs 27:17, Iron sharpens iron, and one man sharpens another.* In sharpening (not honing), both irons lose metal. Similar materials cannot sharpen one another. But both irons/men are sharpened when they together confess Jesus, the Stone that sharpens all!

Therefore, under the law, people brought their sacrifices and confessed their sins in order to be forgiven. But under the new covenant of grace, Grace came and forgave us of all our sins first. We should confess or *homo-logos* that every opportunity we get!

ও 31 ৩

JESUS AND FORGIVENESS

In the last chapter, we talked about confession and its relationship to forgiveness. Let us now examine forgiveness in greater detail. Before the cross, forgiveness was a work. Not only did we have to sacrifice and confess, but we had to forgive as well. The first step must be ours. We had to forgive in order to earn God's forgiveness. We see this in *Matthew 6:14-15, For if ye forgive men their trespasses, your heavenly Father will also forgive you: But if ye forgive not men their trespasses, neither will your Father forgive your trespasses,* and again in *Mark 11:25-26, And when ye stand praying, forgive, if ye have ought against any: that your Father also which is in heaven may forgive you your trespasses. But if ye do not forgive, neither will your Father which is in heaven forgive your trespasses.* This is evident even in what we call the Lord's prayer. *Matthew 6:12* states, *And forgive us our debts, as we forgive our debtors.* Under the law, we had to do something good in order to earn a blessing from God. So we offered sacrifices, confessed our sins and forgave others in order to earn the blessing of forgiveness back from God.

Jesus, born under the law, preached law until He fulfilled the law. *Matthew 5:17* states, *Think not that I am come to destroy the law, or the prophets: I am not come to destroy, but to fulfil.* The law was not destroyed but fulfilled by Jesus' birth, life, and death. Jesus brought the law back to its pristine state in order to show us our inability to fulfill all of its requirements and conditions. His words are to be taken seriously. They were not hyperbole or exaggerated. When we see how sinful we really are then we acknowledge that we need a Savior. Hence, the purpose of the law was to bring us to Jesus, not to make us righteous *Galatians 3:24* states, *Wherefore the law was our schoolmaster to bring us unto Christ, that we might be justified by faith.* Only Jesus could fulfill the law and once fulfilled, the law was no longer needed. It had achieved its purpose of bringing us to Christ.

The pristine law commanded us to not only offer up sacrifices but also to confess our sins and to forgive others. Offering up animals was easy. To confess our sins is difficult as we need to know the whole law in order to confess every time we 'miss the mark' or mess up. But to forgive others who had done us terrible wrongs (especially without their 'full repentance') is near impossible. To just forgive them is downright unnatural. In fact, our natural response is revenge. Revenge seems right to us. Pour burning coals on their heads. Then Zippo them with lighter fluid! Quick and easy. Whooosh!

But the revenge that we sought for was paid in full by Jesus, on Himself. We read in *Matthew 18:21-35,Then Peter came up and said to him, "Lord, how often will my brother sin against me, and I forgive him? As many as seven times?" Jesus said to him, "I do not say to you seven times, but seventy-seven times. "Therefore the kingdom of heaven may be compared to a king who wished to settle accounts with his servants. When he began to settle, one was brought to him who owed him ten thousand talents. And since he could not pay, his master ordered him to be sold, with his wife and children and all that he had, and payment to be made. So the servant[i] fell on his knees, imploring him, 'Have patience with me, and I will pay you everything.' And out of pity for him, the master of that servant released him and forgave him the debt. But when that same servant went out, he found one of his fellow servants who owed him a hundred denarii,[i] and seizing him, he began to choke him, saying, 'Pay what you owe.' So his fellow servant fell down and pleaded with him, 'Have patience with me, and I will pay you.' He refused and went and put him in prison until he should pay the debt. When his fellow servants saw what had taken place, they were greatly distressed, and they went and reported to their master all that had taken place. Then his master summoned him and said to him, 'You wicked servant! I forgave you all that debt because you pleaded with me. And should not you have had mercy on your fellow servant, as I had mercy on you?' And in anger his master delivered him to the jailers, until he should pay all his debt. So also my heavenly Father will do to every one of you, if you do not forgive your brother from your heart."*

Peter, full of himself, came to ask Jesus how many times he should forgive his brother, Andrew. He knew what was written in *Amos 1:3, Thus saith the Lord; For three transgressions of Damascus, and for four, I will not turn away the punishment thereof.* God forgave only three times. The fourth time judgment fell on Damascus, Israel's enemy neighbor to the north. Peter felt pretty good about his question as he had forgiven his brother 7 times already. That was more than double the times God forgave! He expected Jesus to lavishly congratulate him on his ability to forgive.

But Jesus came back with an outlandish answer. He told Peter that he should forgive 77 times! 7 stands for perfection and 77 for divine perfection. Jesus was asking Peter to forgive his brother perfectly and in an unlimited way. Then Jesus told him the parable of the king who forgave his servant 10,000 talents. The debt was an un-payable amount. It was too large. The servant could work his entire lifetime and still fall far short. Hence, under the law the servant would be sold, together with his wife, children and all of his possessions. But the king showed him Grace and forgave him his debt. We know that the debt would be forgiven anyways at the end of every seven years and the servant and his family would be set free. We read this in *Exodus 21:2-3, If thou buy an Hebrew servant, six years he shall serve: and in the seventh he shall go out free for nothing. If he came in by himself, he shall go out by himself: if he were married, then his wife shall go out with him.* But in this parable, the servant was forgiven before the seven year period.

The servant although forgiven first, could not see that he was forgiven. Instead of taking his position as a free person with his debt fully paid, he continued being a servant. He showed contempt for the king and his gift of forgiveness. Failure to see Grace results in a continuation of life under the law. Being unthankful for the free gift, he went out and applied the law on his fellowservant. He demanded payment for the hundred pence that was owed to him. His fellowservant could not pay the sum owed. Seething with anger, he took his fellowservant by the throat. His flesh wanted revenge. Under the law, there would be no forgiveness. The fellowservant was thus thrown into prison. When the king heard that the servant had applied the law, the same law was then applied back to him. Freed from his first debt by the king, he was found owing in many other areas and was delivered to the tormentors until he paid back all. Hence, under the law, we have to forgive in order to earn or merit forgiveness.

But under Grace, forgiveness starts with God. The King forgave first. Every debt was paid for by Jesus. The un-payable debt was paid for by the in-estimable Son. The gargantuan 10.000 talents was deliberate to show that Grace was deliberately much more gargantuan. God supplied forgiveness first. God took the first step towards us without requiring anything from us, then and after. There was no obligation on our part to forgive first in order to earn forgiveness. But because God forgave us so much, we are able to forgive others much as well. Forgiveness cannot start with us because if we succeed in forgiving others, we swell up with pride at our ability and performance. We even try to blackmail God by our thoughts, 'Now God has to forgive me because I forgave first!' However, if we fail, we condemn ourselves as not being holy enough to forgive and end up recriminating ourselves.

Of course, we can choose to not forgive even after God forgave us. But that may bring about consequences. Rejecting Grace and relying on the flesh may result in a root of bitterness growing deep inside of us, manifesting itself in resentment, anger, acrimony, hate, envy, cynicism, and rage. *Hebrews 12:15* states, *Looking diligently lest any man fail of the grace of God; lest any root of bitterness springing up trouble you, and thereby many be defiled;* While we do not lose our salvation because we did not forgive somebody, we become ill tempered, bitter, critical and find fault in and with everyone. We focus obsessively on fruits and forget about the root, who is Jesus!

This principle of God forgiving us first is hard to accept. The people in Jesus' time found it equally difficult that Jesus could and would actually forgive them of their sins without any work on their part. We read in *Mark 2:5-10, When Jesus saw their faith, he said unto the sick of the palsy, Son, thy sins be forgiven thee. But there were certain of the scribes sitting there, and reasoning in their hearts, Why doth this man thus speak blasphemies? who can forgive sins but God only? And immediately when Jesus perceived in his spirit that they so reasoned within themselves, he said unto them, Why reason ye these things in your hearts? Whether is it easier to say to the sick of the palsy, Thy sins be forgiven thee; or to say, Arise, and take up thy bed, and walk? But that ye may know that the Son of man hath power on earth to forgive sin.* Nobody deserved forgiveness by their works. It was unmerited forgiveness followed by unmerited healing. Both given freely by Jesus.

Below are some scriptures where we find that we are not only forgiven in Jesus' name but that our sins were blotted out forevermore. Because of the blood of Jesus, **ALL**, not some, of our sins were cast into the depths of the sea. **His blood has absolute and total sin-killing power!** Because of Jesus, we were forgiven first. Our part is to receive it.

1 John 2:2, And he is the propitiation for our sins: and not for ours only, but also for the sins of the whole world.

Psalm 103:12, As far as the east is from the west, so far hath he removed our transgressions from us.

Isaiah 43:25, I, even I, am he that blotteth out thy transgressions for mine own sake, and will not remember thy sins.

Matthew 26:28, For this is my blood of the new testament, which is shed for many for the remission of sins.

Ephesians 1:4-7, According as he hath chosen us in him before the foundation of the world, that we should be holy and without blame before him in love: Having predestinated us unto the adoption of children by Jesus Christ to himself, according to the good pleasure of his will, To the praise of the glory of his grace, wherein he hath made us accepted in the beloved. In whom we have redemption through his blood, the forgiveness of sins, according to the riches of his grace.

We actually cannot ask for forgiveness as God gave forgiveness to us already. There is no need for searching, crying, examining, asking, begging, shouting, reproaching, castigating, working, or confessing. All works do not earn or win us forgiveness. Only one thing was needed - Jesus! Jesus actually reversed the revenge curse of 7 on Cain in *Genesis 4:15, Therefore whosoever slayeth Cain, vengeance shall be taken on him sevenfold,* and the revenge curse of 77 on Lamech, another murderer and the first polygamist, in *Genesis 4:23-24, And Lamech said unto his wives, Adah and Zillah, Hear my voice; ye wives of Lamech, hearken unto my speech: for I have slain a man to my wounding, and a young man to my hurt. If Cain shall be avenged sevenfold, truly Lamech seventy and sevenfold.* **Jesus annulled the 77 unlimited revenge curse and replaced it with the 77 unlimited forgiveness blessing!**

Grace was given to all men before there were men on this earth. We were predestined to become His children before creation begun. Not just Jews but Gentiles as well. To be accepted in the Beloved. God did not predestine anyone to a destiny of heaven or hell! But He definitely foreknew who would believe in Him! That was the thief who recognized Jesus in *Luke 23:42-43, And he said unto Jesus, Lord, **remember** me **when** thou comest into thy kingdom. And Jesus said unto him, Verily I say unto thee, **Today** shalt thou be with me in paradise.* Under the law, both of the thieves deserved death. The first thief ranted and raved at Jesus, not acknowledging that it was his actions that had brought him to the cross. He tongue-lashed Jesus to act and to save them all. He wanted more works to cover his works. Meanwhile the second thief acknowledged that his actions had brought him to the cross and asked for Grace. **Under the law, by his actions, he merited death. He was disqualified to live. But by Grace, he was forgiven, approved, and awarded eternal life. He was qualified into heaven. Jesus in the middle separated law/death from Grace/Life. The thief under Grace did not confess his sins,**

change his ways, fast or prayed. He did not get baptized nor spoke in tongues. He acknowledged Jesus and received his salvation. The thief was 're-membered' by Jesus on the cross. Jesus guaranteed that the thief's 'when' became his 'today'. He entered heaven, as a member, because Jesus said he could.

Just as the centurions who were at Jesus' crucifixion. We read in *Matthew 27:54, Now when the centurion, and they that were with him, watching Jesus, saw the earthquake, and those things that were done, they feared greatly, saying, Truly this was the Son of God.* Changing their minds about Jesus i.e. repenting, and putting their faith in Him was all that was needed. **That day, the lowly thief and the lowly centurions became much higher than Caesar on his throne. Jesus knew all of this beforehand. It was that easy because He was that good to us!** It is very hard for legalists or for people who are caught up in self-works to believe that Jesus could be that good. How good? Legalist: You let your dog on the sofa? Grace: I would let my dog drive my car!

Let us continue with *Luke 7:36-48, And one of the Pharisees desired him that he would eat with him. And he went into the Pharisee's house, and sat down to meat. And, behold, a woman in the city, which was a sinner, when she knew that Jesus sat at meat in the Pharisee's house, brought an alabaster box of ointment, And stood at his feet behind him weeping, and began to wash his feet with tears, and did wipe them with the hairs of her head, and kissed his feet, and anointed them with the ointment. Now when the Pharisee which had bidden him saw it, he spake within himself, saying, This man, if he were a prophet, would have known who and what manner of woman this is that toucheth him: for she is a sinner. And Jesus answering said unto him…There was a certain creditor which had two debtors: the one owed five hundred pence, and the other fifty. And when they had nothing to pay, he frankly forgave them both. Tell me therefore, which of them will love him most? Simon answered and said, I suppose that he, to whom he forgave most. And he said unto him, Thou hast rightly judged. And he turned to the woman, and said unto Simon, Seest thou this woman? I entered into thine house, thou gavest me no water for my feet: but she hath washed my feet with tears, and wiped them with the hairs of her head. Thou gavest me no kiss: but this woman since the time I came in hath not ceased to kiss my feet. My head with oil thou didst not anoint: but this woman hath anointed my feet with ointment. Wherefore I say unto thee, Her sins, which are many, are forgiven; for she loved much: but to whom little is forgiven, the same loveth little. And he said unto her, Thy sins are forgiven.*

Simon the Pharisee, full of self-righteousness, thought himself superior to Jesus. He wanted to glorify himself so he invited Jesus to his house to see what a great man he was. To his horror, a woman whom he knew intimately barged in suddenly and anointed Jesus' feet with ointment. The woman was a prostitute who frequented Simon's house. She was not an unknown for Simon already knew that she was a sinner. Furthermore, she was let into his house without question. The money that Simon had spent on her sexual services bought the alabaster box of ointment. The prostitute then touched Jesus with her hands, eyes, hair, and lips. The same hands, eyes, hair, and lips that had brought Simon to orgasms! Under the law, that would make Jesus unclean. Simon did not speak but was aghast at her actions. Horrified that he would be found out, he condemned her silently, in his mind. But Jesus, knowing what he was thinking, answered him out loud. Since Simon stood on his works, Jesus questioned him back based on his works. Why had he purposefully given no water to Jesus to wash His feet, nor greeted Him with a kiss as was their custom, nor anointed His head with oil? Simon was thunderstruck. He had wanted to debase Jesus but his works with the prostitute was now laid bare at Jesus' feet. The unworthy prostitute had done what he did not do. She washed, kissed, anointed and wiped Jesus' feet. Based on works which he had so proudly stood upon, the unworthy woman had done more.

Based on Grace, the comparison was even more pronounced. Simon was the man in the parable who owed fifty pence. The woman was the one who owed five hundred. Both owed the law as none could attain the standard. Nobody could pay back what the law required. Only Jesus could pay that debt. Self-works is always insufficient to meet the demands of the law. But the woman was the bigger sinner in that she had committed more sins. Under the law, she owed more. She risked it all on Jesus and hence, more Grace was given to her. She received more. That added to God's glory. The Law scoffed while Grace cried. And because she had been forgiven more, she also loved Jesus more. And the more she loved Jesus, the less desire she had for sin! She could not stop kissing His feet for she was made clean. She did *Psalm 2:12, Kiss the Son!* for His Righteousness was now her righteousness.

There was another Simon mentioned in *Mark 14.* In his house, an ointment of spikenard worth 300 pence was poured over Jesus' head by an unnamed woman. When some of the disciples murmured about the expensive ointment and why it could not have been sold instead, Jesus replied in *Mark 14:8, She hath done what she could: she is come aforehand to anoint my body to the burying. Verily I say unto you, Wheresoever this gospel shall be preached throughout the whole world, this also that she hath done shall be spoken of for a memorial of her.* Here the number 300 stood for the death, burial, and resurrection of Jesus. In *John 12:1-8,* a few days earlier, Mary the sister of Martha, had also anointed Jesus and wiped His feet with her hair with spikenard oil, also worth 300 pence. The number 300 have always stood for victory and life - Enoch's 300 years of life from Methuselah's birth until God took him, Noah's Savior-Ark length of 300 cubits, Benjamin's redemptive 300 pieces of silver, Gideon's victorious army of 300, Sampson's 300 firebrand foxes, and Jashobeam, one of David's mighty men, who slew 300. All of these are memorials to the fact that Jesus is the victorious Gospel! Because of Jesus we have victory over sin, death, and hell. *2 Corinthians 2:15-16 states, For we are a fragrance of Christ to God among those who are being saved and among those who are perishing: to the one an aroma from death to death, to the other an aroma from life to life.* To God, we who smell of Jesus smells of Life. Without the smell of Jesus, we stink of death.

Now that we realize how much Jesus loved us first and forgave us first, we can likewise try to be like Him and forgive others even without their repentance. We read in *Ephesians 4:32,*

And be ye kind one to another, tenderhearted, forgiving one another, even as God for Christ's sake hath forgiven you and again in *Colossians 3:13, forgiving one another, if any man have a quarrel against any: even as Christ forgave you, so also do ye.* Forgiving others is a fruit of being in Jesus. And we who remain in Christ bear much fruit! That was why Jesus told Peter that he could forgive his brother unconditionally and endlessly. **We can forgive because we have been forgiven first! It is effortless because Grace supplied first!**

However, forgiving others does not mean that we have the power to forgive sins! Some churches use *John 20:23, Receive ye the Holy Ghost: Whose soever sins ye remit, they are remitted unto them; and whose soever sins ye retain, they are retained,* to justify their position that they have the authority to forgive sins. But these verses simply mean that the disciples, having received the Holy Spirit, are now new creations. As such, they have the authority to declare Jesus' forgiveness to all. Jesus is the only one who cancelled or remitted all our sins. Jesus' finished work revoked and rescinded our sins entirely and completely. What we are declaring is that Jesus, knowing full well who we are and what we have done, obliterated every sin we ever made. "Do you know what we did?" has been replaced forever by "Do you know what Jesus did?" Believers believe that Jesus already cancelled their sins while unbelievers believe that Jesus did not cancel their sins i.e. they believe that their sins are still held against them or retained.

Actually, if we could go back in time to look for our sins, to correct them, we would find no sins at all to correct! Jesus took every one of our sins upon Himself. There is no quota. Every lie, every deceit, every lustful deed and thought, every manipulation, every selfish action, every greed, every mistake. He became our sin so that sin would die in us and be obliterated forever with His blood which cried out Forgiveness. It is a memorial, a *fait accompli*, that Jesus already corrected every sin that you and I ever made! There are no sins, no, not even the thought of sin, in heaven!

❧ 32 ❦

JESUS AND SIN

Sin came into being when satan wanted to be god. Then sin entered mankind when Adam and Eve wanted to become like gods. Sin was present before and after the cross. The Hebrew word for sin is the word '*chata'ah*' and it means 'missing the mark'. The other two closely connected words are '*pesha*' or transgression, meaning rebelling against God and '*avon*' or iniquities. In *Isaiah 53:5* we read, *But he was wounded for our transgressions, he was bruised for our iniquities: the chastisement of our peace was upon him.* As sin would always be around until the end of time, Jesus defeated it permanently by taking upon Himself not only all our sins but also all our transgressions and iniquities as well.

When Adam fell into sin in the garden of Eden, he hid himself from God. But God still approached him and called out to him. Many people think that God rejected Adam when he sinned. Actually, Adam rejected God. He turned away from God. Sin brought consequences. Sin separated Adam from God. **Sin can separate us from God but sin cannot separate God from us.** Why? Because from God's perspective, it has always been about a relationship. It has never been about rules and works! Just like Peter in *Luke 5:8, When Simon Peter saw it, he fell down at Jesus' knees, saying, Depart from me; for I am a sinful man, O Lord.* But Jesus did not depart from Peter. He drew closer to Peter. Ultimately, in *Luke 5:10, And Jesus said unto Simon, Fear not; from henceforth thou shalt catch men.* From unbelief to a disciple. **Although sin has consequences, our sinful actions do not**

influence Jesus one iota as His love for us is independent of our actions. He will never leave us just because we sinned.

We read further in *John 15:9-12,16, As the Father hath loved me, so have I loved you: continue ye in my love. If ye keep my commandments, ye shall abide in my love; even as I have kept my Father's commandments, and abide in his love. These things have I spoken unto you, that my joy might remain in you, and that your joy might be full. This is my commandment, That ye love one another, as I have loved you. Ye have not chosen me, but I have chosen you, and ordained you.* God the Father loved His Son, Jesus, unconditionally. Then from *John 5:19,Whatever the Father does the Son also does,* as Jesus was loved, He loved us back unconditionally. And because of His love for us, we can now love others the way we have been loved by Jesus. Let us not be like those in *2 Corinthians 6:12* and *2 Thessalonians 3:5* and have constipated love. How? Because our love is the fruit of His abounding love. He loved us first. He chose us first. *1 John 4:19* states clearly that, *We love him, because he first loved us.* Jesus kept all His Father's commandments so we do not have to. Not that we can! We rejoice in this finished work of Jesus. This position of completeness was then given to us. That is our position.

Belief or Unbelief in God	Belief or Unbelief in Jesus

Before the cross, the people could choose whether to believe in God or not. If they believed in God and what He said, as Abraham did, then that was counted to them as righteousness. If they did not believe in God, then that was counted as unrighteousness. Nobody who lived before the cross ever earned salvation by works. Or ethnicity. No one ever got saved by doing the commandments/law or being born Jewish. Under the law, their self-works earned them either blessings or curses, but not salvation.

The cross represented a significant demarcation point in time. Because it was on the cross that Jesus took on the sins of the world. *Romans 5:8-10*, states, *But God commendeth his love toward us, in that, while we were yet sinners, Christ died for us. Much more then, being now justified by his blood, we shall be saved from wrath through him. For if, when we were enemies, we were reconciled to God by the death of his Son, much more, being reconciled, we shall be saved by his life.* Jesus loved us while we were sinners, how much more He love us now that we are His! Because Jesus paid the price for all sinners first, there are no sinners left after the cross. Even though sin is still around and people still commit sin, nobody can be called a sinner as Jesus paid the price for all sinners. That is why God is no longer wrathful nor pre-occupied with sin as He had already dealt with it. All sins, not some, has been judged on the cross. When Paul mentioned he was the chief of sinners in *1 Timothy 1:15, Christ Jesus came into the world to save sinners; of whom I am chief,* he was stating that though he **was** the greatest sinner of all time yet Jesus saved him from his sins! Henceforth, he is no longer that sinner. That is why there is no sin too bad that Jesus cannot save us from! Jesus is exceeding and abundantly good. Good far above our bad!

A debtor cannot remain a debtor once his debt has been paid in full. A sinner cannot remain a sinner once his sin has been removed completely. That is why, after the cross, there is only a choice between believing in who Jesus is and what He did or not believing in who Jesus is and what He did. The people who do not believe in Jesus are called unbelievers and the people who believe in Jesus are called believers. While we commonly refer to unbelievers as sinners, it is not biblically correct. Unbelievers of Jesus are not sinners as Jesus paid the price for their sins too. **Both heaven and hell are full of forgiven sinners. When unbelievers are judged one day, they are not judged because of sins committed or omitted. They are judged because of their unbelief in Jesus.**

We all know that the law was given to the Jews because they asked for it. They wanted God to reward them based upon their own works. Jews do not believe in personal salvation as the law was given to the whole nation. For them, keeping the law by repentance, good deeds, and a lifetime of devotion to the law would earn the whole nation 'salvation'. But the law, in its original pristine form, was un-keepable. It was too difficult, too high, too stringent. So in order to be 'saved' they had to 'dumb' it down. Make it palatable. No cutting off hands or gouging out eyes. No stoning of rebellious children. No shootings/killing of all infidels. Hence, a dumbed-down law is one that does not maim/kill you.

For us, when a person puts his or her faith in Jesus, he or she becomes a believer. Believers are also known as righteous saints. While all believers believe in Jesus, not all believers agree on whether they are saved only by Jesus or whether they are saved by Jesus plus their own works. Those believers who believe that they are saved by Jesus, plus some self-works, practice what we call mixtures. They mix Grace with some law to arrive at a comfortable lukewarm level. They call this lukewarm level a balanced state. Of course, this balance is different for every person, depending on their degree of discipline. The law was vast. Then as time went by, many people added to the law. Nobody can follow the whole law. So, like the Jews, everybody 'dumbs' the law down. A person's determination, strictness, and self-will will decide how dumb he/she makes the law.

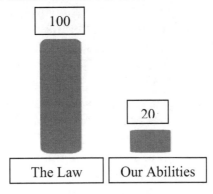

In the chart above, we see that the law in its pristine form stands at 100. It is perfect. To the best of our abilities, we may be able to keep, say an average of 20 out of that 100. Some more disciplined and highly legalistic person may score higher. But the law demands perfection. A score of 99.999 is still failure. Failing spectacularly or by the slimmest margin is still failure. *James 2:10* states, *For whosoever shall keep the whole law, and yet offend in one point, he is guilty of all.*

As the law is too high, we have to dumb it down. We have to cheapen the law to make it keepable. Only by 'dumbing' down the law can we keep it, making it not so damnable! This is illustrated below. The law has been dumbed down to 10. Now we can keep it as our abilities remain at 20.

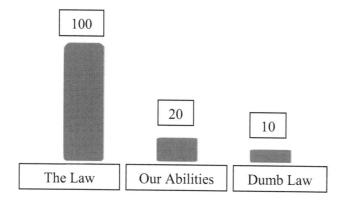

But in doing so, we forget about the absolute holiness of God. We treat sin as a small thing, easily taken care of by some good works. We lessen its severity by modifying the law so it becomes more accommodating to our abilities to uphold it. We say that Jesus died for our sins but after that initial salvation, we are perfectly capable of doing good works to maintain our salvation. We may need Jesus initially but then we grow up and we become self-sufficient and independent. We grow out of needing Him. We have arrived at the point where we believe that our abilities have exceeded the dumbed down law! So we let go of our dependence on Jesus and congratulate ourselves on our well earned degree of self-righteousness. We graduated and will now teach others to become like us; good moral law keepers. We make light of sin and in doing so make light of Jesus' sacrifice for us .

While Grace magnifies Jesus and shows us how perfect He is, doing the law just magnify our sins and show us what bad sinners we are. In recent years, the term 'cheap grace' was coined. That is an unfeasible term because the cheaper/lower grace is, then the law has to be cheaper/lower still for people to be saved by Grace. And we all know that the law is high. **If we know how high the law actually is, then grace has to be higher still for us to be saved by Grace. Hence, a high view of the law produces a higher view of Grace but a low view of Grace produces an even lower view of the law.**

Paul puts it best in *Romans 5:20, Moreover the law entered, that the offence might abound. But where sin abounded, grace did much more abound:* Paul called grace '*Huperperisseuo* Grace' or 'overabounding Grace'. *Huperperisseuo* Grace effectively means that no sin, no matter how bad, can overcome grace. It means that we cannot out sin Grace! The Grace of God, Jesus, is bigger than any sin we can commit or think of. *1Timothy 1:14* states *And the grace of our Lord was exceeding abundant with faith and love which is in Christ Jesus.* Jesus is exceeding abundant or '*hyperepleonasen*' in Grace! And again in *Ephesians 2:7-9, That in the ages to come he might shew the exceeding riches of his grace in his kindness toward us through Christ Jesus. For by grace are ye saved through faith; and that not of yourselves: it is the gift of God: Not of works, lest any man should boast.* Jesus' Grace is exceedingly rich or '*hyperballon*' toward us! Grace is radical and *hyper* and His name is Jesus!

So, rather than dumbing down the law, let us put the law back in its proper place. In the illustration below, let us maintain the law at perfection, at 100. But *Huperperisseuo* Grace is at, say, 500. Five times more, the number five standing for Grace. Where sin abounded, Grace did 'much more' abound! That is why there are 5 'much more's in *Romans 5*! The malady is wide but the remedy is much much much much much wider. Yes, the law is perfect but Jesus is Perfection Perfection Perfection Perfection Perfection. Hence, the worst sinner can be remedied and restored to perfection by Jesus' gift of righteousness. So let us not idolize sin or the law and let it become higher than Jesus!

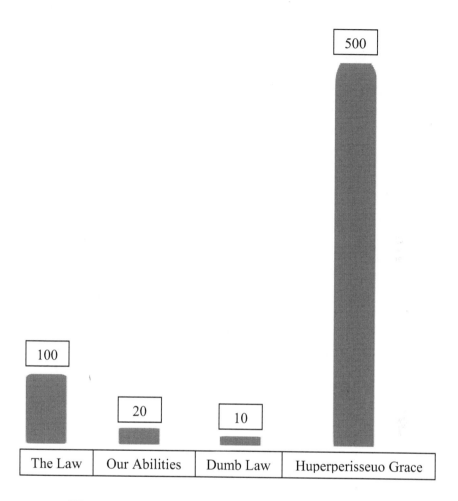

You may ask what is so wrong about mixing Jesus with works? Surely there is nothing harmful to add some good to what Jesus had accomplished? A balance without extremes is good, isn't it? Let us see what God says about this in *Revelation 3:16-19, So then because thou art lukewarm, and neither cold nor hot, I will spue thee out of my mouth. Because thou sayest, I am rich, and increased with goods, and have need of nothing; and knowest not that thou art wretched, and miserable, and poor, and blind, and naked: I counsel thee to buy of me gold tried in the fire, that thou mayest be rich; and white raiment, that thou mayest be clothed, and that the shame of thy nakedness do not appear; and anoint*

thine eyes with eye salve, that thou mayest see. As many as I love, I rebuke and chasten: be zealous therefore, and repent. Lukewarm people are fooled into believing that they have need of nothing. Their works of hay, wood, and stubble; their rags of self-righteousness; and their blinded eyes obscure their inherent need for Jesus. For only Jesus is the rich gold tried in the fire. He is the righteous garment that covers our shame and nakedness and He is the salve that makes us see clearly our impoverished state. Lukewarm people are spiritual adulterers, are under bondage, and have little power over sin. However, God still loves them and wants them to repent or change their mind about their lukewarmness.

Isaiah 43:18-19 states, *Remember ye not the former things, neither consider the things of old. Behold, I will do a new thing; now it shall spring forth; shall ye not know it? I will even make a way in the wilderness, and rivers in the desert.* The former things pertain to the law. It is wilderness thinking and dry as the desert. We are told to not consider it any more. Why? Because God had done a new thing. He brought in Grace. He gave us Jesus. He is The Way (*John 14:6, Acts 9:2, 19:9,23,24:14,22*) where there is no way and He is the life giving river where there is thirst all around. When Grace came, the law was taken away.

We saw this clearly in *Luke 2:21-38, And when eight days were accomplished for the circumcising of the child, his name was called JESUS, which was so named of the angel before he was conceived in the womb. And when the days of her purification according to the law of Moses were accomplished, they brought him to Jerusalem, to present him to the Lord; (As it is written in the law of the Lord, Every male that openeth the womb shall be called holy to the Lord;) And to offer a sacrifice according to that which is said in the law of the Lord, A pair of turtledoves, or two young pigeons. And, behold, there was a man in Jerusalem, whose name was Simeon; and the same man was just and devout, waiting for the consolation of Israel: and the Holy Ghost was upon him. And it was revealed unto him by the Holy Ghost, that he should not see death, before he had seen the Lord's Christ. And he came by the Spirit into the temple: and when the parents brought in the child Jesus, to do for him after the custom of the law, Then took he him up in his arms, and blessed God, and said, Lord, now lettest thou thy servant depart in peace, according to thy word: For mine eyes have seen thy salvation, Which thou hast prepared before the face of* **all people***; A light to lighten the Gentiles, and the glory of thy people Israel…And there was one Anna, a prophetess, the daughter of Phanuel, of the tribe of Aser: she was of a great age, and had lived with an husband seven years from her virginity; And she was a widow of about fourscore and four years, which departed not from the temple, but served God with fastings and prayers night and day. And she coming in that instant gave thanks likewise unto the Lord, and spake of him to all them that looked for redemption in Jerusalem.*

Jesus was the promised Seed. On the eighth day, He was circumcised, fulfilling the law as in *Leviticus 12:2-4, Speak unto the children of Israel, saying, If a woman have conceived seed, and born a man child: then she shall be unclean seven days; according to the days of the separation for her infirmity shall she be unclean. And in the eighth day the flesh of his foreskin shall be circumcised. And she shall then continue in the blood of her purifying three and thirty days; she shall touch no hallowed thing, nor come into the sanctuary, until the days of her purifying be fulfilled.* After forty days (7+33), Mary brought herself and Jesus to the priest to be purified and to be redeemed, respectively. For Mary's own purification, she brought two turtledoves, one as a burnt offering and the other as a sin offering. For Jesus to be redeemed as the firstborn, Joseph and Mary had to pay five shekels, as we know from *Numbers 18:16, And those that are to be redeemed from a month old shalt thou redeem, according to thine estimation, for the money of five shekels, after the shekel of the sanctuary.* Mary had to follow the law, but Jesus the Redeemer of the world was redeemed so as to fulfill the law. He perfectly circumcised every sin ever committed.

In the meantime, Simeon was told by the Holy Spirit that he would not see death before he had seen the Consolation or Comforter of Israel, Jesus. Simeon derives from the root word *shama* or *shema* meaning 'to hear', as found in *Deuteronomy 6:4-*

5, Hear (Shama), O Israel: The LORD our God is one LORD: And thou shalt love the LORD thy God with all thine heart, and with all thy soul, and with all thy might. Solomon asked for a *shama* heart as well in *1 Kings 3:9, Give therefore thy servant an understanding heart to judge thy people, that I may discern between good and bad: for who is able to judge this thy so great a people?* Hence, the Israelites were commanded to *shama* or hear the law. The law waited until Grace was born. Simeon (symbolizing our shame before the law) heard, then departed. We saw a shadow of this before when Jacob said to Joseph in *Genesis 46:30, Now I am ready to die, since I have seen your face again and know you are still alive.* For their eyes saw Salvation who was Alive and who was for **all people**, Jews and Gentiles. At the end, all that matters is that JESUS IS ALIVE! Because He is alive, even when we depart, we do not see death! Alive now and forevermore because Jesus is alive!

In the instant that Simeon left, Anna or Hannah appeared. She was the daughter of Phanuel. As *Penuel* or *Peniel* means the face of God, Anna from Phanuel, literally meant Grace from the face of God! She was from the tribe of Asher whom Jacob prophesied over back in *Genesis 49:20, Out of Asher his bread shall be fat, and he shall yield royal dainties.* Anna was widowed for 84 years old and out of her mouth, she spoke all about Jesus, the anointed/fat Bread, who would give royal/kingly dainties or delights of healing and redemption. Even a crumb of Him will heal us. The number 12 stands for government and 7 for perfection or 12x7=84. Jesus' perfect government had come. Jesus, the face of God, has arrived! He would replace the long widowed condition of the people. Jesus would be their perfect 'new' husband as in *Isaiah 54:4-5, for thou shalt forget the shame of thy youth, and shalt not remember the reproach of thy widowhood any more. For thy Maker is thine husband; the LORD of hosts is his name; and thy Redeemer the Holy One of Israel.*

Grace is the new cloth in *Matthew 9:16-17, No man putteth a piece of new cloth unto an old garment, for that which is put in to fill it up taketh from the garment, and the rent is made worse. Neither do men put new wine into old bottles: else the bottles break, and the wine runneth out, and the bottles perish: but they put new wine into new bottles, and both are preserved.* It cannot be sewn together with the inflexible dry cloth of the law. The new would tear away from the old. Grace is also the new wine. It cannot be put into the old, dry bottles or wineskins of the law. The fermentation of the new wine would break the bottle. The new would always break the old. Any mixture would ruin both the old and the new.

This was illustrated beautifully in *Acts 9:36-41, Now there was at Joppa a certain disciple named Tabitha, which by interpretation is called Dorcas: this woman was full of good works and alms deeds which she did. And it came to pass in those days, that she was sick, and died: whom when they had washed, they laid her in an upper chamber. And forasmuch as Lydda was nigh to Joppa, and the disciples had heard that Peter was there, they sent unto him two men, desiring him that he would not delay to come to them. Then Peter arose and went with them. When he was come, they brought him into the upper chamber: and all the widows stood by him weeping, and shewing the coats and garments which Dorcas made, while she was with them. But Peter put them all forth, and kneeled down, and prayed; and turning him to the body said, Tabitha, arise. And she opened her eyes: and when she saw Peter, she sat up. And he gave her his hand, and lifted her up, and when he had called the saints and widows, presented her alive.*

Tabitha, or in Greek, Dorcas, trusted Jesus. But she also trusted in her good charitable works, that of making coats and other garments for the poor. She, in time, fell sick and died. When Peter was shown into the upper chamber, all the widows pointed to the garments and coats that Tabitha did! She did so much. Surely God would see that. None pointed to what Jesus did. So, Peter had to put all these works outside. With the complete removal of all her works mixture, Grace raised up Tabitha. Life fell on her just as it fell on the disciples in the upper room in Jerusalem. Her eyes opened to see Grace. She saw none of her good works. For only Grace could give Tabitha life. For Grace is Life! Jesus is Life!

ঌ 33 ঌ

JESUS AND THE NEW MAN

The life that we had before Jesus is symbolically known as the Old Man. The old man is spiritually dead. Though spiritually dead, it is possible for the old man to experience a changed life. A changed life means having our lives changed from bad to good (or good to better). It can also be called behavior modification. This is usually due to our own persistence and diligence in doing many good works. Many church testimonies actually center around this theme. "I was bad, then I did something about it and now I am good!" cries the Old Man. The whole congregation whoops in delight, applauds enthusiastically, and fists bump each other in joy. However, with time, that same person would start to make mistakes. The congregation that had so enthusiastically cheered him on before would roundly condemn him now. Come to church drunk the first time and everybody welcomes you. Come back to church drunk the next week and everybody condemns you. Feeling guilty, rejected, and a failure, the old man forsakes church forever. If the old man can become good by his work, then he can also become bad through his work.

The New Man is the life that we have after putting our faith in Jesus. We were dead but now we are alive. The new man is spiritually alive because Jesus made him alive. He has an exchanged life, not a changed life. That was the exchange! He is not an old man, changed. He is not a better old man. He is a completely new person. Therefore, an exchanged life can only take place because of Jesus. This is illustrated in the diagram below.

| Old Man - Changed Life
From Bad to Good | New Man - Exchanged Life
From Dead to Alive |

No man can exchange his life for a new one by his own effort. Even if all the angels died myriad deaths it would not result in even one exchanged life. An exchanged life can only happen because of Jesus' finished work on the cross. We who were dead have now been made alive by Jesus. We had a heart/spirit head/soul transformation. Only God can make dead things alive again. The old man died and does not exist anymore. The new man which never existed before, now exists, and is 'alive' forevermore. The new man has a new heart or spirit, together with a renewed mind. He has the power to say 'No' to sin. He does not want to sin because of his new heart. He awoke to righteousness in Christ and he does not sin as written in *1 Corinthians 15:34, Awake to righteousness, and sin not.* He is dead to sin. Sin has no attraction for him. Paul said that all things are lawful for him but he acknowledges that not all things are beneficial to him. He is not under the power of sin even though sin has not lessened. In his spirit, he cannot sin. In his new mind, he does not want to sin. Sinning makes as much sense to him as the prodigal son wanting to return to eat from the pig's trough while feasting at the father's table. Sinning just feels wrong and stupid!

Of course, a person who claims that he or she is a New Man but sins all the time is suspect. A person living continuously under sin is probably not living under Grace. We read in *Romans 6:1-7,14, What shall we say then? Shall we continue in sin, that grace may abound? God forbid. How shall we, that are dead to sin, live any longer therein? Know ye not, that so many of us as were baptized into Jesus Christ were baptized into his death?...like as Christ was raised up from the dead by the glory of the Father, even so we also should walk in newness of life. For if we have been planted together in the likeness of his death, we shall be also in the likeness of his resurrection: Knowing this, that our old man is crucified with him, that the body of sin might be destroyed, that henceforth we should not serve sin. For he that is dead is freed from sin. For sin shall not have dominion over you: for ye are not under the law, but under grace.* **The old man died with Christ. The new man was resurrected with Christ. He is now one with Christ. The sole reason why the new man does not sin even more under Grace is because he is now one with Christ. Sin has no dominion over him because sin has no dominion over Christ.** Grace is the first and only resort, never the last resort, for sin. No self works made the new man and as such, no self works can condemn the new man. Jesus made the new man and He said that there is no condemnation of death from sin for the new man because the new man has put on Christ as in *Galatians 3:27, For as many of you as have been baptized into Christ have put on Christ.*

There is only one way whereby the old man can become the new man. That way is through repentance (in Greek *metanoia,* meaning a change of mind). **Hence, repentance means a change of mind concerning Jesus and our salvation.** As the old man, we did not believe in Him. After a change of our minds, we now do. We become the new man. We acknowledge His goodness that brought us to repentance as in *Romans 2:4, Or despisest thou the riches of his goodness and forbearance and longsuffering; not knowing that the goodness of God leadeth thee to repentance?*

Contrary to popular opinion, repentance has no action in it. So, what happened? Well, it began in the 4th century when the 'hedonistic-who-became-ascetic' Jerome translated *metanoia* as *paenitentiam agite* (in Latin meaning perform acts of penance). Many years later, his translation became the official Latin bible of the Catholic church. Repentance now meant that people had to atone for their sins by acts of punishment administered by the pope, clergy, as well as the law. Hence, to this day, we still see repentance as an action i.e. stop doing something bad and start doing something good, admitting to sin, turning from sin. To somehow do something to earn our way back to God.

But it is not our repentance that brought in the goodness of God! God is good to us no matter what we do or not do. He gave us Jesus while we yet sinners! Hence, it is not about us making reparations and restitutions for our mistakes. It is not about us repairing our own broken lives. It is not about us turning our backs on sin. *Acts 5:31* states, *God exalted Him to His right hand as Prince and Savior, to give repentance to Israel, and forgiveness of sins.* Here, we see that repentance itself is a gift! It is simply about us receiving this gift of repentance and then changing our minds (we were wrong) about Jesus!

Repentance has no works in it as we cannot repent from the very same sins that Jesus already took away. In *Acts 20:21*, we read, Testifying both to the Jews, and also to the Greeks, *repentance toward God, and faith toward our Lord Jesus Christ.* We are called to repent towards God. We change our minds and lineup our thoughts according to what God said about His Son, Jesus. With this in mind, we should repent all the time! Begin with repenting about repentance. Without Jesus or Grace, there can be no repentance. Only with Jesus or Grace can we repent. Repentance in Hebrew is *teshuvah* (תשובה). Reading from right to left, we get *tav* (cross) *shin vav bet* (to return) *hei* (grace). Hence, repentance in Hebrew meant a return to Grace because of the cross. It is always 'when I see the blood I will pass over you'.

In the well known story of Paul's experience on the road to Damascus, we find that only when Jesus was revealed could Paul repent. We read this in *Acts 9:7-9, 17-18, And the men which journeyed with him stood speechless, hearing a voice, but seeing no man. And Saul arose from the earth; and when his eyes were opened, he saw no man: but they led him by the hand, and brought him into Damascus. And he was three days without sight. And Ananias went his way, and entered into the house; and putting his hands on him said, Brother Saul, the Lord, even Jesus, that appeared unto thee in the way as thou camest, hath sent me, that thou mightest receive thy sight, and be filled with the Holy Ghost.*

And immediately there fell from his eyes as it had been scales: and he received sight forthwith.

Paul desiring to kill as many disciples of Jesus as possible went to the high priest, Caiaphas, and received letters of introduction to the synagogues in Damascus. But en route, he encountered the new High Priest called Grace, fell to the ground, and was blind for three days. He fell from his old way of thinking but rose again to a new way of thinking about Jesus. The 'old' Paul, who was 'blind', became blind. But the 'new' Paul, who can now 'see', saw Ananias. Ananias meant 'the Grace of God'. Paul saw Grace and immediately started sharing Jesus! The Saul of the OT persecuted David while the Saul of the NT shared about the Son of David. Paul did not repent from his sins but he sure changed his mind about Jesus! He could never again un-see Grace! Once again, without Jesus there can be no repentance. Without Jesus, who or what would we change our minds to? Who do we repent to? We can only repent or change our minds to what God said about His Son, Jesus!

This is shown clearly in *Acts 2:36-38, Therefore let all the house of Israel know assuredly, that God hath made that same Jesus, whom ye have crucified, both Lord and Christ. Now when they heard this, they were pricked in their heart, and said unto Peter and to the rest of the apostles, Men and brethren, what shall we do? Then Peter said unto them, Repent, and be baptized every one of you in the name of Jesus Christ for the remission of sins, and ye shall receive the gift of the Holy Ghost.* The Jews, who had thought earlier that the disciples were hammered, were now pricked in their hearts by Peter. If they were wrong about the Holy Spirit then they could be wrong about Jesus! They inquired of Peter what they should do next. Peter told them to repent. Repent from what? The Jews rejected Jesus before and now had to repent or change their minds about who Jesus is and what He had done. There was really nothing for them to 'do' but line up their thoughts to what God said about Jesus.

And what did God say about His Son and our salvation? In *Hebrews 10:16-17, This is the covenant that I will make with them after those days, saith the Lord, I will put my laws into their hearts, and in their minds will I write them; And their sins and iniquities will I remember no more,* we read that Jesus is in our hearts and our minds. Our sins have been forgiven and will no more be remembered. Our salvation depends solely on Jesus and His finished work. The old man, no matter how hard he tries or how many good works he does, cannot save himself.

The new man is a complete new creation. We do not flip the old man and, *viola,* we get a new man. The new man is not an extreme makeover of the old man. He or she never existed before. But because of Jesus, this man now exists. *Galatians 2:19-21* states, *For I through the law am dead to the law, that I might live unto God. I am crucified with Christ: nevertheless I live; yet not I, but Christ liveth in me: and the life which I now live in the flesh I live by the faith of the Son of God, who loved me, and gave himself for me. I do not frustrate the grace of God: for if righteousness come by the law, then Christ is dead in vain.* The old man is truly dead. He has been crucified with Christ. The old has to die so that the new could be born. The new man is alive in Christ. He is righteous only because of what Jesus did for him. Righteousness comes only through Jesus, never by doing right works!

The Pharisees spoke and looked like believers but were not. They were 'old man' trying to look like 'new man'. But it is also possible for believers to go back and follow the law. They are the 'new man' but behave like the 'old man'. Both are an abomination to God as the two men in *Proverbs 17:15, He that justifieth the wicked, and he that condemneth the just, even they both are abomination to the LORD,* as they are both doing fleshly works. For the one-legged 'old man' in an ass-kickin' righteousness competition will fall. However, the 'new man' being rooted and established in Jesus' righteousness cannot fall, even while doing fleshly acts, as in *Psalm 121:3, He will not let you fall.* So while both old and new man can and will do fleshly acts (acts not dependent on Jesus), only the new man cannot fall as Jesus will not let him fall!

We read in *Galatians 2:11-16, But when Peter was come to Antioch, I withstood him to the face, because he was to be blamed. For before that certain came from James, he did eat with the*

Gentiles: but when they were come, he withdrew and separated himself, fearing them which were of the circumcision...But when I saw that they walked not uprightly according to the truth of the gospel, I said unto Peter before them all, If thou, being a Jew, livest after the manner of Gentiles, and not as do the Jews, why compellest thou the Gentiles to live as do the Jews?...Knowing that a man is not justified by the works of the law, but by the faith of Jesus Christ, even we have believed in Jesus Christ, that we might be justified by the faith of Christ, and not by the works of the law: for by the works of the law shall no flesh be justified.

Peter and some other Jewish believers were having a great time fraternizing and eating with the Gentiles when news reached them that James and others 'of the circumcision' were coming into town. As the law forbade eating unclean food (pulled pork, meat sacrificed to idols, etc) they quickly removed themselves from their Gentile brothers and pretended to be living under the law, eating only kosher food. Paul confronted Peter and the other pretenders directly and told them that they were not 'walking uprightly according to the truth of the gospel'. The truth of the gospel is Jesus. **We are not saved by Jesus so that we can follow the law.** Jesus set us free from the law. Peter did not have to pretend. James, who was a prominent leader in the early church, often emphasized the Torah over faith in his brother, Jesus! It must have been a brother thing. Also, belief in Jesus did not instantly erase a lifetime of law keeping and other traditions. In *Acts 15*, James actually settled this issue at the Council of Jerusalem when he agreed with Peter that salvation was by Jesus as Grace. He decreed that no Gentile believer ever need follow the Mosaic law. But at the end, despite his own decree, he could not help slipping in some works! Now you know why the book of James is packed with 'works' amidst grace.

Actually, Paul and Peter's ministries were to be separate, as in *Acts 2:7, But on the contrary, seeing that I had been entrusted with the gospel to the uncircumcised, just as Peter had been to the circumcised.* No need for pretense. Paul would share with the Gentiles about Grace while Peter and the other eleven (Matthias replaced Judas) would share with the Jews presumably a 'mixed' culturally sensitive message of Jesus, ethnicity, purity, and works. Unconditional with some conditions! After *Acts 13:2*, the Holy Spirit no longer recorded the acts of the twelve, only Paul's or only if they interacted with Paul! However, despite their different understandings of Grace, all of Jesus' disciples except John, were martyred for their faith in Jesus,

We read in *Philippians 2:12-13, my beloved...work out your own salvation with fear and trembling. For it is God which worketh in you both to will and to do of his good pleasure.* The new man should recognize that his salvation and new life is only because of Jesus. **Work out your salvation does not mean work for your salvation!** Salvation is not earned nor maintained by works on our part. God saved us and He keeps us saved. It is entirely God's will and good pleasure that we become completely new. Once we work out that our salvation is entirely God's work, then we stand in awe and trembling at what has been achieved. This is exactly what God promised to Israel in *Jeremiah 33:8-9, And I will cleanse them from all their iniquity, whereby they have sinned against me; and I will pardon all their iniquities, whereby they have sinned, and whereby they have transgressed against me...and they shall fear and tremble for all the goodness and for all the prosperity that I procure unto it.* The whole nation of Israel would be in awe at the goodness of God. That is the meaning of fear and trembling! Similarly, we should all be wonderstruck and open-mouthed at what Jesus did for us.

A clear picture of this awe and amazement at what Jesus did can be found in the story of the woman who had an issue of blood for twelve years. Having spent all her money on physicians she did not become better but worse off. She was now penniless, still sick, and treated as an untouchable. She was the old man, exhausted and defeated by her own self efforts. We know this from *Leviticus 15:25-27, And if a woman have an issue of her blood many days out of the time of her separation, or if it run beyond the time of her separation; all the days of the issue of her uncleanness shall be as the days of her separation: she shall be unclean.* But she had faith in Jesus! So she pressed, which was not lawful for her to do, through the crowds and touched the fringe of Jesus' garment. Her touch did not heal her but her faith in Jesus did. For we know that Jesus is the Sun of Righteousness with healing in His wings from *Malachi 4:2, The Sun of Righteousness shall arise With healing in His wings.*

We continue reading in *Mark 5:32-34, And he looked round about to see her that had done this thing. But the woman fearing and trembling, knowing what was done in her, came and fell down before him, and told him all the truth. And he said unto her, Daughter, thy faith hath made thee whole (sozo); go in peace, and be whole of thy plague.* The moment she was healed, she started fearing and trembling knowing what was already done in her. She was *sozo*-ed! Unclean made clean! Sick made whole! Old made new! She trembled with awe and wonderment at her Healer's feet. No doctors could heal her. No works worked. But Jesus did it! **Jesus' power extended even to the fringe of His garments or wings! She was not trembling with fear at what was going to happen to her but at what had already happened to her!** She was not trembling because of the crowds and what they might do or say. She was trembling because of what Jesus did! Healed and made righteous at the same time! And then to be called daughter! From outcast to family! Small wonder she trembled in bewildered reverence of Jesus! She trembled at her newness! At Grace! This was repeated by Paul in *1 Timothy 4:16: Take heed unto thyself, and unto the doctrine; continue in them: for in doing this thou shalt both save (sozo) thyself, and them that hear thee.* Even today, hearing the doctrine of Grace gives us physical healing (part of *sozo*) just as it did for Timothy!

Right after the healing of this woman who had been sick for 12 years, Jesus raised Jairus' 12 years old daughter from the dead. Twelve stands for government or a body of people. A whole body of people are physically sick today. But when they hear Grace, they will realize that they are already healed. Also, generations of people who are spiritually dead will become spiritually alive in Christ as well. It is as written in *Hosea 3:5, In the last days, they will tremble in awe of the LORD and of his goodness.* Jesus is awe-fully, awe-fully good! Awesome! Awesome! Awesome! Awesome Jesus!

☙ 34 ❧

JESUS AND GOOD WORKS

People under the law had to work in order to pay off the mountain of debt they owed to the law. So they worked out of obligation, bondage, and indebtedness. When they finally got saved by Jesus, they were mistakenly taught that they had to continue on with this debt repayment. The debt was never wiped out. It was just transferred. Now, they have to pay Jesus back. Jesus gave all so what are they giving back to Him? All these works to pay Jesus back are called dead works.

But there is another type of work as described in *1 Corinthians 15:10, But by the grace of God I am what I am: and his grace which was bestowed upon me was not in vain; but I laboured more abundantly than they all: yet not I, but the grace of God which was with me.* Paul who was under Grace, worked harder than all other people. Why? Because Paul knew that he had the prize of Jesus already. His position as a son was secure and everlasting. However much works he did, great or small, he would always be 'good enough' to God because of Jesus in him. He knew that God delighted in him, as in *Psalm 16:3, As for the saints who are on the earth, They are the excellent ones, in whom is all my delight!* Therefore, his abundant work was pure joy and not counted as dreary, as Jesus worked through and in him - *according to His energy, working in me in power (Colossians 1:29).* These works are known as good works.

Good works begin after we rest and receive from Jesus. This is evident in *Luke 10:38-42, Now it came to pass, as they went, that he entered into a certain village: and a certain woman named Martha received him into her house. And she had a sister called Mary, which also sat at Jesus' feet, and heard his word. But Martha was cumbered about much serving, and came to him, and said, Lord, dost thou not care that my sister hath left me to serve alone? bid her therefore that she help me. And Jesus answered and said unto her, Martha, Martha, thou art careful and troubled about many things: But one thing is needful: and Mary hath chosen that good part, which shall not be taken away from her.* When Jesus and His disciples came to Mary and Martha's house, Martha thought that the proper thing to do was to serve and feed Him. But because He had brought all His friends, they had to be fed too. So she banged pots and pans in the kitchen as she stirred and fretted away before the hot stove.

Meanwhile, Mary chose to rest in the presence of Jesus, at His feet, and to receive from Him, as in *Isaiah 55:1-3, Ho, every one that thirsteth, come ye to the waters, and he that hath no money; come ye, buy, and eat; yea, come, buy wine and milk without money and without price. Wherefore do ye spend money for that which is not bread? and your labour for that which satisfieth not? hearken diligently unto me, and eat ye that which is good, and let your soul delight itself in fatness. Incline your ear, and come unto me: hear, and your soul shall live.* In the hot kitchen, Martha stirred up a storm of self-works in her labor that satisfied not. When Martha could not take it any longer, she burst into Jesus' gathering and condemned Mary with the long end of her kitchen spoon. However, Jesus did not commend Martha for her diligence and hard work. Instead, He corrected her accusing kitchen spoon finger lovingly.

Time with Jesus, not laboring, satisfies. Receiving bread and fatness freely (zero cost not some cost) from Him leads to restoration and fullness. Taking from Jesus is the one needful thing we all need to do. Mary, having received from Jesus, continued to rest in Him for her brother's resurrection and later, anointed the feet of Jesus with expensive spikenard ointment. We know it was expensive because Judas admonished her for that action. While we do not know for sure, Mary could have been one of the women at the foot of the cross. She followed Jesus all the way! However, Martha, not having received from Jesus, ran and served until she became empty. She wanted to feed God, forgetting *Psalm 50:12, If I were hungry, I would not tell you, for the world is Mine, and the fullness thereof.* We do not hear of her anywhere near the cross.

In this world though, we are often told to be like Martha and not Mary. We read this in *Luke 14:26-35, If any man come to me, and hate not his father, and mother, and wife, and children, and brethren, and sisters, yea, and his own life also, he cannot be my disciple. And whosoever doth not bear his cross, and come after me, cannot be my disciple. For which of you, intending to build a tower, sitteth not down first, and counteth the cost, whether he have sufficient to finish it? Lest haply, after he hath laid the foundation, and is not able to finish it, all that behold it begin to mock him, Saying, This man began to build, and was not able to finish. Or what king, going to make war against another king, sitteth not down first, and consulteth whether he be able with ten thousand to meet him that cometh against him with twenty thousand?... So likewise, whosoever he be of you that forsaketh not all that he hath, he cannot be my disciple. Salt is good: but if the salt have lost his savour, wherewith shall it be seasoned? It is neither fit for the land, nor yet for the dunghill; but men cast it out.*

This passage has been used exclusively to show believers the high cost of being a believer or a disciple. The explanation goes something like this. Many people were following Jesus at that time but He knew they were not real followers. To distinguish superficial from dedicated followers, He demanded the people to examine themselves. Were they willing to pay the price? Following Jesus would cost them everything. To the point of hating parents and other loved ones who would come between them and Jesus. Forsake all. Sell all. Count the cost and pay any price because Jesus is worth it. Anything less means that you are just a spectator and not a true follower. You are salt that is not salty. You are not even fit for the dunghill but to be cast out completely. Jesus accepts only those who are willing to lay down their lives, bear their cross, for Him.

For most of us there is little hope if the above interpretation is correct. The cost is too great. The bar is too high. The standard is too perfect. We are too ordinary! Or maybe there is an another explanation for the parable? First, Jesus was actually using *Micah 7:6-7, For the son dishonoureth the father, the daughter riseth up against her mother, the daughter in law against her mother in law; a man's enemies are the men of his own house. Therefore I will look unto the LORD.* Micah is lamenting that all people are unrighteous, so who can he turn to? He then answers his own question. He will turn to Jesus! Jesus is not asking us to make a choice between Him and our loved ones. He is asking us to turn to Him alone as only He can make us righteous.

The King is God the Father. He sat down and counted the cost for going to war against sin, the 'other' king. There could not be peace with sin but the cost of going to war against sin would be enormous. Even if God sacrificed all of His angels, cherubims and seraphims, He would still not win. Only one thing could win the war but that would cost Him everything. Therefore, God forsook all He had. He gave up His everything, which was Jesus! When sin was defeated, all sinners became righteous. That was the price that He paid for you and me. We paid nothing but because God paid everything, you and I won!

Similarly, God built the tower or the cross to redeem us. God never called anyone else to build a tower. Many people gathered at the cross to mock the Foundation Stone, Jesus. He started the work but can He finish the work? In *Isaiah 66:17, They that sanctify themselves, and purify themselves in the gardens* (the unbelieving Jews) *behind one tree in the midst* (Jesus on the cross), *eating swine's flesh, and the abomination, and the mouse* (the Gentile Romans), *shall be consumed together, saith the LORD.* Then Jesus shouted *'Tetelestai!'* Jesus' finished work on the tower would stand forever. He gave us His righteousness. Not father, mother, spouse, children, or siblings.

This parable was given to the multitudes after the parable where the Pharisees accepted the invitation to the feast but only if they could pay back for the meal. They came loaded with self-works as well as self-righteousness. All these works were to be hated. *1 Chronicles 29:14* states, *Everything we have has come from you, and we give you only what you first gave us!* **We need to understand that we cannot make God love us more or less by our works. He loves us independent of our works, good or dead. We do not become righteous by our good works and we do not become unrighteous by our dead works. We become righteous solely because of Jesus. It is His work, not ours. Salt is good but without the salty savor, it is useless. Good works are good but without Jesus, they become dead works.**

It is very important to understand that a person's good works count for naught if he does not have Jesus. We read in *Luke 12:16-21, The ground of a certain rich man brought forth plentifully: And he thought within himself, saying, What shall I do, because I have no room where to bestow my fruits? And he said, This will I do: I will pull down my barns, and build greater; and there will I bestow all my fruits... But God said unto him, Thou fool, this night thy soul shall be required of thee: then whose shall those things be, which thou hast provided? So is he that layeth up treasure for himself, and is not rich toward God.* The ground of a certain rich man had produced enormous quantities of good works. Perceiving the many good works that he had performed and accumulated over the years, he felt very contented and satisfied. The 'barns-full' of good works would earn him his salvation. He felt that he merited his salvation. But he was called a fool for only a fool would trust in his good self-works. All our treasured self-works, all our medals of self-centeredness, are nothing to God. **It is right standing with God that mattered, not right doing.** Without Jesus, our copious quantities of good works are all in vain.

This is explained further in *Matthew 5:13-15,19-20, 48, Ye are the salt of the earth: but if the salt have lost his savour, wherewith shall it be salted? it is thenceforth good for nothing, but to be cast out, and to be trodden under foot of men. Ye are the light of the world. A city that is set on an hill cannot be hid. Neither do men light a candle, and put it under a bushel... Whosoever therefore shall break one of these least commandments, and shall teach men so, he shall be called the least in the kingdom of heaven: but whosoever shall do and teach them* **this one***, the same shall be*

*called great in the kingdom of heaven. For I say unto you, That
except your righteousness shall exceed the righteousness of the
scribes and Pharisees, ye shall in no case enter into the kingdom of
heaven.   Be ye therefore perfect, even as your Father which is in
heaven is perfect.*

Salt is salty because of the sodium (or other alkali metals)
ions in it. We are called the salt of the earth because of Jesus in us.
If we do not have Jesus in us or if salt does not have sodium, then
we are no good even if we look good. Salt without sodium may
look like salt but is unsavory. That is why all the offerings in the
temple had to be salted. A person without Jesus may look alive but
is not alive. We are cast out not because we lose our Savior, but
because we do not have the Savior in the first place. An unbeliever
will be trod down upon by other men in this world whereas a
believer will be protected and raised up by the Son of Man. We are
called to be like a brightly lit city on top of a hill, resplendent with
Jesus. But many times we do not shine that way because satan has
tricked us into focusing our lights under a bushel or basket; under a
vessel; and under a bed (*Luke 8:16*). Bushels were made for grain,
vessels for drink, and bed is our comfort/shelter. Therefore, we do
many insignificant self-works because we worry about our wellbeing; namely food, drink, and comfort/shelter. We never lose our
salvation or Light, who is Jesus, but we end up worrying about
many things and not shining brightly as we were meant to be. We
forget that when we have Jesus, we already have everything
because He is everything.

In *Mark 7:8,* the Pharisees *disregarded the commandment
of God to keep the tradition of men.* They broke the law
consistently and taught men as such. They would be called the
least in the kingdom of heaven. But whosoever teaches about 'this
one' (in Greek *houtos,* meaning the person just named) would be
called great in heaven. The one just named is Jesus! Our
righteousness exceed those of the Pharisees, not because we broke
less laws, but solely because Jesus gave us His righteousness. We
are perfect as our Father in heaven is because of Jesus' perfection
in us. It is all Grace, never works!

৯ 35 ৬

JESUS AND FRUITS

We read in *Colossians 1:10, That ye might walk worthy of the Lord unto all pleasing, being fruitful in every good work, and increasing in the knowledge of God.* Good fruits are produced by those who are attached to Jesus. Jesus is the root, the stem, the branch, and the vine. He is the Seed and the Tree of Life. As we are grafted into Him we take on His Life nature and produce good fruits. With Jesus, we produce good fruits. Without Jesus, we produce bad fruits, which are impressive sins and very dead.

We can walk in love because He loved us first. *John 13:34* states, *A new commandment I give unto you, That ye love one another; as I have loved you, that ye also love one another.* Love is no longer a work as the old commandment in *Leviticus 19:18, thou shalt love thy neighbour as thyself,* but a response to 'as I have loved you'. We can forgive one another because He forgave us first. We can accept one another as He accepted us first. We can be kind to one another because He showed kindness (*checed* or Grace) to us first. We can give to one another because He gave to us first. These are fruits of being in Christ as stated in *Philippians 1:11, Being filled with the fruits of righteousness, which are by Jesus Christ, unto the glory and praise of God.*

We read in *Matthew 25:34-36, Then shall the King say unto them on his right hand, Come, ye blessed of my Father, inherit the kingdom prepared for you from the foundation of the world: For I was an hungred, and ye gave me meat: I was thirsty, and ye gave me drink: I was a stranger, and ye took me in: Naked, and ye clothed me: I was sick, and ye visited me: I was in prison, and ye came unto me.* Jesus prepared His kingdom for us as an inheritance. We inherit His kingdom first. We were hungry and He gave us the Bread of Life. We were thirsty and He gave us the Living Water. We were strangers and foreigners and He gave us His name and adopted us as sons and daughters into His family. *Psalm 27:10* states, *Even if my father and mother abandon me, the LORD will take care of me.* We were naked and He clothed us in His righteousness and glory. We were sick in our bodies, and He visited, inhabited, and healed us. We were imprisoned by the law and He came and fulfilled all the requirements of the law so that the righteousness of the law might be fulfilled in us. He set us free from the shackles of the law. We were dead and He gave us life. Only after we received all from Him could we give meat and drink, provide hospitality, sustenance, and share the gospel.

Ephesians 4:30-32 states, *And grieve not the holy Spirit of God, whereby ye are sealed unto the day of redemption. Let all bitterness, and wrath, and anger, and clamour, and evil speaking, be put away from you, with all malice: And be ye kind one to another, tenderhearted, forgiving one another, even as God for Christ's sake hath forgiven you.* Forgiving one another is a fruit because God forgave us first. God was also kind and tenderhearted towards us. So we can likewise produce similar good fruits.

However, works that spring from our flesh may result in bad fruits such as bitterness, wrath, anger, clamor, and evil speaking. He is grieved when we do that. Jesus spoke to His disciples in *John 14:15, If ye love me, keep my commandments.* Because of His love for us, He wants to see us well. That is why He tells us to keep His commands. When we do what He says, or at least try, we avoid all types of hurts, disappointments, and frustrations. Our behavior matters to Him because we matter to Him. And we matter very much to Him. So when we participate in sinful behavior that destroys us, He is grieved. He is not grieved because of sin as He already dealt with it. He is not infuriated with us because we broke His rules. He is not angry or disappointed with us because we misbehave. He is grieved because of what sin can do to us. We are His sons and daughters and He does not want to see us destroyed by the consequences of sin, as in *1 Timothy 3:6, and fall under the same judgment as the devil.* The consequence of sin makes us fall, just as the devil.

Because of His love for us first, we love Him back. And because we love Jesus, then it just follows that we will do what He says. However, it does not mean we must obey in order for Jesus to love us. **Love is not conditional upon obedience. Under the law, we obey to earn love. But under Grace, we are loved into obedience. When we do what He says, that is our fruit of His loving us first.** In *John 14:23-24* we read, *Jesus answered and said unto him, If a man love me, he will keep my words: and my Father will love him, and we will come unto him, and make our abode with him. He that loveth me not keepeth not my sayings: and the word which ye hear is not mine, but the Father's which sent me.* A person who does not know or rejects Jesus, does not love Him and will not do what He, or the Father, says. It has nothing to do with disobedience. An unbeliever can produce copious quantities of fruits too. But they are called bad fruits simply because he is not attached to Jesus.

As the new man, our conduct should follow that as in *1 Peter 1:13-16, Wherefore gird up the loins of your mind, be sober, and hope to the end for the grace that is to be brought unto you at the revelation of Jesus Christ; As obedient children, not fashioning yourselves according to the former lusts in your ignorance: But as he which hath called you is holy, so be ye holy in all manner of conversation; Because it is written, Be ye holy; for I am holy.* We were made holy by Jesus. It is a gift. So let us behave like the holy people we already are. To be holy is to be uncommon. We can be holy in our conversation, holy in our thoughts, and holy by our obedience. We do not act holy. Our actions are holy or uncommon because we are already holy. It is a good fruit of being in Christ.

We read in *Luke 8:4-18, And when much people were gathered together, and were come to him out of every city, he spake by a parable: A sower went out to sow his seed: and as he sowed, some fell by the way side; and it was trodden down, and the fowls of the air devoured it. And some fell upon a rock; and as soon as it was sprung up, it withered away, because it lacked moisture. And some fell among thorns; and the thorns sprang up with it, and choked it. And other fell on good ground, and sprang up, and bare fruit an hundredfold. And when he had said these things, he cried, He that hath ears to hear, let him hear. And his disciples asked him, saying, What might this parable be? And he said, Unto you it is given to know the mysteries of the kingdom of God: but to others in parables; that seeing they might not see, and hearing they might not understand. Now the parable is this: The seed is the word of God. Those by the way side are they that hear; then cometh the devil, and taketh away the word out of their hearts, lest they should believe and be saved. They on the rock are they, which, when they hear, receive the word with joy; and these have no root, which for a while believe, and in time of temptation fall away. And that which fell among thorns are they, which, when they have heard, go forth, and are choked with cares and riches and pleasures of this life, and bring no fruit to perfection. But that on the good ground are they, which in an honest and good heart, having heard the word, keep it, and bring forth fruit with patience.*

No man, when he hath lighted a candle, covereth it with a vessel, or putteth it under a bed; but setteth it on a candlestick, that they which enter in may see the light. For nothing is secret, that shall not be made manifest; neither any thing hid, that shall not be known and come abroad. Take heed therefore how ye hear: for whosoever hath, to him shall be given; and whosoever hath not, from him shall be taken even that which he seemeth to have.

Let us examine this seemingly simple parable. The Seed is Jesus. The wayside people are unbelievers. They reject Jesus and trod on Him. Satan seizes this opportunity and quickly robs them of any chance of Jesus taking hold *lest they should believe and be saved*. However, the stony ground and the ground infested with thorns are believers! Jesus took hold of their hearts but satan caused them to fall away. They produce little to no fruit. While satan has no power to steal their salvation, satan kidnaps their joy and chokes them with thorns and works. The ground may lack moisture and depth, but the people in these two categories are still saved because it is neither the water level nor the root depth that saves, but the Seed that was planted. Only one ground was fruitful and that was the ground that was Jesus conscious. Good fruit bearing comes only from God. We read in *1 Corinthians 3:6-7, I have planted, Apollos watered; but God gave the increase. So then neither is he that planteth any thing, neither he that watereth; but God that giveth the increase.* A man or woman cannot bear good fruit apart from Jesus. Note that out of the four types of ground mentioned in this parable, three of them received Jesus, albeit only one produced an abundance of good fruit. But regardless of the ground, Jesus still sowed Himself for all! He loved every ground, even those who rejected Him! He is never stingy with Grace even though He knew that many would reject Him. **It is all about the Seed, never the ground. It is all about Jesus, never about us.**

This fruit producing ground was also told in a parable in *Mark 4:26-29, And he said, So is the kingdom of God, as if a man should cast seed into the ground; And should sleep, and rise night and day, and the seed should spring and grow up, he knoweth not how. For the earth bringeth forth fruit of herself; first the blade, then the ear, after that the full corn in the ear. But when the fruit is brought forth, immediately he putteth in the sickle, because the harvest is come.* Jesus causes all the increase and growth in the ground while men sleep and rise. Only the seed or Jesus matters. Stony or thorny ground can become good ground once deception is lifted from them. The harvest from the good ground is a bumper crop of believers.

The fruit from this good ground can be found in *Titus 2:11-15, For the grace of God that bringeth salvation hath appeared to all men, Teaching us that, denying ungodliness and worldly lusts, we should live soberly, righteously, and godly, in this present world; Looking for that blessed hope, and the glorious appearing of the great God and our Saviour Jesus Christ; Who gave himself for us, that he might redeem us from all iniquity, and purify unto himself a peculiar people, zealous of good works. These things speak, and exhort, and rebuke with all authority. Let no man despise thee.* The Grace of God, Jesus, gave to all men first. It is Grace that makes us zealous of good works. When we become fully conscious of Jesus and what He did for us, we take our sinful thoughts captive. The only way to overcome sinful thoughts and actions is to bring into captivity every thought and every fleshly reasoning, not to our obedience, but to the obedience of Christ. When we are Jesus conscious, we can live soberly and righteously in this world.

We read this in *2 Corinthians 10:5, Casting down imaginations, and every high thing that exalteth itself against the knowledge of God, and bringing into captivity every thought to the obedience of Christ;* **It is because Jesus obeyed and overcame sin that we become righteous before God. He obeyed unto death. Once again, it is the obedience of Christ that matters and not our obedience to Christ. For we can never obey like Jesus did. When our every thought is captive to the finished work of Jesus, then we can start to apprehend good works. Our good fruits start after we receive from Jesus.**

After we receive from Jesus, we will want to do good works. *Ephesians 2:8-10* states, *For by grace are ye saved through faith; and that not of yourselves: it is the gift of God: Not of works, lest any man should boast. For we are his workmanship, created in Christ Jesus unto good works, which God hath before ordained that we should walk in them.* These good works, prepared and gifted by God for us to do, are for other believers and not for God.

We see this in *James 2:14-26, What doth it profit, my brethren, though a man say he hath faith, and have not works? can faith save him? If a brother or sister be naked, and destitute of daily food, And one of you say unto them, Depart in peace, be ye warmed and filled; notwithstanding ye give them not those things which are needful to the body; what doth it profit? Even so faith, if it hath not works, is dead, being alone. Yea, a man may say, Thou hast faith, and I have works: shew me thy faith without thy works, and I will shew thee my faith by my works. Thou believest that there is one God; thou doest well: the devils also believe, and tremble. But wilt thou know, O vain man, that faith without works is dead? Was not Abraham our father justified by works, when he had offered Isaac his son upon the altar? Seest thou how faith wrought with his works, and by works was faith made perfect? And the scripture was fulfilled which saith, Abraham believed God, and it was imputed unto him for righteousness: and he was called the*

Friend of God. Ye see then how that by works a man is justified, and not by faith only. Likewise also was not Rahab the harlot justified by works, when she had received the messengers, and had sent them out another way? For as the body without the spirit is dead, so faith without works is dead also.

Abraham and Rahab were praised for their faith in God, not rebuked for their sins. Because of that, they produced good fruits. Similarly for us, we want and delight in doing good works for others. Why? So that we can be justified before others that our good works are a result of being saved by unmerited Grace! The moment we repent and agree with God, we can do these works, as in *Acts 26:20, that they should repent and turn to God, and do works meet for repentance.* **Works for the new man is the by-product of being connected to Jesus. As the new man is led by the Holy Spirit, he automatically and effortlessly bears good fruit. The root, who is Jesus, produces the fruits.** As we are the new man in Christ, we can do all as written in *Colossians 3:3,5-10, For ye are dead, and your life is hid with Christ in God. Mortify therefore your members which are upon the earth; fornication, uncleanness, inordinate affection, evil concupiscence, and covetousness, which is idolatry: For which things' sake the wrath of God cometh on the children of disobedience: In the which ye also walked some time, when ye lived in them. But now ye also put off all these; anger, wrath, malice, blasphemy, filthy communication out of your mouth. Lie not one to another, seeing that ye have put off the old man with his deeds; And have put on the new man...*

The new man, in Christ, produces good fruits. Good fruits can also be called living works as the works are a response to the Living God in him. John the Baptist mentioned it back in *Matthew 3:8, Bring forth therefore fruits meet for repentance.* The first fruit is the confession or a lining up of our thoughts to the obedience of Christ. Speak and agree that Jesus has perfectly obeyed the Father. We do not have to obsess over our need to improve and achieve for Jesus has perfected us. When we understand who we are, then and only then can we begin to deny ungodliness and worldly lusts. As stated before, the moment we take our thoughts captive to the obedience of Jesus, we can avoid all types of corrupt behavior patterns. *Ephesians 4:22-24* states, *That ye put off concerning the former conversation the old man, which is corrupt according to the deceitful lusts; And be renewed in the spirit of your mind; And that ye put on the new man, which after God is created in righteousness and true holiness. Wherefore putting away lying, speak every man truth with his neighbour: for we are members one of another. Be ye angry, and sin not: let not the sun go down upon your wrath: Neither give place to the devil. Let him that stole steal no more: but rather let him labour, working with his hands the thing which is good, that he may have to give to him that needeth. Let no corrupt communication proceed out of your mouth, but that which is good to the use of edifying, that it may minister grace unto the hearers. And grieve not the holy Spirit of God, whereby ye are sealed unto the day of redemption. Let all bitterness, and wrath, and anger, and clamour, and evil speaking, be put away from you, with all malice: And be ye kind one to another, tenderhearted, forgiving one another, even as God for Christ's sake hath forgiven you.*

For example, we read in *Exodus 21:17, And he that curseth his father, or his mother, shall surely be put to death.* Under the law, we honor our parents to become righteous. Then in *Ephesians 6:1-3* we read, *Children, obey your parents in the Lord: for this is right. Honour thy father and mother...That it may be well with thee, and thou mayest live long on the earth.* Under Grace, we are already righteous. Just as Jesus had already honored His Father, we can similarly honor our parents. We no longer honor our parents to become righteous but we honor them because we are already righteous. We honor our parents not because of any obligation but because that is the fruit of being in Jesus.

James 1:21-25 states, *Wherefore lay apart all filthiness and superfluity of naughtiness, and receive with meekness the engrafted word, which is able to save your souls. But be ye doers of the word, and not hearers only, deceiving your own selves. For if any be a hearer of the word, and not a doer, he is like unto a man beholding his natural face in a glass: For he beholdeth himself, and goeth his way, and straightway forgetteth what manner of man he was. But whoso looketh into the perfect law of liberty, and continueth therein, he being not a forgetful hearer, but a doer of the work, this man shall be blessed in his deed.* The Engrafted Word is Jesus. We receive Him first. Then we hear. Only after that, we do. Always inside out. We are called to continuously look at the Perfect Law of Liberty who is Jesus. We are called to behold Jesus and not to behold ourselves. If we begin to start looking at ourselves and our own righteousness (outside in) then we become forgetful hearers. Our works become works of the flesh (not dependent on Jesus). We forget who we are. Only in Christ can we lay aside all filthiness and superfluity of naughtiness. This is stated clearly in *James 2:26, For as the body without the spirit is dead, so faith without works is dead also.* We do these works not to be justified again before God, for we are already justified, but for man to see.

We should be as described in *1 John 2:3-6, And hereby we do know that we know him, if we keep his commandments. He that saith, I know him, and keepeth not his commandments, is a liar, and the truth is not in him. But whoso keepeth his word, in him verily is the love of God perfected: hereby know we that we are in him. He that saith he abideth in him ought himself also so to walk, even as he walked.* Because we know Jesus, we keep His commandments. We walk and agree with Jesus. Conversely, if we do not know Jesus we do not keep His commandments. We do not walk nor agree with Jesus. Jesus is the Love of God perfected. So when we know that we have the Love of the Father, Jesus, in us then we keep His word and bear much good fruit.

We are not kicked out of God's kingdom every time we stumble and commit a work of the flesh and then admitted back in when we stop. Either we are in or we are out. There is no revolving door in the kingdom, where people pirouette endlessly in and out, round and round, until they die. We rest in the fact that Jesus had already obeyed, now we can also effortlessly do what He had already done. If we fail in our works, we can still look to that Blessed Certain Hope, Jesus Himself, who redeemed and purified us perfectly. We remain righteous in our walk of righteousness.

We are made free from sin to not sin. We have dominion over sin. We can do righteous actions which are a fruit of our abiding in Jesus. *Romans 6:18-23* states, *Being then made free from sin, ye became the servants of righteousness. I speak after the manner of men because of the infirmity of your flesh: for as ye have yielded your members servants to uncleanness and to iniquity unto iniquity; even so now yield your members servants to righteousness unto holiness. For when ye were the servants of sin, ye were free from righteousness. What fruit had ye then in those things whereof ye are now ashamed? for the end of those things is death. But now being made free from sin, and become servants to God, ye have your fruit unto holiness, and the end everlasting life. For the wages of sin is death; but the gift of God is eternal life through Jesus Christ our Lord.* We produced no good fruit while servants of sin, the end result being death. But being servants of righteousness, we bear good fruits unto holiness, the end result is having eternal life with Jesus. The power to do right is because we are now servants to righteousness. In the original Greek, the word servant is *doulos,* meaning 'belonging to another'. We belonged to sin but we belong now to Righteousness, who is Jesus. The fruit of serving Righteousness is righteous living.

To produce good fruits we need to rest in Jesus. We read in *Hebrews 4:9-11, There remaineth therefore a rest to the people of God. For he that is entered into his rest, he also hath ceased from his own works, as God did from his. Let us labour therefore to enter into that rest, lest any man fall after the same example of unbelief.* Unbelief happens when we try to rest in our own or fleshly works! The Israelites could not enter the Promised Land because of unbelief. The people in Jesus' own hometown did not receive healing because of their unbelief (all those who believed were healed). The Pharisees could not receive Grace because of their unbelief. We too cannot receive all that God has for us if we have unbelief. Self-works is an elusive rest that is no rest at all. We cannot rest in ourselves but only in someone else. That someone is Jesus. Let us therefore labor to enter into His rest. In Jesus' rest, we bear much good fruit effortlessly.

ॐ 36 ॐ

JESUS AND SALVATION

To be saved requires only one thing and that is to believe in Jesus and what He did on the cross. Salvation is never progressive. Never a work-in-progress! We do not do more, try harder, and over time arrive at salvation. There are no ten-steps program to earn salvation. Jesus is our Savior. No one and nothing else saves us. We receive salvation by Grace alone and His name is Jesus. *Romans 10:13*, states, *For whosoever shall call upon the name of the Lord shall be saved.* It does not depend on what we do or not do. It does not depend on our moral fiber or our zeal for God. Either we believe in Jesus or we do not. Either we have Jesus or we do not have Jesus. It is either a 'Yes' or a 'No' to Jesus. *John 5:24* states, *Verily, verily, I say unto you, He that heareth my word, and believeth on him that sent me, hath everlasting life, and shall not come into condemnation; but is passed from death unto life.*

Let us examine some popular church dogmas surrounding salvation. The first has to do with something called 'Lordship Salvation'. Basically, it means that Jesus has to be Lord over every aspect of our lives before He will give us salvation. If we forsake every aspect of our lives to Him, then and only then will He accept us. Salvation is based exclusively on our ability to surrender all. That is a prerequisite. Even if there is one tiny aspect of our lives that remains under our control, then Jesus would deny us salvation. We have to please Him. We have to obey Him. Our behavior must change. This often requires drastic changes in our lifestyles, clothing, friends, jobs, behavior, possession, and dietary habits before we are considered worthy to be saved. Of course, different churches would impose different levels of surrender and submission, making the whole process fraught with uncertainty, fear, guilt, and control. This salvation by self-works reeks of law and condemnation. Under Lordship salvation, we believe we are saved because we gave our lives to Jesus but the truth is that we are saved because He gave His life to us.

    Romans 10:9 states, *That if thou shalt confess with thy mouth the Lord Jesus, and shalt believe in thine heart that God hath raised him from the dead, thou shalt be saved.* **Our salvation rests squarely on our belief in Lord Jesus' actions alone. As Lord, He chose to give us salvation apart from our actions.** Jesus is Lord regardless of whether every aspect of our life is surrendered to Him or not. We cannot make Him what He already is. As Lord, He justified us freely into eternal life. As Lord, He made us righteous. As Lord, not only did He took us into the throne room, but get to sit with Him on the throne of Grace as well. We read this in *Hebrews 4:16, Let us therefore come boldly unto the throne of grace, that we may obtain mercy, and find grace to help in time of need.*

    A second dogma taught is that salvation is by Jesus, but maintenance of that salvation is by our good works. This maintenance requires surrender and persistence. Since we are unable to surrender everything at once, we have to gradually surrender aspects of our life to Him. We try our best to earn the holy carrot dangling at the end of the religious stick. When we fail, we ask for forgiveness and strength to try again. Persistence, fortitude, and grit is key. When we fail yet again, we ask for grace to work harder. We pull harder on our bootstraps to lift ourselves up. We use grace to make up for our lack. We keep seeking forgiveness for our failures. We tell ourselves that God knows our weaknesses. He knows we tried our best. We did our part. He will reward us with a partial carrot for our partial goodness. We call this progressive sanctification or sin management. We maintain our salvation apart from Jesus.

    This sounds good until we realize that under the law, it is an all or nothing deal. Either we are perfect in our every deed, thought, and word or we are not. There is no progressive righteousness before a perfectly righteous God. Either we are in or we are out. There is no in-between state. No partial goodness. No partial righteousness. The only way to be perfectly righteous is to accept the gift of perfect righteousness who is Jesus. We are saved by Jesus and our salvation is maintained by Jesus alone, apart from works. Jesus wants us, not us and our works.

A third dogma is that we have to be sorry for our sins in order to receive salvation. *2 Corinthians 7:9-10, Now I rejoice, not that ye were made sorry, but that ye sorrowed to repentance: for ye were made sorry after a godly manner, that ye might receive damage by us in nothing. For godly sorrow worketh repentance to salvation not to be repented of: but the sorrow of the world worketh death,* is often misquoted as being necessary for salvation. To this sorrow we then add weeping, sobbing, wailing, moaning, and self-affliction. But this Godly sorrow was about a believer who had an incestuous relationship in the church. It is not for an unbeliever. Paul also corrected other errors in that church and rejoiced when they came back to the centrality of Jesus. Emotions are not necessary for a person to be saved. Some people may feel joy, others freedom, sadness, tears of relief, or nothing at all. In the end, none of these emotions count, only the belief in their hearts. We do not have to be sorry for our sins because the price for sin has already been paid in full.

Similarly, we do not ask Jesus into our hearts to earn salvation. So where did this asking Jesus to come into our hearts spring from? Well, it came from *Revelation 3:18,20, that the shame of thy nakedness do not appear; and anoint thine eyes with eyesalve, that thou mayest see. Behold, I stand at the door, and knock: if any man hear my voice, and open the door, I will come in to him, and will sup with him, and he with me.* This verse was for the Laodicean church which was lukewarm and was practicing mixtures. As works cannot mix with Grace, Jesus was kicked out. Removing Jesus made the church naked and blind. And though Jesus was kicked out, yet He still stood outside the church and knocked, waiting for the door to be opened so that He could cloth their shame in white raiment and put healing ointment on their sightless eyes. Jesus is our Beloved from *Song of Solomon 5:2, it is the voice of my beloved that knocketh, saying, Open to me, my sister, my love, my dove, my undefiled.*

Praying aloud with our mouths in order to be saved is another act that I have huge problems with, as my church has worked with deaf and mute people before. To exclude a section of the populace because they cannot speak is just another righteous self-work. *Romans 10:9-11, That if thou shalt confess with thy mouth the Lord Jesus, and shalt believe in thine heart that God hath raised him from the dead, thou shalt be saved. For with the heart man believeth unto righteousness; and with the mouth confession is made unto salvation. For the scripture saith, Whosoever believeth on him shall not be ashamed,* has often been used to substantiate this requirement. Yet, the scripture is perfectly clear. It is the belief in the heart that makes one righteous. It has nothing to do with praying aloud with the mouth. If possible, the mouth then confesses or agrees with the heart about what God says about Jesus. Note also that prayers do not save. More as well as louder prayers do not equal salvation. Only Jesus saves.

Another dogma concerns water baptism as a prerequisite for salvation. It is erroneous. In the old testament, as the Israelites walked upon the dry seabed of the Red Sea, it was raining upon them. *Psalm 77:17-20* states, *The clouds poured out water: the skies sent out a sound: thine arrows also went abroad. The voice of thy thunder was in the heaven: the lightnings lightened the world: the earth trembled and shook. Thy way is in the sea, and thy path in the great waters, and thy footsteps are not known. Thou leddest thy people like a flock by the hand of Moses and Aaron.* The rain was a shadow of the Living Water or Jesus pouring upon His people, giving them life. We see this clearer in *1 Corinthians 10:1-4, Moreover, brethren, I would not that ye should be ignorant, how that all our fathers were under the cloud, and all passed through the sea; And were all baptized unto Moses in the cloud and in the sea; And did all eat the same spiritual meat; And did all drink the same spiritual drink: for they drank of that spiritual Rock that followed them: and that Rock was Christ.*

The 'baptism' which saved them was none other than Jesus. Water does not save. It just makes people wet. Water baptism is only for believers and is a symbol of Jesus' death, burial, and resurrection. Paul mentioned that Jesus sent him to preach the gospel and not to baptize. The gospel is about Jesus and Jesus alone. *1 Corinthians 1:14-17, I thank God that I baptized none of you, but Crispus and Gaius; Lest any should say that I had baptized in mine own name. And I baptized also the household of Stephanas: besides, I know not whether I baptized any other. For Christ sent me not to baptize, but to preach the gospel: not with wisdom of words, lest the cross of Christ should be made of none effect.* Baptism is a believer's profession, in public, that he or she believes in Jesus. *Genesis 1:20* states, *Let the waters bring forth abundantly the moving creature that hath life,* The creature already has life because of Jesus. He/she just comes out of the water. Only the blood of Jesus saves, never the water of baptism. Remember Jesus as we do, re-do, re-turn, or re-member our baptism!

We turn now to the biggest dogma in the church. Is the work of repentance and turning away from sins a prerequisite for salvation? In the old testament, there are fifteen different Hebrew words for salvation but none of them consistently refer to repentance. However, two words *'shub'* (meaning to turn back) and *'naham'* (meaning to be sorry) come closest to what we call repentance. But they generally mean Israel or God turning towards or away from each other. This turning action and being sorry for wrong actions brings either blessings or curses. It does not refer to nor bring salvation. Furthermore in *Genesis 15:6, And he believed in the Lord and he counted it to him for righteousness* and in *Habakkuk 2:4, Behold, his soul which is lifted up is not upright in him: but the just shall live by his faith,* we see clearly that salvation is by faith in God alone and what He said about the coming *Yeshua Hamashiach* (Jesus the Messiah or Jesus Christ). That belief is counted as righteousness. We can conclude that nowhere in the old testament can we find salvation by turning away and being sorry for one's sins. Salvation is based solely on one's belief in God by faith.

Works cannot earn us salvation. A servant who does many works is still a servant as illustrated in *Luke 17:7-10, But which of you, having a servant plowing or feeding cattle, will say unto him by and by, when he is come from the field, Go and sit down to meat? And will not rather say unto him, Make ready wherewith I may sup, and gird thyself, and serve me, till I have eaten and drunken; and afterward thou shalt eat and drink? Doth he thank that servant because he did the things that were commanded him? I trow not. So likewise ye, when ye shall have done all those things which are commanded you, say, We are unprofitable servants: we have done that which was our duty to do.* The servant who worked all day under the heat of the sun is still a servant when the day is done. He still has to first serve his master after coming in from the field. It does not matter how diligent the servant is. A cartload of good works, habits, or virtues cannot earn him the position of son. Does the servant deserve thanks for all his hard work? We would like to say 'Yes' but the word 'thank' here in Greek is *'charis'* or Grace. Does the servant deserve Grace for his hard labor? Jesus' answer was a 'No'. Grace is always unmerited and it is still the only way whereby servants are adopted and transformed into sons and daughters. Belief in Jesus resulted in the new birth. The new birth gave us our identity and position, which in turn gave us our rights and privileges.

If not for what Jesus accomplished on the cross, everything we believe in would be in vain. He died for us, He was buried for us, and He rose again for us. And because He was resurrected, so we will be one day. The gospel is about Jesus and His work alone. He gave us salvation freely by His Grace and that is what we stand upon. Let us keep this in our memory. This is explained in *1 Corinthians 15:1-4, 13-17, Moreover, brethren, I declare unto you the gospel which I preached unto you, which also ye have received, and wherein ye stand; By which also ye are saved, if ye keep in memory what I preached unto you, unless ye have believed in vain. For I delivered unto you first of all that which I also received, how that Christ died for our sins according to the scriptures; And that he was buried, and that he rose again the third day according to the scriptures: But if there be no resurrection of the dead, then is*

Christ not risen: And if Christ be not risen, then is our preaching vain, and your faith is also vain...For if the dead rise not, then is not Christ raised: And if Christ be not raised, your faith is vain; ye are yet in your sins. To believe in any other gospel other than Jesus is to believe in vain. If Jesus did not finish the work, then we are all still in our sins. And dead we remain! But He is the resurrected Christ! That is how we know that all our sins are forgiven. In the resurrected Jesus there is life. In all others, there is death.

Jesus is the only way to salvation. Grace is the only answer to sin. But the moment we share Jesus as Grace, there will come opposition. Many people, who genuinely love God, but are caught up in legalism, will persecute us. *Matthew 10:17-18, But beware of men: for they will deliver you up to the councils, and they will scourge you in their synagogues; And ye shall be brought before governors and kings for my sake, for a testimony against them and the Gentiles.* But do not be afraid of these people when we are persecuted by them. They can only hurt our bodies in this life. But being spiritually dead i.e. not knowing Jesus will destroy both our soul and body as in *Matthew 10:28, And fear not them which kill the body, but are not able to kill the soul: but rather fear him which is able to destroy both soul and body in hell.*

We read in *Galatians 4:28-31, Now we, brethren, as Isaac was, are the children of promise. But as then he that was born after the flesh persecuted him that was born after the Spirit, even so it is now. Nevertheless what saith the scripture? Cast out the bondwoman and her son: for the son of the bondwoman shall not be heir with the son of the freewoman. So then, brethren, we are not children of the bondwoman, but of the free.* The Pharisees always persecuted/denied Jesus. They are the ones who committed the 'unpardonable' sin by continuously rejecting Jesus as we see in *Matthew 12:31-32, Wherefore I say unto you, All manner of sin and blasphemy shall be forgiven unto men: but the blasphemy against the Holy Ghost shall not be forgiven unto men. And whosoever speaketh a word against the Son of man, it shall be forgiven him: but whosoever speaketh against the Holy Ghost, it shall not be forgiven him, neither in this world, neither in the world to come.* They were against Jesus. They accused Him of having a devil, thus blaspheming the Holy Spirit who testified that Jesus was the Son of God. This paralleled *Isaiah 63:10, But they rebelled and grieved His Holy Spirit. So He turned and became their enemy, and He Himself fought against them.* During the exodus, the Israelites rejected God. They asked for the law and became an enemy to Grace. Hence, rejecting God or rejecting Jesus grieves the Holy Spirit. Jesus referred to those who rejected Him as vipers and murderers, as in *Matthew 23:33, Ye serpents, ye generation of vipers, how can ye escape the damnation of hell?*

Similarly, legalists would always persecute those who preach Grace. Ishmael would persecute Isaac. The bondwoman, Hagar, against the freewoman, Sarah. Galatians' believers against Paul. Same father but different mothers. We stand wholly upon Grace or Jesus. Legalists stand upon works. Either one or the other has to be cast out, as Grace and works cannot coexist together and be joint heirs. There can be no mixtures. Hence, Hagar and Ishmael were cast out. Similarly, we are told to cast out the law for we have nothing in common with it.

We read in *Matthew 10:31-33, Fear ye not therefore, ye are of more value than many sparrows. Whosoever therefore shall confess me before men, him will I confess also before my Father which is in heaven. But whosoever shall deny me before men, him will I also deny before my Father which is in heaven.* These verses have nothing to do with Jesus accepting us first and then denying us later before His Father! Jesus does not change His mind. When Jesus sent out His disciples, He told them that there would be Jews who would deny Him i.e. legalistic unbelievers. These people would be denied entry into heaven solely because they do not have Jesus when they stand before God.

This is similar to the nation of Israel who was denied entry into the Promised Land because of their works. In *Deuteronomy 1:37-39,* we read, *Also the Lord was angry with me for your sakes, saying, Thou also shalt not go in thither. But Joshua the son of Nun, which standeth before thee, he shall go in thither: encourage him: for he shall cause Israel to inherit it. Moreover your little ones, which ye said should be a prey, and your children, which in that day had no knowledge between good and evil, they shall go in thither, and unto them will I give it, and they shall possess it.* But their children, who had no knowledge of good and evil and did not stand on their works, were given entry.

But for all those of us who confess Jesus, not works, let us not be afraid. For we are guaranteed heaven by Jesus! So do not worry too much when we are criticized or persecuted because we are much more valuable than sparrows. Sparrows are not worth much but God still takes care of them. How much more will God take care of us.

We read in *Luke 13:23-25, Then said one unto him, Lord, are there few that be saved? And he said unto them, Strive to enter in at the strait gate: for many, I say unto you, will seek to enter in, and shall not be able. When once the master of the house is risen up, and hath shut to the door, and ye begin to stand without, and to knock at the door, saying, Lord, Lord, open unto us; and he shall answer and say unto you, I know you not whence ye are.* The Pharisees mocked Jesus by asking Him why so few were saved. Saved here is not salvation as Jesus had not died or been resurrected yet. Saved here meant as 'why are there so few disciples following you?' Jesus answered them by making a distinction between a gate and a door.

There were many Pharisees striving to enter in at the gates, by their works. Gates are places of judgment as we see in *Deuteronomy 16:18, Judges and officers shalt thou make thee in all thy gates...and they shall judge the people with just judgment.* We read another mention of gates in *Matthew 7:13-14, Enter ye in at the strait gate: for wide is the gate, and broad is the way, that leadeth to destruction, and many there be which go in there at: Because strait is the gate, and narrow is the way, which leadeth unto life, and few there be that find it.* Gates are meant to keep people out. When judged by the law at the gates, everybody would be found short. None would enter! Many people end up at the 'wide' gate to be judged. They were all disqualified to enter beyond. But some people lived an ascetic live and ended up at the 'narrow' gate to be judged. However, committing even a single sin will disqualify them as well. Hence, nobody enters in by the gates to everlasting life.

But Jesus! He made an opening in the gates! We saw a shadow of this in *Judges 16:3, And Samson lay till midnight, and arose at midnight, and took the doors of the gate of the city, and the two posts, and went away with them, bar and all, and put them upon his shoulders, and carried them up to the top of an hill that is before Hebron.* At the gates of Gaza, judgment awaited him. An ambush was all set up. Samson would be found guilty. He would be killed. But that did not happen as Samson tore the doors of the gate, the posts, and the top bar away. The post and the top bar made a cross. The gates of judgment were now irreparably torn. This was a picture of Jesus' strength prevailing against the gates of hell. We read of this in *Matthew 16:18, And I say also unto thee, That thou art Peter, and upon this rock I will build my church; and the gates of hell shall not prevail against it.* The gates of hell or death were defeated at the cross as Jesus opened up a door.

We can now enter in without fear of judgment, for Jesus took the judgment for sins upon Himself at the cross. At the gate, Jesus was judged worthy. In doing so, He opened up an entrance. It is called the door and it is wide open! The Door is Jesus as in *John 10:7,9, Then said Jesus unto them again, Verily, verily, I say unto you, I am the door of the sheep. I am the door: by me if any man enter in, he shall be saved, and shall go in and out, and find pasture.*

Jesus is not the gate but the door. All those who know Jesus simply walk in. Into Life. There is no death in Jesus. There is also no striving to enter in. At present, this door is wide open. Its double hinges are the wide open arms of Jesus. Embracing us in. We call this period of open door the period of Grace. It has been opened now for about 2000 years. All are invited to come in through this door. Jesus is available to all. But while Jesus is available to all, not all want Him. Many people refuse to enter in. But for all those who are in, Jesus keeps them completely safe. No thieves can approach us because of Jesus. Nobody can steal, kill, or destroy us. Why? Because Jesus is the Door and satan cannot pass by Him to hurt us.

❧ 37 ❧

JESUS AND OUR SALVATION

Salvation is a free gift given to us by Jesus. **We cannot lose our salvation because it is not of ourselves. It is not of us, from us, nor by us, but it is for us.** Those of us whose faith rests upon Jesus are sealed together with Him forever. We know that those who come to Jesus cannot be cast out because Jesus will never cast us out. God never changes His mind about us. *Romans 11:29* states, *For the gifts and calling of God are without repentance.* We will never be blotted out of the book of life, as we read in *Revelation 3:5, He that overcometh, the same shall be clothed in white raiment; and I will not blot out his name out of the book of life, but I will confess his name before my Father, and before his angels.* We say Amen to all that God said about His Son, Jesus. *2 Corinthians 1:20-22* states, *For all the promises of God in him are yea, and in him Amen, unto the glory of God by us. Now he which stablisheth us with you in Christ, and hath anointed us, is God; Who hath also sealed us, and given the earnest of the Spirit in our hearts.* Salvation has everything to do with Jesus' faithfulness. Salvation has nothing to do with our faithfulness. Salvation is nothing about what we did or did not do. We did not fix it and likewise we cannot un-fix it. Salvation is all about what Jesus did.

But many people believe that they earned their salvation because of their many good works. Or they believe that they have to continue with good works in order to maintain their salvation. They like to quote *1 Timothy 1:18-20* which states, *This charge I commit unto thee, son Timothy, according to the prophecies which went before on thee, that thou by them mightest war a good warfare; Holding faith, and a good conscience; which some having put away concerning faith have made shipwreck: Of whom is Hymenaeus and Alexander; whom I have delivered unto Satan, that they may learn not to blaspheme.* They maintain that Paul charged Timothy to fight the war of salvation with tenacity. Otherwise, Timothy would be delivered to satan just like Hymenaeus and Alexander. Everybody who does not fight the good fight would lose their salvation, be shipwrecked, and burn in hell.

But Paul was actually advising Timothy to hold onto his faith in Jesus. Because with Jesus, all wars have a foregone conclusion of victory. We never fight for victory. We fight from a position of victory. It is good warfare when we know we have won. But some people, like Hymenaeus and Alexander, have shipwrecked their faith in Jesus and returned to works. Paul called this action blasphemous. Having 'shipwrecked faith' did not mean that they lost their salvation. But it did mean that they now trusted in their own works. From the verses above, we are unsure whether they genuinely had faith in Jesus at all. However, one thing is for sure. Hymenaeus and Alexander turned away from Grace. We read this at the start of *1 Timothy 1:3-7, that thou mightest charge some that they teach no other doctrine, Neither give heed to fables and endless genealogies, which minister questions, rather than godly edifying which is in faith: so do. Now the end of the commandment is charity out of a pure heart, and of a good conscience, and of faith unfeigned: From which some having swerved have turned aside unto vain jangling;* **Desiring to be teachers of the law;** *understanding neither what they say, nor whereof they affirm.* Paul charged that there be no other teaching or doctrine besides Grace. But Hymenaeus and Alexander wanted to become teachers of the law. Paul called them teachers with no understanding, teaching fables and endless genealogies, and raising more questions than simple faith in Jesus.

We read more about this in *2 Timothy 4:3-4, 14,17, For the time will come when they will not endure sound doctrine; but after their own lusts shall they heap to themselves teachers, having itching ears; And they shall turn away their ears from the truth, and shall be turned unto fables. Alexander the coppersmith did me much evil: the Lord reward him according to his works... Notwithstanding the Lord stood with me, and strengthened me; that by me the preaching might be fully known, and that all the Gentiles might hear: and I was delivered out of the mouth of the lion.* They had itching ears as they turned away from the sound doctrine of Grace, back to the law. Going back to the law is to go back into the lion's mouth to be devoured.

1 Peter 5:8-9 states, *Be sober, be vigilant; because your adversary the devil, as a roaring lion, walketh about, seeking whom he may devour: Whom resist stedfast in the faith, knowing that the same afflictions are accomplished in your brethren that are in the world.* Satan is the roaring lion whom Paul was delivered from. And just like Daniel, satan's mouth is shut up against us. We read in *Daniel 6:22, My God hath sent his angel, and hath shut the lions' mouths, that they have not hurt me.* Satan has no direct power over believers. Jesus has shut his mouth against us forever. Although he roars, he cannot afflict us.

All teaching other than Jesus is profane and vain babblings. *2 Timothy 2:16-18* states, *But shun profane and vain babblings: for they will increase unto more ungodliness. And their word will eat as doth a canker: of whom is Hymenaeus and Philetus; Who concerning the truth have erred, saying that the resurrection is past already; and overthrow the faith of some. Nevertheless the foundation of God standeth sure, having this seal, The Lord knoweth them that are his.* Teaching that a person cannot be resurrected from sin to righteousness by Grace overthrew and shipwrecked the faith of some in Christ. It may also mean that the believer has no resurrection body to look forward to that is free from sin. People with 'shipwrecked faith' will in turn, shipwreck the faith of others. There is now no assurance of salvation. Salvation by works brings insecurity and anxiety. Jesus did not finish the work as it is now Jesus plus our works. We are unsure of how much work we have to add to Jesus' finished work to win the war! That shipwrecks and make a shambles of our faith that the war has already been won.

1 Corinthians 1:8-9 states, *Who shall also confirm you unto the end, that ye may be blameless in the day of our Lord Jesus Christ. God is faithful, by whom ye were called unto the fellowship of his Son Jesus Christ our Lord.* Jesus confirms those that are His and proclaims them blameless, free from all sin and guilt. Jesus started the work in them and will keep them flawless till the end. We read of this in *Philippians 1:6, Being confident of this very thing, that he which hath begun a good work in you will perform it until the day of Jesus Christ* and in *1 Peter 1:5, Who are kept by the power of God through faith unto salvation ready to be revealed in the last time.* Jesus saved us, kept us saved, and will declare us saved. He guarantees our salvation. Even shipwrecked people belong to Him. He works in us. Not us for Him. It is all His work. Hence, He knows perfectly well those that are His.

We, on the other hand, do not have such knowledge. As such, we cannot say with certainty whether those mentioned by Paul; namely Hymenaeus, Alexander, and Philetus, were saved or not. But we know that those who are His are sealed and assured of their salvation. Note that it was Paul who handed them over to satan, not Jesus. The objective was not to punish them, but so that they will learn not to blaspheme what they have been given freely, namely Jesus or Grace.

Many of Jesus' disciples have similarly walked away from Him. Many of them appear to have not placed their faith in Jesus at all as we read in *1 John 2:19, They went out from us, but they were not of us; for if they had been of us, they would no doubt have continued with us: but they went out, that they might be made manifest that they were not all of us.* Although they walked with Jesus, they were not of Jesus. This meant that they did not believe in nor have a relationship with Jesus. If they had a genuine relationship with Him, they would no doubt have stayed. And again in *John 6:64-66, But there are some of you that believe not. For Jesus knew from the beginning who they were that believed not, and who should betray him. And he said, Therefore said I unto you, that no man can come unto me, except it were given unto him of my Father. From that time many of his disciples went back, and walked no more with him.* Some of His disciples did not even believe in what Jesus was teaching! They followed Him for other reasons. Because Jesus could see into their hearts, He knew exactly who had faith in Him and who were dissimulating, as in *John 2:23-25, many believed in his name, when they saw the miracles which he did. But Jesus did not commit himself unto them, because he knew all men, And needed not that any should testify of man: for he knew what was in man,* and in *Isaiah 29:13, Therefore the Lord said: These people draw near to Me with their mouths and honor Me with their lips, but their hearts are far from Me. Their worship of Me is but rules taught by men.*

Those who believed in Him remained saved even though they walked away. Those who did not believe in Him remained unsaved even though they remained with Him. A perfect example of the latter was Judas Iscariot. Whether remaining or walking away 'profiteth nothing'. Some people have claimed that Judas lost his salvation because of his betrayal of Jesus. This is not so. Even though Judas knew Jesus, yet he rejected Jesus as the Son of God. He did not believe in Jesus and therefore betrayed Him. Judas did not lose his salvation as he never had salvation in the first place. Judas perfectly reflected Ahithophel, David's grandfather-in-law, the one who told Absalom to sleep with David's concubines on the rooftop. Just as Judas, Ahithophel ended up hanging himself too in *2 Samuel 17:23.*

Let us read further in *Matthew 10:1,7-8, And when he had called unto him his twelve disciples, he gave them power against unclean spirits, to cast them out, and to heal all manner of sickness and all manner of disease...And as ye go, preach, saying, The kingdom of heaven is at hand. Heal the sick, cleanse the lepers, raise the dead, cast out devils: freely ye have received, freely give.* Jesus' disciples were given power to cast out unclean spirits, raise the dead, and to heal all types of sicknesses and diseases. Yet these supernatural abilities did not earn them their salvation. Salvation comes but by one way only and that is by believing in Jesus.

Works do not qualify us for salvation. We see this clearly in *Matthew 7:21-23, Not everyone that saith unto me, Lord, Lord, shall enter into the kingdom of heaven; but he that doeth the will of my Father which is in heaven. Many will say to me in that day, Lord, Lord, have we not prophesied in thy name? and in thy name have cast out devils? and in thy name done many wonderful works? And then will I profess unto them, I never knew you: depart from me, ye that work iniquity.* These groups of people did the exact same works as the disciples but were not accepted by God. They did not lose their salvation as they never had it in the first place. Why? Because there is only one work that is required by God and that is to believe in His Son, Jesus. Another example is Demas, who was consistently with Paul, even when he was imprisoned twice in Rome. A fellow-worker, full of works, but one day upped and left Paul in *2 Timothy 4:10, For Demas hath forsaken me, having loved this present world, and is departed unto Thessalonica.* Demas was revealed as loving the world. As discussed in *1 John 2:15-16,* the person who loves the world is an unbeliever who does not have the love of the Father in him.

    John 6:26-29 states this clearly, *Jesus answered them and said, Verily, verily, I say unto you, Ye seek me, not because ye saw the miracles, but because ye did eat of the loaves, and were filled. Labour not for the meat which perisheth, but for that meat which endureth unto everlasting life, which the Son of man shall give unto you: for him hath God the Father sealed. Then said they unto him, What shall we do, that we might work the works of God? Jesus answered and said unto them, This is the work of God, that ye believe on him whom he hath sent.* There is to be no labor involved in receiving Jesus. Otherwise, it will be called the meat that perishes because we labored for it. We are to simply receive the meat of everlasting life who is Jesus. **Once again, there is only one work required and that is to believe in Jesus! All believers in Jesus cannot ever lose their salvation as it is everlasting! We cannot lose our salvation! Asking whether we can lose our salvation is the wrong question. Rather we should ask whether Salvation, who is Jesus, can ever lose us! As Jesus is everlasting so is our salvation in Him. My salvation is secure in Jesus. Your salvation is secure in Jesus. It is all because of Jesus!**

APPENDIX A

HOW TO READ YOUR BIBLE

As believers, one of the most basic and important things we have to learn is how to read our bibles. The bible is God's word. But after more than thirty years of ministry, I have concluded that many people are more confused than enlightened by it. For example, we learn about an angry God in the old testament and then, a loving Jesus in the new testament. We learn about punishment in the old testament and grace in the new testament. So, is God angry or is He loving? Does He punish us or does He not? We end up very confused.

Actually, the bible is quite easy to read and understand. A few guidelines on how to read the bible will help us greatly. God came close to us so that we could examine His goodness close-up. While we may never understand fully how good God is, we can comprehend that He is indeed very good to us. Jesus became the Son of Man so that we could be related by blood. He became one of us and lived with us. Not in another galaxy, far, far, away. The Word was made flesh so we could not only see but understand Him as well. At the end, He became one with us.

The whole bible is inerrant and very useful to us. We read in *2 Timothy 3:15-16, And that from a child thou hast known the holy scriptures, which are able to make thee wise unto salvation through faith which is in Christ Jesus. All scripture is given by inspiration of God (God breathed), and is profitable for doctrine, for reproof, for correction, for instruction in righteousness.* God breathed life into His word. That is why our salvation to Life and righteousness is only through faith in His Word, Jesus. It is profitable indeed to study the word like Timothy.

But in *2 Timothy 2:15,* we read, *Study to shew thyself approved unto God, a workman that needeth not to be ashamed, rightly dividing the word of truth.* Timothy, like us, was called to rightly divide this word of truth. The Greek word here for dividing is '*orthotomeo*'. It means 'to cut straight', like a carpenter cutting a straight line or an engineer designing a straight roadway. Therefore we are called to precisely and accurately cut straight the word of God towards the Word of God, Jesus!

To accurately interpret any scripture, we need the Holy Spirit. Without the Holy Spirit, our flesh would, by default, rise up. In our flesh, we cannot help but interpret scripture from a fleshly self-perspective. *1 Corinthians 2:10* states, *But God hath revealed them unto us by his Spirit: for the Spirit searcheth all things, yea, the deep things of God.* The Holy Spirit was in creation, in the temple, in prophets, kings, priests, judges/warriors,and individuals (even Balaam). He was in Jesus and known as the Spirit of Christ. Before Jesus physically left the world, the Holy Spirit only rested on people temporarily. After Jesus left, the Holy Spirit rested in people permanently!

Jesus actually spelled out exactly what the Holy Spirit would do for us in *John 16:7-15, Nevertheless I tell you the truth; It is expedient for you that I go away: for if I go not away, the Comforter will not come unto you; but if I depart, I will send him unto you. And when he is come, **he will reprove the world of sin, and of righteousness, and of judgment: Of sin, because they believe not on me;** Of righteousness, because I go to my Father, and ye see me no more; Of judgment, because the prince of this world is judged. I have yet many things to say unto you, but ye cannot bear them now. Howbeit when he, the Spirit of truth, is come, he will guide you into all truth: for he shall not speak of himself; but whatsoever he shall hear, that shall he speak: and he will shew you things to come. He shall glorify me: for he shall receive of mine, and shall shew it unto you. All things that the Father hath are mine: therefore said I, that he shall take of mine, and shall shew it unto you.*

The Holy Spirit reproves the world, or unbelievers, of sin. Singular 'sin', not plural 'sins'. That singular sin is the sin of unbelief in Jesus. They believe not on Me! All other sins are irrelevant insofar that Jesus paid in full the price for those sins. Because unbelievers are spiritually dead, the Holy Spirit cannot talk to them directly. So the Holy Spirit shows them the law and the law in turn shows them how far they have sinned. *1 Timothy 1:*

8-9 states, *But we know that the law is good, if a man use it lawfully; Knowing this, that the law is not made for a righteous man, but for the lawless and disobedient, for the ungodly and for sinners.* The Holy Spirit disconcerts unbelievers and shows them their need for Jesus. God takes no pleasure in seeing unbelievers perish or be destroyed by sin. *2 Peter 3:9* states, *The Lord is not slack concerning his promise, as some men count slackness; but is longsuffering to us-ward, not willing that any should perish, but that all should come to repentance.* Even though Jesus paid the price for all sins, sin is still around and continues to destroy lives. That is why God hates sin. God's will is that none to perish. God never hates unbelievers. He wants them to repent or change their minds about Jesus. From unbelief to belief.

The Holy Spirit is our Comforter. He is not the Un-Comforter or Discomfiter. Because Jesus paid the full price for all our sins, the Holy Spirit never convicts the believer of sin. There are no sins left as Jesus paid for them fully. He paid for our past, present, and future sins. No sin is ever lost or misplaced - all are fully paid for! Therefore, the Holy Spirit does not try to make us un-Comfort-able by reproving us of sins already paid for in full by Jesus. Instead, whenever we sin, He reminds us of who we are in Christ. Since Jesus physically went to be with the Father and we see Him no more, it is now the role of the Holy Spirit to remind us that we are the righteousness of God in Christ. He takes everything of Jesus and teaches it to us. Without the Holy Spirit, we can learn nothing spiritual. All His teachings, of things present and things to come, has only one aim and that is to point to Jesus. And once we become fully aware of Jesus, we have very little desire to sin. Hence, the Holy Spirit continuously remind believers of who they are in Christ. Finally, judgment is reserved for the prince of this world or satan. The Holy Spirit reminds him and us of that.

Many times, scholars use big words to tell us how to read the bible. They tell us that we should practice exegesis (draw the meaning out) and not eisegesis (impose our interpretation in). But all exegetical reading is useless without revelation by the Holy Spirit. God reveals the whole bible to us, even the deep things, by the Holy Spirit. As the Holy Spirit points only to Jesus and only He can correctly interpret scripture for us, therefore all scripture should point us to Jesus. *1 John 5:6* states, *This is he that came by water and blood, even Jesus Christ; not by water only, but by water and blood. And it is the Spirit that beareth witness, because the Spirit is truth.* The bible, as testified by the Holy Spirit, is all about Jesus! If we read the bible and interpret it based on our fleshly viewpoint, it becomes very subjective. Every person would have his or her own interpretation. To rightly divide the word of truth, we have to read the bible from Jesus' perspective. If not, we would end up like every educated Jew, who without Jesus, would interpret the *Tanakh* (Hebrew Bible) in his own way. Or in the early church where the fathers would commonly hold contradictory positions without even an awareness of such inconsistencies!

Many people say that the word bible is an acronym for Basic Instructions Before Leaving Earth (B.I.B.L.E.) It is not! We are not building a space ship to leave Earth. And the Rapture does not involve alien space ships either! Also, the rapture was not invented by Darby in 1830 but was a word *directly from the Lord* in *1 Thessalonians 4:15*. Others say that the bible is full of moral stories. When we read it, we should ask what the Moral Of The Story (M.O.T.S.) is. It is not that either. Morality saves no one. The bible is not about instructions, spiritual checklists, or commands of do's and don'ts. So what is the bible about then? Well, very simple. From Jesus' perspective, the bible is a record of Him delighting in doing the will of His Father. *Psalm 40:7* states, *Then said I, Lo, I come: in the volume of the book it is written of me, I delight to do thy will, O my God.* Jesus said that the bible was about Him and what He did! Jesus revealed this also to Cleopas and the other purposefully unnamed disciple (so that you can put your name there) on the road to Emmaus, in *Luke 24:27, And beginning at Moses and all the prophets, he expounded unto them in all the scriptures the things concerning himself.* Their hearts burned within them as Jesus talked with them! We recall that it was a meal that opened the eyes of Adam and Eve after they ate the fruit from the tree of right and wrong, and saw themselves naked. Now it was another meal that opened the eyes of these two disciples as they ate bread with Jesus, a picture of the Lord's Supper, and they recognized Him.

Jesus died on the cross for us. Therefore, the cross is another point that divides the bible. Before the cross God says, 'You shall or you shall not' (*Exodus 20:3-4*) but after the cross God says, 'I will' (*Hebrews 8:8*). There are literally, life and death differences between what comes before and what comes after the cross. Because of the finished work of Jesus on the cross, commandments and instructions that were extremely important before the cross may have no relevance for us whatsoever due to Jesus' finished work. For example, let us read *Psalm 51:10-11, Create in me a clean heart, O God; and renew a right spirit within me. Cast me not away from thy presence; and take not thy holy spirit from me.* While it was fully appropriate for David to say these verses, it is irrelevant for us today. Why? Because all believers after the cross were given a new heart, His heart, and a righteous spirit. Furthermore, Jesus would never cast us away. He cannot reject Himself as He is one with us, just as the Holy Spirit would never be taken away from us. Before the cross, atonement and sacrifices were necessary for sins to be covered. Punishment was common. After the cross, all sins were forgiven by the perfect sacrifice, Jesus. All sins meant ALL, not some, as in *Psalm 90:8, Thou hast set our iniquities before thee, our secret sins in the light of thy countenance.* Yes, even secret sins were forgiven! The wrath of God on sin was spent on Jesus and is no more. Hence, it is very important for us to consistently ask ourselves whether the scripture that we are reading is before or after the cross.

We know that God is good all the time. He is not good some of the time and at other times, He is bad. The word gospel comes from the Greek word '*euaggelion*' which means good news (not good law). We do not make the news good or deep fake it so that it looks and sounds good. We do not wrap bad news in an attractive wrapper and sell it as good news. It is good news solely because it is all about Jesus who is all good. Unlike the news from the world, the gospel has no bad news in it. It is good without a single drop of bad in it. So when we read scripture that seems to suggest that God is bad; or that God is angry or wrathful with us;

or that we are to be punished for sins; we have to carefully examine the context of that scripture. Look at the other verses coming before and after that verse of scripture. Pay attention to the theme or subject matter of that chapter. And the whole book. Also, look up parallel scriptures from other books.

Let scripture interpret scripture. For example, Paul mentioned about a thorn in his flesh in *2 Corinthians 12:7, And lest I should be exalted above measure through the abundance of the revelations, there was given to me a thorn in the flesh, the messenger of Satan to buffet me, lest I should be exalted above measure.* The common explanation is that God gave Paul a disease, or some type of problem with his body, to keep him humble. This explanation makes God bad so it cannot be correct. Hence, let us look up other scriptures to explain this scripture. *Numbers 33:55* states, *But if ye will not drive out the inhabitants of the land from before you; then it shall come to pass, that those which ye let remain of them shall be pricks in your eyes, and thorns in your sides, and shall vex you in the land wherein ye dwell.* We also read in *Judges 2:3, but they shall be as thorns in your sides.* From these parallel scriptures, it is obvious that the thorn in Paul's side was a person who persecuted him for his abundance of Grace revelations. This persecutor was called a messenger of satan. Satan cannot attack a believer directly, but as god or ruler of this world, he can influence others to attack believers. This messenger tried to take Paul down who was exalting Jesus as Grace.

1 Corinthians 1:27-29,31 states, *God hath chosen the weak things of the world to confound the things which are mighty; And base things of the world, and things which are despised, hath God chosen, yea, and things which are not, to bring to nought things that are: That no flesh should glory in his presence. That, according as it is written, He that glorieth, let him glory in the Lord.* Paul wanted to boast about Jesus, not himself. Hence, this evil messenger buffeted Paul continuously to hinder the message of radical Grace. This way, Jesus would not be exalted by Paul! But the more the messenger tried to take Paul down, the more radical Grace shone through. Restraining Paul was to restrain un-restrainable Grace! Paul's weaknesses were perfect for Jesus to supply him with unmerited strength, as in *2 Corinthians 12;10, for when I am weak, then am I strong.* Paul could take all types of suffering because Jesus suffered for him first. Paul worked because Jesus worked in him. Jesus is sufficient no matter what we go through.

Many people, under the Holy Spirit inspiration, wrote the bible and it was written to many people. We have to ask ourselves who a particular book or scripture was written to. For example, the book of Matthew was written to the Jews. The book of James was written for the Jewish diaspora. Similarly, the law was written specifically to the Jews as God had a covenant with them (the Mosaic Covenant). The Mosaic Covenant was not made with us, Gentiles! While we can definitely say that the bible is 'for' us, we cannot claim that everything was written 'to' us. Also, we have to ask whether verses or portions of scripture were written for believers or for unbelievers. Obviously, we do not want to claim what is written for unbelievers. If I have a headache, I may take an ibuprofen. I am certainly not going to take a cocktail of chemotherapy drugs. We should not take someone else's medicine.

Due to the many writers and the period of time the bible covered, we should try to understand the geography, the culture, and the historical background of scripture as well. The more geography, culture, and history we know, the richer our understanding of scripture. For example, many scriptures about women as being inferior, about their covering, about their submission to men, about their ability to teach and share, stem from geography, culture and history. Gentile cities, and there were many of them around the Sea of Galilee, would have very different norms than Jewish cities.

Lastly, the bible was written in Hebrew, Aramaic, and Greek. Many words do not have proper equivalents in English. When in doubt, try to go back and look up the word in its original Holy Spirit inspired language. A whole book, like the book of Job, can take on a different meaning from the proper understanding of the true meaning of just one word. I highly recommend using Strong's Concordance with Hebrew and Greek lexicons for this task.

Jesus Revolution 2 (1993-2017, 2024 revised) Book 2 in the Jesus Revolution trilogy. Jesus as Grace everywhere!
To order more copies of this book, please go to www.amazon.com
You are welcome to leave your comments about this book at Amazon too. Get others to see Jesus!

Other bestseller books by Dr. Billy Ng (available at www.amazon.com and at local bookstores):

Jesus Revolution (1993-2014, 2017, 2024 revised) Book 1 in the Jesus Revolution trilogy. Jesus as Grace!

Jesus Revolution 3 (1993-2024) Book 3 in the Jesus Revolution trilogy. Jesus as Grace eternally!

Witnessing To Dracula: A Memoir of Ministry in Romania (2010) This is a bestselling book on missions.

You can also write or send bulk order inquiries for any book to jesusrevolutionbook@gmail.com